IN CONTEXT

Understanding Police Killings of Unarmed Civilians

By

Nick Selby
Ben Singleton
Ed Flosi, MS

Forward by
Commissioner Lawrence Mulvey
Nassau County Police Department (ret)

Afterword by
Clint Bruce
Former LT, Naval Special Warfare

Contextual Press
an imprint of CIAI Press
135 Jenkins St., Suite 105B-237
St. Augustine, FL 32086

Quantity sales: Special discounts are available on quantity purchases by law enforcement officers, police associations, universities, and others. For details, contact Contextual Press at the address below.

Printed in the United States of America
First Printing, 2016

978-0-9801817-0-8

Criminology
Criminal Law
Jurisprudence
Constitutional Law > Civil Rights
Education & Teaching > Criminal Justice & Law Enforcement

Contextual Press, an imprint of CIAI Press
135 Jenkins St, Suite 105B
Box 237
St. Augustine, FL 32086
http://contextualpress.com

Distributed by Calibre Press

Cover by David Wenk. Cover photo, *Police Tape*, by Tony Webster, cc 2008.

This book is dedicated to the memory of Jeremy Mardis.

Also by Nick Selby:

Blackhatonomics:
An Inside Look at the Economics of Cybercrime;
With John Pirc, Will Gragido and Daniel Molina

Investigating Internet Crimes:
An Introduction to Solving Crimes in Cyberspace;
by Todd Shipley and Art Bowker (Nick Selby, Technical Editor)

Nick is a regular contributor to Calibre Press

Also by Ed Flosi:

SUDDEN in-Custody DEATHS:
Exploring Causality & Prevention Strategies
Flosi, Ed, MS.
Forensic Examiner 20.1 (Spring 2011): 31-48

Contents

FOREWORD

By Lawrence W. Mulvey

We ascribe extremely complex and demanding responsibilities to our police, which require that they make life and death decisions many times in a matter of seconds. On one extreme, we train and require that police engage in lifesaving measures such as CPR to a heart attack victim, or administer Narcan to an overdose victim, and even deliver a baby in an emergency situation. On the other, we train and legally sanction an officer to take the life of another.

Because police chiefs delegate to our police officers this awesome responsibility, they must provide the training, policies and procedures to fully prepare them for the job. Chiefs must give their officers clear guidance and direction, to equip them to fulfill their duty.

Yet the research, studies and data on police use of deadly force available to the chief is very limited. The FBI tracks fatal police shootings, but officials acknowledge that their data is far from complete.

Police agencies are not required to report police shootings, and while many police departments don't, the FBI has no mechanism to check the completeness or accuracy of reports that are forwarded from agencies that do. Projects from other agencies to account for arrest related deaths did occur over a span of several years, but have since been suspended, because of deficiencies in the data collection, and poor data quality.

I believe that it is this lack of research and analysis that has allowed the media to run unchecked with a narrative that claims the police are killing unarmed people of color at an alarming rate. When the narrative is repeated over and over and over again, it becomes an accepted perception for many. Unfortunately, without thorough research and analysis of these encounters between police and citizens, there is scant evidence to refute or sustain that perception.

The cop on the street is caught in the middle of this. Don't misunderstand, the overwhelming majority of agencies have policies and procedures and training on the use of force. Most agencies refined their policies following the 1985 Supreme Court decision that said police could only justify using deadly force if the suspects posed a threat to the officer or others. All officers generally know the criteria for use of deadly force.

But can we go further, can we fine-tune it; should we take a step back and rethink our approach. Unfortunately this comes at a time when municipal budgets have been slashed and many mental health programs have been cut. The police now encounter more subjects with mental health issues than they have heretofore. Since the Columbine tragedy and the repeated active shooter incidents that followed, we have trained our police not to wait for help; they must rush in, do not delay and aggressively take out the shooter.

Does this training influence the police officer's thinking or perception in other encounters? In order for the police chief to implement proper training and promulgate effective policies and procedures on the use of force, he or she must keep abreast of trends. The chief needs comprehensive and specific details on police encounters that result in the death of subjects, particularly unarmed subjects. Until now, that data has been difficult to find.

Nick Selby's book, "*In Context: Understanding Police Killings of Unarmed Civilians*," fills that important void for the police chief. Nick and his co-authors have outlined, with much specificity, all 153 cases wherein the police have killed unarmed subjects in 2015. A neutral, factual account is laid out clearly for you to make your own judgments, and the authors provide their commentary separately from these accounts.

The analysis in In Context shows that there are instances of unjustified, excessive force by some police officers. The value of human life is of extreme importance in our society and we put great trust and have high expectations that our police will serve us and protect us. Putting this in the proper perspective, what clearly comes through in the book is that the police, thrust into dangerous, tense and stressful situations, act properly in the overwhelming majority of the cases cited.

A police department's policies and training philosophy provides the foundation for positive outcomes. Many police chiefs have been concerned about repeated instances in which officers have been clearly justified in using deadly force to protect themselves or others, from vehicles that are essentially being utilized by offenders as a weapon against them. The book mentions several cases of this. In some cases, the officers were clearly justified, and in some cases, the officers might have used different tactics for a better outcome. Perhaps better tactical training on how to approach a suspect vehicle and keep out of harm's way will enhance the officer's safety and reduce the use of deadly force.

Another concrete finding in the book is that we as a society need to put more money and funding into treating the mentally ill. In Context examines 29 cases wherein the police killed an unarmed person suffering from mental illness. Certainly expanding and creating Crisis Intervention Teams (CIT) to assist the police would be helpful, but we are light years away from having this resource available to the cop in the moment he or she needs it. So I believe we need to focus more on situational scenario-based training.

If a department has an Electronic Control Device (ECD, such as TASER) program, perhaps the training component should include de-escalation tactics before resorting to an immediate deployment of the ECD. Delaying actions, without putting an officer in grave risk of harm, are an option. At any given moment in time situations change; deadly force might be indicated in one moment, but perhaps there is another less deadly option one or two seconds later.

I believe we need to promote the training of officers to tactically retreat in some situations. Many cops have the mindset that retreat is failure. But sometimes stepping back and containing a situation is the better option. Officers should be aware, however, that acts of omission as sworn officers can carry the same amount of liability as intentional overt actions. This illustrates just how difficult the policing profession is.

I have found In Context to be quite insightful. It should serve as an important resource for all law enforcement leaders. For the media, it's time to correct the record. The inaccurate narrative they have put forth has had repercussions. The way the police profession has been portrayed both reflects and creates public mistrust. Have police officers been verbally and physically assaulted because of the sentiment? Have potential high quality police candidates sought work elsewhere? At least the discourse should no longer be one-sided.

-Lawrence W. Mulvey
Long Island, New York

Commissioner Mulvey retired in 2011 as the Commissioner of the Nassau County, New York, Police Department. His career in law enforcement spanned 38 years. Commissioner Mulvey has a Bachelor of Science degree in Criminal Justice from John Jay College of Criminal Justice, and a Master of Science in Criminal Justice from Long Island University. He is a graduate of the FBI National Academy (189th session), and an FBI Certified Hostage Negotiator. Commissioner Mulvey was awarded the Purple Heart after being stabbed three times in the chest in the line of duty.

INTRODUCTION

By Nick Selby

Since 2015, the media and the public have paid more attention than ever before to the use of deadly force by American police officers. That's a *great* thing. The more questions the public asks, the more the public demands police produce believable, transparent evidence that they are treating people fairly, the better off our nation will become. You will see how true this is throughout this book, but until 2015, not many Americans had noticed that the data gathering done by the government on this subject was, to put it mildly, really bad.

In the United States, these incidents are reported on a voluntary basis for many of the important data points that ultimately comprise government statistics related to lethal use of force. American criminal justice system statistics about deaths related to law enforcement operations (of officers and of suspects/convicts) are compiled mainly by the Federal Bureau of Investigation[1] a national law enforcement agency with no real power to compel local, county, state and tribal police departments to actually report these numbers, and which provides few, if any, rigorous standards or definitions around what specifics are reported. Since 2010, The Bureau of Justice Statistics has been testing an absolutely excellent open-source program to capture deaths in custody, but it has not yet been officially unveiled.

Now, this lack of useful data on police use of force hasn't gone entirely un-noticed — it's just that those who noticed it didn't get any attention. They tended to be nerds; academics and others with a professional interest in the topic, and because crime was at all-time lows and life was generally pretty safe, there simply wasn't the kind of driving force required to precipitate change at a macro, or societal, level.

There were some exceptions. Some good reporters, some criminal justice professors and academics, and certain activists did notice this paucity of police use of force data, and they tried to do something about it. These efforts, though, were generally relegated to, "toil in obscurity" status. One such project was started in 2012 by D. Brian Burghart, a journalist in Reno, Nevada, who began to count every killing of a citizen by police since 2000.

Burghart's insight came to him serendipitously. He was perusing federal justice statistics and he came across a statistic he found odd and, frankly, unbelievable: according to the FBI statistics, police in Florida had never had an officer-involved justifiable killing – at least in the years Burghart reviewed. Knowing both cops and Floridians, Burghart sensed that this could not possibly be correct. The serendipity was that Florida was the only state that had never participated in reporting its officer-involved deaths.

"From a journalist's ironic point of view," Burghart told me, "it was the lack of transparency that caused the exposure. If I had picked almost any other state, I probably just would have said, 'Oh, that's interesting,' and continued to believe the stats put out by the FBI and the mainstream media and moved on."

Instead, Burghart began to Google.

He soon came across many articles about police involved killings in Florida, and across the country, and he came to realize that the FBI figures were wrong everywhere – and badly so. He realized that he could do something about it in the same way he just proved his point: through open source research and statistical analysis. Thus the Fatal Encounters project was born.

In America, a sea change began in 2012 and 2013. Empowered by the Internet and social media, and an increased ability to gather, analyze and quickly and cheaply disseminate data, new groups began to bring attention to issues around police use of force and abuse of their authority. CopBlock, CopWatch and other groups determined to hold police accountable for their actions, and to highlight what they said was the hypocrisy of cops enforcing laws unfairly or flouting laws themselves, began to use video and data to prove their point. Police militarization – the use by police of equipment originally made for the military but sold at steep discounts to local police departments – became a related subject of particular concern.[2]

Burghart's project, Fatal Encounters, became more important in 2014 when several high-profile killings by police of unarmed black men were referred to in the mainstream media as a trend. Newspapers began to dig in. In the aftermath of the burning of the QT gas station in Ferguson, MO, which was set ablaze by protesters angered by the shooting death by Officer Darren Wilson of Michael Brown, journalists were better able to quantify the anger of protesters using Fatal Encounters data. The genuine grassroots movement to question how often police killed people – and more specifically, how often white police killed black people – was ultimately bolstered by the protesters' access to this trove of data.

The questions these activists ask are crucial. They are questions that we as law enforcement officers and administrators and researchers, at the local, county, state and federal level, have failed to answer in a manner that people can understand, believe and, most important, trust.

By early 2015, two major newspapers – the Guardian and the Washington Post – had begun their own projects to count some of these killings. Each placed upon their projects a slightly different spin. Both the Post's "Fatal Force" and the Guardian's "The Counted" series based their initial count on Fatal Encounters' data, but then quickly moved on to their own gathering and reporting systems. Their methodologies varied – the Post stayed focused on police shooting deaths, while the Guardian opened its scope to all kinds of killing by police, regardless of method and regardless, at times, of whether the death actually involved police, per-se.

The Guardian statistics, for example, included deaths that occurred in federal prisons, off-duty personal disputes, and even traffic accidents in which a police vehicle was involved. This broader methodology upped the total of "police killings" and many of these were included in The Guardian's reported totals. But "The Counted" was broadly popular, and very culturally significant. Through beautiful graphical visualization and personal stories of each decedent, The Counted was ultimately most successful in humanizing and democratizing the statistics about police killings, and bringing them to the mainstream reader. In April, 2016, Wesley Lowery's and The Post's efforts resulted in the well-deserved award of a Pulitzer Prize for national reporting. All of this focused the attention of unprecedented numbers of Americans on questions about how they are policed.

As 2015 progressed, more database projects sprang up, also based on Fatal Encounters, and run by many groups. They became better at counting the high-level number of people killed by police, but important facts were not considered in the analysis, such as why the decedent was killed. There were often no details, or only the ones that served a narrative, but other key data were absent. There was no context.

In short, the reporting I saw, for various reasons, was missing some important points. As a police officer myself, I was aware that many incidents in which police use force begin with a civilian threatening another person or the officer. As someone who runs a company that provides data analytics to law enforcement, I was in a position to recognize that the data in the news stories was incomplete

Let me be clear at the outset; my objective is to be objective. This was not a project I marched into to defend the officers indiscriminately or to exonerate the guilty. Rather, the media narrative I was seeing did not have a foundation based on robust data or rigorous process, which makes it impossible for the police to learn from mistakes and build on strengths. It was analysis, but analysis that did not take the whole picture into account.

This doesn't mean the cops always look good, and the media is not by any means the only side withholding context. The shooting of Laquan McDonald in Chicago is the best example of where honest people, relying solely on public proclamations and officer statements, could have easily written that we saw a completely legitimate and even heroic effort by police to stop a knife-wielding assailant. Then the in-car video was disclosed. It showed clearly that the officers were not in the immediate danger they claimed, but instead that McDonald was 20 feet from any officer when Officer Jason Van Dyke fired multiple times, killing the young man in the street. It is a case that now looks unjustified, and VanDyke was soon indicted for murder.[3]

In the same way, media coverage of officer-involved deaths can lead to inaccurate impressions. Filimoni Raiyawa died while battling officers in San Francisco in July, 2015. The Guardian said that Raiyawa had, "been involved in a traffic collision, fought with another individual at the scene, had run away from, and then allegedly fought with and injured, two officers before becoming unresponsive." This account may be factually true as far as what it states, but there was some extremely important information relevant to context that was left out of their summation.

A deeper investigation into even the media reports that were publicly available at the time of the original reporting surrounding the case would add the following to this narrative; that Raiyawa, who was 6 feet tall and weighed 265 pounds, was the caregiver to 96-year-old Solomon Cohen, whom Raiyawa had just beaten to death half an hour earlier. Soon after, Raiyawa rear-ended a BMW and pushed it across a street and into a parked car. When its driver got out of the BMW, Raiyawa began making disturbing statements about God and "God's will," and chased the driver around the block. When police responded, Raiyawa beat a female officer several times about the head and shoulders until she lay barely conscious on the ground. Raiyawa then grabbed the officer's standing partner by the wrist, and threw her to the ground.

Witnesses saw two female police officers trying and failing to subdue Raiyawa. One said, "Nothing was going to get him to stop moving." Raiyawa continued to fight officers and finally collapsed after he tried to break into a restaurant.

When putting all of the information together you get a clearer picture, where you can derive that the two officers used tremendous restraint by not using their guns. When Raiyawa died, his death was due to existing health issues aggravated by the physical exertion of murdering one person, attempting to murder another, and attacking others. That is a lot of valuable context to leave out when arguing the case of police negligence.

In the middle of 2015, I began a project to track killings by police of unarmed civilians. I decided that it should not have any text or prose because any attempt to describe an incident was inherently editorial. I wanted to ask questions to which the answer would be "Yes," "No," "Unknown," or "Not applicable."

I chose to inquire into police killings of unarmed civilians because it was my fear that other projects were creating body counts seemingly with the intent of clocking numbers that were higher and higher, using methodology that seemed designed to maximize "head count." The Guardian and the Post added much needed attention to serious shortcomings, and what they ultimately did was incomplete.

If we seek to use the data to affect outcomes, to change things, to inform training and policy and debate, the non-obvious question was, in addition to just "deaths," what *else* should we be counting?

When I look at what should be counted, I start at the goal: to differentiate killings by police who are behaving badly from those in which cops were doing what we want them to do – that is, standing between civilians in danger of losing their lives and those who would take their lives from them.

In short, I wanted to know when officers behaved as they should behave, as I say they did in the Raiyawa case I mentioned previously.

The PKIC database gave no opinion whatsoever. In this book, which is entirely separate from the PKIC project – my co-authors and I give opinions. In doing this, there is a risk: there are some cases (like that of Mr. Raiyawa, or Samuel DuBose) that may seem obvious at the outset. But there are others that aren't really so clear, or are even misleading based on initial public information given through the police and the media.

The task we set ourselves, in laying out the cases in this book, was to search as far and wide as possible to get context from witness statements, review every video and audio recording, and examine every available coroner report and any other objective evidence available before offering any opinion. We read all available media reports, watched all available video, searched for and found medical examiner or coroner reports, toxicology reports, witness statements, and other information available publicly wherever we could.

In this book we stake out positions that may well be proved incorrect after new evidence comes to light. In many cases, we bemoan the lack of evidence, and cite this as another example of how police agencies must try and disclose as much evidence as early as possible without undermining the integrity of the investigation. And make no mistake, while there are many cases in which we find the police action apparently justified, there are many other cases in this book in which we opine that the police are just, plain wrong. No one has cherry-picked to demonstrate a particular opinion: all cases for the year are included.

No one complains when a police officer uses deadly force to end a hijacking in progress, a school shooting, or an armed robbery. What no one likes is when it appears that police are using their authority and deadly force abusively, which results in taking the lives of people without justification.

I decided that the only way to tell the difference between these kinds of events is to ask as many questions as you can about how the police got involved, what happened when they did, and what specific actions lead to the use by the police of deadly force against a person who was, presumably, unarmed and therefore not dangerous.

The answers are revealing. They show that more than 70% of the unarmed civilians killed by police in 2015 were in the middle of committing crimes such as robbery, carjacking, assault, serious destruction of property or burglary. It is important to note that these crimes themselves are not necessarily justification for the use by police of deadly force. This simply says, seven in every ten unarmed people killed by police were engaging in actions that brought the police to them, most often at the direct request of the community.

Unarmed people killed by police in 2015 had already injured and assaulted civilians in 26 cases, and murdered other civilians in 2 cases – this despite the fact that the decedent was not armed.

It is a mistake to equate "unarmed," to always mean "not dangerous."

...

I am a law enforcement expert, and more specifically, an expert on police data and statistics. My project set out to answer these kinds of questions. I sought to look back at the entire group of unarmed people who were killed during encounters with the police, with the benefit of lack of political pressure, lack of commercial media requirements, and the fact that I am not personally involved in any of these cases.

This book is co-authored by Ben Singleton, a 10-year veteran officer who has worked patrol, traffic enforcement, field training, SWAT, narcotics, and criminal investigations; and by Ed Flosi, a 27-year police veteran who currently owns and operates a company that provides use of force and defensive tactics training for law enforcement agencies. Flosi's firm also offers consultation and expert witness services for both defense attorneys and prosecutors in cases in which officers were alleged to have used excessive force The book has been reviewed by several other officers, administrators, statisticians, citizen oversight experts, authors and editors.

We wanted our work to be as useful and immediately applicable as possible. The intent of this book is to make these results, these statistics, actionable. Because people rightly distrust statistical analyses, we have provided more than 500 source reference links, and of course the underlying PKIC data is open and freely distributable, so that people may check our work and present alternate analysis.

We want to change the debate from one of blame to one of *action*, to review and update policies and procedures.

Body counts make for great headlines. If you are in the business of selling newspapers, it's a fact that reporting on the more than 1,200 people who were killed in 2015 by the police will sell a lot of newspapers and significantly drive online traffic. What it won't do is change anything about how the nearly 18,000 law enforcement agencies in the United States operate or use force.

America is a very violent place. Its police must address violence not on a statistical level, but on an individual, face-to-face, at bad-breath distance, in person encounter. While we study numbers on killings, it is crucial to remember that there's nothing theoretical about the danger of doing police work in America.

It is important to consider context. While I am, of course, not saying that any unjustified death is acceptable – I absolutely do not say that - it's important to keep in perspective how many deaths we are talking about that appear to be unjustified. As we will see in this book, in most cases in which the police killed a civilian, they were justified.

Another controversy is that killings by police are not objectively and thoroughly investigated. We believe that failure to do so is a travesty. Investigations in which slanted or omitted questions to witnesses, or ones in which leading questions to involved law enforcement officers destroy objectivity are no better. Part of the purpose of this book is to show that honest police officers believe these statements to be true, and in this, we stand firmly on the side of society. We have found cases in this book (for example, here) in which an officer may have been found to be justified by the department, and we respectfully disagree.

The fact is, though, that until society understands the process, the law, and the methodology of investigations, it will continue to react to investigations with general distrust. It is a truth that one cannot detect "abnormal" until one understands what "normal" looks like. It is our contention that too much of the public debate has been held on emotional, as opposed to factual and legal grounds.

To begin, I would like to give some high-level lessons that we have learned studying the 153 incidents during 2015 in which an unarmed civilian lost his or her life after an encounter with an American police officer.

– Nick Selby
Arlington, Texas

ABOUT THE DATA

This book is based on the project that was begun by a group gathered at StreetCred Software, Inc.: The StreetCred® Police Killings in Context (PKIC) database. PKIC is a peer-reviewed, open-standard database that includes incidents during 2015 in which an unarmed civilian was killed by any cause, except vehicle accidents, that occurred within the United States during an encounter with American police who were acting (whether on-, or off-duty) in an official capacity, from the time of first contact through booking.

Note: this book is separate from the PKIC project in all respects, and is not sponsored, promoted, endorsed or published by StreetCred Software or the PKIC project. In fact, anyone who disagrees with analysis provided in this book is free to use the data from the PKIC database to create their own analysis. The data is freely available at https://github.com/StreetCredSoftware/PKIC.

PKIC sought to provide, in as transparent and accurate terms as possible, contextually relevant facts on deadly force incidents in which American police acting in an official capacity kill unarmed civilians. It sought to enable serious researchers, reporters, legislators, agency administrators and others to understand issues of improper police use of deadly force.

Researchers, journalists, activists, and others may use PKIC data to ask questions, such as, "Of all unjustified or potentially unjustified killings by police, what were the commonalities?" and, "Are our police treating our communities fairly?" These are incredibly important questions that deserve answers.

The goal is to give stakeholders the tools they need to better understand whether law enforcement is fairly and justly treating the public it is sworn to protect. The goal is not to stanch criticism or suppress controversy. It is to produce clean, clear and actionable data that both sides can use to intelligently and meaningfully debate the way forward.

Deciding What To Gather

It was the stated goal to be able to ask for data on as many contextually relevant data points as could be found, so that a person looking at just the answers to our questions could have a hope of understanding what happened.

The first things we needed to determine were entirely technical, and these were questions of methodology. For example, we needed to consult with scientists and statisticians and database experts and make decisions about things like:

- Data quality (is the data accurate and as complete as possible?);
- Data structure (does our methodology make sense, and how can we improve it?);
- Data normalization and de-duplication (are we providing data that can be used by everyone? In a form that assures duplicates don't exist?);
- Errors and omissions (how do we know what we have wrong; what can we add or subtract to make it right?); and most important,
- Bias: how do we succeed in our project goal to gather un-biased and objective data, and how do we uncover bias in our figures?

These questions were very important, and we came up with some equally important policies. First, there could be no editorializing within the project: StreetCred PKIC could not draw conclusions as to culpability or blame for any incident, and could not have any opinion on any incident or its outcome.

We needed to ensure that the dataset would be maintained entirely separate from any analysis by any party (including StreetCred Software, Inc.) of any datum or data within. That means that, even if we don't like the way an incident went, we can't change it or soft-pedal it: the data are what the data are.

We provided a mechanism for gathering errata and publishing corrections. This was accomplished through a special mail form at the StreetCred Software website, and announcement of the publication of errata would be done through the official StreetCred PKIC Twitter account.

StreetCred PKIC also maintains a page that would document every change made to the data, so that anyone could go back and read every change to find how our data have changed over time. There were 49 additions or changes in 2015, including two major updates that removed some cases from the DB that did not meet the published criteria, but had been erroneously included. Some six incidents were removed from the database for this reason on December 21, 2015 alone.

When these records were removed, we posted a notice, such as:

> 3 DEC 2015 21:39: Removed Joshua Jozefowicz, after department issued a press release stating that Jozefowicz was armed with a firearm at the time of his death.

What Was Gathered

Many of the data types we got were pretty obvious, and dictated by necessity, but adapted by us for better normalization – as an example, The Guardian lists name like, "John Q. Public," but we believed it basic database best-practices to have individual columns for last name, first name, middle name or initial, prefix (like Dr., Mr., Mrs.) suffix (III, Jr., etc.) and other columns, such as race, age, etc.

We had noticed in reviewing other projects that that the media used several conventions that were probably unhelpful, as they used terms that were not necessarily clear to all, but which most people "felt" they understood.

A perfect example of this is the use of the word, "Homicide." The definition of Homicide is somewhat confusing to those outside the criminal justice system – and we blame television for this. As a medical finding, "homicide" means "death at the hands of another." The crucial thing to recognize is that, a medical finding of homicide is not a statement of culpability, an indictment for a crime or even, for that matter, a finding that a crime took place - not all homicides are crimes. We mention this a number of times throughout the book.

Since we were about to undertake a project in which we would count deaths of unarmed people, the definition of the word, "Armed" became important as well. During 2014, the fatal shooting by police of Tamir Rice, a 12-year-old boy who was in a park brandishing an airsoft gun at passers-by, raised many questions about whether an officer has a reasonable responsibility to determine whether a weapon is real before firing.

A more complex discussion regarding the answer to this will come up in our chapter on Defining "Armed", but the simple answer, upheld repeatedly in case law, is that the officer does not have such a responsibility. The reason why is that it's not reasonable to ask anyone, even a police officer, to know the difference between a fake weapon and a real one, or even whether something presented in a manner consistent with the way one would wield a weapon, is indeed a weapon of any kind. The legal standard remains that if an objectively reasonable person would feel that they are under an imminent threat of death or serious bodily injury given the information they had at the time, they are permitted to defend themselves. Finding out later that the gun was fake does not negate the person's conclusion at the time of the incident. Just as police cannot legally shoot you now for a murder you committed five minutes ago, we cannot judge what the police decided five minutes ago by what they learned just now.

Race

Another major consideration was race, both of the decedent and the officer(s) involved in an incident. Almost all news reports of a killing of a civilian by police report on the race of the decedent. The race of the officer(s) involved is much less frequently stated. In order to determine the race of the officer involved, we read primary and secondary sources, seeking specific articulation of the race of the officer. This includes sentences such as, "Officer X, who is white…" or confirmation to that effect.

Other constructs, such as: "Mr. Y, a black man, was killed by a white police officer" are only acceptable if the source provides further information about the provenance of this determination. We have read several news articles that state constructs that later turned out to be false – someone's race was misidentified. A photo of the officer in an article that is not accompanied by a specific statement of the race of the officer is not acceptable evidence of the officer's race. "Further information," can be the name of the officer and his rank, or, if the name is not released, a reference to an official statement by police that contains the racial characteristics of the officer involved.

Another relatively common problem was that news reports are often wrong and imitate one another. In December, 2015, a man named Miguel Espinal was killed by NYPD officers after a car chase that led to a wooded area along the Saw Mill River Parkway in Yonkers, New York. By the next day, media reported that Mr. Espinal was black, but no official comment on his race could be located. On September 18, 2015, Cecil Lacy was killed after a confrontation on the Tulalip Indian Reservation with officers from the Tulalip Tribal Police. Correspondence with the Washington State Police and Tulalip Tribal Police did not result in confirmation that Mr. Lacy was Native American, as was reported by many news outlets. PKIC went to great lengths to confirm race of officers and decedents wherever possible.

This confusion over race was part of a larger trend we discovered in our analysis of the data: a widespread media inconsistency in reporting on race. According to our analysis of 679 media reports gathered by PKIC on the killings of unarmed civilians, in 2015, the news media was more than three times more likely to name the race of the officer involved in a police killing of an unarmed person if the decedent was black.

Gender

Almost all news reports cite the gender of the decedent. The gender of the officer(s) involved is less frequently stated. In order to determine the gender of the officer involved, we read primary and secondary sources seeking specific articulation of their gender. This, however, is not as specific as race. Many articles will specifically state "female officer," while others will do it indirectly, saying, for example: "Police have not released the name of the officer involved in the shooting, but state she is a six-year veteran of the force," or "Police say the officer deployed his TASER…" It is also marginally acceptable to infer the gender of the officer through the officer's obviously male or female name, such as "Michael" or "Elizabeth," however great care was taken when dealing with names that are dual-gender in the American culture, such as "Ashley," "Blair," "Sydney," and the like. This is especially important as even smaller agencies become more supportive of transgender officers in their ranks[4], because we did not want to presume the gender of an officer. A photo of the officer in an article that is not accompanied by a specific statement that the officer pictured is the officer involved in the incident is not acceptable to PKIC as gender identification.

Types of Data Gathered

The 79 data points gathered by the PKIC data project for each incident are neither complete, nor final. Some (like, 'Armed') are currently all listed as 'N' – but the category was left in for later expansion should the project ever decide to collect data on armed decedents.

Others represent a cluster of questions about a single topic. Consider the columns: '911 Call for Service', '911 Caller Reported Armed', 'Decedent Described In 911 Call for Service', 'Alarm Triggered', and 'Other Community Contact.' They all help fill in gaps in understandings and answer questions about how the police come in contact with someone.

To those outside law enforcement, it's not always obvious that there is a limited number of ways in which people come in contact with the cops, and they can be broken into rough categories of, "Calls for service," and "Self-initiated." Calls for service involve flagging down an officer in some manner, calling the local non-emergency or 911 emergency numbers, pulling the signal on a call box, pushing a panic button, or setting off an alarm. Self-dispatched calls are those in which the officer observes a crime or event in progress, such as a traffic infraction, or a robbery, or smoke coming from a building, or a suspicious person. It could be from the work of a detective who has uncovered the identity of someone who he wants to have a conversation with, or arrest.

It was important to us at PKIC to separate these types of contacts, because one of the primary questions Americans have for their law enforcement is whether law enforcement unfairly targets minorities like black people. By discovering how the officer first came in contact with a person, we can better determine whether the officer was engaging in racial profiling. For example, if someone calls the police and reports a robbery in progress, then describes the suspect as a black male, 6 feet tall, wearing a bowler hat and white pants, and the officer arrives on scene and spots a six-foot-tall black man wearing a bowler hat and white pants holding a knife, we can safely say that the officer did not target the suspect through racial profiling.

Another important aspect is whether the caller reports the person as armed. If the suspect ultimately turns out to be unarmed, but the 911 caller reported that the suspect was armed, that is context that may affect the behavior of the officer when he comes in contact with the suspect.

We went through similar exercises about mental illness. Even before we began the project we knew that some behavior exhibited by the mentally ill is indistinguishable to the layman from acute narcotic intoxication. We had entered a column for "Apparent Mental Illness," but Elisabeth Nybo at the Santa Barbara Sheriff's office immediately suggested another column, 'Prior diagnosis of serious mental illness.' Adding this column gave us unprecedented insight into one of the most important trends in 2015: that of the mentally ill in deadly force situations. We now know, for example, that

19% - nearly one in five unarmed people killed by law enforcement in 2015 – were apparently mentally ill, and 11% had prior diagnoses of serious mental illness (See the Mental Health chapter). These are truly staggering numbers, and they allow us to make very aggressive recommendations about mental health programs, like Crisis Intervention Team training.

Some of the other columns here are about drug and alcohol use, types of offenses (robbery, assault, burglary, vandalism), whether the decedent had killed or assaulted another civilian, or the officer; whether video and/or audio was available. This last proved to be inspired when the Chicago Police Department official video in the Laquan McDonald case – the most controversial case it has had in years – turned out to be without audio. We include columns on whether there were non-police, civilian witnesses and whether those witnesses supported or disputed the official police account (or both); whether the incident began on a traffic stop; whether the officer involved had been fired, or indicted, etc. One set of questions seeks to find whether the decedent had any convictions of violent crime in the past, and whether the officer involved had had any complaints of excessive force in his past – placing the higher standard rightly upon the officer.

Candidates

The StreetCred PKIC dataset considers any death that occurs within the United States, that occurs during an encounter with American law enforcement, from first contact through booking, except vehicle accidents, in which the decedent is unarmed.

We do not consider vehicle-wreck fatalities. These are incredibly difficult to track, and data on them is very dirty and unreliable.

We do not consider deaths in county jail or in Municipal jail after booking. A jail is a confinement facility designed to hold people awaiting trial, or serving short sentences; typically of less than one year. Jails are typically managed either by the office of the county Sheriff, or by a municipality, or a county government. Jail officers are generally not police officers, even if they are working as a corrections officer or as a jailer run by a county Sheriff. It is true that they ultimately are responsible to, and the Sheriff is ultimately responsible for, the jail. These are outside the scope of this data set. There are cases in this book in which fights broke out in the jail, resulting in the death of the decedent, but these were in pre-booking when the person was still in the officer's custody.

We do not consider deaths in prison. A prison is a confinement facility, usually run by the state or federal government, which generally houses prisoners convicted of crimes punishable by one year or more. Corrections officers in prisons are almost always not police officers.

We do not consider unofficial acts committed off-duty. A personal dispute between family members or friends, who happen to be police officers, that turns deadly, is not in the scope of this database. This database seeks to highlight killing of unarmed civilians by police, whether on- or off-duty, who are acting in an official capacity.

Sources

This project seeks relevant, factual, non-biased news sources. The source of each data entry should be documented, in the dataset Links columns, and/or bibliography – note that the bibliography contains URLs not included in the Links columns in cases when all three links columns are already occupied and we have more links to provide. The order in which sources are checked, trusted and then used are as follows:

- Official Coroner reports, releases, or statements;
- Official district or county or state attorney reports, releases, or statements;
- Grand jury reports, records, transcripts, indictments, or evidence;

- News reports (print, web or television/video) by reputable news sources that quote more than one source and do not have a demonstrable bias towards any given version of the story; and
- Official police reports, statements, or releases.

Note: official police reports are written by police officers either directly involved with the incident, or based upon interviews with those directly involved in an incident. It has been demonstrated that officers have lied in the preparation of their statements and reports. This is an enormous challenge and impediment to our work. These lies can be direct, or they may be lies of omission. There are criminal penalties for falsifying these reports and statements, which are in public records. The chances of dishonesty being uncovered get higher each year with the increased scrutiny of civil litigation attorneys, investigative reporters, public advocacy groups, and projects including this one. Civil lawsuits, when filed, especially tend to bring forth many more documents and testimonial records than prior to litigation.

We recognize fully that basing our analyses on these sources comes with risks and challenges. Even if you don't believe our analysis is better, we believe it is different from those of the available analysis in the press. We of course believe that our formal training in use of force and subject-matter expertise in law enforcement make our analysis better.

By focusing on the sources previously mentioned, in the order stated, StreetCred PKIC makes every effort to remain unbiased and factual.

In general, local television news, local newspaper and news sites and other traditional local, county, state, regional and national news sources provide acceptable depth and acceptably unbiased reporting to be included as primary or secondary sources.

In certain cases, articles in various Patch outlets, New York Newsday, The Huffington Post, The Daily Kos, The Washington Times, The Guardian (UK), PhotographyIsNotACrime, etc., are acceptable only as secondary sources.

Articles on the websites of groups with an overt agenda – CopBlock, We Support Our Police, and similar groups – are legitimate outlets to discuss issues, but are not, in our view, sufficiently objective, and are only used in cases in which there are no other sources and there is evidence that an event occurred. We believe that the watchdog aspects that call attention to potentially illegal activity by police that these groups provide are an important First Amendment-protected activity. However it is often difficult to verify the veracity of claims that are made.

Known Limitations of Data

The StreetCred PKIC methodologies are designed to reduce to the lowest number possible those incidents in which we only have the word of the police as to what happened in an incident. Specifically, records that contain official autopsy data, prosecution or grand jury testimony, information that comes from witnesses (who either support or dispute the account of the police), video and audio (taken by police, surveillance cameras or bystanders), timestamps on 911 calls, interviews with 911 callers, computer-aided dispatch records and other objective records, are more reliable than those that do not contain these entries.

There are incidents in the PKIC database in which it is impossible to verify claims and statements made by police, and we acknowledge this. Such is the nature of policing. This means that researchers are unable, in some cases, to verify claims by police as to specifics of an incident. It also means that researchers are unable to reach conclusions as to whether the police behave differently in cases when they know that they are being observed by others. There are incidents in the PKIC database for which the only sources are media reports. While sub-optimal, using our methods and techniques to assure multiple references and quotes from officials, we feel these records are better than no record.

Racial & Ethnic Identifier Terms

The Criminal Justice Information Services Division (CJIS) of the Federal Bureau of Investigation (FBI) produces the nation's authoritative criminal statistics set, the Uniform Crime Report (UCR). We have adopted for our project and this report a slightly modified version of UCR racial and ethnic naming conventions. The UCR categories include, "White," "Black or African American," "American Indian or Alaska Native," "Asian," "Native Hawaiian or Other Pacific Islander," and "Hispanic or Latino." This is particularly confusing because, since 1997, the federal Office of Management and Budget has required all federal agencies to use a minimum of five race categories: White, Black or African American, American Indian or Alaska Native, Asian, and Native Hawaiian or Other Pacific Islander.

Note the lack in the federal OMB requirements of the term, "Hispanic or Latino." Since the 2010 Census, the U.S. Census Bureau has treated "Hispanic or Latino" as an ethnicity separate from race (White, Black, American Indian, etc.). The Census Bureau's document, "Overview of Race and Hispanic Origin: 2010", attempts to clarify: "'Hispanic or Latino' refers to a person of Cuban, Mexican, Puerto Rican, South or Central American, or other Spanish culture or origin regardless of race." While this is probably ultimately the correct decision, it has created heaps of confusion in the statistics and demographics community, and resulted in a large range of descriptions from non-statisticians and non-demographers that conflate "race" with "ethnicity."

In this book, and in the PKIC project, we use "White," "Black," "American Indian," "Asian or Pacific Islander," and "Hispanic." "Semitic," refers to those peoples who speak in a family of languages that includes Hebrew, Arabic, and, constituting the main subgroup of the Afro-Asiatic family.

Similar Projects

PKIC is itself a derivative work of, and an expansion of a small subset of, the excellent Fatal Encounters. D. Brian Burghart, the founder of Fatal Encounters, was incredibly generous and gracious about his cooperation. The partnership between PKIC and Fatal Encounters is one of a number of similar ones that comprise projects that span the political spectrum: from Black Lives Matter, Mapping Police Violence and The Guardian, to the Washington Post and PKIC, Fatal Encounters' thorough and balanced approach has been a boon to citizens in the United States who have had to tolerate a highly incomplete approach toward this type of data from our government.

It is important to note the importance of the attention to this problem area by The Guardian and The Washington Post. Without the coverage by these very well-read publications, it is almost certain that counting this kind of data wouldn't have been given the priority within the US Department of Justice it's been given. In 2016, two highly important developments have already taken place, and more are expected to come.

The first major development was the release by the Sunlight Foundation of their Hall of Justice Project, which seeks to serve as a curated clearinghouse of links to datasets from every state in the nation. This is an ambitious project from a necessary organization that does great work.

The second has been the revamping by the California Department of Justice of their OpenJustice portal. The CADOJ initiative tries to make the data accessible to everyone (through beautiful visualization), while staying very aware that any visualization is, by definition, editorializing—something they don't seek to do.

In their words: "OpenJustice advances Attorney General Kamala D. Harris's "Smart on Crime" vision by leveraging statistical data maintained by the California Department of Justice (CA DOJ) and other publicly available datasets."

Unlike many projects that deal with analysis of law enforcement data, CADOJ is trying its best to play this as objectively as possible. That is a hard road to walk, and we can see CADOJ is really trying to get it right.

OpenJustice tries to bring some clarity to race and ethnicity questions, and in some ways succeeds, while in others it works hard to bring contextual data to the fore. As an example, a comparison of the race and ethnicity of those arrested against the racial composition of the state would appear to be a data point, but demographers know better predictors of criminality include issues of poverty, substance abuse, education, nutrition, and other factors long discussed by social scientists—race comes almost dead last in this list.

OpenJustice is working admirably to provide Californians meaningful statistics—information, not just data—here and in future revamps. Of course, the most exciting thing to me is that the data is open and being provided with tools to help understand the data they are seeing, without special software. That is very important. It also speaks to where California DOJ is going with this. Obviously they have decided that transparency—sunlight—is the best solution for problems.

DEMOGRAPHICS

When considering demographics, it is important to understand that these are presented without context. We have seen newspaper reporters make the highly tempting, and utterly wrong, leap to comparing the proportion of black males in this cohort to black males in the United States. This is wrong for many reasons, explained later in the book.

In this chapter we set forth some raw demographic data that will serve as the basis for analysis later in the book.

Decedent Demographics

One hundred and fifty three cases fit the criteria for inclusion in the StreetCred Police Killings in Context Database in 2015. Of these, two (1.3%) were Asian or Pacific Islander; 59 (38.56%) were black or African American; 22 (14.37%) were Hispanic or Latino;[5] 1 (0.65%) was Native American; 2 (1.3%) were Semitic, 12 (7.84%) were of unknown race; and 55 (35.94%) were White.

Of the 153 cases, there were 149 (97.38%) males, and four (2.61%) females.

Geography

The cases were spread throughout the United States. Twenty percent of states (California, Florida, Georgia, Maryland, New York, Ohio, Oklahoma, Texas, Virginia and Washington) accounted for nearly 64% of the total – some 97 incidents occurred in these ten states.

There were 32 decedents in the state of California alone, which was the state with by far the most police involved killings. The Los Angeles Sheriff's Department and the Los Angeles Police Department each had five incidents each.

Florida had 13 incidents, though no agency in Florida had more than one incident.

Texas had 11 incidents among 11 agencies.

Oklahoma had eight incidents among seven agencies.

The state of New York had seven incidents, of which the City of New York Police Department had four incidents. Ohio had seven incidents, among six agencies.

Maryland had six incidents, spread among six agencies each.

Georgia had five incidents; two of these occurred at the DeKalb County Sheriff's Department.

Two states, Virginia and Washington, had four incidents, each among four agencies.

In nine states, Arizona, Colorado, Indiana, Kansas, Michigan, Minnesota, Mississippi, North Carolina and Pennsylvania, there were three incidents at three agencies, each.

In eight states – Connecticut, Iowa, Kentucky, Louisiana, Missouri, Nebraska, South Carolina, and Tennessee - there were two incidents, each at different agencies.

Thirteen states had one incident each: Alabama, Arkansas, Delaware, Hawaii, Illinois, Massachusetts, New Jersey, New Mexico, Oregon, Rhode Island, Utah, Wisconsin and West Virginia.

There were no incidents in ten states: Alaska, Idaho, Maine, Montana, Nevada, New Hampshire, North Dakota, South Dakota, Vermont and Wyoming.

Police Demographics

According to the Bureau of Justice Statistics[6], of the 477,000 full-time and 26,790 part-time police officers nationwide in 2013, about 58,000 were Black (11.51%), and the same number were female.

About 55,000 Hispanic officers (10.9%) were employed by local police departments in 2013. We assume that the BJS, a federal agency, is treating "Hispanic or Latino" as an ethnicity, not a race (see the About the Data chapter for more information).

Of the StreetCred PKIC's record of 153 unarmed people killed by police in 2015, we do not, in 129 cases, or 84%, know the race of the officer involved. This is not necessarily police departments being cagey or reluctant to release the information. In many agencies where there is union representation, there are restrictions on the department's release of personal information about officers. Other agencies are in states where privacy laws dictate non-release of personal information. And still in other cases, sometimes reporters are not as good at requesting pertinent information as one would hope. Finally, there is the chance of an error in PKIC's compilation of available data.

To compile this information, we analyzed the data in 679 media articles covering the 153 incidents in our database (see About the Data). We found that there were two incidents in which a black officer acted alone in the killing of an unarmed decedent; and one incident in which two black officers were involved in the killing of an unarmed decedent.

There were 12 incidents in which a white officer acted alone in the killing of an unarmed decedent; one incident in which a white officer and a black officer were involved in the killing of an unarmed decedent, and one incident in which a white officer and two black officers were involved in the killing of an unarmed decedent. There were also two incidents in which two white officers were involved in the killing of an unarmed decedent; three incidents in which three white officers were involved in the killing of an unarmed decedent, and two incidents in which two white officers and one black officer were involved in the killing of an unarmed decedent.

Table 1. describes these incidents:

Table 1 Race of officer(s) involved in use of deadly force incidents, 2015

Race of Officer 1	Race of Officer 2	Race of Officer 3	count
BLACK	BLACK	NONE	1
	NONE	NONE	2
WHITE	BLACK	BLACK	1
		NONE	1
	NONE	NONE	12
	WHITE	BLACK	2
		NONE	2
		WHITE	3

To read this chart, follow from the left to the right. For example, starting at the bottom, there were three incidents in which Officer 1, Officer 2 and Officer 3 were White.

There were two cases in which a black officer acting alone killed a black decedent, and one in which two black officers killed a white decedent.

There were nine cases in which a white officer acting alone killed black decedents, one in which a white officer acting alone killed a Native American decedent, and two in which a white officer acting alone killed a white decedent. There was one case in which a white officer and a black officer were involved in an incident in which a black decedent was killed. There was one incident in which a white officer and two black officers killed a black decedent.

There was one case in which two white officers killed a Hispanic decedent, and one in which two white officers killed a white decedent. There was one case in which two white officers and one black officer killed a black decedent, and one case in which three white officers killed a black decedent.

Table 2 Race of Officer(s) and Decedents

Race of officer 1	Race of Officer 2	Race of officer 3	Race of Decedent	count
BLACK	BLACK	NONE	White	1
	NONE	NONE	Black	2
WHITE	BLACK	BLACK	Black	1
		NONE	Black	1
	NONE	NONE	Black	9
			Native American	1
			White	2
	WHITE	BLACK	Black	2
		NONE	Hispanic	1
			White	1
		WHITE	Black	3

To read this chart, follow from the left to the right. For example, starting at the bottom, there were three incidents in which Officer 1, Officer 2 and Officer 3 were White, and the decedent was black.

Gender

There were 126 incidents in which male officers were involved with killings of civilians (more than one officer is involved in many individual incidents); there were two incidents in which one male and one or two female officers were involved. There were ten incidents in which women were involved as primary officer; there was one incident in which a female was primary and a male was secondary officer, and one in which female officers were primary and secondary officers.

POLICE-CITIZEN CONTACTS,
& DEADLY FORCE

In this book we ask several questions about how we are being policed, including whether police are treating citizens fairly, with respect for their lives and Constitutional rights. To address these questions, it's significant to know how citizens come into contact with police, because the dynamics are vastly different between types of contacts. The best definitions available on the use of deadly force and non-deadly force have to be provided. This chapter sets forth some of these fundamentals.

It has been often said that all policing is local. We cannot stress enough the basic truth of this concept, and its importance. In the media, and in television and film portrayals, police are often depicted as part of a cohesive national force. A key to analyzing police behavior is in understanding that policing differs between cities and suburbs, between counties and states, and even between large cities – the police in New York City are very culturally different from those in Boston or Baltimore. And all three are different from policing in smaller cities and towns across the country.

In the introduction we mentioned that there were around 18,000 law enforcement agencies in the United States. Three-quarters of America's 12,300 local police departments employ 24 or fewer officers; 48% employ fewer than 10 officers, and, in 2015, 5% employed a single officer. If we add to this America's 3000-some-odd county sheriffs, and 50 state police departments we begin to see the fragmented nature of American policing. The rest of the agencies include a couple thousand federal police agencies, various state and county police departments, and other jurisdictions that exist outside the mainstream of American life – and some of these agencies were involved in killings of unarmed civilians in 2015.

For example, in Cincinnati, Samuel DuBose was killed by an officer from the University of Cincinnati Police Department. Six-year-old Jeremy Mardis was killed by two officers from the Marksville City Marshals, Ward 2. A man named William Dick was killed in a struggle with rangers from the US Forest Service. All policing is local, so to better understand how these issues could have taken place, we look to the commonalities.

Deadly Force

The main thing law enforcement has in common throughout the country are the Constitutional limitations of officers' use of deadly force. The overriding law of the land that is most often looked to in cases in which officers use any force option, including deadly force, is Graham v. Connor (490 U.S. 386 (1989)). In this case, the US Supreme court ruled that an, "objective reasonableness" standard should apply to a civilian's claim that law enforcement officials used excessive force in the course of making an arrest, investigatory stop, or other "seizure" of his person.

Along with clarification of issues surrounding seizures, the court's ruling stated that, "[t]he 'reasonableness' of a particular use of force must be judged from the perspective of a reasonable officer on the scene, rather than with the 20/20 vision of hindsight." What this established was that the crucial element was how the officer measured the situation and its elements at the time, regardless of what may have been discovered later.

The court continued, "the 'reasonableness' inquiry in an excessive force case is an objective one: the question is whether the officers' actions are 'objectively reasonable' in light of the facts and circumstances confronting them, without regard to their underlying intent or motivation."

It also noted that the test for reasonableness ... "is not capable of precise definition or mechanical application," and therefore the test's "proper application requires careful attention to the facts and circumstances of each particular case."

One part of the Graham ruling dealt with some questions that could be used to balance the officer's rights versus those of a citizen's. These included the severity of the crime, whether the threat posed by the subject poses an immediate threat to the safety of the officers or others, and whether the person is actively resisting arrest or attempting to evade arrest by flight. Since the decision, later cases have added other factors to the analysis such as: the pace of the event; the number of officers versus number of suspects; injury or exhaustion level; mental illness; drug use; special skill demonstrated by subject; prior contacts with violence; and environmental factors.

Attempting to evade arrest by flight in a deadly force application is covered in another landmark case on deadly force from the 1980s: Tennessee v. Garner (471 U.S. 1 (1985)). In that case, the Supreme Court ruled that, under the Fourth Amendment, when a law enforcement officer is pursuing a fleeing suspect, he may only use deadly force to prevent escape when; (1) the officer has probable cause to believe that he has committed a crime involving the infliction or threatened infliction of serious physical harm, and (2) "the officer has probable cause to believe that the suspect poses a significant threat of death or serious physical injury to the officer or others." Tennessee v Garner was directly referenced in at least one case within this book.

Because this book deals in analysis of actions by officers that resulted in the deaths of civilians, it's crucial that the reader understand the legal definition of the terms of art, "deadly force" and "non-deadly-force." Note that the term, "less-lethal," listed by Black's Law Dictionary as, "jargon," is not included in these descriptions. While policing is local, and while all police departments have the ability to set their own policies about the use of force, the standard against which all officers and police departments in the United States are ultimately judged are standards that have been set through case law, generally at the United States Supreme Court, but sometimes from decisions of lower federal courts. These are the standards that, for example, were used by the United States Department of Justice when examining the actions in Ferguson, MO in 2014.

Deadly force is defined as: violent action known to create a substantial risk of causing death or serious bodily harm. (Black's Law Dictionary 9th Edition (2009), Garner, B., Thompson-Reuters, St. Paul, MN)

Many circuit courts have a similar definition, for example the 9th Circuit Court of Appeals defines Deadly Force as: Force that creates a substantial risk of causing serious bodily injury or death.

Many legal experts agree that "substantial risk" means that it is more likely than not.

Non-Deadly Force:

Force that is neither intended nor likely to cause death or serious bodily harm; force intended to cause only minor bodily harm. (Black's Law Dictionary 9th Edition (2009), Garner, B., Thompson-Reuters, St. Paul, MN)

In the 9th Circuit Court of Appeals, they have divided "Non-Deadly Force into two categories:

1. Non-Deadly Force: force that poses a minimal risk of injury or harm

2. Non-Deadly Intermediate Force: force capable of inflicting significant pain and causing serious injury. Examples of Non-Deadly Intermediate Force would be:

    a. TASER device in probe mode

    b. OC Spray

    c. Baton Strikes

    d. Police Service Dogs (K9)

When may an officer use Deadly Force? In direct defense of self or of others against deadly threat

- An officer may use deadly force to protect himself or others when there is an objective and reasonable belief the he/she is, or another person is, in imminent danger of death or serious bodily injury given the totality of the facts and circumstances known at the time (i.e., Graham Standard)

To seize a fleeing suspect, deadly force may be used if:

- The officer has probable cause to believe that the suspect has committed a crime involving the infliction or threatened infliction of serious physical harm; and
- The officer has probable cause to believe that the subject poses a threat of death or serious physical harm, either to the officer or others, if allowed to escape
- A warning should be given if feasible

Police-Citizen Interactions

At a high level, it is easiest to separate contacts into two broad categories: citizen-initiated and self-initiated. Generally speaking, most self-initiated encounters are traffic stops. Of deadly incidents in 2015, 73% did not begin on a traffic stop, and 27% began on traffic stops.

There are five primary ways people come in contact with police.

911 Call

The most common, according to the PKIC data, is a police response to a 911 call from a member of the community who generally describes a crime or complaint. One example from PKIC data of this type of incident is that involving Andre Larone Murphy, Sr. Police received a "series of 911 calls" requesting assistance for a "disturbance" at a Super 8 motel in Lincoln, NE, and fought with Murphy after their arrival and investigation.

911 Call With Suspect Description

The next most-common is a 911 call from the community that specifically describes a suspect. Nearly 78% of 911 calls fall into this category. This is when a police dispatcher receives a 911- or other emergency call from a member of the community in which the caller specifically describes the suspect either by name, or by a description complete enough to be recognizably the person with whom the police ultimately contact and engage with. An example of this is the incident involving Chase Alan Sherman, whose mother called 911 to report that Sherman was out of control and intoxicated and harming people and himself after experiencing a drug-induced "psychotic break."

Traffic Stop

The third most-common way people come in contact with police is an officer-initiated traffic stop. This is a situation in which the officer observes a vehicle (and, possibly, the occupants of that vehicle) and based on the officer's determination as to whether the vehicle has broken a traffic law or otherwise provided the officer with probable cause for a traffic stop, effects a traffic stop. In police terminology, this is a "self-dispatched" or self-initiated event. The most infamous of these incidents this year was perhaps that of Walter Scott, who was stopped for a traffic infraction and subsequently killed by the officer. This would also include pedestrian stops and other such "observational contacts."

Other Community Contact

The fourth most-common scenario is a community contact other than a 911- or emergency call. This includes waving down a traveling police officer, or approaching an officer engaged in an unrelated activity and reporting directly to that officer information about a crime or incident in progress. It also includes officers spotting someone who is the target of an arrest warrant signed by a judge, or a known fugitive. An example from the PKIC database of this kind of encounter is the incident involving Dajuan Graham, who was described to a police officer by witnesses who flagged down the officer while he was on an unrelated traffic stop; the witnesses reported that Mr. Graham was running wildly down the street, half-naked and shouting.

Alarm Activation

The fifth most-common way police come in contact with people is when police respond to an alarm, either through a security company dispatcher or an automated alarm, or a 911 or other call prompted by an alarm. One example of this is the incident involving Christian Taylor, who found destroying vehicles and property at an Arlington, TX car dealership after police were summoned by the alarm system.

Other Means

After these, there are other ways that people come in contact with the police. These contacts are more dramatic and attention-garnering, but statistically they are the least common. These include "sweeps" by task forces (DWI, fugitive, prostitution, etc.); checkpoints (Driver license, weapons [such as in New York City, when officers perform bag checks], etc.), and most rare, accidental contact as a result of unrelated police action or activity. One horrible tragedy in the StreetCred PKIC database is of the latter nature: Felix Kumi was an innocent bystander killed as a result of officers shooting at suspects in an illegal gun-purchasing sting operation.

DEFINING "ARMED"

When we tell people we are writing a book on killings by police of unarmed people, the number of people who think that the most controversial part of that concept is how we tell if someone is "unarmed" is high.

The methodology of the StreetCred Police Killings in Context project was very clear on this, and our interpretation is explained in more detail here.

In this book, we consider a person to be armed if they are holding or displaying in a threatening manner, or moving overtly or covertly to grasp, a gun, knife or deadly weapon. What constitutes a deadly weapon is highly subjective. "I killed the president of Paraguay…with a fork," said the fictional Martin Q. Blank, in the movie Grosse Pointe Blank. The fact is, many things can be a deadly weapon in the hands of someone determined to be deadly, and the law is very clear (and most people would agree) that someone who is yelling at you that they want to kill you, while charging at you with a brick raised above their head should be considered "armed," for the purpose of whether you would be justified to defend yourself from an attack that poses a significant threat of death or serious physical injury.

Note the modifiers – someone with a folded knife in their pocket that they have made no attempt to grasp (as was the case with Freddie Gray), or with a gun or fake gun in their glove-compartment that they have made no attempt to reach for or present (as was the case with Ernesto Canepa), would be considered, "unarmed" for the purposes of this book (which is why Freddie Gray is included).

But this goes both ways: someone holding an object in a manner that would appear to a reasonable person to be a gun, knife, or any object that may be used as a deadly weapon, or if they are behaving in a manner that a reasonable person would confuse for that of a person drawing, displaying or otherwise brandishing a deadly weapon would also be considered armed. This is controversial, but it's not decided by the police.

While some civilians and many of those who have not taken police or deadly-force training sometimes have a difficult time understanding how a police officer could mistake an air gun or a replica for a real gun, it is a matter of law and precedent. Law enforcement officers have been exposed to a much wider range of weapons than most civilians, and have seen or read reports of killings by the most unusual people.

Take children, for example: there are frequently killings in America by children with weapons. In February, 2016, a 12-year-old boy fatally stabbed his 15-year-old brother[7], and in December, 2015, an 11-year-old Tennessee girl was shot dead by her 12-year-old classmate[8]. These incidents are common. It is not, therefore, an unusual situation when a 12-year-old boy points what looks like a gun at a police officer and is shot dead[9], nor it is reasonable to ask police officers to delay reacting to what looks very much like a deadly threat simply because of the age of the person presenting it.

There are weapons that are very small, actual, functioning pistols that are painted to look like toys that have been confiscated from criminals, and they are displayed for law enforcement officers to familiarize themselves with. Make no mistake, these are actual guns, designed to look like toys. So when a person points something that looks anything like a gun at an officer, the officer is absolutely justified to consider that threat to be real, even if the gun is pink – the website ArmedInHeels.com has a wide selection of pink highlighted firearms, which they market to women.

This also extends to those who face down officers and then make overt movements that are identical or substantially similar to that of a person reaching to draw a weapon from concealment. As an example of this, on September 23, 2015, Keith Harrison McLeod, a 19-year-old Washington, DC man, who had tried passing a fake prescription at a pharmacy confronted officers responding to the call from the business. McLeod led officers on a foot chase across the street, into a dead-end alley, and started screaming and making threats at an officer. A Baltimore County Officer, Officer Earomirski, gun drawn and retreating from McLeod, watched as McLeod reached around to the waistband at the small of his back (a common place in which people carry pistols concealed), and then suddenly whipped his hand around in a manner we can only describe as totally consistent with someone drawing from concealment and pointing a gun. Officer Earomirski fired several times, knocking McLeod to the ground (to view surveillance video of this account in its entirety, follow the link in the end-note[10]).

In the review process of this book, one of our early readers questioned, "Have you ever seen an unarmed reaching for a waistband shooting on video? The only two I can think of the officer was charged." And as it happened, we had recently re-viewed the video of the McLeod incident, so we were able to answer in the affirmative.

Often, when officers allege that a suspect moved towards their waistband, the account is second-guessed in the way our reviewer did. This may be because officers have used this explanation for their use of deadly force in a multitude of cases in which witnesses and/or video ultimately showed that it was untrue. Our attitude is that we don't know: if an officer alleges it, we will tend to believe that account so long as there is no evidence to contradict it. It's better, of course, if the evidence supports it.

Gunfights typically take place at close range, and are finished in well under three seconds[11]. Officers, who typically use retention holsters that take somewhat longer to unlock, are trained to identify overt or covert movements consistent with that of a person drawing and pointing a gun, with an imperative on speed. While some may think that the era of the quick-draw ended in the Wild West, make no mistake: officers' lives hang in the balance while identifying and responding to those movements rapidly as quickly as possible.

It is precisely because this is true that some despondent people, determined to commit what is colloquially referred to as, "suicide by cop," will engage in exactly these actions. For the record, we have a hard time thinking of a more cowardly and horrible way to kill oneself: those who engage in this force another human being to live for the rest of her life with the kinds of second-guessing, and "if only" calculations, that arise every time one of these incidents occurs.

A driver who aims a moving vehicle at police officers who are unable to get out of the way is absolutely armed. This does not mean that any time an officer sees a person in a vehicle, that that officer is justified in shooting that driver. In this book there are several cases in which officers shoot at people in vehicles. We opine that some, based on the evidence available in the public domain, seem justified. There are others we seriously question. We express great trouble with officers shooting at vehicles in some cases.

Consider this analysis by Ben Singleton of a case in June

> "The purpose of shooting at the driver is to stop the acceleration of the car, preserving the lives of the officers or others in its direct line of travel. To use the fact that the vehicle is being driven, in opposition to the police officer's orders and in the general direction of the officers, as justification to shoot at the car, has less to do with the preservation of officer lives and more to do with a preconceived justification to shoot. What further complicates this case is that the passenger, who did not have control of the vehicle, was shot. Was the passenger targeted, or was his death unintentional? The only acceptable target, if the goal is to stop a vehicular assault, is the driver of the vehicle…"

In some cases, the shooting of someone using a vehicle as a weapon is controversial – we include one of these cases, that of Nicholas Johnson in September, 2015, in this book. Here is analysis from Nick Selby on that case:

> "Johnson was fleeing a violent crime at speeds that passed 100 mph, in a 5,300-lb. vehicle going the wrong way on a crowded freeway. He sent the Tahoe crashing into oncoming traffic. This man,

whether he was armed, was by any reasonable conclusion, dangerous and deadly. Johnson was, in my opinion, engaging in activities that can reasonably be described as those which would clearly lead, without intervention, to deadly results. This justifies the use of deadly force to stop Johnson's actions."

Despite the previous statements, the authors have also considered cases in this book in which people were holding objects (for example, a cell phone) or driving recklessly or crashing vehicles, simply because the public outcry over the incident and common misunderstanding of the person as being "unarmed" led us to consider the case.

In summary, this book considers cases in which decedents did not have, or behave substantially as if they had, a weapon.

WHY TRACK KILLINGS
OF THE UNARMED?

By Nick Selby

As police officers and law enforcement data specialists, we seek data on unjustified killings by police. Incidents in which people with weapons threaten the police or other people don't fall into that category. When someone is imminently threatened with serious bodily harm or death, our federal, state and local laws, and common sense prevail: officers, and even civilians for that matter, have the right to use deadly force to stop the use of deadly force against them or any other person.

The main purpose of the research that went into the StreetCred Police Killings in Context data project was to understand better how deadly force incidents involving police and unarmed civilians unfold, and to determine what lessons can be gleaned to reduce their incidence in the future through policy changes and training advances[12]. To the casual observer, it sometimes seems pretty easy to tell when a use of force seems unjustified.

Sometimes, it even is.

Often, however, we as a society leap to conclusions that may not be appropriate. Sometimes, even incidents that seem to be clear cut are in fact more complex than we might think.

When someone points a weapon at a police officer, or at another person, the legal justification for use of deadly force is fairly clear-cut. When the decedent is unarmed, the justification is less clear, and discerning it requires serious examination of all the facts of the case. The seeming simple nature of cases that are actually more complex under the surface is often a great source of difference and controversy.

We reduced the scope of our data set, therefore, to include only those who were unarmed at the time that they were killed by police. By doing this, we maximized the group that is most likely to contain unjustified killings.

Another equally important reason to focus on the killings by police of the unarmed is that there is a common misconception in the United States that "unarmed" means "not dangerous."

We urge you to separate "unarmed" from the danger posed by a person bent on hurting someone. As the 174 US persons murdered in 2011 by "strangulation" or "asphyxiation" can attest, "unarmed" does not mean that someone isn't engaged in an act of deadly physical force – it simply refers to whether they have a weapon. The opposite is also true. Someone can be armed and not engaged in a use of deadly physical force—if I am carrying a holstered gun in the supermarket while I squeeze the tomatoes, I'm armed but certainly not dangerous.

In England, where strict national weapon control makes guns in the hands of criminals extremely rare, and where front-line police are traditionally and most often unarmed, we see different dynamics. We also see that assaults against English police by unarmed civilians are very common. In the UK's fiscal year ending in March 2015, there were 7844 assaults against police officers in England, or 21 a day[13].

While not delving into the differences between the UK and US styles of policing[14], this serves as further illustration of the concept that, unarmed does not necessarily mean, "not dangerous."

In the next chapter, Case Studies, we highlight three incidents in which the initial media response was misleading or mistaken, and how this led people to have a really simple –and incorrect – view of those incidents. Sorting out what happened in a situation in which someone dies after a confrontation with the police is a very involved process. In the chapter, Police-Citizen Contacts and Deadly Force, we set forth some of the legal standards that are the basis of analysis for any investigation. Without getting into detail here, the media accounts of incidents are often missing crucial details which lead them to simplify investigations and smooth over matters essential to evaluation by legal standards.

In this book, we hope to make clear some of the ways investigators approach these cases, to give some insight into the process that can allow you to ask questions that will elicit those details and nuances. Since we have found that these cases are often more complex than has been reported, we hope you find that the way we drill down into these complexities is in fact more interesting and ultimately more accurate according to legal standards – even if what is found can't be summed up in a few terse words.

The authors do not seek to protect officers from criticism, nor do we seek to persecute officers. Instead, we seek to make genuine criticism of officer misconduct more persuasive - based on context, and the totality of the circumstances - that they might serve as compelling stimulus for change.

CASE STUDIES

In the last chapter we mentioned how simplifying the discussion of deadly encounters with police glosses over details that can have crucial meaning. This does not necessarily mean that it shows the police were right – sometimes, a deeper dive into an incident does reveal that officers did the best they could in a bad situation, and conducted themselves in a manner that was legally and morally justified. Sometimes, the opposite is the case. Sometimes the investigation reveals a set of facts that are too ambiguous to make a judgment in either direction.

And sometimes, we find cases that are outliers – cases in which, while the actual use of force may have been justified, the circumstances leading up to the use of force were handled in a manner that aggravated problems, intensified animosity or simply escalated a situation that might have been, in a better world, handled differently. These details are only revealed after investigation.

In this chapter we present three case studies, from June and July, 2015. The case of Samuel DuBose is almost a perfect example of how quickly an incident can turn violent, and how unclear things can be when an unarmed person is killed by a police officer, even if the media reports it as a slam-dunk one way or another.

Samuel DuBose

Samuel DuBose, a 43-year-old black man, was pulled over by Officer Ray Tensing of the University of Cincinnati Police Department, as DuBose drove his car in the Cincinnati suburb of Mt. Auburn on July 19, 2015. We don't propose that this incident was justified – it looks, in fact, terrible. But we do say the event was more complex than has been portrayed in the media. After you read this we hope you will agree that context can change perspective.

The police said Officer Tensing pulled over Mr. DuBose for failure to display a front license plate. There are many times when it is appropriate to use no-front license plate as a probable cause for a stop - after all, it is right there in the traffic code along with speeding and requirements for, say, working headlamps and tail-lamps. We will come back to this with a thought a little later.

Tensing pulled over DuBose, and politely chatted with him. Having watched the official police video[15], in our opinion, Tensing behaved in a professional and courteous manner throughout the stop. Tensing properly introduced himself to DuBose. After discerning that DuBose owned the vehicle, he informed DuBose that he was being stopped for failure to display a front license plate. He asked DuBose repeatedly whether he could produce his driver license.

For his part, DuBose appeared in the official police video to be avoiding the question about his license. About 40 seconds into the video, Tensing observes a bottle of what turns out to be Barton's Gin on the driver-side floor of the vehicle and requests DuBose hand it to him. Tensing asks again the direct question, "Do you have a driver license on you?" and when DuBose finally admits that he does not, Tensing asks DuBose to honestly state whether he, DuBose, is driving on a suspended license.

"OK, be straight up with me: are you suspended?" Tensing asks, and DuBose denies that he is. This is an important contextual moment. To police, when people don't have a driver's license with them, it is often because their license has been suspended. Furthermore, just prior to making the traffic stop, Tensing had entered the license plate of DuBose's vehicle into his computer and learned that the owner of the vehicle's license was suspended.

Since Tensing had already confirmed with DuBose that Dubose was the owner of the vehicle, Tensing now knew that DuBose had lied to him[16]. This is, of course, not justification for Tensing's use of deadly force, but it is a contextual clue as to Tensing's interpretation of DuBose's words, and the filter through which Tensing would have likely viewed DuBose's actions.

The incident begins to turn physical soon after this exchange. Tensing states that until he can discern Dubose's license status and identity, he would be detained. While reaching to open the driver side door, Tensing asks DuBose to remove his seatbelt and get out of the car. DuBose prevents Tensing from opening the driver side door. In the official video at around 1:50, Tensing is seen reaching to open the door.

At 1:52 we see both Tensing's and DuBose's hands on the door, struggling with it. Between 1:53 and 1:54 we see a brief struggle between DuBose and Tensing, who has already drawn his pistol. At 1:55, a single gunshot rings out that presumably is Tensing shooting DuBose. We then see the camera perspective change as Tensing apparently falls backwards. We hear and then see DuBose's vehicle driving away.

Tensing later claimed that, at the time of the shooting, he was being "dragged" by DuBose. Hamilton County prosecutor Joseph Deters said the body-camera evidence completely contradicted this account. In a blunt assessment of the officer's conduct, Deters told the media that Tensing had "purposely killed" DuBose and that Tensing "should never have been a police officer." The Associated Press reported, "Deters says the shooting of motorist Samuel DuBose in a 'chicken crap' stop over a missing front license plate was 'asinine,' and 'without question a murder.'" Deters also said the university shouldn't be in the policing business at all. The prosecutor said he thinks now-fired Officer Ray Tensing lost his temper because, "DuBose wouldn't get out of the car."[17]

Several things are happening here. We will not comment on (because we don't know) whether Tensing felt his life in danger at the moment he drew his pistol and fired. That is up to a jury to decide, and we won't second-guess what the officer was feeling in the moment. We will say that, in our professional opinions, the video isn't anywhere near as clear-cut as the media believes it is, and we were surprised, when we watched the entire video, to see that Tensing did not appear angry, hostile, or defensive, nor did he even appear to me to be escalating the situation unnecessarily. In fact, up to the moment of the scuffle, it would appear that Tensing was being courteous, polite and reasonable. As, in fact, Mr. DuBose also was, albeit while the latter was withholding information and lying.

The scuffle, as with most incidents in which law enforcement interactions turn violent, was very fast, and its dynamics are confusing. After the gunshot, the vehicle leaped forward and continued to another point, with Tensing giving foot pursuit. No one can tell whether this was due to Mr. DuBose attempting to flee, or whether Mr. DuBose had died and his leg extended involuntarily and depressed the accelerator. Given what is visible on the video, and with the strong caveat that we were not present when the incident took place, it would not appear to have been an unreasonable belief on the part of Officer Tensing that Mr. DuBose was attempting to flee. And since Tensing ended up on the ground after the scuffle and saw the vehicle driving away, it might not be unreasonable to believe that Tensing believed DuBose tried to drag him. We are not saying that happened, just that it is conceivable that this was Tensing's belief. It is also entirely possible that Tensing began to cover his tracks from the moment after he fired, and that what we see on the video is theater. We just don't know.

When the vehicle crashed and stopped, Tensing and another officer approached the vehicle with what looks like apparent genuine concern for their safety, judging their manner of approach and communication. This dynamic change in conditions and foot chase could conceivably change the perceptions of a reasonable person in this situation. As we said, Tensing's statements about, "being dragged," could just as easily have been personal confusion as fabrication: when a situation turns from conversation to deadly force within a two-second window, many people become confused.

We don't have any idea what really happened here, and neither do you. The video is not as clear as we would hope, and even if it were, there are elements of this incident that could not be captured by it. We could not, for example, see Officer Tensing's facial expressions or actions until they became visible in the frame. Video is a good, but not perfect, record of an event.

There's no doubt that the media coverage of this event and the official incident report added to the confusion. We watched on television shortly after this incident as NYPD Deputy Commissioner of Intelligence & Counterterrorism John Miller stated flatly on The CBS Morning News that Tensing was a murderer. That Tensing is white and DuBose was black became as much a part of the media retelling of this story as the facts of the case - and by doing this, the media knitted this incident into a national narrative of issues that fully transcend those of the case at hand in a way that isn't helpful.

Ultimately, our point in discussing this incident is to say that it is emblematic of the main reasons we began this research project: to understand better how deadly force incidents involving police and unarmed civilians unfold, and to try and determine what lessons can be learned from them to reduce their incidence in the future through policy changes and training advances.

This cuts both ways. As the prosecutor mentioned, the stop could be referred to as "chicken-crap." However there are two things worth considering when this video is viewed through a law enforcement lens. Officer Tensing cited the lack of a front license plate as probable cause for the stop, and we have seen evidence that this was true: DuBose himself admitted that the plate was not affixed to the front of the vehicle, and DuBose pointed to an object in the glove-box that he stated was the front license plate. Officer Tensing commented correctly and not in a hostile way that the glove box was not the legally required place to display the front plate. So there is no doubt that Officer Tensing did indeed have probable cause to make this stop.

More important, though, and rarely commented upon by the media, was the fact that early in the stop, Officer Tensing discovered an opened bottle of alcohol on the driver-side floor of the vehicle. What we still do not know – even after reading the critical Kroll report, which is silent on the topic - is whether officer Tensing used the pretext of the front license plate to effect the stop in an effort to investigate what he suspected was a driver under the influence of alcohol.

The media has condemned Tensing for a murder before the trial[18], but many facts of the case have not yet emerged. The Kroll report was largely critical of Officer Tensing's actions and failure to de-escalate, but it did not refer to the autopsy or toxicology report of Mr. DuBose, other than to mention it was unavailable at the time of the report's drafting by Kroll.

Ultimately, the co-authors agree that, given the evidence in the public domain, the shooting by Tensing of Samuel DuBose was an unreasonable and unjustified use of deadly force. Whether he should be charged or convicted is a separate matter. This case is just not as simple as was cast in the press.

Ryan Bolinger

The next case we will look at is that of Ryan Bolinger, a 28-year-old white man who pulled his 2000 Lincoln sedan closely alongside a police cruiser at about 10:15 pm on the night of June 9, 2015. Bolinger was clearly behaving in a bizarre manner. He pulled his vehicle up and very closely alongside the patrol car of Officer Ian Lawler, who was engaged in an unrelated traffic stop, in such a manner that the officer could not get out of his car.

Bolinger then got out, and began acting in a manner that Lawler later described as "dancing, or making unusual movements" in the street, and engaging in "odd, erratic behavior." Bolinger got back in his car and blocked the road, while Lawler kept yelling at Bolinger to pull into a nearby lot. A police spokesman said that Bolinger "peeled out his tires and whipped into the lot." He then drove off, with Officer Lawler in pursuit, at about 35 miles per hour. Lawler announced the pursuit over the radio.

About a mile south, Bolinger made a U-turn and stopped abruptly. Officer Lawler pulled his vehicle in front of Bolinger's vehicle at an angle to stop Bolinger from continuing. Senior Officer Vanessa Miller stopped a short distance behind Bolinger's car[19]. At that point, Bolinger rapidly got out of his car and charged, or "walked with a purpose," toward Miller's squad car. When he was a short distance from Miller's driver's side window, she fired one round, shattering the rolled-up window and hitting Bolinger in the torso[20].

Our view is highly restricted in the in-car video of Senior Officer Miller's vehicle. We hear Officer Miller speaking on the radio and announcing that Bolinger was making the U-turn, stating her physical position, and then stating that Bolinger had emerged from his vehicle and was running. We see her react, apparently to Bolinger running towards her, by leaning far over to her right, and drawing her pistol and firing a single shot. Immediately afterwards she announces on her radio: "Shots fired." As Officer Miller exits her vehicle, we hear a male officer (presumably Lawler) shouting instructions, presumably to Bolinger, to get on his stomach and stop moving. Miller later stated that she felt in fear for her life because of the way Bolinger was charging towards her vehicle.

Police Chief Dana Wingert told The Des Moines Register that Miller's actions were "consistent with what a reasonable person would do in that situation," Wingert said. "There is not a policy violation. It was (Miller's) reaction in that moment. That's the standard not just for a police officer, but any reasonable person. It's the standard used by the grand jury[21]."

Wingert stated that Bolinger had been acting erratically, and had made an aggressive move towards the officer's car. "The squad car isn't a magic shield. If the suspect had had a gun, he could have shot her right through the window," Wingert told the Register[22].

An internal police investigation cleared Miller, finding that she did not violate any administrative policies in the shooting[23].

What is absolutely astonishing to us – speaking as police officers and a trained and qualified use of force expert – is that not only could Senior Officer Miller claim to have been in fear for her life because someone was running towards her car, but that this could get through an internal investigation and a grand jury and result in no disciplinary action.

This will definitely sound like Monday-morning quarterbacking, but the chief's comments about "if" Bolinger had a gun notwithstanding, Bolinger had not exhibited any weapon and the chase itself was conducted at the relatively stately pace of 35 miles per hour. While Bolinger was clearly behaving in a manner consistent with mental illness or acute drug or alcohol intoxication, he had not conducted himself – by the officers' own testimony or the audio audible on the video recording from Miller's in-car camera – in a manner that overtly suggested a deadly threat.

Miller did not shout any command, like "stop." We have no doubt that she was afraid. One can see on the video her reaction was visceral; a recoil in fear. We do not suggest that she was unafraid. But we all question whether she was afraid for her life to an extent that a reasonable person in her position would have felt articulable fear for their life.

Simply put: the idea that an officer can open fire at someone for "purposefully walking" towards a police officer stands contrary to everything about this country that protects people.

Yet this incident has had no national controversy. CopBlock writers followed the case aggressively, and did a pretty good job of articulating their outrage. In one of the more printable passages[24], they put forth three reasons for their anger:

- Not once in human history has anybody ever been killed by being 'walked purposefully' towards. Nobody has ever even sustained a minor injury whose direct cause was damage inflicted by a mindful gait.
- Ryan did not have a weapon, nor did Officer Miller ever even claim to have even imagined seeing one. Never was there any hint that anything besides his willful stride led her to fear for her life.
- No citizen would ever be exonerated for killing another human being because they observed them committing an act which itself presented no danger whatsoever.

Outside a local protest organized by CopBlock[25], this incident didn't reach anything like the controversy over Samuel DuBose, Freddie Gray, Jamar Clark, or several other similar incidents. Whether this is because both the officer and the decedent were white, or whether this incident seemed less "cut-and-dried" than others is something we cannot figure out. But the media coverage of this incident seems far less aggressive than we would have expected it would be, especially given the heated environment around police killings in 2015.

Jermaine Benjamin

The last case study is that of Jermaine Benjamin, a 42-year-old black male. At 3:42 a.m., on June 16, 2015, deputies responded to multiple 911 calls[26] of a disturbance in the 4300 block of 35th Avenue in Vero Beach, FL. Callers said Benjamin was "acting crazy" and "tripping," and that several people were holding him down[27]. The sheriff's office reported that calls had been made to the house at least 70 times[28] in the past.

Arriving deputies found Benjamin on the ground, with several people attempting to control him. Sheriff Deryl Loar stated that Benjamin was, "out of control" when deputies arrived.

The deputies were not wearing body-cameras, so we have no video of the scene. Deputies stated that they moved to restrain Benjamin and were able to handcuff him. Soon after he was restrained and deputies had turned him back over, they realized that Benjamin was not breathing and they began CPR.

Family members claim a deputy who was subduing Benjamin put his knee into the back of his neck and kept his face pressed against the ground[29]. Benjamin was transported to the Indian River Medical Center where doctors pronounced him dead. The Medical Examiner ruled that Benjamin died of excited delirium after taking Flakka[30].

Even with the few facts we have, two things are clear to us. First, police were in this case called to a narcotics overdose in progress. Remember that we are not doctors, but in our experience and training, the likelihood that Benjamin would have died whether the police were there is very high. Flakka is a street name for alpha-Pyrrolidinopentiophenone, or Alpha-P, or "bath-salts," a synthetic stimulant that has been around since the 1960s, but which has been making a comeback across the country. It is a psycho-stimulant drug that typically comes as a white or off-white, odorless crystalline powder.

Public information and law enforcement experience with Flakka is that those who overdose on it experience hyper stimulation, paranoia, hallucinations that lead to violent aggression, insomnia and self-injury. These adverse effects can persist for several days. Flakka can dangerously raise body temperature. It is not uncommon to see people with fevers over 105°F. Flakka can cause kidney failure. A joint study in 2015 by Europol and the European Monitoring Centre For Drugs and Drug Addiction showed that overdose of the drug has led to tachycardia, hallucinations, agitation or anxiety, tremors, hypertension, hyperthermia, convulsions, seizures[31], and many other symptoms.

When deputies showed up to Mr. Benjamin's house after multiple 911 calls about behavior completely consistent with acute Flakka intoxication, to a house that had been the target of 70 prior calls, they did, according to media and witness accounts, everything they could to save his life.

The autopsy results that were released to the media (they have since been removed from the Sheriff's Department Facebook page, and the Sheriff's Office media relations phone went unanswered in March, 2016) stated that the cause of death was Flakka-induced excited delirium.

Some of the most frustrating cases in law enforcement come when officers do the right thing, the thing that is expected of them, and they are blamed for a negative outcome. In this case, the media chose to highlight the horrors of Flakka ("First death attributed to Flakka in Indian River County," said the local CBS affiliate[32] in a typical headline). This sad death is listed in all databases as a "police-involved death." That is technically appropriate, because the police were present and involved when it happened, and the incident should absolutely be studied for ways in which officers might be better able to respond in future. But we want to be clear that this almost certainly was not a police-*caused* death.

We have chosen to make this the last of the case studies because it illustrates almost perfectly the fact that the police frequently arrive at the worst times in a person's life. Often many things have gone wrong before the police become involved.

It is important, when looking at police killings, to get the details that separate cases like that of Mr. Benjamin from others, like those of Mr. DuBose or Mr. Bolinger, so that we can focus our attention where it needs to be: finding answers to the questions about whether we are being policed fairly and justly.

We hope this book is a start.

KEY FINDINGS

Every killing by police of a civilian is investigated, but there are reasonable questions as to exactly *how* they are investigated. An internal investigation that is not transparent, or an external agency? An investigation by a special prosecutor? The answers to these questions vary throughout the country. Most, though not all, police-involved killings are ultimately determined to be legally justified. However, this determination is rarely made by a judge. Most often, police investigations determine no charges are warranted; or prosecutor investigations stop shy of criminal charges; or cases are brought to a grand jury which "no-bills" – that is, declines to prosecute. In this book there are examples of at least two cases in which these processes have completed in favor of the officer, and the authors disagree with that decision. Only rarely are police involved killings adjudicated in court and judged to be justified, though that number is increasing as a direct result of the data projects we have mentioned, and books like this.

We also note that this determination is a matter of criminal law. Under civil law the outcome may be an entirely different matter, and getting statistics on the national numbers of cases that are settled, for how much, and under what terms, is out of the scope of this book.

Beyond the question of legal justification, though, is a separate question, in the words of Professor Peter Moskos: "Was the deadly force used morally and tactically appropriate?"[33] For an overview of the basics of how police interact with civilians, and the laws governing police use of deadly force, please see the chapter on Police-Citizen Interaction & Deadly Force.

As we said previously, we selected killings of unarmed people to maximize the possibility of finding unjustified use of deadly force by police. We find it compelling that the number of cases that involved less than fully and obviously justified use of deadly force was higher than any of us expected. There were also more cases than we might have expected involving use of deadly force by an officer where the deadly force was legally justified, but only because of conditions that were themselves avoidable – such as a solo officer who didn't wait for backup before confronting a group of suspects. To be clear, the authors' findings are those of subject matter experts expressing opinion. They are not findings of fact informed by access to investigative files.

Based on their independent review of information available in the public domain at the time of writing, using standards described in the chapter on Police-Citizen Interaction & Deadly Force, of the 153 cases in the database, the authors independently concluded that the same ten (6.5%) cases appeared to involve the unjustified use of deadly force by a police officer. The authors believe that an additional number of cases - 9 (Singleton), 12 (Selby) and 14 (Flosi) - involved police actions that either were "partially justified," or were considered justified but the authors expressed some reservations about aspects of the case or the information available for review. These are preliminary opinions, based on the limited amount of information that has been released publicly, and the authors reserve the right to return to each case should more information become available.

The cases with unjustified or partially justified use of deadly force highlighted for all of us the inherent value of this kind of data-driven examination of police behavior. Unless officers, administrators, civilian oversight commission members, city leaders, policy-makers, journalists and activists can examine data in an open and transparent way, we can't learn the lessons of incidents, whether they were mistakes, or "by-the-book" incidents that confirm the value of, or suggest a needed update to, a policy or procedure. Anecdotal surveys conducted by the authors found that in general, those identifying themselves as police supporters expected one or two cases to involve unjustified use of force, whereas activists and other police skeptics felt a much higher number, as high as 30, would be found. This highlights our primary key finding that none of us in the public has enough information from either the police or the media, to actually form an opinion about how we are being policed – we are, all of us, being led by narrative.

This book seeks to inform the way police approach and use force, so our key findings are those that are significant to jumpstart change. It also seeks to better inform dissent. Too often, activists speak in the language of emotion, not policy. To effect systemic change, it's often useful to speak in the language of the system.

Most often, the person killed by the police was in the process of an attack that had a significant likelihood of causing death or serious injury. That conclusion is not just our analysis, and it isn't just in killings of the unarmed. Of the 986 fatal police shootings in 2015 counted by The Washington Post (including shootings of armed and unarmed suspects), nearly three-quarters (74%) involved a suspect who had already fired shots, brandished a gun or attacked someone, and another 16% involved a direct threat[34]. In the analysis of the Washington Post, nine out of ten shootings involved police acting correctly. Their headlines tout the total number of those killed by police as if each is worrisome, but they could very well have as accurately read, "Police thwart hundreds of potentially deadly attacks in 2015." [35]

Simply put, in order to answer important questions as to how we are policed and when and if police should be held accountable for use of force, better data is essential.

Here, then, are our key findings.

Police Must Release More Data, and Do It Sooner

The key finding that can drive the greatest impact from a policy perspective was informed by the very difficulty we faced finding data to support the police account of incidents. This was true regardless of when during the year the incident occurred. Law enforcement agencies simply must find better ways to release more data, and to release it earlier. There is a significant public interest in this data, and the public has a legitimate right to understand how it is being policed. We call for agencies to release more data, more quickly. In America, we believe that sunlight is the best cure for most challenges between government and the people. Police agencies failing to release information look like they're hiding something, and alternatively, agencies that release what they have, when they have it are invested with the trust of their communities.

It has been shown in agencies across the country that substantial portions of the known material can be placed in the public domain early, and updated as necessary, without negatively affecting the integrity of the investigation. There are even proved compensating controls to mitigate the legitimate concern that people who have seen video or read information released by the police would come forward claiming to have seen the incident. Release early, release often, put a face to the investigation, and don't even appear to be hiding.

Drugs & Mental Illness, Not Race

While media, political and activist attention has been centered on race, in our research the most significant findings by group of decedents involved illegal drug use and mental health issues. Almost half the cases, 46%, involved suspected or proved acute narcotic intoxication, and/or mental health crises. This did not surprise the authors, but we recognize that, from a public health standpoint, that is an astonishing number.

Acute narcotic intoxication, methamphetamine-induced psychosis, PCP and synthetic drugs were the trigger of 42 cases (see the Drugs & Alcohol chapter). That is 27% of the total. In almost every case involving acute narcotic intoxication, these decedents fought with the police and others, and after they were immobilized, suffered heart failure or heart attacks. In 70% of these, the behavior led to deaths after officers used tools intended to be non-deadly, such as TASER, pepper-spray, clubs, or their hands.

Twenty nine cases (19%) involved people suffering from apparent mental illness, of which 16 (11% of the total) involved a person who had received a prior diagnosis of a serious mental illness. (For more information, please see the Mental Health chapter.)

No Systematic Illegal Use of Force

The main question Americans have been asking is whether the police have been systematically and illegally using deadly force against civilians. The objective answer to this question is: no, they have not. In this book we set forth narratives on each of the 153 cases in which in an unarmed civilian was killed by a police officer, and we invite you to compare our analysis to your own and point out where you disagree. The underlying data is freely available for review, and we encourage those who disagree with our conclusions to download the free dataset at https://github.com/StreetCredSoftware/PKIC, and create alternate analyses. We welcome both collaborative as well as competitive projects.

By saying that most of the cases were not representative of a systemic or illegal use of force, we certainly do not mean to imply that all killings by police of unarmed civilians in 2015 were justified. Far from it. Criminal prosecutions of police officers have increased dramatically with the public attention on officer conduct, including in some of the very incidents we cover in this book. Not all of the officers were justified in their use of deadly force in 2015. There were several cases of killings that appear to us (and sometimes, also, to the public) be unjustified, some of them involving people whose names have become synonymous with cries of police brutality: Freddie Gray, Walter Scott, and others. There were cases, like that of Samuel DuBose, which saw the media and even law enforcement leaders immediately condemning the officer under circumstances that, as we will see, might not be at all as clear as we first were led to believe. There were some that never raised national attention, but about which unanswered questions still swirl, such as the case of Kris Jackson in South Lake Tahoe, CA.

Police Not Targeting Minorities For Special Attention…

The next key finding is two-fold. First, in initial contacts of those unarmed civilians who ultimately died after a confrontation with police in 2015, police did not selectively target by race. Second, based on the data we collected, it is not possible to determine whether, once contact is made, police treated black or Hispanic people differently from white people. The distinction is nuanced, and it is critical as America considers ways to consider whether there is unfair policing and biased behavior by officers.

To illustrate the difference, consider this: if a computer selected at random cars to pull over, officers would not be able to select drivers to stop based on race. But if an officer gave more tickets to black drivers than to white drivers once the computer selected the car, the officers would be treating black drivers differently.

These are nationally important questions related to race that must be addressed: are police targeting minorities for special attention? Do officers behave differently or use greater force when confronting a black suspect than a white one? To address these questions, we must separate them. First, let's look at how citizens first come into contact with police, because the dynamics are vastly different between certain types of contacts.

At a high level, it is easiest to separate contacts into two broad categories: citizen-initiated and self-initiated. Generally speaking, most self-initiated encounters are traffic stops. Of deadly incidents in 2015, 73% did not begin on a traffic stop[36], and 27% began on traffic stops.

Citizens Initiate Most Contacts

The PKIC data reveal that it is citizens who initiate most of the deadly encounters that don't begin with traffic stops. In 88% of those cases, citizens — and not the police — initiated the encounter by asking an officer for help[37].

As we can see from this graphic breakdown, these killings did not involve people selected by the police for bad treatment, but rather, people selected by the citizenry themselves as being dangers to their community:

2015 NON-TRAFFIC INCIDENTS

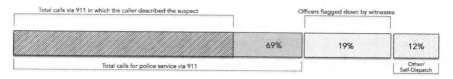

Put another way, when considering the 73% of cases in the database that did not start with traffic stops, the number of minorities contacted by police, and proportion of black people to white people to Hispanics, is not relevant to the question of officer targeting of minorities. This is because in nine out of ten cases, it was a member of the community and not a police officer who selected the person to be contacted.

Media narratives that state the police are more likely to target black people in deadly encounters are, statistically speaking, demonstrably wrong.

911 Callers Describe The Suspects Officers Target

Moreover, in nearly 80% of the emergency calls[38], the caller specifically identified or otherwise described the suspect who ultimately died[39]. There were no false identifications. Put another way, 911 callers specifically described these decedents in their call to 911, and there was never a time when an officer arrived on scene and selected a suspect who was different from the person described by the 911 caller.

Considering further non-traffic cases:

- In the 11 cases in which the incident was initiated by a 911 call to the police that did not include a description of the suspect being reported by the community, 4 (36%) of the decedents were black, 6 (55%) were white, and 1 (9%) was Hispanic.

- In the 21 cases in which the incident was initiated by a citizen contact with a police officer during which a description of the suspect was not given, 9 (43%) of the decedents were black, 9 (43%) were white,

2 (10%) were Hispanic, and one (5%) was Native American (rounding makes numbers >100).

These breakdowns are important because they demonstrate that, in the vast majority of the 110 non-traffic incidents in which people died, race was not a factor in the commencement of the incident.

We therefore know the following:

The police did not select most of the people they confronted

Just about 70% of unarmed people who died at the hands of police were reported to the police by citizens as being a danger to the community, rather than selected by police for attention;

Even When The Police Select, The Racial Composition Is The Same

The racial composition of the group reported to the police by the community does not differ significantly from the racial composition of the group the police self-dispatched.

Most of Those Killed Were Engaged In Deadly Activities

As we have shown, the majority of those ultimately killed by police were themselves engaging in behavior that was criminal (which brought the police to the scene), and posing direct threats to law enforcement or other civilians (which most often precipitated the use of force);

...But We Don't Know If Police Treat Races Differently Once Contact Is Made

Note that the previous section does not answer the question of whether the police treat white people differently once an event begins – this is a separate question that must be answered using a much wider array of contextual data. We are unable to address this question in this book.

Cause of Death is Often Not Shooting

Belying a powerful media narrative to the contrary, nearly half of the 153 cases involved no shooting, and the decedent died by other cause. In cases where death did not result from the deployment of a firearm, the cause of death was most often an abnormal reaction or complication after officers deployed tools or techniques with the intent of using of non-deadly force. This includes the drug-related and mental-health related deaths described previously, as well as other incidents in which decedents with chronic health conditions attacked or resisted officers or others.

For the purpose of clarity, if an officer deployed OC-spray with the intent of gaining compliance through the use of non-deadly force, and the subject died after due to complications related to a chronic breathing disorder or heart failure, we would consider this a death that followed the application of force intended to be non-deadly. As we described in the Police-Citizen Contacts & Deadly Force chapter, the legal standard at work here is the definition of Non-Deadly force being that which poses a minimal risk of injury or harm; and Non-Deadly Intermediate Force is that force *capable* of inflicting significant pain and causing serious injury, but not force with a significant likelihood of causing death. A TASER may be *capable* of causing death, but so for that matter is a butter knife. In practice, and in studies, TASER does not have a significant likelihood of causing death[40].

In 23 of the 83 cases (27%) in which there were shootings, officers deployed a TASER prior to shooting. In our analysis, this is a clear indication that officers were attempted to subdue using non-deadly force, which would be consistent with current best-practices. Specifically, the data show that, almost one-third of the time, officers attempted non-deadly force before using deadly force.

Shooting Deaths

The most high-profile and controversial cases involved the shooting death of an unarmed Black citizen. Of 83 shooting-death cases year-to-date, 32 (39%)

were Black, 33 (40%) were White, and 14 (17%) were Hispanic, 2 (2%) were Semitic and 2 were of unknown race.

The US census figures of the United States show that just under 13% of the population is black. Some have raised the question as to whether equal representation of black people to white people in this mix is evidence that blacks are more likely to be killed by police. We do not believe that a reasoned statistical analysis would show that. Instead, we would point out that poverty, drug use and alcohol abuse are far better predictors of criminality than race alone. That more minorities are poor is a matter of national discourse, but blaming the police for larger systemic issues is counter-productive. One thing is true: Police are the most visible nexus of government & the people.

That insight raises a better question: "It would seem that black people are over-represented in the group of those killed by police. Is this indication of police bias or prejudice? Or is the fact that black people seem to come into contact with law enforcement at a rate higher than one would expect based on their representation in the national racial composition evidence of a larger set of national policy issues?" To that question we believe the answer is clearly the latter.

Some data points that our research uncovered that support this systemic national trend, as opposed to an isolated police trend are as follows:

The Most Controversial Cases Were Resistive, Not Combative, In Nature
The most controversial shootings were those involving people not involved in deadly activities. These are primarily instances in which the resistive is treated as assaultive; and often (not always) where the suspect is black and described as larger, older and more fearsome than they may have been. It is in that group that many people are concerned the disparity is found. This book cannot answer questions about this group, other than to note that (a) it exists, and (b) it exists in a small but important minority of incidents.

Witnesses to Shooting Deaths

According to the PKIC data, which draws from media accounts and counts witnesses quoted in the press, there were non-police, civilian witnesses to 38 (46%) of the 83 shootings. Note that this does not suggest that we have conclusively added up all witness accounts, only that we have counted those listed in media accounts.

2015 WITNESS ACCOUNTS
Shooting Incidents

Non-police, civilian witnesses – 45%			No witnesses – 55%
Exclusively Dispute Police Account 7%	Support & Dispute Police Account 12%	Exclusively Support Police Account 26%	

Generally speaking, in cases where there were witnesses quoted in the media, the witnesses described facts that were consistent with the police account more often than they disputed it. We point out the obvious: part of the reason for this book is that we perceived a trend towards media being critical of police in reporting on police killings. We also note that this trend bucks that trend.

Witnesses exclusively made statements containing facts consistent with the officer's account in 22 cases (58% of shooting cases with witnesses, and 26% of all shooting cases). Some witness statements are consistent with, and some contradict the officer's account in 10 cases (26%/12%). Witness statements exclusively contradicted the police account of shootings in six cases (16%/7%)

Officers Need Appropriate Non-Deadly Force Training

In case after case as we reviewed them for this book, the authors were struck by several incidents in which officers reached for tools, like TASER or pepper spray, in situations that might have easily been addressed by going hands-on. Remember, all the subjects in this book were unarmed at the time of their encounter with the police. As we wrote the book, we had conversations in which we all mentioned concerns that some officers had resorted too often, and too quickly, to tools as opposed to their hands or their voices. And when these tools don't have the desired effect, those officers go to their firearms. In some cases, one or more of the authors opine that the officer may have had more options had they gone "hands-on" as opposed to relying on their TASER. When the TASER was ineffective, the officer felt it appropriate to escalate to firearms.

We point out that this statement is controversial. Some in law enforcement, including very experienced professionals for whom we have the utmost respect, disagree with this basic premise. Commissioner Mulvey, who wrote the Foreword to this book, is among them. "If the research shows that cops go to their tools too soon, then additional training should address that issue. But going physical or engaging in a physical fight, in my view, will lead to more police injuries and offender injuries, and perhaps more public relations issues which the police do not need."

This, like many of the statements we make in this book, is intended to start conversations, not to make pronouncements of what is "right". We want to inform and inspire conversations, especially those about topics that promote debate about how to improve public safety and save lives.

It used to be an expectation of police work that officers would sometimes have to fight. To be clear, there is no expectation that officers need to suffer injury. We don't mean abusive behavior, but sometimes, people are getting rowdy and they need to be grabbed and secured. Sometimes in securing them, they fight. Officers should be expected not to treat every assault as a life and death situation, and should be trained sufficiently to keep their cool in situations in which someone who is a little drunk or a little unruly may take a swing at you. That training should include methods to physically defend against to punch and to counter it with reasonable force.

Instead, many younger officers are actually being told in the academy that, "you're not paid to fight," and to treat attacks as if they are assaults on your very life. We disagree. Officers should be well-trained in basic hands-on techniques including blocking and countering drills. We believe that the tools officers carry on their duty belts are there to augment, not replace, an inherent ability to go hands-on. In fact there are cases in this book in which that choice may well have saved a life.

The personal investment in the violence of action - the very cost of physicality - has been reduced dramatically by these tools. That is not to say that they don't have their place, but to remind officers that, before TASER, before pepper spray, if feasible and the situation allows, we needed to stay much more adept on the art and science of negotiation and de-escalation, and the practice of verbal persuasion. TASER is an excellent tool, but our reliance on it has diminished some of the prerogative to engage in those inter-personal skills, and may even make us quicker to use force.

This is a tough line, because officers do a job that is dangerous. When people opine that police work is not as dangerous as, say, factory work or coal mining, we would point out that the difference is that the danger in police work is intentional - other human beings working to hurt the officer. Industrial accidents are horrific, but a table saw never followed anyone down the street and attacked. Obviously we are not suggesting that officers should shrink from using tools in self-defense. But we are saying that an over-reliance on TASER or pepper spray has its own set of dangers. Officers who do not practice fighting – using the defensive tactics training offered by their agency or another training school, risk being surprised by physicality, over-powered or out-maneuvered by those they confront, or just plain scared. Boxing, or martial arts like Brazilian Jiu-Jitsu, Krav Maga or other fighting, can be very good training, but ensure your trainer has actual law enforcement experience and isn't just teaching you stuff that looks awesome on the mat but has no practical application in real life.

In police work, too much fear can have deadly consequences. Officers find themselves panicked when fights end up on the ground (secret: many fights end up on the ground), but those who practice their physical skills are mentally and physically prepared. Recently a video made the rounds in which an officer at a gas station took on a man who was at least a foot taller and at least 75 pounds heavier.

But the officer used physical control techniques to control the situation and the suspect - no deadly force was used, and the subject surrendered.

Officers should also train in the appropriate decision making process of using reasonable and appropriate force, whether it be deadly or non-deadly force. The training should include when it is appropriate to use no force as well, supporting the fact that most incidents don't require any force response at all. The majority of arrest situations only require the amount of force to put on the handcuffs. The question in the officer's mind shouldn't be, "Can I shoot?" as if they're seeking permission, but rather, what is the appropriate force response to effect the arrest, overcome resistance, prevent escape, or to defend yourself or others. In other words, officers should understand their response must be balanced to the actions and behaviors of the subject.

In the police academy, Nick was told, "Go in to a boxing gym and say, 'I'm a cop! Who wants to fight?' The instructor's point was that we all need to experience physicality – getting punched, moving, getting punched again - and regularly, in order to maintain an understanding of force, an understanding of our limits, and an understanding of the real damage that can be inflicted by a punch to the face.

Officers who plan to rely on tools where their hands, feet, fists, wits, and breathing are forgetting Mike Tyson's wisdom: "Everybody has a plan until they get punched in the mouth."

More Police Video Must Be Deployed…Correctly

Video was only available in 26% of cases. In two 2015 cases, witness video was crucial to show officers were not truthful with investigators. It fully exonerated the officers in two other cases in 2015. In all four of these cases, video was photographed by bystanders or surveillance cameras, rather than by police-supplied video.

Agencies are aggressively working to expand their video coverage, but the size and scale of this undertaking hampers the effort. Properly-handled, stored and released video will increase transparency and thus promote justice.

This is an effort that can't be delayed any longer. Without video, officers are not protected from accusations, and the agency loses community trust. But video is not a panacea. Before rushing headlong into an age of ubiquitous police cameras, there should be some consensus on a question of equal interest to everyone from the most staunchly anti-police to the most virulently pro-police: What do we want cameras to accomplish? Our answers will shape the resulting policies in radically different ways.

Video Must Be Deployed With A Plan

As this was written in the spring of 2016, no clear national goals have been established for police video, other than some vague statements about "police oversight."

This is a huge issue that doesn't get considered that often. Policies about what the cameras are supposed to do are radically different depending on the outcome desired. For example, for police oversight, it's likely we would want all video released publicly, and as much recording as possible of interactions between police and civilians. But for civilian oversight, and evidentiary purposes, we would likely want the video kept secret as long as possible, and only retain it for minimal periods[41].

Which raises another really important question: when should officers be recording? The fact that so few of the killings by police of the unarmed in 2015 were recorded speaks to this. The CSI Effect suggests that the public (and therefore trial outcomes) are affected by the television program and its spin-offs, which wildly exaggerate and glorify forensic science. We extend this to video because the media has so widely celebrated cases in which either video recorded officially by police, or video taken by bystanders, has been used to contradict the testimony of cops who have lied.

Therefore, the 'CSI effect' on juries informs our prediction that, three years from now, if video is unavailable, the police will be disbelieved on principle.

While laypeople and some police officers can interpret the public's cry for video evidence to support officer testimony to be presumptive societal acceptance that police are liars, there is ample evidence to interpret it in a different way: that the memory of officers is simply not the best available tool. In the Mississippi Law Journal, Richard Myers argues that the standard of the Terry v. Ohio[42] rule, of "reasonable and articulable" suspicion, is an incomplete thought.

"Expert police officers," Myers says, "process much of the critical information on which they rely at a subconscious—and therefore inarticulable—level. The better they get at their job, the less likely they are to make conscious note of classes of information, especially in the potentially life-threatening situations that may lead to frisks for weapons."[43]

As open source intelligence expert Eric Olson has stated, referring to the way some cops can stand on the side of a highway and select, out of hundreds driving by, the car driven by the narcotic smuggler, "That cop probably couldn't tell you how he knows. But he knows, and this kind of information, which is often so difficult to articulate, is exactly the kind of thing we hope to help analysts articulate."[44]

Olson states:

> "Anyone who has gone on a ride-along can tell you that it's astounding what patrol officers can see – that guy, running behind him? The inspection sticker out-of-date by one month on the car passing the opposite direction, two lanes over? That guy entering the building, who looks as if he doesn't live in that building? All those kinds of things are examples of something that patrol officers see because they have worked, since the first day they hit the streets under a Field Training Officer, to become finely-tuned anomaly detection devices. If it's weird, the officer will likely notice it."[45]

So, according to Myers, "reasonably articulable suspicion," is really just a subset of "reasonable suspicion based on credible evidence."

Civilians don't often think through the statement that officers should be expected to record whenever they are working, or whenever they are interacting with the public. Generally that's true, but there are some really notable and significant exceptions. The first thing to remember is that, once it is recorded, it is publicly discoverable. This means that, generally speaking, give or take, anything that is recorded can be obtained by John Q. Public through a public records request.[46]

Body-worn video is not by any means a punitive measure. And even though officers are granted extraordinary powers in this society, and even though it is right to expect a higher level of monitoring of and transparency into the activities of officers, there must be some recognition of this basic human right to privacy.

Obviously, we don't want video recordings of officers on the toilet. Or officers eating lunch. You can't just (as some have suggested) turn the cameras on at the beginning of the shift and turn them off at the end, because even if the video weren't publicly discoverable, it would be a grotesque invasion of privacy. Who among us would want recorded every personal telephone call, or every personal in-person conversation?

So, too, are there legitimate reasons why those who come into contact with the police would expect privacy. Consider the reaction of a confidential informer when there is a body-camera in the room in which he is about to describe criminal activities. Think about the battered person describing, on camera, to the police how their spouse or roommate beats them. Or the witness to a murder. Or as the officer enters your home on a call of a burglary. Or on a call of domestic assault. You get the idea.

Finally, there has already been a push for more innovation, like wearable technologies that sense an officer's movements and heart rate. This raises another set of yet-to-be-answered policy decisions: how to handle the resulting trove of data on the minutiae of policing, and the personal lives of police officers on the job. Policies must govern carefully the tracking and recording of every moment, from donut shops to confidential informant meetings to murder investigations, to protect the rights of all. This would include the citizens captured in those millions of hours of video. Consider the uproar that resulted simply from people's images captured by Google's mapping vehicle license plates and houses. This would be a whisper compared to the roar that would result from indiscriminate, publicly discoverable, video of the constant interactions between police and the community.

The processing and sharing of the video data - indexing, mining it, running facial recognition and automated license plate recognition systems against it, audio transcription and other methods of data dissemination will need to be addressed, because the amount of data resulting from a data surveillance state is both useful and terrifying.

A Brennan Center study[47] discusses their findings on policies surrounding the decision about when to record in various large agencies around the country. These policies, as a whole, are rather fascinating, because they reveal the different thinking of policy committees throughout the country, and while often they are in agreement, often they are not. One thing clear is that these video policy committees are not collaborating as much as one would expect based on media coverage of the video issue.

All this is to raise the basic point that, while methods and technologies to turn on the camera are going to be developed, things are not as simple as they might initially appear.

Indictments

There have been indictments of 15 officers in eight of the 153 incidents that occurred in 2015. Eleven officers were indicted in the killing of six Black decedents; four officers have been indicted in the killing of two White decedents. One of these officers (a white female officer who shot and killed a white male) was acquitted. One was convicted. The trial of Baltimore Police Officer William Porter (in the Freddie Gray death) was declared a mistrial after a deadlocked jury[48], and it is unclear as we write whether prosecutors will re-try him.

Traffic Stops

For most agencies outside major urban areas, traffic stops remain the single most common place for self-dispatched calls. We saw no pattern of racism in terms of selection of drivers, however several of the most controversial cases began on traffic stops. For this reason, the calls for officer-worn and dashcam video are perhaps loudest. The public simply needs better insight into and transparency of traffic stop activities.

There were 41 traffic stops that led to the death of an unarmed citizen. Two of the most high-profile and highly-suspect cases involved the death of an unarmed black citizen that began with a traffic stop. Three indictments involved traffic stops of unarmed civilians that turned deadly. Two involved a black driver, one a white driver.

No agency had more than one traffic stop of an unarmed person that turned deadly. Unarmed black and white people were represented about equally in car stop incidents that resulted in the death of the driver.

Six of the traffic stops were prompted by a 911 call for service; two each for black and white drivers, and one each by a Hispanic and an Asian or Pacific Islander driver.

DRUGS AND ALCOHOL

There were 42 cases, more than 27% of the total, in which officials suspect or know that acute drug intoxication was either the direct cause of death, or a significant contributing factor. That in itself is a truly remarkable figure. This means that drugs played a role in more than one in every four deaths of unarmed civilians. We suppose this shouldn't be surprising, but it remains surprising quite possibly because the cost of drug abuse has been so high, for so long, despite our nation's incredibly expensive and disruptive "war on drugs."

Statistics

The average age of a person who died in an incident that involved an acute narcotic intoxication related death was 34.23 years. The youngest was 18. The oldest was 55. In the 42 cases in which officers, neighbors or community members who called police stated that the decedent was intoxicated, we have autopsy or toxicology reports, or official statements quoting those reports in 27. In 30 of the 42 cases, officers used a TASER. Eight of these people were shot by police. Of those, three had been TASERED prior to being shot. Non-deadly force was exclusively used in 29 (69%) of drug cases.

In eight of the 27 cases in which we have toxicology reports, decedents had two drugs in their system, and four had three or more drugs in their system. For example, the cause of death of Jeremy Linhart, a white male who was shot on June 9 as he reached for a .40 caliber pistol secreted under his seat, was primarily a gunshot wound to the chest, with a "significant condition" listed as, "acute combined drug intoxication." Linhart was found to have had amphetamine, methamphetamine, cocaine, ephedrine, oxycodone, and phenylpropanolamine in his system, and heroin, cocaine, and methamphetamine were found in the vehicle. Seven people died after taking synthetic drugs, like N-Bomb, Spice, and flakka. Eight took methamphetamine, five took cocaine, three took PCP, among other drugs including opiates/oxycodone, alcohol, and marijuana.

Overview of Acute Narcotic Intoxication

By Ben Singleton

Some of the statements we make when concluding that a use of force was reasonable rely on the assertion that particular drugs make one more dangerous to the police than a person who is simply violent, or psychotic. To explore this idea, we must first understand the drugs that police are seeing on the street and how they affect behavior, psychology, and physiology.

Methamphetamine is one of the most prevalent and destructive illicit drugs in use today. Users can be easily identified by someone with a trained eye, as the drug causes users to scratch and pick at themselves due to intense itching and sometimes the actual belief that bugs are crawling beneath the skin. It also causes rapid tooth decay, commonly called "meth mouth," and rapid weight loss.

Users often binge on Meth for days at a time. During this time, they experience intense euphoria, hyperactivity, and sleep deprivation. At the end of the binge, users begin a downward spiral into an intense psychosis in which they are disconnected from reality and experience vivid hallucinations. But this isn't the purple elephant kind of hippie euphoria that we think of when we hear the word hallucination. Because these hallucinations happen after days of sleep deprivation and at the end of a binge, they are often horrific and dark. Users see and hear things that don't exist. The intense paranoia that accompanies the hallucinations causes users to genuinely believe that everyone is against them.

Bob Pennal, a retired meth investigator from the California Bureau of Narcotic Enforcement put it this way when explaining recent murders by people in apparent meth rages, "Your children and your spouse become your worst enemy, and you truly believe they are after you[49]."

This drug lifts the boundaries and limitations of what is rational.

Years ago I responded to a disturbance at a local gas station to find a tweaked out meth-head wielding a hypodermic syringe, and pointing it at everyone, because he was convinced that everyone in the store had convened there to kill him. Mothers have even murdered their own children as a result of this psychosis.

Like methamphetamine, PCP, and synthetic drugs such as bath salts and flakka, bring users to a state of intense psychosis. Family members frequently use the phrase, "He was not himself" in describing the behavior of someone who was under the influence of these mind-altering drugs.

What makes dealing with someone in this state such a dangerous proposition for police is that users are completely disconnected from the sensory mechanisms that police officers use to bring normally functioning people under control.

Drug use can eliminate a person's ability to listen to reason. One of the most important tools in an officer's arsenal is his ability to de-escalate a potentially deadly situation through reason and rationale. Drug users experiencing this psychosis are irrational and completely unpredictable. Attempting to calm someone in this state is often a futile endeavor. Their brain has been hijacked by horrific thoughts and paranoia.

They also don't experience pain in the same way that someone with a normally functioning brain would. Efforts to gain compliance through pain, whether via the use of a baton, pepper spray, or other means, are often met with even more aggression. What police are faced with is an ever escalating encounter. The user does not know when to quit. This is why so many of these encounters result in the death of the user. They fight until their bodies collapse and cease to function.

When, for example, someone who is not in a drug-induced state of psychosis is pinned down by the police, they will usually give in to exhaustion, recognizing that they have lost, and comply. Someone in a psychotic state, caused by a stimulant like methamphetamine, does not recognize the feeling of exhaustion, and will continue to fight until their body shuts down entirely.

What this means for police is an elongated struggle, a higher propensity toward injuries, and the possibility that the encounter will become deadly. We reviewed some cases in this book in which officers used deadly force to end a violent struggle with intoxicated subjects. In my opinion, these subjects would have fought until their bodies shut down.

An officer who has normal physiological responses cannot outlast someone in this state, and will ultimately succumb to exhaustion before his intoxicated adversary.

Fighting Someone On Meth

One of the most violent and injurious fights of my career was with a 115-pound woman who had been binging on methamphetamine for a week. The ferocious, savage, and relentless aggression with which she fought myself and two other officers was truly astonishing. We fought her for what seemed like an eternity. Having finally handcuffed her and put her in the patrol car, my fellow officers and I leaned up against the car, drenched in sweat and blood, and completely exhausted. The woman in the car though, kicking and screaming, had not slowed down.

The reason TASER is so valuable in combating this kind of subject is that it provides an opportunity to stop the escalation in seconds. A correctly executed TASER exposure can allow officers to subdue and handcuff a subject while they are immobilized, ending the struggle. The media coverage of its use has made it the scapegoat for deaths that would likely have occurred anyway. Virtually no coverage has been publicized on the massive reduction in officer injuries that have resulted from the use of TASER. Injuries declined significantly after the adoption of ECD devices[50]. Further, there is no evidence of any increase in in-custody deaths as a result of the adoption of TASER. Of the 250,000 annual ECD field uses in the United States, only 1 in 4000 is involved in an arrest-related death[51]. Many of these deaths can be attributed to drug overdose.

This is not to abdicate police responsibility to care for those in custody, nor to excuse excessive force. It is to give the reader some context as to why police view acute narcotic intoxication as such a dangerous situation, and to explain why the rate of death in custody is so much higher when police confront people who are in states of acute intoxication.

Prevention of In Custody Deaths
By Ed Flosi

After my graduate program, my peer-reviewed and published final paper was titled, "Sudden In-Custody Deaths: Exploring Causality & Prevention Strategies." The goal was to explore the tools and tactics used by law enforcement that had been claimed to have caused the death in subjects that died proximate to the arrest process and to explore into the validity of those claims. I wanted to see if there were any strategies that law enforcement could provide to mitigate these in-custody deaths.

I did research into a few tactics and tools including: (1) positional asphyxia caused by the total appendage restraint position (TARP), sometimes referred to as "hogtying," (2) the carotid restraint, (3) OC Spray, and (4) TASER. The overwhelming evidence that I discovered was that these tools and tactics had very little (if anything) to do with the subject's death. In the large majority of cases, it was apparent that the real cause of death was the subject himself/herself.

The pattern that emerged in the cases I studied was how a combination of factors was involved, including a subject's poor physical condition (including cardiomyopathy and obesity), mental illness (diagnosed or undiagnosed/suspected), and poor lifestyle choices (alcohol and/or drug abuse). The fact that many of the subjects had also engaged in prolonged strenuous activity prior to and during the arrest process adds to creating a much higher risk for sudden in-custody death.

In many of these cases, the officers acted according to their training and using current best practice tactics, but the subject died anyway. What we see and read in the media is often that an officer used some tactics or tool, and then the subject died, leading some to draw the conclusion that the tactic or the tool used by the officer was the reason for the death, which is almost certainly incorrect. This logic was identified centuries ago as the "post hoc, ergo propter hoc" logic flaw. One can't draw a causal relationship conclusion about events correlated in time and space without further exploration and evidence.

MENTAL HEALTH

Of the 153 unarmed civilians killed by police in 2015, 29 (or 19%), had apparent mental illness, of which 16 (11% of the total) had a prior diagnosis of a serious mental illness. From one angle, this issue simply must be judged in the context of how many times it occurred in this, a nation of 320 million people, in which there are some 50 million annual police-citizen interactions, between citizens and one of 800,000 cops serving in 18,000 police agencies. In that context, 15 does sound like a pretty low number.

Digging in further, consider that, in the past year, about 1.4 million people were arrested who suffer from both severe mental illness and illicit drug and alcohol use disorders. That's about 25% of the 5.7 million people arrested[52]. That's a huge number. Here's another one: 2 million jail bookings involve a person with mental illness, and approximately 15% of men and 30% of women in local jails have a serious mental illness.[53]

One school of thought states that, given all standard disclaimers about how every life is precious, if cops are annually handling about 2 million people who are in the throes of a violent mental health crisis and 15 of them die, this might not be an important part of the bigger picture.

We are not sold on that worldview.

The intersection of law enforcement and the mentally ill is gaining particularly close scrutiny, as well it should. And it is of special concern to me as a police officer and someone who looks at these statistics because mental illness can manifest in so many ways.

In our opinion, we need to move beyond "whether" the intersection is appropriate by any theoretical standard and get to the real discussion: the reality is that law enforcement is the first and last option for the treatment of a great number of mentally ill people in this country. Until systemic changes are made to affect that calculus, not training officers to deal better with mental health and addiction-specific behavior is simply negligent. This should not be a surprise (even though it seems to surprise many): the current state of affairs is a result of a series of moves by the United States Congress over the past 50 years.

In 1965, Congress was very specific that its new Medicaid program would not fund state and local psychiatric hospitals. Since the early 1960s, under the Kennedy administration, a re-emphasis to drive mental patients to local and community clinics (and pump them up with Thorazine[54]) had pressed resources. The Carter administration saw expansion of community mental health centers' remit to handle substance use disorders, but Reagan era cutbacks led Congress to cut federal mental health funding significantly.[55] The "emptying" of America's mental health facilities that began in the 1980s has resulted in today's circumstances.

"It is safe to say that a third to a half of all use-of-force incidents involve a disabled civilian," said David Perry and Lawrence Carter-Long, writing in a white paper from The Ruderman Family Foundation. This may not be an unreasonable estimate. Our data captured apparent or prior-diagnosed mental illness at a rate of almost one-in-five. By the Ruderman methodology, which is an intersectional study based on media accounts covering the three years from 2013-2015 that includes all manners of physical and psychological disability, it is quite possible that 33% is correct. The paper also agrees that the trend behind these numbers is a pattern in which police have become the default responders to mental health calls.[56]

What we don't want to do is harm in the name of "doing something." In the same way that state laws to reduce drunk driving and scofflaws can act as an unintended and regressive tax on the poor (while looking to all the world like police picking on blacks and Hispanics[57]), so too are people blithely looking at cops as the place to focus when thinking about mental health issues. When a mentally ill person dies in a struggle with the police, it's looked upon as a "police issue." Mental health patients shunted down to the cops for treatment is an awful thing, but if we let the deaths of those in the throes of a mental health episode push us towards unconsidered, solutions, we might miss the larger problem.

The larger problem, of course, is not just how we regard mental illness in America in general, but the fact that the mentally ill behave in ways more likely to bring them in regular contact with the cops. The mentally ill are more likely to be arrested: The prevalence of an arrest in the past year in the 44.5 million adults suffering from of mental illness of any severity was 5.4%; compare this to the 1.8% prevalence of arrest in the past year among those without mental illness. According to The National Alliance on Mental Illness[58] (NAMI) about 10 million adults, or 3.1% of Americans, experience a serious mental illness in a given year that substantially interferes with or limits one or more major life activities.[59]

"Community mental health systems lack the resources they need and, as a result, many individuals with mental illness are homeless or unemployed, circumstances that correlate with encounters with police," wrote Robert Bernstein, President and CEO of the Bazelon Center for Mental Health Law, in a March, 2015 letter to the President's Task Force on 21st Century Policing. "Individuals with mental illness have higher rates of arrest than the general population, and the rate of arrest among public mental health service recipients is roughly 4.5 times higher than those observed in the general population."[60]

It is also fascinating is to see the failure of our drug and alcohol policies through this prism: in the last chapter we highlighted drug and alcohol use among cases in our database, but nationally the prevalence among those with a substance abuse problem who were arrested last year was 13%, compared to the prevalence of those without a substance abuse problem of 1.5%. Having a substance abuse disorder increased the likelihood of arrest among adults, regardless of the presence or level of mental illness. But it is also interesting to note that 48% of mentally ill inmates are charged with drug-trafficking-related crimes.[61] At least some of these are due to self-medication by the mentally ill unable to obtain treatment.

When mental illness and drug abuse are mixed and matched, we see increasing likelihoods of getting arrested - for example, the prevalence of past year arrest was 2.8% for adults with mental illness but no drug or alcohol problem, but a stunning 16.1% for the mentally ill with an illicit drug use disorder.

To the layman, an acute mental health crisis is indistinguishable from an acute narcotic overdose. The fact that "only" 16 unarmed, severely mentally-ill people died last year at the hands of police is indeed a low number, but it's not a reason to stop thinking of increasing the things we do that work to keep that number low and try and make it lower.

More clearly: excellent police work and great training has made it so that small numbers of mentally ill people die each year at the hands of the police. Let's do better: Crisis Intervention Team training has been proven to save lives, save taxpayer dollars and perhaps most important, improve the lives and treatment of the mentally ill. It does this by ensuring better follow-up, fewer crisis admissions to hospitals, and fewer violent confrontations with police.

Work to improve the policing of the mentally ill is among the lowest-hanging fruit. It must be a top priority. The need for a proactive approach, such as mental health Crisis Intervention Teams and a "Follow-up Based Approach," is clear and compelling.

Mental Illness & Race
Mental illness strikes without respect to race or ethnicity. Of those with prior diagnoses of serious mental illness killed in 2015, six were black, five were white, two were Hispanic, one was Asian or Pacific Islander, and one person's race was unknown. Those with apparent mental illness and no prior diagnosis comprised four people who were black, five who were white, one who was Hispanic, one who was Native American, and one person of unknown race.

CRIMES IN PROGRESS

Officers alleged that 71 (46%) decedents attempted to flee arrest.

Fugitives

Of the 153 decedents, 24 (16%) were fugitives; some were wanted on misdemeanor charges, many were wanted for felonies. Three (13% of fugitives, or 2% of the total) were escapees from jail or prison. Of the 24 fugitives, 18 (75%/12%) attempted to flee arrest.

Four fugitives (17%/3%) were engaged in acts of domestic violence; one in both acts of domestic assault and assault on other civilians. Three fugitives (13/2%) were engaged in acts of robbery. Seven (30%/5%) committed acts of vehicular assault against the police or others. Despite being unarmed at the time of his encounter with police, one of the fugitives had shot at another civilian; six (25%/4%) had assaulted other civilians, and one had killed a civilian. Five (21%/3%) injured a police officer.

Violent Crime & Property Destruction

All told, 70% of the total were in the process of violent crimes or property crimes at the time of their fatal encounter with police. When they encountered police, 17 (11%) decedents were in the process of robbery or carjacking; 26 (17%) were committing domestic violence; 32 (21%) committing assault against other civilians; 29 (19%) committing serious vandalism or burglary (five were committing both robbery and vandalism or burglary - that's - 17% of those committing vandalism or burglary or 3% of the total). Vandalism in most of these PKIC cases was destruction of vehicles or businesses - smashing vehicle windows, jumping up and down on vehicles to destroy roofs and hoods, smashing plate glass store windows and destroying stock and merchandise, etc.

Narcotics

At least 42 (28%) of the decedents were under the influence of narcotics; ten (7%) were under the influence of alcohol; of these, nine were under the influence of both narcotics and alcohol (21% of the decedents under the influence of narcotics, or 6% of the total). Twelve people (27%/8%) were under the influence of methamphetamine; and three (7%/2%) under the influence of prescription drugs. See the Drugs & Alcohol chapter for more information.

Prior Convictions

There were 33 decedents (22%) with prior convictions for violent crimes. This compares to nine officers (6%) with a history of complaints for excessive force. Note that the bar in PKIC was much higher for police, for whom we would accept accusations of prior violent acts, versus decedents, for whom we sought only convictions of violent crime in the past. However, we must note that when it comes to the officer histories, it is highly likely that there are false negatives (that is, it is highly likely that although no media or public statement about the officer's history is released, some of the officers involved had prior accusations of excessive force). This is not necessarily an intentional misleading by the police of the media. In many departments, especially those with unions and collective-bargaining agreements, departments are unable to release personal information about an officer prior to a conviction. This is also why it is so difficult in some cases to get descriptions of officers' race, gender, age or name.

TASER DEPLOYMENTS
AND AUTOPSIES

The StreetCred PKIC dataset provides significant insights into TASER use that are contrary to conventional wisdom. TASER-related incidents are among the most controversial and complex to understand. There is much disagreement about the contribution of the TASER to a death. TASERS, like batons, and chemical agents such as OC spray, are categorized as, non-deadly tools. However, in some cases in which a TASER is deployed, people have died.

Narcotics were involved in 25 (39% of all) TASER cases; methamphetamine in six of those cases (24% of narcotics cases and 9% of TASER cases) and alcohol in five cases (20%/8%). We will discuss more thoroughly acute drug intoxication and "excited delirium" in the Drugs & Alcohol chapter, but below is information on TASER itself.

The StreetCred PKIC dataset contains 64 cases of TASER deployment. In 15 (23%) of these, the decedent assaulted a civilian immediately prior to being TASED, and 44 (69%) of these, the decedent assaulted the officer prior to being TASED. In 13 cases the decedent assaulted both another civilian and the officer. In 16 of the 44 cases (36%) of the cases in which the decedent assaulted the officer, the officer was injured; and in six cases (14%) in which the decedent attacked the officer, the decedent had also reached for or struggled for the officer's gun.

There are known witnesses to 64% of all TASER deployments, and these witnesses generally supported the account of police (see Witnesses to TASER Deployments below). In 45% of TASER activations the decedent had attempted to flee arrest.

TASER Deployment & Autopsies

The StreetCred PKIC data contains 28 cases of death of unarmed people after a confrontation with police in which both a TASER was involved and for which an official autopsy is available.

In these deaths following TASER deployment, the official autopsy showed primary or secondary cause of death factors such as overdose from drugs including methamphetamine, phencyclidine (PCP), alcohol and flakka in 10 cases (36)%.

In three cases (11%), the autopsy found the cause of death also stemmed from significant health issues, including thyroid disorder, pulmonary emphysema and cardiac complications.

Nationwide TASER Use & Safety

According to a National Institute of Justice report[62]:

> "Taser use has increased in recent years. More than 15,000 law enforcement and military agencies use them ... A study by Wake Forest University researchers found that 99.7 percent of people who were shocked by [TASERs] suffered no injuries or minor injuries only. A small number suffered significant and potentially lethal injuries. This NIJ-sponsored study included six police departments and evaluated the results of 962 "real world" [TASER] uses. Skin punctures from [TASER] probes were common, accounting for 83 percent of mild injuries."

TASER Deployments Prior to Firearm Deployment

In 23 (27%) of the 84 cases in which police shot an unarmed person, officers first used a TASER before using deadly force. This is a clear indication that officers in these 23 cases made one or more attempts to use lesser intrusive levels of force before using deadly force. In all these 23 cases, the TASER was ineffective for a number of known reasons.

In some, clothing, or a miss, prevented the full contact that is necessary for neuromuscular incapacitation (NMI[63]). In at least one case, an officer attempted a "drive-stun" (full contact with the front end of the TASER) prior to using deadly force.

In one case that led to an indictment (the officer and decedent were both white), the TASER was deployed and gained compliance, but the decedent subsequently was said by the officer to have moved his body and hands in a manner the officer considered threatening and she deployed her firearm. The officer was acquitted after a trial in late 2015.

Witnesses to TASER Deployments

Most cases in which TASER was deployed and in which the person being TASERED subsequently died were witnessed by non-law enforcement (civilian) witnesses, or video, or audio, or all. There were non-law enforcement (civilian) witnesses in 39 (61%) of all TASER deployments. In 29 cases (74% of TASER cases with witnesses, or 45% of all TASER cases), witnesses exclusively support the officers' version of events. In seven cases (18%/11%) some witnesses support, and others dispute the police account. In three cases (8%/5) witnesses exclusively dispute the police account.

In 18 (28%) of the 64 TASER deployments, there is video available of the incident. In 11 (17%) TASER deployments there are both civilian witnesses and video.

EDGE CASES

During the last year, words like "homicide" were – perhaps unintentionally – often misused by reporters. After a controversial death (such as the 2014 death of Eric Garner in Staten Island, NY), reporters would say that the coroner found the cause of death to be homicide, the implication being that homicide is synonymous with murder. Homicide is a word that confuses those outside the criminal justice system. As a medical finding, "homicide" means: "Death at the hands of another." The medical finding of homicide is not a statement of culpability, or an indictment for a crime. But in story after story, the use of this term ultimately angered people who were later confused when charges were not filed against officers.

Not all homicides are crimes. For example, a killing by one person of another self-defense, or in the defense of another, is generally not a crime. Here's a scenario to make this understandable: You're lying in your bed one night and a man bursts into your bedroom, pointing a knife at you. You remove a loaded handgun from beneath your pillow, point it at the intruder and order him to stop, and to drop the knife. But the intruder tightens his grip on the knife and, holding it outward towards you, begins to purposefully advance upon you – so you shoot him in the heart.

You were just in a relatively unrealistic situation, but one in which you felt that you were in imminent danger of death or serious bodily injury and you took action to stop the threat. Any objectively reasonable person in the same condition would have recognized the reasonableness of feeling that those circumstances presented a threat to their life.

What you've just seen is the textbook definition of self-defense, and it is your right – not just in all 50 states, but also in most countries around the world. Self-defense is indubitably not a crime, but the manner of death of the person killed would be listed in their autopsy as a homicide. Therefore, an autopsy finding of manner of death of "homicide" does not necessarily mean that a crime has been committed. It is included to distinguish the manner of death from other manners of death, such as "natural causes," "suicide," "drug overdose," "accidental death," and others.

While there is no crime of homicide, when the acts of the killer and circumstances demonstrate criminal culpability it is generally referred to and charged as the crimes of capital murder, or murder, or manslaughter.

DISCLAIMER

In each of the 153 incidents identified for this study you will find brief analysis done by each of the authors. It is important to note that in none of the cases did the authors have the complete set of facts and circumstances known to the officer at the time of the incident.

It is also important to understand that the authors did not have access to the investigative case files. The authors were limited to only that information that was available mostly through open sources.

Therefore any analysis or opinion rendered by the authors on any particular case would not necessarily be the same had the authors been given full access to the entire set of circumstances and facts of the incident.

The authors reserve the right to revisit any case and modify their opinion should new information come to light.

SECTION II: THE CASES

JANUARY, 2015

Roberto Ornelas, 18, Hispanic Male

Key Largo, FL, January 1

At about 4:00 am, Roberto's father, Guadalupe Ornelas, called 911 because Roberto was exhibiting "wild, bizarre, behavior" and throwing things around their home. Two Monroe County Sheriff's deputies found Roberto was in his bedroom with the door locked. Deputies reported he was breaking objects and screaming incoherently[64].

The deputies forced their way into the bedroom and found Roberto "sweating profusely" on the floor and punching the wall. When the deputies got his attention, he stood up. Deputy Bryan Cross reported that Roberto was "staring right through them" with a wide-eyed blank expression, and was foaming from his nose and mouth. The deputies saw blood on the floor and walls.

Deputy Garcia grabbed Roberto by the arm, but Roberto broke free. Roberto spit in Deputy Cross's face, and lunged at him. Deputy Cross fired his TASER, hitting Roberto in the torso. Roberto stood up and began spitting at officers again. Roberto was TASERED a second time, handcuffed, and hobbled.

Roberto was transported to Homestead Hospital where his condition continued to worsen. Roberto was taken off of breathing machines on January 6[65].

Roberto's sister told investigators that her brother may have taken LSD for the first time on the night the police were called to his home. Roberto had previously been arrested by Monroe Sheriff's narcotics deputies on a felony charge for intent-to-sell. Toxicology showed no drugs in Roberto's system, but the Medical Examiner ruled his death a result of "delayed complications of acute drug toxicity[66]."

Analysis

The Medical Examiner's finding that death was caused by complications of acute drug toxicity even as toxicology shows no drugs is unusual. Given that, and given Ornelas' behavior, the failure to detect drugs in Ornelas' system strikes me as strongly indicative of a badly conducted drug-screen, or a drug-screen that didn't screen for the right drugs. Setting aside the drugs, this seems to be a case of clearly justified deadly force use by officers, who attempted non-deadly force multiple times, but who reasonably feared for their lives.

– Nick Selby

The deputies were confronted with a young man exhibiting erratic, destructive, and violent behavior, who was foaming at the mouth and covered with blood. Once the door to Roberto's bedroom was slightly opened, Roberto was seen on the floor punching the wall repeatedly. There are so many new and synthetic illicit drugs on the market, that traditional tests often don't detect them. Roberto's behavior and drug test results are consistent with a synthetic drug like flakka or bath salts.

This situation presented a number of risks to officers. Although not commonly a part of public discussion, the risk of an officer contracting blood-borne diseases such as HIV or hepatitis is very high. Medical personnel dealing with this subject would not be permitted to treat him without protective gloves, and possibly facemasks. Despite this, Deputy Garcia attempted to get Roberto to comply by grabbing his arm. Roberto spit in Deputy Cross's face, further exposing the deputy to bodily fluids, and limiting his ability to see and defend himself. Then Roberto lunged at him. This is almost a textbook example of why the TASER was created. It is my belief that no other force option available to the deputies at the time would have ended the violence safely. Deputy Cross deployed his TASER in an effort to end the violence and the risks posed to those present, a reasonable decision.

– Ben Singleton

This is one of those unfortunate events that police officers must deal with on a daily basis. The officers had a lawful objective to control Roberto's action to prevent further harm. They were working with limited or no information as to the cause of Roberto's condition. They operated in accordance with current law enforcement standards and training, but Roberto still died proximate to the seizure.

The officers were faced with a tense and rapidly evolving situation that required quick decision making skills. The situation and environment dictated that this encounter would be close quarter. Officers understand that a person in Roberto's condition can be difficult to control and dangerous. When officers' attempts at using physical control to stop Roberto from further harming himself failed, and the threat was articulated in the form of the Roberto spitting and the potential for blood borne pathogen exposure, the officers used a TASER in order to control Roberto. This is an appropriate use of the TASER and in the proper manner as trained in contemporary law enforcement standards. From the information provided, it appears unlikely that the TASER had any causal relationship to Roberto's death.

– Ed Flosi

John Quintero, 23, Hispanic Male

Wichita, KS, January 3

Police received calls from Quintero's relatives who described him as armed with a knife, under the influence of alcohol, "not all there right now," and threatening himself or others[67].

Dispatch received at least three additional 911 calls in which callers stated that Quintero was under the influence of alcohol and armed with a knife.

Officers arrived, and approached the vehicle occupied by Quintero and his father. The father came out of the vehicle compliant with the officers. Quintero was belligerent, confrontational, and refused to comply with officers' commands. Officers repeatedly ordered Quintero to show his hands. When Quintero did not comply, one of the officers deployed a TASER, but the TASER had no effect. Quintero advanced toward the officer, and as

Quintero reached for his waistband, another officer fired two shots from her patrol rifle, hitting Quintero in the middle of his body. [68]

He was transported to Wesley Medical Center where he died a few hours later.

Quintero tested positive for alcohol, methamphetamine, and marijuana.

Analysis

This is one of a surprisingly large number of cases in this book in which a person under the influence of multiple intoxicants, or acute mental-health crises, or both, attacks officers undeterred by the use of TASER non-deadly force. Officers typically count on the TASER as an effective tool to immobilize and then deter further aggression, but several issues we are tracking as we write this book, and in the PKIC project, support research in the law enforcement community about two crucial issues. The first is about the over-reliance by officers on TASER, and the second is training of officers in better handling incidents that involve this type of aggressive person. In this case, it would seem that officers were justified in their use of deadly force, because of the clear threat of deadly force by Quintero.

Some have asked about the "reach to the waistband," which sounds flimsy to those outside law enforcement. Remember that these officers had been told Quintero had a knife. I have been trained to take this kind of intelligence entirely seriously. One interesting note is that Commissioner Lawrence Mulvey, one of the co-authors of this book, was stabbed three times by a suspect when Larry didn't recognize the suspect had a knife until after the second stab wound had been inflicted. He tells me that, during the 1981 incident, he did not realize he had been stabbed – he felt no pain – but recognized that his chest was wet and he saw the glint of steel. He didn't unholster his weapon until after he realized what had already happened. The sheer speed with which knives can be produced and deployed is shocking.

– Nick Selby

The officer who shot Quintero was forced to make a decision based on the information available to her at the time. Callers reported Quintero was armed with a knife, intoxicated, and threatening to others. When Quintero refused to show his hands, was unaffected by the TASER deployment, advanced on fellow officers, and reached for his waistband, the officer had to make a split-second decision. This officer knew that had Quintero had a knife, as multiple callers reported, and had she waited for Quintero to display it, she wouldn't have time to react before Quintero used it to injure or kill officers. It was her responsibility as a cover officer – the person protecting the other officers - to make sure that Quintero didn't have that opportunity.

Remember, these life or death decisions have to be made in an instant. There is no time to thoroughly evaluate a situation like this. Officers are forced to rely on their training. This officer's training likely included a concept referred to as the "21-foot rule." This concept refers to the theory that an assailant, armed with a knife, can advance 21 feet or less in the amount of time it takes a human being to recognize the threat and react. While the 21-foot rule has come under controversy in early 2016, it is still a broadly applicable general rule-of-thumb by which officers can safely gauge the immediacy of the danger. The speed with which knives can be produced and deployed is truly surprising.

When Quintero advanced on officers and reached into his waistband, it would have been reasonable for the cover officer to believe that Quintero was about to attack officers with the knife she was told he had at the time of the initial calls.

– Ben Singleton

At first glance, it appears that the officer's use of deadly force would be appropriate under the circumstances. There are however several unknown variables that could confound this opinion. The distance between Quintero and the officer(s) is not specifically stated, but it would be reasonable to conclude that the distance was less than 25 feet, due to the mention of a TASER device probe deployment, an assumption based on the fact that most law enforcement agencies are using probe cartridges of either 21 or 25 feet.

We don't know why the TASER device had no effect on Quintero. Although this would cast little weight for judging the deadly force response, it would be interesting to know if the TASER deployment failed due to operator miss, device malfunction, or if Quintero was impervious to the pain.

I am not an advocate of the "21-foot rule," as it's too overly simplistic to be effective. When determining the threat of an edged weapon attacker, officers have to consider several factors including; (1) distance, (2) speed of aggression, (3) direction of movement, and (4) path of aggression, including any obstacles. An officer need not wait until they see the actual weapon, or wait until the weapon is used to determine actual intent. In this case, officers had previous information that Quintero was armed with a knife. The overt action of Quintero reaching for his waistband could lead a reasonable officer to believe Quintero was in the act of arming himself.

– Ed Flosi

Brian Pickett, 26, Black Male

Los Angeles, CA, January 6
Police received a call from Pickett's mother, who reported that Picket was under the influence of drugs and threatening to kill her. Deputies arrived at the home and confronted Pickett. Pickett charged the deputies when he saw them. Deputies deployed a TASER, subdued Pickett, and handcuffed him[69].

Paramedics were called to remove the TASER darts. While being treated by the paramedics, Pickett stopped breathing[70].

Pickett was taken to a hospital, where he died.

Analysis
This is another of the cases in which we see the potentially deadly combination of acute illicit drug intoxication, aggressive behavior, and attempts by officers to stop the threat using non-deadly force that results in the suspect dying. There are details missing, but the officers seemed to have

handled the situation appropriately by responding with what they intended to be non-deadly force.

– Nick Selby

Unfortunately, we do not have important details about Pickett's demeanor from the officers' perspectives. If for example, Pickett was naked, sweating profusely, and seemingly possessed, officers likely would have recognized these as signs of PCP intoxication. Subjects under the influence of PCP often possess super-human strength and are impervious to pain. Similar effects can be attributed to high doses of methamphetamine and cocaine.

Regardless of Pickett's drug of choice, we know that he charged officers and they responded with what they intended to be non-deadly force. It is reasonable that the deputies made the decision to subdue Pickett and used a non-lethal method to do so.

What made the encounter lethal is likely the drugs ingested by Pickett. Although TASER has been cited as a contributing factor in some in-custody deaths, it is unlikely that the outcomes in these cases would have been different had another use-of-force option, such as a baton, been used by the officers.

– Ben Singleton

Although the details in this circumstance are limited, the officers were called because Pickett was threatening to kill his mother. Time was of the essence for the officers to stabilize the situation from escalating. The officers tried to use non-deadly force to overcome Pickett's aggression as he charged at them. This would be an appropriate response.

– Ed Flosi

Autumn Steele, 34, White Female

Burlington, IA, January 6
Officer Hill responded to a domestic disturbance at the residence of Steele

and her husband. When Officer Hill arrived, he began attempting to quell the disturbance, and was then attacked by the couple's German shepherd. Upon the dog's attack, Hill fired two shots, with one hitting Steele in the torso[71]. She was later pronounced dead at the hospital.

Officer Hill was treated for at least one dog bite[72].

Analysis

I've never been attacked by a dog, but I have had dogs straining at the leash to come towards me. In both cases, I reached for my TASER and not my firearm. I have had discussions with other officers who disagree with me on my choice, and I am fortunate not to have had to find out who of us was right. I can't opine further on this case because I don't think there is enough information on why the officer fired his pistol and struck Steele.

– Nick Selby

Officer Hill was under attack by a German shepherd, but more details are needed to determine if negligence, lack of training, or unusual circumstances were factors in the death of Steele. Was Steele caught in crossfire while attempting to restrain the dog? Was Steele behind the dog when Officer Hill fired at the dog? Or did Officer Hill fire his weapon without taking aim and hit Steele as a matter of haphazard negligence?

The county attorney stated that the decision not to charge Hill criminally with the death of Steele was based on body camera evidence, suggesting that Hill was not negligent, and that Steele's death was the result of an unfortunate accident. It is even possible that Steele jumped between Hill and the dog as Hill was firing his weapon, and was hit by his bullet as a result.

– Ben Singleton

It appears that Steele was not the intended target in the shooting. Hill was being attacked by a German shepherd and appears to have been targeting the dog. Many factors are still unknown. In the use of force analysis one must consider the actions of the officer at the time of force response as to, "Was the force used an intentional act?" In this case, it would be unlikely to rise to the level of a Constitutional violation, as the act appears to be unintentional. It gives rise to a discussion regarding a negligence claim, though, and how much of the negligence could be assigned to Steele herself.

– Ed Flosi

Andre Murphy, 42, Black Male

Norfolk, NE, January 7

Norfolk Officers Bahns and Martinez responded to a domestic disturbance at a Super 8 Motel. Officers deployed a TASER to subdue Murphy and take him into custody. An officer sustained minor injuries during the incident.

Toxicology reports indicate there were: "very, very high levels of methamphetamine" in Murphy's system[73]. The presence of K2 was also found in his system.

A grand jury found the cause of death to be accidental, and found that no officers were guilty of any crimes surrounding the death of Murphy[74].

Analysis

There is too little public information about this case to conclusively assert a position on reasonableness. But with the information available, we find that officers used non-deadly force to subdue and apprehend a subject who was under the influence of drugs. Murphy later died of drug overdose.

– Nick Selby

This is another case of a subject succumbing to drug toxicity after having contact with the police. In cases where subjects are highly intoxicated, TASER is often the only non-deadly option. Highly intoxicated people often exhibit super-human strength, extremely high pain tolerance, and severely diminished cognitive ability. This means traditional pain compliance methods, such as baton strikes, are ineffective. If this subject was highly intoxicated, as the toxicology report states, the officer's decision to use the

TASER as a non-deadly force option to subdue this intoxicated subject was reasonable. I believe his subsequent death was a result of the fatally toxic levels of methamphetamine found in his system.

– Ben Singleton

There are far too many unknown facts to make a reasoned opinion as to the appropriateness of using the TASER. This even includes the lack of information as to the effectiveness of its use. Circumstantial information, such as the coroner's report and the grand jury's decision, lead me to believe there was no criminal culpability in this case.

– Ed Flosi

Artago Howard, 36, Black Male

Strong, AR, January 8

A Union County deputy responded to an alarm call at a pharmacy. Upon arrival, he saw a broken window and found Howard inside. The deputy confronted Howard, and a fight ensued. A struggle for the deputy's weapon reportedly led to the discharge of one round into Howard[75]. Howard attempted to flee, but was caught and taken into custody by the deputy. Howard died at the scene. Two other suspects in the burglary were arrested and charged.

Analysis

There are many crucial details of the struggle missing from these reports and it would be great to know if there was video, or if there were witnesses to the incident. As an officer I'm biased towards belief of the officer's account in this case, considering that some of the aspects of the case – the alarm, the broken window, Howard's presence in the Pharmacy – that would tend to support the deputy's account. I don't understand why he chose to go in alone when he had reason to believe more than one suspect was inside.

– Nick Selby

The deputy found himself fighting a burglary suspect for control of his gun while attempting to take him into custody. The likelihood that a deputy's gun will be turned against him, if obtained by a suspect, is statistically high. The deputy surely knows this.

We must also understand that this deputy was all alone, and the only means of defending himself was being taken from him by a criminal with unknown intentions. Although media reports merely state that the gun discharged as a result of the struggle[76], I believe the deputy was faced with the choice to give the suspect control of his deadly weapon, or fire the weapon.

While fighting Howard, the deputy also had to consider the remaining burglary suspects, and the potential threat they posed. Had the deputy not fired his weapon, he would have been outnumbered three to one, and unarmed.

Officers killed with their own guns make up about 8% of law enforcement officers killed every year by criminals[77].

– Ben Singleton

The deputy was alone inside a building searching for a burglar suspect. This raises a concern with me. Why was the decision to go in solo made? There might be good reasons for this and there may not have been. I can't make that determination without further exploration of the circumstances. If the decision was found to be unsound, would have the presence of another deputy mitigated the assault and the eventual shooting?

If the decision was found to be tactically sound, there are still questions that remain about the firing of the pistol. Officers are trained to understand that deadly force may become needed to prevent another person from gaining control of their weapon.

But the questions remain: What was the level of struggle? How did the pistol get out of the holster? Did Howard remove it in his attempts to gain control of it? Was the gun intentionally fired by the deputy and, if so, what were the factors that would justify a shooting (not to imply that they are not there, I just don't know)? Was the gun fired unintentionally as a direct result of the struggle? Please note, these questions are meant to clarify and not to cast doubt upon the deputy's actions.

– Ed Flosi

Joshua Garcia, 24, Hispanic Male

Tahoka, TX, January 26

A Lynn County deputy attempted to stop Garcia after a traffic violation that led to a pursuit. Garcia ultimately collided with a police vehicle, and was arrested. After being handcuffed and placed in a patrol car, Garcia slipped his handcuffs from behind his body to the front of his body. Garcia then attempted to steal the patrol car[78]. Deputies discharged their firearms into the patrol car, killing Garcia[79].

Analysis

I tend to be skeptical of the old "he's in the police car and therefore a deadly threat" school of thought. Sure, officers keep weapons in the vehicles, but they are typically locked – and while the security of these locks is not Fort Knox, neither is it trivial to overcome, and it is (and this is more important) transparent when someone is attempting to overcome it. It used to be that the mere act of stealing the police car was cause for deadly force, but I'm not sure in this case. If Garcia was aiming the car at the officers, or making an overt attempt to obtain a weapon, or if he had unlocked the weapon and was preparing it to fire, then I can absolutely see the exigency for deadly force. But mere car theft doesn't quite cross the line for me in terms of deadly force, so more information is needed before I can state an opinion.

– Nick Selby

More details are needed to adequately analyze this incident. However, it is probable that the police vehicle was forward-facing during the incident, where the officers were working. That's generally the way officers position their vehicles for many reasons including traffic control, in-car video positioning, and visibility into the patrol car from the scene. Given the reported distance that Garcia drove the police vehicle (only a few feet), and the assumption that the vehicle was nose-in to the incident, it is reasonable to believe that the vehicle was being driven toward officers who were ordering him to stop.

If Garcia was driving the stolen police vehicle toward the officers or otherwise endangering the lives of others, the decision to use deadly force against him was absolutely reasonable. If Garcia was again attempting to evade police, this time by fleeing the scene in the stolen patrol car, and did not pose a threat to the officers' lives, this shooting was unnecessary. A fleeing suspect does not pose an immediate threat to officers.

– Ben Singleton

Here is another case where more information is needed to make a reasoned opinion. It can be reasonably inferred that the suspect was searched prior to being placed in the police vehicle (and if not we have another issue to explore) and therefore not personally armed.

It's not evident whether the suspect was attempting to gain access to any weapons that were in the vehicle, or if there were any weapons in the vehicle that he could access. If the suspect was pulling at a shotgun in the magnetic lock and the officer was able to hear or see the mechanism release, then we have a different set of facts that may support the use of deadly force. If the vehicle was moving, this would be extremely difficult to imagine happening.

If the suspect was endangering the officer or other motorists with the vehicle, it could lead to an appropriate use of deadly force, but the only information here is that the suspect was attempting to steal the police vehicle, and there is no movement or direction of potential travel mentioned. Indeed, most agencies now train officers to get out of the path of a moving or potentially moving vehicle to avoid "having to shoot" the driver.

One simply cannot use deadly force only because they think the suspect "might" do something. There must be specific facts which would lead a reasonable officer to believe the suspect "will" do that act. If the officers in this case shot only to prevent the stealing of a police vehicle, I believe it may fall short from being appropriate.

– Ed Flosi

Jessica Hernandez, 17, Hispanic Female

Denver, CO, January 26

Denver Police Officers responded to a suspicious vehicle complaint in an alley. Upon arrival, the investigating officers found that the vehicle was previously reported stolen. The vehicle was occupied by five juveniles, ages 15 to 17[80]. The juvenile occupants noticed the officers' presence and attempted to flee. During the attempt, Officer Jordan found himself between the front of the suspect vehicle and a brick wall, or a fence. Officer Jordan heard the vehicle engine rev, and he saw the car speed toward him from a distance of about 10 feet. Officer Jordan yelled for the driver, Jessica Hernandez, to "stop!" multiple times. The event took place in a narrow alley where Officer Jordan had no means of egress. Officer Jordan and another officer fired into the vehicle when they say the vehicle closed the distance, and became an immediate threat to Officer Jordan's life[81]. The driver, Jessica Hernandez, died as a result of the gunshots fired by Officer Jordan.

An eyewitness stated that she saw an officer get hit by and "bounce off of" the front of the stolen car immediately before shots were fired. She also stated that she heard the car engine rev as the car accelerated toward the officer. The crime scene report states that three bullets pierced the front windshield, three pierced the driver side front window, and one pierced the rear driver side window. It also states that the evidence supports the officers' statements regarding their positions relative to the vehicle at the time of the shooting. Officer Jordan's shell casings were found three feet, six inches from the fence that was behind him when he fired.

Analysis

I want to comment on the inclusion in this book of this incident, since a vehicle is clearly a deadly weapon. We left it in the database because of its dynamics, the involvement of teenagers, and public expressions of doubt at the time the incident took place that the teenagers had not, in fact, driven towards the officers. It was highly contested in local media at the time of the original reporting, so we chose to leave the incident in.

– Nick Selby

Officer Jordan was dispatched to a vehicle which he found to be stolen and occupied. This is a dangerous situation for police officers. Department policy usually requires officers to proceed on occupied stolen vehicles with deadly force options at the ready, as Officer Jordan did. When Officer Jordan heard the engine rev and saw the car, a 3,000 pound deadly weapon, speeding toward him, he fired on the driver. Officer Green, also on scene, also fired upon the vehicle. In his statement Officer Green says, "I had my gun out and was preparing to shoot because I was afraid that he (Officer Jordan) was going to get run over."

"Officer Jordan's shell casings were found three feet, six inches from the fence that was behind him when he fired."

Officer Jordan had no other reasonable options. He reasonably believed that the stolen vehicle that was being driven toward him was going to crush him and kill him. Fearing for his life, and at the last possible moment, he discharged his weapon into the driver of the vehicle.

– Ben Singleton

This incident made national news and was the direct cause of a major policy shift within the agency. The new policy states that officers may not shoot at the driver of a vehicle unless there is some other threat than to the vehicle itself. I don't agree with the policy shift at all.

A vehicle itself is a weapon that creates a significant risk of serious bodily injury or death, which by definition is deadly force, regardless of the age or gender of the driver. Officers are trained and understand that they may use deadly force themselves if they reasonably believe their life or the life of another is in imminent danger of serious bodily injury or death.

In this case, Officer Jordan had no escape route. Hernandez demonstrated clear intent to strike him. After being given opportunities to not hit him, Hernandez chose to drive the vehicle in the officer's direction. It is clear to me the use of deadly force to stop her deadly threat was fully appropriate.

– Ed Flosi

Ralph Willis, 42, White Male

Stillwater, OK, January 29

Stillwater fire crews responded to an apartment fire, where they found a dead body. Witnesses reportedly saw Ralph Willis leave the scene of the fire. He was listed as a person of interest, and he was located. He led officers on a foot chase, during which he ran to a nearby neighborhood, scaled a fence, and was confronted by an officer. Willis reportedly made "an aggressive move" toward the officer. The officer fired his weapon once, killing Willis[82].

Analysis

The devil, of course, is in the details of "an aggressive move." I don't have enough to form an opinion other than the observation that you can't shoot someone right now for something he did 30 seconds ago – let alone five-minutes-and-a-reasonably-involved-foot-chase ago. We need more details.

– Nick Selby

The officer was engaged in a foot chase with a murder suspect. At the conclusion of the chase, Willis made an aggressive move toward the officer. There is insufficient information about the incident to make a conclusive assessment. We do not know what use of force options were available to the officer at the time, and lack a sufficient description of events regarding the escalation of the contact.

At the conclusion of a foot chase, officers are often fatigued. A fatigued officer, alone, and with gun in hand, must do something to stop the suspect from attacking and disarming him. But this must be thoroughly investigated. If the officer had time to better assess the threat and evaluate other force options, he should have done so.

– Ben Singleton

There is a clear lack of details in this account. It seems clear that the officers would have reasonable suspicion to conduct an investigatory stop on Willis especially after he fled the contact. He was eventually found after a foot chase in a yard. These situations can be dangerous, but the level of the threat must be in line with whatever force is used. I am unsure what an "aggressive move" truly means. It could be anything from a body posturing that indicates a possible physical attack to a life-threatening action of drawing a weapon. Also, what was the distance between Willis and the officer? Were other officers there and, if there were, how many were there? A lot of questions are still unanswered.

– Ed Flosi

FEBRUARY, 2015

David Kassick, 59, White Male

South Hanover, PA, February 2

Officer Lisa Mearkle, a 14-year veteran of the Hummelstown Police Department in Pennsylvania, attempted to stop a vehicle for displaying an expired inspection sticker. The driver, David Kassick, took off. Officer Mearkle gave chase. Kassick eventually stopped in front of his home, exited the car and ran. Officer Mearkle stopped him using her TASER, which incapacitated Kassick, and he fell to the ground, face down[83]. Officer Mearkle ordered Kassick to show his hands. He did not. Officer Mearkle then fired two shots into Kassick's back. Kassick was unarmed[84]. On November 5, 2015, a Dauphin County jury acquitted Hummelstown Officer Mearkle of third-degree murder, voluntary manslaughter and involuntary manslaughter[85].

Analysis

This incident troubles me. Without second-guessing what the officer saw, and with the caveat that the video I have watched has inherent visual limitations, it did appear to me that Kassick was ignoring Mearkle's commands to show his hands. This is a real challenge for an officer, and can be quite frightening especially because from the police academy on, officers are trained that Kassick's behavior could lead to his producing a weapon and opening fire. I have been lucky and never faced this situation, but I know from sitting in the police academy watching dashcam videos of officer after officer killed for hesitation in situations exactly like this one that the main thing I determined was never to allow myself to hesitate should this situation present itself. The main reason this case troubles me, then, is because my training and academy-determined mindset would have potentially led me to make the same mistake as Mearkle did. In 20-20 hindsight, there were other options available to her.

I do not imply Mearkle acted illegally, but rather that this incident is squarely in the realm of what cops refer to as, "Lawful but awful."

– Nick Selby

In my opinion, Officer Mearkle did not appropriately control her fear and deal with the situation using a reasonable amount of force. People unable to control their fear and use good judgment in the midst of chaos are not fit to work in law enforcement.

Her use of deadly force may have been legally justified, but it was completely unnecessary and driven by fear rather than sound judgment.

– Ben Singleton

This case has some serious problems. The fact that the officer was acquitted of criminal culpability doesn't relieve the case from moving forward as a civil rights lawsuit, nor does it protect the officer from administrative sanctions.

I have noticed a trend in law enforcement that is reflective of society's "no tolerance for violence" of any type, including self-defense actions. Children are told that even if they hit another student in self-defense that they will get suspended. Many law enforcement recruits have never been in a physical altercation prior to entering the profession, whether it was on the school yard or even in sports. These recruits are sometimes afraid of physical confrontation and leery to put their hands on others in fear that they "might" get hurt. While it is possible that anybody "could" be armed, too many law enforcement instructors fill their heads with thoughts that everybody "is" armed, further exacerbating the fear.

Looking at the facts presented here, it seems possible pure fear drove the officer to use her firearm. I see nothing to suspect that officers believed Kassick to be armed, nor is there any evidence of any overt act or circumstance that would lead someone to believe Kassick was attempting to produce a firearm.

– Ed Flosi

Wilber Castillo-Gongora, 35, Hispanic Male

Electra, TX, February 3

Castillo called 911 multiple times from inside his vehicle along Highway 287, each time reporting a different occurrence. When deputies arrived on scene, they found Castillo to be upset and behaving erratically[86]. Castillo began running out into the roadway, at which point deputies began trying to control him. TASER was deployed twice by the officers, and Castillo was handcuffed. Castillo became unresponsive and stopped breathing[87].

Analysis

This is another of the cases from 2015 that haunts us, in which arriving officers are given their pick of terrible choices and struggle to make best with the least bad ones. In this case, I believe the officers' intent was to subdue Castillo for his own protection, but his health condition made deadly what is otherwise non-deadly force.

– Nick Selby

Although investigating authorities intended to order toxicology tests to determine levels of alcohol or drug intoxication, the results have not been released. Clearly Castillo was in the throes of some kind of psychotic episode. Whether it was drug-induced is not necessarily relevant. In-custody deaths following non-deadly force are most often cases where subjects are found to be in a state of psychosis, whether drug-induced or not.

As to whether the use of the TASER was appropriate, I believe it was. We have limited information upon which to base an opinion, but attempting to take control of a person in this condition, in the middle of a state highway while negotiating traffic, is dangerous for everyone involved. TASER allows officers to incapacitate a subject quickly and, in most cases, safely. These officers appear to have been making an effort to save Castillo's life.

– Ben Singleton

This is a case with a repeated theme. Officers used an appropriate non-deadly force based on the threat Castillo would have presented to himself and the public if he ran out on the active roadway. Their use of the TASER was consistent with current law enforcement training and practices to stop Castillo causing harm to himself and others. But for conditions unknown to us, Castillo died proximate to the arrest process.

There is no way for the officers to determine the cause of Castillo's condition or anybody that is "upset and behaving erratically." There are too many reasons why a person might behave this way including; (1) simple anger and confusion, (2) mental illness, (3) intoxication, or (4) excited delirium. In any case, an officer faced with having to make quick decisions to prevent harm is not required (and well advised not to) make a diagnosis of the condition prior to using force.

– Ed Flosi

Joaquin Hernandez, 28, Hispanic Male

Phoenix, AZ, February 4

A US Marshals Fugitive Task Force was looking to arrest Salvador Muna for outstanding warrants. The task force officers located Muna, at which point he jumped into a car driven by his friend Joaquin Hernandez. Hernandez led police on a short chase that ended when police pinned the car at an intersection[88]. Muna pulled out a gun and pointed it at officers. Four officers opened fire, killing Muna.

Media accounts differ regarding the circumstances of Hernandez' death. One account states that after police fired on Muna, Hernandez made a "movement that officers perceived as threatening," so officers directed fire at Hernandez. Other accounts state that Hernandez was simply "killed in the crossfire."

Analysis

This is one of a small number of similar 2015 cases in which a person not directly in the process of attacking police is killed by police stopping a legitimate, active threat. In this case, whether by crossfire or intent, the officers were in a situation in which deadly force was clearly justified, and Hernandez, who chose to drive his friend and chose not to put his hands in the air and exit the vehicle, was killed by police stopping a legitimate threat[89]. Hernandez' death is lamentable, but it would seem very difficult for the police to have avoided it while defending themselves.

– Nick Selby

While we should never view "crossfire casualties" as acceptable, the decedent in this case was not an innocent bystander. We don't know whether officers targeted Hernandez.

If immediately after Muna engaged officers in a gunfight, Hernandez made some furtive movements inside the car and the officers targeted him as a result, theirs is a justifiable use of deadly force. Officers should not have to wait to receive fire before engaging. If Hernandez wanted to disengage and surrender, he had the ability to do so at any point prior to his death.

If Hernandez was simply "hit by crossfire," we must ask whether his death occurred as a result of officer negligence. The reports suggest that there were a total of about four to six total shots fired. This is not suggestive of a barrage of haphazard gunfire by overzealous police. It is possible that Hernandez put himself in the line of fire or was hit by a ricochet. It is also possible that one of the four officers who fired on Muna fired a round off target. Without a forensic analysis of the physical evidence, we just cannot answer these questions.

Muna engaged in a fatal encounter with the police and Hernandez stayed by his side throughout. He refused to surrender when given the opportunity and was, in my view, complicit in the events that drew gunfire from police officers.

– Ben Singleton

Here again we must look into the question: "Was the force used on Hernandez intentional?" If we answer "yes," and Hernandez was a perceptible deadly force threat, then the use of deadly force would most likely be deemed appropriate and consistent with current law enforcement training and standards. The argument would be that Muna had a gun and pointed it at officers, that Hernandez was a willing participant in the escape and did not surrender when the opportunity was given, and finally, that Hernandez may have acted as if it appeared he was attempting to present a firearm, forcing the officers into making a split-second decision.

If the answer to the question is "no," then again, it may rise up to a negligence claim. Based on Hernandez's actions and apparent voluntary participation in the event, the percentage portion of negligence assigned to him in this case would have to be considerable.

– Ed Flosi

Jeremy Lett, 28, Black Male

Tallahassee, FL, February 4

Officer Stith of the Tallahassee Police Department responded to a burglary in progress at an apartment complex. He located Jeremy Lett there, laying on the front stoop of the complainant's apartment. Lett had one hand in his pocket, so Officer Stith instructed him to show both. Lett yelled, began getting up, and then charged Stith, attempting to tackle him.

Stith holstered his weapon, and drew his TASER. Again Lett charged Officer Stith. Officer Stith fired his TASER, but missed Lett with one of the darts. Stith then fruitlessly attempted to make direct contact between the TASER and Lett to deliver the exposure. Lett charged Stith again. Stith dropped his TASER, and drew his firearm. Lett charged Stith a last time and Stith found himself on the ground. Stith fired multiple rounds into Lett as he came down on top of him.

A grand jury found Officer Stith's use of deadly force was justifiable under Florida law[90].

Analysis

This may have been reasonable, but I think perhaps it was avoidable. The over-reliance by officers on TASER is becoming a real problem, as officers feel increasingly that their two options are TASER or firearm. There are in fact a range of other options, but some require officers to behave differently – choosing de-escalation techniques, backing off and waiting for backup, or just old-fashioned going "hands-on" and using holds and immobilization techniques. Part of the issue would seem to be officers feeling that they can't allow themselves to be seen as retreating, which I think may push officers to escalate, rather than de-escalate. Ultimately, I don't know if the actions of Lett rose to the point that would justify a fear for Stith's life.

– Nick Selby

Police Departments all over the country are utilizing advanced tools like the TASER to deal with violent subjects. TASER is a fast, safe, and effective way to drop a suspect to the ground without incident. It really is a great tool. But many officers today are unprepared for its occasional failure.

Before TASER, police officers fought people. It was part of the job. As I read the grand jury's description of this incident, I think about similar incidents occurring before TASER in which the officer and suspect may have walked away beaten, battered, and bruised, but neither died.

Police officers need to be prepared to fight unarmed suspects, without the use of deadly weapons. There are those few exceptions where a fight leads to serious injury, and the officer must make that life or death decision. In this case however, I find no reference to injuries sustained by the officer. In fact, except for an inferred intent to "tackle" Stith, I find no reference to an actual physical assault by Lett.

Are we at a point in the pursuit of officer safety where we are willing to excuse officers from a fight, instead allowing them to use their firearms, because they have not prepared for such an occurrence? Justifiable or not, I believe this death was unnecessary.

– Ben Singleton

Unknown information about what happened prior to the contact could factor into the evaluation of this case. Why did Officer Stith choose to contact Lett without a cover officer present? Were there extenuating circumstances that made it not feasible to wait? Too often, we see officers unnecessarily rush into an event, only to have their actions end with terrible consequences.

Officers are not required to use lesser force options in order to escalate up to the appropriate force necessary to subdue the subject. The danger of an officer being taken to the ground should properly be avoided. If Lett was perceived as a viable threat in his aggressively charging a uniformed officer, then the use of baton strikes, TASER, or OC Spray would be appropriate. The TASER had no effect due to a missed probe and the attempted at a drive-stun (indicating very close proximity) also failed. I have little concern about the TASER device use here.

The potential rub comes in with the use of deadly force. Taking an officer to the ground is a dangerous situation, but attempting to tackle an officer does not necessarily rise to the level for using deadly force. Other factors would need to be articulated to support such a decision.

– Ed Flosi

Jonathan Pierce, 37, White Male

Port St. Joe, FL, February 11

Pierce was arrested for Felony Theft. Sgt. Garner, of the Port St. Joe Police Department interviewed him. During questioning, Pierce grabbed a firearm, and killed himself with it.

Sgt. Garner gave two different, and conflicting, accounts of the incident. Initially he told a Gulf County deputy that he saw Pierce with a gun, so he took cover. When a fellow Port St. Joe officer arrived, Garner told him that he removed his backup pistol from his pocket when Pierce rushed him, knocking the pistol to the floor. Pierce then picked it up and shot himself with it[91].

Media reports state that Sgt. Garner did not follow normal police procedures with respect to the securing of prisoners, or the operation of body-worn cameras. Pierce remained unrestrained during the interview and was later found to have secreted a razor blade in his mouth. Garner also deactivated his body-worn camera before the shooting took place[92].

Garner refused to answer further questions regarding the incident. No charges were filed against him.

Analysis

We struggled with whether to put this in to the PKIC database and this book because the killing was of a person armed at the time of his death. We ultimately decided to leave it in when it was clear that the firearm Pierce had was one he never should have had access to. Therein is the issue with this case. There were so many issues with this interview procedure that I personally consider Garner to have been responsible for Pierce's death: as a police officer you are in my custody from the moment I take control of you, in a situation from which you are not legally permitted to leave of your own free will. In this case, Garner's multiple failures (to properly check Pierce for weapons, to properly secure his own weapon, to properly secure Pierce during the interview, to fail to video record the interview) amount in my opinion to culpability for Pierce's death.

– Nick Selby

First, Garner received condemnation for his refusal to answer questions about the incident. I take issue with this. Garner is a police officer, but as an American citizen, he is also afforded the rights under the 5th amendment. His refusal to answer questions cannot be considered a sign of guilt. Attorneys will tell you that refusing to answer questions is the smart thing to do, and I agree.

Now, as to Garner's procedural shortcomings; he should not have deactivated his camera. He should not have given two conflicting accounts of the incident. He should not have pulled his backup weapon out of his pocket. We will never know exactly what happened, but Sgt. Garner's extremely poor judgment was definitely a contributing factor.

– Ben Singleton

Some strange facts are presented in this incident. A supervisor (one would assume to have been an officer for some time) observed a person with a gun.

In response, the sergeant sought cover, which is an appropriate decision. From here the reported facts get so convoluted that it is difficult to even form a reasoned opinion. How did Pierce get into a position that he could "rush" Garner? That Pierce was able to rush Garner from the initial position where he was observed would call into question the appropriate use of distance and cover. If Pierce was directed to Garner's position, why was he not better controlled? Current law enforcement practices would dictate a search, and potentially handcuffing Pierce until the situation was deemed safe.

Perhaps most troubling is the fact that the body worn camera was deactivated just prior to the shooting. This happened prior to the sergeant removing his backup weapon, which was ultimately taken and used by Pierce, according to Garner. Officers are trained that a backup gun is just that, a backup. I cannot find any material that would support the decision to remove the backup weapon from the pocket.

– Ed Flosi

Chance Thompson, White Male, 35

Marysville, CA, February 15
The Yuba County Sheriff's Office received a 911 phone call from a security guard working at a concrete distribution facility. The security guard reported a white male jumping on rocks near the main gate.

Sheriff's deputies arrived and found Thomson standing atop a concrete wall, in a fighting stance, punching and kicking. Thompson did not respond to deputies, speaking incoherently. Deputies believed that he was under the influence of drugs. Deputy Trumm grabbed Thompson's back pocket, and pulled him down from the wall. Thompson landed on his feet, and began fighting the Deputy, ultimately getting Deputy Trumm in a head lock.

Deputy Knacke deployed her TASER and brought Thompson to the ground. She activated her TASER several more times as she and Trumm attempted to subdue Thomson, who was still actively resisting. After handcuffing Thompson, the deputies still couldn't control him. Deputy Knacke activated her TASER several more times to gain control of Thomson, a total of seven times during the incident. Each time Thompson received a five-second exposure.

After the seventh exposure, Thompson began to have difficulty breathing. An ambulance was requested, and Thompson was transported to the hospital, where he later died.

High quantities of methamphetamine, amphetamine, and alcohol were found in Thompson's blood[93].

Thompson was removed from life support by his family[94].

Analysis

This incident highlights two distinct trends – an overreliance on TASER and the challenges of dealing with people under the influence of acute methamphetamine intoxication. In this case, it does appear to me that Knacke overused the TASER. I don't believe that the TASER was responsible for Thompson's death – the toxic narcotic and alcoholic brew he self-administered, in addition to any other health issues he may have had, were likely responsible. I will say that using the TASER on a man who is in handcuffs is something that should be looked at more closely from a policy perspective.

– Nick Selby

Thompson was under the influence of methamphetamine, which causes hallucinations, paranoia, and aggressive behavior. Deputies recognized his condition almost immediately. So when Thompson began fighting Deputy Trumm, Deputy Knacke used her TASER. She used her TASER three more times during the struggle to get Thompson in handcuffs. After handcuffing Thompson, she used her TASER three more times.

As stated earlier regarding other TASER uses, it is a valuable and effective tool for bringing someone to the ground safely and effectively. Unfortunately, TASER has become a substitute for hands-on police work for some officers. I don't believe that TASER was the cause of Thompson's death. Thompson had ingested toxic levels of methamphetamine and engaged in a struggle with the police, which we know can be a deadly combination. A TASER, however, wasn't designed to be used seven consecutive times on one person. It is designed to be used one time to completely incapacitate someone, allowing that person to be handcuffed safely. TASER training encourages officers to handcuff the recipient of the exposure as they are receiving the exposure to minimize harm to all involved. Instead these officers used TASER as a pain compliance tool, expecting Thompson to comply after having received the exposure. One correctly executed exposure may have shortened the struggle, and resulted in a different outcome.

– Ben Singleton

It is unclear to me if the TASER in this incident was used in probe mode or drive-stun mode. This incident occurred in California, which is part of the 9th Circuit Court of Appeals. In this Circuit, officers are directed and trained that for the use of the TASER in probe mode to be deemed reasonable, the subject must be presenting a credible threat to the officer or others and a warning must be given, if feasible. In order to use the TASER in drive-stun mode, there are other lesser factors, but the subject has to be at least actively resisting. It cannot be used without a warning and can only be used if the subject had an opportunity to recover from the pain experienced and is able to understand the consequences of failing to comply with the warning (some agencies have actually eliminated the drive-stun completely due to this ruling).

Prior to handcuffing Thompson, the deputy attempted hands-on tactics, but Thompson was able to get the deputy into a headlock, which made him a credible threat to the deputy. I have no issue with the TASER uses prior to handcuffing, as long as this threat to the officers continued. There are TASER guidelines that speak to the number of cycles that should be used, but it is important to remember that these represent only manufacturer's guidelines and are not a legal standard. Some organizations such as the Police Executive Research Forum (PERF) have also opined on this topic.

Here we must remember that such organizations do not have legal standing or the authority to create legal standards. The legal standard remains as, "Was the force objectively reasonable under the totality of the circumstances?"

The remaining TASER uses after Thompson was handcuffed would need further examination to determine if they were appropriate. Just as we have learned that unarmed does not mean not dangerous, we also know that handcuffing does not always mean the person cannot be a threat. There isn't enough information available to make any determination as to why the officer used additional cycles after Thompson was handcuffed.

– Ed Flosi

Michael Ireland, 31, White Male

Springfield, MO, February 17
Springfield Officers were dispatched to a suspicious activity call. They arrived and saw Ireland, who was on parole and wanted for municipal warrants. Ireland ran from officer Bath, who pursued him on foot. Officer Bath caught up with Ireland, and during that contact, Officer Bath shot Ireland in the chest, killing him[95].

Analysis
We don't have enough facts here to form any opinion.

– Nick Selby

As in other cases, there is too little information from which to derive an opinion on this case. There is an open and ongoing investigation into this shooting. But we do know that Ireland was unarmed, and Bath resigned immediately after the shooting[96].

– Ben Singleton

In this case, there is a total lack of any real facts as to why the officer shot Ireland. It can be inferred that Ireland was no longer running away at the time of the shooting and was facing the officer. Absent other facts, it is impossible to opine either way on this case.

– Ed Flosi

Ruben Garcia-Villalpando, 31, Hispanic Male

Euless, TX, February 20

Grapevine Officer Clark attempted to stop Garcia when he was found in the parking lot of a business where an alarm had sounded. Garcia briefly fled in his vehicle. When Garcia stopped, Officer Clark ordered Garcia out of the car at gunpoint, and clearly ordered him to stay at the rear of his car. Garcia refused to remain at a safe distance from Clark, and continued to advance. As seen on video, Officer Clark tells Garcia to "backup!" more than 20 times during the incident. Garcia advances on Clark despite Clark's repeated orders to stop. When Garcia closes the distance and comes within a few feet of Clark, he is shot two times in the chest by Clark. The last moments before the shooting are off camera[97].

Garcia was transported to a local hospital where he died[98]. Toxicology results state that Garcia's blood alcohol content was 0.14[99]. A grand jury reviewed the evidence and chose not to charge Officer Clark with a criminal offense.

Analysis

I believe that in order to understand the dynamics of this incident one must view the video. After reviewing it, I can say that this case exemplifies why second-guessing officers after the fact is sometimes so difficult. I can see that all the elements were there, especially in the demeanor and what I perceive is the intent of Garcia to fight to the death in a case of suicide by cop. These pre-assaultive indicators were ultimately, I believe, sufficient, given the totality of these circumstances, to make the officer reasonably fearful for his life. Ultimately, I must say that I believe that Garcia would have engaged Clark in more plainly deadly force had Clark not acted when he did. I would have liked to see this end peacefully, but I do not believe that the officer behaved unreasonably.

– Nick Selby

A review of Officer Clark's in-car video is necessary to fully understand the events leading up to the shooting. While Garcia had his hands up at times, he was clearly advancing on Clark in defiance of Clark's orders. He moved deliberately toward Clark, ignoring repeated orders to "STOP!" and "backup!" Garcia spoke in English, and responded to Clark's commands, which were in English throughout the incident. Garcia even tells the officer, "Kill me" at one point.

As I watch the in-car video footage of this incident, I see Garcia advancing on Officer Clark with motive. Garcia is intentionally defying instructions to stop, instead choosing to advance on the officer. I believe had Officer Clark not fired on Garcia, a fight over Clark's weapon would have ensued. Without this video footage, it would be very hard to fully understand the gravity of the situation that Officer Clark found himself in, and to assess the threat posed by Garcia.

– Ben Singleton

The video tells of a very dangerous situation. Garcia led the officer on a pursuit that placed the lives of many motorists at risk, demonstrating a complete lack of respect for life in his escape attempt. Although it is not seen in the video, after the stop, the officer radioed that Garcia was previously "trying to reach" for something. The officer then advised that his cover units should respond quickly because Garcia was asking Clark to kill him. This is a known tactic by subjects that are attempting "suicide by cop."

Based on the manner of Garcia's approach (deliberate and steady towards a uniformed police officer with a weapon drawn) even after being lawfully ordered to stay at an appropriate distance, the officer could have perceived that his intentions were to engage Clark in a fight. Indeed, Garcia displayed many pre-assaultive behaviors while outside the vehicle. If the officer believed that Garcia was reaching for a weapon, it would be appropriate for him to have his firearm drawn and ready. Most agencies do not train their officers to consider lesser force options in a "duel force" deployment in these situations (i.e., deploying the TASER in the non-weapon hand while still holding the firearm). Single officer "duel force" is a dangerous tactic for all included.

Clark was placed in a situation where it was appropriate to have his pistol deployed and to have to make a critical decision once Garcia was close to contact range through his own actions.

– Ed Flosi

Terry Price, 41, Black Male

Tulsa, OK, February 21

Price, who had been banned from Osage Nation casino property, entered the casino twice. After returning the second time, he was chased by Osage Nation police officers, and fought the officers. Officers used a TASER to subdue Price and handcuff him. Once handcuffed, Price began having difficulty breathing, and officers began CPR. Price was transported to a local hospital where he died.

Toxicology reports reveal that Price had PCP in his system at the time of his death[100].

The cause of death was "sudden cardiac death associated with acute phencyclidine intoxication (PCP) and an enlarged heart[101]."

Analysis

While many civilians don't understand the prevalence of PCP, its usage is still common. Incidents like this happen more often than one would think given media concentration on methamphetamine and heroin use in the United States. This drug-related death is another of a cluster of cases in 2015 in which the decedent's choices and behavior led to his death, and the application of TASER by the officer was intended to be non-deadly, and was both appropriate and necessary.

– Nick Selby

Price was under the influence of PCP. People under its influence often exhibit super-human strength and an extremely high tolerance for pain. A TASER is often the only effective method available to safely subdue suspects who exhibit these behaviors. The officers subdued Price quickly, and then immediately began providing emergency medical care to him when his breathing slowed.

Officers in this position just don't have many options, and are forced to use the tools at their disposal to control the situation. The use of the TASER on Price was completely reasonable. His use of PCP caused his unfortunate death.

– Ben Singleton

As soon as Price began to fight and physically resist (assaultive resistance) the use of the TASER would be an appropriate solution to overcome his resistance and to effect the arrest. It is unknown how many cycles were used, but as long as Price remained a credible threat it could still be reasonable to use multiple cycles. It does not appear that the TASER was used after Price was controlled so that question needs no address.

– Ed Flosi

Calvon Reid, 39, Black Male

Coconut Creek, FL, February 22
Margate Fire Department paramedics responded to a gated community in response to a 911 call. They found Reid in the parking lot and described his demeanor as "agitated, combative, and incoherent." They also reported that Reid had numerous cuts on his hands, arms, and chest, and that his clothing was torn and bloodstained.

The paramedics summoned police. When police arrived, Reid refused to comply with orders and TASER was used multiple times to subdue him[102].

The cause of death was ruled by the Medical Examiner to be "complications of an electro-muscular disruption device."

Cocaine use, alcohol intoxication, and an enlarged heart were noted as other significant conditions contributing to Reid's death[103].

The manner of death was homicide, but there have been no charges brought against the officers involved.

Analysis

This is another in the same cluster of cases in which narcotic and alcohol intoxication lead to behavior making the TASER use appropriate and justified. I cannot argue with a Medical Examiner as to the TASER being the cause of death, but its use was reasonable given the decedent's behavior, and the ME states the TASER's intended non-deadly effect was made deadly by the behavior and choices of the decedent.

– Nick Selby

Although the Medical Examiner in this case cited the use of the TASER as the cause of death, the familiar combination of drugs, alcohol, erratic behavior, and apparent mental instability are present.

We need more research into the excited delirium phenomenon to fully understand what happens to the body when this deadly combination of elements is present. The fact is, however, that officers are faced with few options when confronting a person in this condition. Furthermore, there is no evidence that TASER is more likely to cause the death of a person in this condition than other force techniques available to officers.

TASER remains the safest and most effective method of subduing suspects in this condition, and should continue to be utilized by officers in these situations.

– Ben Singleton

This case has some nuances that may not be apparent to a casual observer. Reid was certainly in the throes of some episode driven by emotional distress, mental illness or drug abuse. Reid was reported to have been cut and bleeding presenting blood borne pathogen exposure possibilities. Reid was described by medics as "agitated, combative, and incoherent." The question that is unanswered is, "What was Reid doing at the moment when the officer used the TASER device?"

If it was a simple refusal to obey commands, but the behavior had changed to that of being passively noncompliant, the use of the TASER device would not be appropriate. The problem is that critical facts are unknown.

If Reid was; (1) presenting a threat to the officers or others, and (2) the TASER was used to effect a lawful arrest, prevent escape or overcome resistance (and hopefully the officers were able to articulate specific facts supporting this) then I would opine that the use of the TASER was appropriate.

– Ed Flosi

Daniel Elrod, 39, White Male

Omaha, NE, February 23
While en route to a reported robbery at a Family Dollar, officers located the suspect, Danny Elrod, in a parking lot nearby. Officers ordered Elrod to show his hands and get on the ground. Elrod refused to comply with those orders[104].

Elrod jumped onto a car and continued to disobey orders. TASER was deployed, but failed to gain Elrod's compliance[105].

A press release states that the shooting officer, Officer Lugod, "perceived Elrod's actions and statements to be a threat toward another officer." Lugod discharged his duty weapon several times, and Elrod was critically injured by the gunfire[106].

There were four officers on scene when the shooting occurred.

Analysis
In this case, while I believe that we do not have enough information to support any specific analysis of the ultimate killing of Elrod, I feel it important to point out that this was one of the few cases in which witnesses dispute the specific police accounting of Elrod's actions immediately prior to the shooting. In most cases within PKIC, non-police witness accounts generally support the police, and in most of the non-police witness accounts that

dispute the officer's account, the witness generally disputes not the actions of the decedent as described by the police, but rather they dispute whether the level of force used by the police was appropriate. This is not the case here. An eyewitness specifically states that Elrod's actions immediately before the shots were fired were that Elrod threw his hands in the air in an act of surrender. The agency's decision to release terse and vague statements has not helped the public understand this incident.

– Nick Selby

This is another case on which we unfortunately have very little information. The department press release states that Elrod's actions and statements were perceived as a threat, but does not elaborate at all on what those actions or statements were. We have got to improve our communication strategies on events like this with our communities. Limited explanations like this warrant a negative response from the community. This shooting is an unjustified shooting, based on the limited information that is available. There were four officers on scene. TASER was attempted once before deadly force was used. The suspect was unarmed.

– Ben Singleton

Here we have another case of limited information to opine on the appropriateness of the officer's use of deadly force. There is no real information to support the appropriateness other than some vague comment that Lugod, "perceived Elrod's actions and statements to be a threat toward another officer." This is similar to the old "for officer safety reasons" or "I was in fear for my life" statements that sound official but which in reality carry no real weight. These overarching statements must be backed up with specific and objective facts and circumstances that would lead a reasonable officer to believe their safety or life was in danger.

Of four officers, Lugod was the only officer who fired. Why didn't the other officers perceive the same threat? This is not to imply that Lugod was wrong; we all understand differences in perceptions, but it is a question that needs exploration.

– Ed Flosi

Alexander Long, 31, White Male

Terre Haute, IN, February 25

Multiple officers and agencies were involved in a short pursuit with Alexander Long, who was wanted for rape. Officers attempted to "box-in" the suspect vehicle with police vehicles. Long began ramming police vehicles with his own. Officers demanded that Long stop and surrender, but Long continued to drive forward and backward ramming police vehicles and refusing orders by police. Officers broke out the side windows of Long's vehicle and fired a TASER at Long, but the TASER was ineffective.

The suspect put his right hand inside his heavy winter coat, and began pulling his hand out as if he was holding something, causing officer to believe that he was pulling out a gun. Officer Brinegar of the Terre Haute Police Department discharged his firearm through the passenger window of Long's vehicle, hitting Long.

Three other officers on scene made statements in which they said they were prepared to shoot Long when he began pulling his hand from his coat, but did not shoot because they did not feel they could have done so without putting other officers at risk[107].

Long was shot in the right torso. He died as a result of the gunshot wounds[108].

No weapons were found in the vehicle, but ammunition was found.

The owner of the vehicle that Long was driving, who was also Long's girlfriend, stated "He ran from you because he wanted you to shoot him because he felt like he had no chance in court. Because it was [her] word against his and he was already a sex offender and he didn't want to sit in jail for the rest of his life and have to see his kids through glass. So, he ran from you and he pulled the 'gun' out because he wanted to die because he wanted you to shoot him because he didn't want to be alone." This statement was made on record for police[109].

Analysis

In hindsight, this was a fairly clear case of suicide by cop. I considered not including it because of the vehicle ramming, but it was clear to me that the vehicle ramming was not the matter that precipitated deadly force use by officers. The reach inside the coat was an overt act that, in my opinion, was designed to provoke officers into shooting. Again, similar incidents have been excluded from other counts as "armed." There is an argument here to exclude this case from PKIC because of the movement that indicated he was armed. I ultimately chose to leave it in because of the reported time to action – in hindsight, I might have removed it earlier and been safer for doing so.

– Nick Selby

It is apparent to me that Long did not intend to surrender. While boxed in, and with no place to go, he continued ramming police vehicles, refusing orders, and ultimately reached inside his coat and began pulling something out. In my opinion, and in the stated opinion of his girlfriend, he intended to give officers the necessary cause to shoot him.

Officer Brinegar had no choice but to shoot Long. He presented an immediate threat to the officers on scene, and it is apparent that he intended to present such a threat so that officers would respond as they did.

– Ben Singleton

Although in hindsight this case appears to have been a "suicide by cop" event, the officer on-scene at the time of the force application had no way to know this, and therefore it cannot be used to evaluate the force response. This case is different than the previous case listed. There are specific objective facts and circumstances listed that would lead a reasonable officer to believe Long was reaching for a gun. Indeed, the other three officers directly support the action in their own statements. The officer used appropriate deadly force based on the totality of the facts and circumstances known at the time. The actions of the officer are consistent with current law enforcement training and standards.

– Ed Flosi

Glenn Lewis, 37, Black Male

Oklahoma City, OK, February 25

Oklahoma Police Officers attempted to pull over Glenn Lewis for a traffic violation when Lewis led officers on a vehicle pursuit. During the pursuit a passenger jumped from the vehicle and was later apprehended. The driver, Glen Lewis, continued to flee in the vehicle, until coming to a dead-end, at which point the officers exited their police vehicles and began issuing orders for Lewis to stop and surrender. Lewis turned his vehicle around, and accelerated toward the officers. Officers Sweeney and Cholity state that they were in the path of the accelerating vehicle, so they opened fire[110].

Lewis had an active warrant for his arrest[111].

Analysis

It's my strong opinion that officers faced a deadly threat and that their reaction with deadly force was entirely appropriate. As this case involved someone using a vehicle as a deadly weapon, there are questions about the appropriateness of it being included in this book.

– Nick Selby

In this case, officers were confronted with a deadly situation. A vehicle was being driven toward them by a noncompliant suspect, who refused to surrender. Lewis, in accelerating toward the officers, posed a significant and imminent threat to the lives of the officers. Their response was a justified use of deadly force, and a direct result of Lewis' decision to put their lives in danger.

– Ben Singleton

There is no doubt that a vehicle driven directly at an officer creates a significant risk of serious bodily injury or death. In a situation where an officer is being targeted by a moving vehicle, that officer may use deadly force to prevent the vehicle from striking the officer. There is also little doubt that Lewis, by his own actions, created the risk. Unfortunately in this situation, that singular answer does not necessarily answer all the questions.

Current law enforcement training and standards in shooting at (the driver of) a moving vehicle have changed. There is case law on-point for these situations that will ask certain questions of the officer's actions. Did the officer have a reasonable opportunity to move out of the vehicle's path? Did the officer intentionally move into the vehicle's path? As a long-time trainer, I have to ask these questions as well. Even if the officer is "right" in making the decision to shoot at (the driver of) a moving vehicle, that vehicle could still easily strike the officer, potentially making him or her "dead right."

– Ed Flosi

Ernesto Javier Canepa Diaz, 27, Hispanic Male

Santa Ana, CA, February 27

Santa Ana Officers were searching for a robbery suspect when they spotted a man matching the description of the robbery suspect sitting inside a car. After making contact with the suspect, he was shot by police, and later died[112].

A BB gun was found in the suspect's vehicle[113].

Analysis

This case is frustrating because the description of the involvement of the BB gun is vague, yet it seems from my reading that Diaz wasn't holding the BB gun at the time officers used deadly force. We don't really have enough facts with which to create an informed analysis here. This would seem to be another example of the kind of incident – as in the Elrod case – in which police administrators have withheld from the press information about the incident in an attempt to control public opinion. The result, as it always is in these kinds of cases, is that the public believes the worst. There are much better ways, in my opinion, that agencies can control the flow of outbound information sufficiently to ensure the integrity of an investigation without leaving the media in a data vacuum.

– Nick Selby

An analysis of this incident is impossible without a detailed description of events. What we know is that Diaz matched the description of a robbery suspect, and that he had a BB gun in his possession. We don't know if Diaz threatened officers with the gun. BB guns are often indistinguishable from, and made to look like, real firearms. They are also frequently used in robberies.

But we don't know what happened during the encounter. Any analysis would be purely speculative.

– Ben Singleton

This is yet another case without enough information to support an opinion. The mere presence of a BB gun would not in itself justify the use of deadly force, no matter how real it looked. Reading from what is known, it could be taken as the officer walked up to the car and shot Diaz while he sat motionless in the car, and, oh by the way, we later found a BB gun in the car.

Vague statements create more damage than good. Some agencies still believe that they have to hide all facts of the incident in order to maintain the integrity of the investigation. While some facts may need to be kept hidden, the basic facts should not be. We, as a profession, must be willing to call situations what they are, based on the facts. If the force response appears to be obviously unjustified, we must be willing to say so, rather than trying to make up excuses or convolute and omit facts to lead others to believe that we support such acts. The public already has a trust issue with law enforcement; if we try to cover for the unjustifiable actions of only a few officers, it damages the trust of even the most stringent law enforcement supporter.

– Ed Flosi

Thomas Allen, 34, Black Male

St Louis, MO, February 28
Thomas Allen was a backseat passenger in a car pulled over by Wellston

police. While the officer was interviewing the driver of the vehicle, outside of the vehicle, Allen climbed into the driver seat, and took off in the vehicle[114].

The officer jumped into the passenger side of the vehicle, where a struggle ensued. The officer unsuccessfully tried to get Allen to stop the vehicle. As Allen accelerated the vehicle, the officer, in fear for his life, fired three shots into Allen[115].

There was a 5-year-old girl in the backseat of the vehicle throughout the incident.

Allen's criminal history includes two counts of statutory rape and child molestation. He is listed as a noncompliant offender in the state's sex offender registry.

Analysis

There are many things we don't know about this incident, such as whether the officer knew Allen's criminal history, or about the presence of the girl in the back. What we know is that Allen's actions were, by any reasonable interpretation, life threatening to the officer, who acted appropriately.

– Nick Selby

This is a dangerous situation for an officer to be in. Allen was in control of the vehicle and, in my view, the officer's life. Fighting a suspect in a moving vehicle, one being controlled by the suspect, is a deadly situation that justifies the use of deadly force.

The involved officer reportedly received treatment for injuries at a local hospital, indicating that he may have been dragged by the vehicle or otherwise injured by the incident, further supporting his use of deadly force.

As to why the officer jumped into the vehicle, sometimes officers know that there is something amiss. This feeling usually starts with conflicting stories from the passengers of a vehicle, improbable explanations for their behavior, or intriguing responses that warrant the officers further attention. The fact that this officer was interviewing the driver outside of the vehicle would indicate that the officer was going a step further than a typical traffic stop. He was trying to figure out what was going on with these two men, and the 5-year-old child. When Allen jumped into the driver seat and started driving off, the officer tried to stop him. We can only speculate about what the officer believed was happening. But it would make sense that the officer believed the 5-year-old may be in danger. Having seen Allen's criminal history, I would say that she was.

— Ben Singleton

I have a different spin on officers jumping into moving (or about to be moving) vehicles. Unless there are extenuating circumstances that creates an exigency for the officer to do this, they should not. Looking at the facts known from the reading, there appears to be no exigent circumstances to jump into the vehicle and create this potentially life threatening situation. Keep in mind, there is no information that the officer knew anything about the criminal history of Allen to be able to state he was a threat to the female child. According to the article, Allen and the vehicle had already been searched and Allen was cleared to go back into the vehicle.

It is also unknown if the officer that jumped into the car was actually able to get into a seated position or if he was hanging from the window. If the officer was in a seated position, I would be interested to know how his life was endangered by the driving of Allen and how shooting Allen would make it less dangerous. If the officer did the "jump through the open window" maneuver I would have to ask, "What exactly did you think would happen and how were you planning to stop the car?"

This incident may very well be deemed lawful, but I believe there are some serious training considerations to be addressed. No good usually comes when an officer reaches deeply into or jumps into a moving vehicle, and this practice should be avoided whenever feasible.

— Ed Flosi

Deven Guilford, 17, White Male

Roxand Township, MI, February 28

Eaton County Sheriff Sgt. Frost stopped a vehicle driven by Guilford for repeatedly flashing his high beams at him. Guilford refused to provide Sgt. Frost with his driver license. Guilford protested the stop and refused an additional six requests by Sgt. Frost to produce his driver's license.

Sgt. Frost requested backup. Guilford then began to make a phone call, at which point Sgt. Frost opened the driver door and began pulling Guilford from the car. The seatbelt interfered, however, and Guilford's resistance further prevented him from doing so. Frost backed off, drew his TASER and ordered Guilford out of the car.

Sgt. Frost ordered Guilford to the ground and attempted to place him in handcuffs. Guilford resisted. Frost made repeated attempts to get Guilford to place his hands behind his back and stop resisting. Sgt. Frost then backed up and fired his TASER, striking Guilford, but achieving no effect. Guilford stood up and attacked Sgt. Frost. During this altercation, Sgt. Frost shot Guilford seven times.

Frost reported that immediately prior to shooting, Guilford knocked him to the ground, sat on his hips, and punched him repeatedly in the face. Frost said his vision was blurred by blood, he tasted blood in his mouth, and felt as though he was going to lose consciousness[116].

Guilford died at the scene.

No charges were filed against Sgt. Frost[117].

Analysis

The stated probable cause for the stop, that Guilford was repeatedly flashing his high beams at Frost's oncoming vehicle, is, to me, extremely questionable. According to media accounts, "several" other drivers had also flashed their lights at Frost that evening, and by media accounts, Frost's vehicle had exceptionally bright low-beam lights. It may well have even been that the low-beams had been misadjusted. Whether that is true, after multiple drivers signaled Frost about his high beams, Frost's use of Guilford flashing high beams at him is technically legal, but in my opinion, pretty damned unreasonable. Obviously this does not mean that Guilford was entitled to attempt to hold court on the side of the road, or to dispute the stop. It does not excuse Guilford from refusing lawful orders from Frost. Frost's account is generally and largely corroborated by the video and audio of the account. While I believe the ultimate use of deadly force was appropriate, I strongly maintain that it would not have been necessary had Frost not been so petty in the first place.

– Nick Selby

This case is illustrative of one of the most justifiable reasons to use deadly force on an unarmed suspect. Sgt. Frost was receiving repeated blows to the head and face, such that blood was running into his eyes and mouth. This is a situation that could easily have cost Sgt. Frost his life.

He said he felt as if he was about to lose consciousness, and feared that Guilford would take his gun and kill him with it. This is a reasonable fear.

Sgt. Frost was wearing a body camera, which captured much of the altercation, but was knocked off of his body during the scuffle. What can be seen and heard on the video corroborates Sgt. Frost's account.

– Ben Singleton

It appears to me that Frost believed he had proper probable cause to effect the stop. A person that is lawfully detained by a police officer does not have the right to interfere or obstruct the officer in the performance of his/her duties. Once Guilford refused to identify himself as required in order for a citation to be issued, Frost had little choice other than to take Guilford into custody. A person being arrested has no right to physically resist the arrest. By Guilford's own actions, a force response was appropriate to effect the arrest and overcome his resistance.

It appears that the TASER use was appropriate at the time but unfortunately failed. Again, it would be interesting to learn why the device failed, but for now it is unnecessary to know to evaluate the event.

Eventually Frost was on the ground and being pummeled by Guilford, who was in a low-top mount position causing Frost to believe he would lose consciousness. Unconsciousness is considered as serious body injury in itself, but an armed police officer who is unconscious creates an entirely new threat level to the officer, other responding officers and the public in general. The use of deadly force in this situation is appropriate and consistent with current law enforcement training and practices.

– Ed Flosi

MARCH

Charly Keunang, 43, Black Male

Los Angeles, CA, March 1

Charly Keunang engaged in a fight with police on the side of the road. He swung at officers, and resisted arrest throughout the encounter. While officers were attempting to subdue, Keunang reportedly reached for an officer's gun. The officers discharged their firearms, killing Keunang[118]. A bystander recorded the incident and publicized it[119]. Kenneth Thompson, a witness to the incident, said that during this fight he saw an officer's weapon hit the ground and heard the officer say, "He has my gun![120]"

Analysis

This was one of the most polarizing incidents in California last year, the first of a small series of incidents involving officers and mentally ill civilians. Ultimately the video shows an incident that is justified. At the same time, Chief Beck was right in responding to community concerns and stepping up training of officers in interaction and de-escalation techniques for incidents involving the mentally ill.

– Nick Selby

A review of the video reveals Keunang assaulting officers, and aggressively resisting arrest. Officers get him to the ground, and struggle to gain control of his arms and legs. It is very difficult to pinpoint precise movements by Keunang or the officers due to the poor quality of the video, but it was a brutal fight taking place on the ground.

I believe the officer's gun was removed from his holster during the scuffle. The officer believed that Keunang had his gun. These officers were dealing with a subject who appeared to be very intoxicated, mentally unstable, and

155

very violent. When a very intoxicated and mentally unstable person actively engaging in a brutal fight with police gains control of a deadly weapon, there are no options left for the police. It was, in my opinion, reasonable for the officers who heard the words, "He has my gun," to react with deadly force.

– Ben Singleton

This is a good example of video helping in some aspects, but only raising questions about others. The video doesn't show the how the encounter started. It only picks up when the subject was already engaged with the officers. Based on the material provided, there is no way to know of the officers did or did not use good communication techniques. I am an advocate of training, but sometimes when agencies jump to training it creates an appearance that the officers were not properly trained or acted improperly, and therefore need training.

There are many potential threats in this area of Los Angeles. Keunang was known to use illicit drugs and was apparently suffering from mental illness. A person in this condition can create a sudden threat if the incident is not quickly controlled, as indicated by the second subject picking up an impact weapon and looking is if he was getting ready to use it on the officers while they were not looking.

This is also a good case to illustrate what perception was at the time of the incident versus what was learned later. The officer believed his weapon has being taken by the subject and according to the witness, it was. The officer had no idea that the weapon had fallen to the ground. He knew he was no longer in possession of it, coming to the reasonable conclusion that the subject had taken it. This made him shout that the subject had his gun.

Once this happened, any officer who heard this would have reason to believe that all the officers were in imminent danger of serious bodily injury or death, based on the totality of the facts and circumstances perceived at that moment. In that event, the use of deadly force would be appropriate and consistent with current law enforcement training and practices.

— Ed Flosi

Darrell Gatewood, 47, Black Male

Oklahoma City, OK, March 1

Police responded to a disturbance call at an apartment complex where a man, Darrell Gatewood, was reportedly "breaking things" and "fighting with the air." When officers arrived, Gatewood assaulted them. Officers used a TASER on Gatewood, but while attempting to take him into custody, he stopped breathing[121].

A media account states that Gatewood was bleeding heavily when police arrived and that prior to using the TASER, officers tried pepper spray on Gatewood, but were unable to gain compliance.

The state medical examiner's report indicates the probable cause of death as "cardiac arrhythmia due to cocaine-related toxicity coupled with police action[122]."

Analysis

Another of the series of incidents in which intoxicated, bleeding and psychotic individuals present officers with limited choices, in which officers' use of non-deadly force became deadly due to the decedent's drug use and health conditions.

– Nick Selby

This is another example of the combined effect that heavy drug use and physical stress have on the human body. Engaging in a fist fight with a bloody, intoxicated, violent, and mentally unstable person can have disastrous consequences for officers. And, there is no evidence to support the claim that Gatewood would have survived, even absent the use of TASER.

These officers used the tools that they had available to subdue Gatewood as safely as possible. His death is unfortunate, but not a result of poor judgment by the police.

– Ben Singleton

Gatewood was a credible physical threat by both his demonstrated behaviors and actions, and the fact that he presented as a possible blood borne pathogen exposure threat. The use of non-deadly force options, such as OC Spray and TASER, in these situations is appropriate and consistent with current law enforcement training and practices.

— Ed Flosi

Derek Cruice, 26, White Male

Deltona, FL, March 4

Volusia County narcotics deputies entered a home to serve a search warrant on Cruice, when he reportedly advanced on a member of the SWAT team, Deputy Todd Raible, in the doorway and was shot in the face[123]. Cruice was taken to a local hospital where he died. There were five other people inside the home when the shooting happened, but none were injured. Two of the witnesses, friends of Cruice, told reporters that Cruice was wearing only basketball shorts, and did not threaten or resist the deputy[124].

Raible's defense attorney said when Raible tried to kick-in the door the first time, it was "rigid, as if someone was leaning against it." He said: "Then the second kick, the door did go swinging open and the first movement was that of a person coming with his hands about chest level, both together, and coming towards the first officer, so it appeared to the first two officers who were making entry that the person had something in his hands and was coming directly towards them with whatever it was[125]." It was also very dark inside the home, according to officers.

Analysis

It does not say in the material we reviewed, but it seems clear that this was a drug search warrant. No-knock raids (officers coordinate a dramatic and rapid entry designed to "shock and awe" sufficiently to secure those within the area quickly enough to stave off any violence) are a perfect example of the barely lesser of two awful choices. There are reasons why these tactics are as they are, and I wish they were not necessary. Arguing this is an endlessly circular process for me: we cannot leave people inside dangerous houses (and the potential inside drug houses for illness, generation of poison gas or explosions is all too high), but at the same time those with dealer-quantity drugs are most likely to possess weapons, behave in a paranoid way and fight back when the cops arrive. Unfortunately the higher likelihood of violence makes officers as well as the targets of these no-knock raids very nervous. I cannot opine further on this particular case.

– Nick Selby

More information is needed to properly evaluate this case. There is an investigation under way which should shed more light on the incident. Narcotics raids are dangerous. Guns almost always accompany large amounts of drugs. No-knock warrants are usually used because evidence in these cases is easily disposable. They allow officers to get in and take control of a scene before any of the occupants have time to dispose of drugs or arm themselves.

During my ten-year career as a police officer, I participated in many no-knock narcotics raids like this one. When everything goes as planned, they are much safer for everyone involved. The team usually enters the home and takes control of all occupants before they realize what has happened. However, things do not always go as planned.

In this case, the first attempt to breach the door was unsuccessful, alerting the occupants to the fact that someone was breaking into the house. This undoubtedly gave deputies a heightened sense of urgency and danger, knowing that they no longer had the element of surprise, and suspecting that people inside might be actively arming themselves.

If Cruice did advance in darkness with his hands in front of his chest as if he was holding a weapon, the deputies may have seen what they perceived to be a genuine threat. Identifying what Cruice had in his hands would have been difficult. In that case, Raible reacted as he was trained to react, and was reasonable in eliminating the threat posed to himself and fellow officers.

– Ben Singleton

It would be difficult to render any reasoned opinion as to the appropriateness of the deadly force application in this case. We don't know what Raible perceived at the moment he pulled the trigger. If Raible perceived that Cruice was presenting a deadly threat at the moment based on the position of his body and a perception that Cruice was armed, then the deadly force would likely be deemed as appropriate.

On the other hand, if Raible only fired due to being startled by the presence of a figure in the doorway it would not be an appropriate response.

— Ed Flosi

Sergio Navas, 35, Hispanic Male

Los Angeles, CA, March 5

Los Angeles Police Officers attempted to stop Navas, who was driving a stolen vehicle, when he fled and led them on a 6-minute pursuit. That pursuit ended on a cul-de-sac where the vehicle driven by Navas collided with a police vehicle[126]. There were two officers in the police vehicle.

The two vehicles were facing the same direction, side by side, after the collision. One officer was trapped in the passenger seat of the police vehicle.

The officer in the passenger seat of the police vehicle fired at Navas as he sat in the driver's seat of the stolen vehicle, hitting him.

Navas evaded on foot for about 200 feet before he collapsed. He was pronounced dead on scene[127].

Analysis

This case, which occurred just days after the Charly Keunang incident, further polarized Angelenos. In my opinion, we don't have enough information about what happened while the two vehicles were stopped and sitting side-by-side. I can understand how the officer might have felt trapped and fearful that Navas, who had just crashed his vehicle into a police car, presented an active threat. I do not know what prompted the ultimate use of deadly force.

— Nick Selby

The shooting officer in this case was pinned in his police vehicle. But without the ability to review his report, it is unclear what the perceived threat was. Was Navas continuing to crush the police vehicle by smashing into it repeatedly, causing the officer to fear for his life? Did Navas reach under the seat of the vehicle leading the officer to believe that he was retrieving a weapon? Without these details, we cannot form an opinion on reasonableness.

If the officer's decision to shoot was based solely on the fact that he was trapped in his patrol car, and the suspect was still attempting to flee, I believe his decision was unreasonable. If there were other perceived threats, such as those previously stated, his decision may have been completely reasonable.

– Ben Singleton

There aren't enough facts known here to form an independent reasoned opinion on the appropriateness of the deadly force option. This is another case that will hinge on whether the facts and circumstances perceived at the time the officer pulled the trigger support his use of deadly force.

— Ed Flosi

Naeschylus Vinzant, 37, Black Male

Aurora, CO, March 6

Vinzant was on parole for a prior assault conviction. He cut off his monitoring bracelet and fled after beating his wife, stealing her wallet and taking their 2-month-old child.

As Vinzant walked down the street, Officer Jerothe and other tactical team members attempted to arrest him. Officer Jerothe and other tactical team members said they believed Vinzant was about to pull a gun and open fire. Officer Jerothe shot Vinzant one time in the chest. It was later discovered that Vinzant was unarmed.[1]

A grand jury, having reviewed the evidence, chose not to indict Officer Jerothe.

Analysis

I wish we had more information on this case. There's not enough here to form an opinion.

– Nick Selby

More details are needed to form an opinion on this case. There are no details available regarding Vinzant's actions during the encounter.

Although media reports made note that "He was black, and Jerothe is white[128]," there is no indication that race had anything to do with the Officer's decision to use deadly force. It is unfortunate that the media, apparently in pursuit of readership and ratings, subliminally indict white officers with charges of racism for no other reason than the decedent was black.

– Ben Singleton

In this case, as with the two previous cases there is not enough specific information to make a reasoned determination on the appropriateness of the deadly force application. There are some hints as to the overarching reason being that the officers felt Vinzant was about to pull a gun. If the officers honestly and reasonably believed Vinzant was reaching for a gun then the deadly force application would most likely be appropriate. It appears that more than one officer had the same perception, so that would strengthen this argument.

As a training matter, it is important to point out again that officers cannot merely rely on nebulous statements such as, "The subject might have had a gun" or "I feared for my safety." These fears must be substantiated with objective facts that would lead another officer to come to the same or similar conclusion.

–– Ed Flosi

Tony Robinson, 19, Black Male

Madison, WI, March 6

Officer Matt Kenny was dispatched to a disturbance at an apartment where Robinson was reportedly "acting insane" and attacking people. Caller said Robinson was punching holes in walls and "going crazy."

After hearing what he believed to be an assault in progress, Officer Kenny entered the apartment. Officer Kenny reported that Robinson hit him with a closed fist when he entered, and knocked him into a wall inside the apartment. Robinson continued swinging at Officer Kenny hitting him multiple times. Fearing further assault, Officer Kenny fired his weapon, hitting Robinson seven times.

Officer Kenny had minor injuries, including a minor concussion[129].

No criminal charges were filed against Officer Kenny.

Analysis

It's so rare that someone on mushrooms becomes this violent, that I wonder if some mental health issues were also playing a role. In any event, the officer's injuries are consistent with his account, and the repeated assault after a surprise attack would certainly seem to rise to the level at which I think a reasonable person would fear for his life.

– Nick Selby

According to witnesses, Robinson was under the influence of psychedelic mushrooms, and other substances. He had been walking down the street and assaulting people at random.

When Officer Kenny entered the apartment, he was hit by Robinson without provocation. Robinson hit Kenny in the head, with a closed fist. A punch like this can cause immediate disorientation. It causes one to become dazed, and greatly diminishes one's ability to fight back. Officer Kenny believed that if he took many more punches of this kind, he would lose consciousness or be otherwise unable to defend himself.

His decision to shoot Robinson was made out of desperation. Officer Kenny was losing the fight, and feared he would be killed if he did not end it. This is a reasonable use of deadly force.

– Ben Singleton

We have to look at what was known to the officer in all force analyses. The officer believed that Robinson; (1) was most likely under the influence of some drug, (2) had been involved in physical acts of violence towards others and (3) was still in the process of harming others inside the apartment. Based on this, the officer decided to make entry and proceed to the second floor, where he was immediately attacked with a fisted strike to the side of his head causing him to fall back into the wall again, striking his head on the wall.

The officer articulated several important details, including that he felt like he was about to lose consciousness. The fight was at the top of a stairway that he could have fallen down or been pushed down if the subject continued his attack. Any of these reasonably foreseeable conclusions would lead an officer to believe they were in imminent danger of serious bodily injury or death. The use of deadly force in this incident appears to have been appropriate and consistent with current law enforcement training and practices.

– Ed Flosi

Michael McKillop, 35, White Male

Claymont, DE, March 8

Delaware State Trooper Cpl. Mauchin responded to a burglar alarm at a Rite Aid. He observed a running vehicle parked behind the store.[1] McKillop emerged from the store, carrying cartons of cigarettes, and went toward the vehicle.

Cpl. Mauchin ordered McKillop to "get down." McKillop refused the order and jumped into the vehicle. Mauchin ran to the vehicle and attempted to get McKillop to come back out. McKillop took off, driving forward and backward, slamming into Mauchin's patrol car multiple times, and dragging Mauchin, who was still attempting to get him to stop the car.

Mauchin fell out of the vehicle and found himself in the direct path of McKillop's only available direction of travel. Mauchin fired on McKillop.

McKillop was transported to the hospital where he died.

During this incident, Mauchin sustained a puncture wound to his left knee (requiring stitches), scrapes, cuts, and contusions to his legs, swelling to his right hand, bruising to his upper right shoulder, and bruising under his right eye. He was also transported to the hospital where he was treated[130].

Analysis

This case was included because Mauchin was out of the police car when it was used as a weapon, and he was attempting to arrest McKillop when McKillop dragged him, while he continued to attempt to stop the vehicle. Given these facts, and that his account is supported by his serious injuries, Cpl. Mauchin was justified in his use of deadly force.

– Nick Selby

During this incident, Mauchin sustained a puncture wound to his left knee (requiring stitches), scrapes, cuts, and contusions to his legs, swelling to his right hand, bruising to his upper right shoulder, and bruising under his right eye.

Cpl. Mauchin received these injuries while being dragged by McKillop, a scenario that authorizes the use of deadly force. McKillop drove back and forth, violently slamming his car into the building and Cpl. Mauchin's police car multiple times, while dragging Cpl. Mauchin. Cpl. Mauchin was punching McKillop throughout, trying to get him to stop. But not until Cpl. Mauchin was injured and believed that McKillop was going to run him over, did he use deadly force. This was completely reasonable.

– Ben Singleton

As noted in a previous case analysis, I have a different spin on officers jumping into moving (or about to be moving) vehicles. Unless there are extenuating circumstances that create an exigency for the officer to do this, they should not do it. While in the long run the officer's use of deadly force may be deemed as appropriate, sometimes we have to sit back and wonder if a tactic creates more problems than it solves. In this case we have a property crime and no articulated threat to anybody. When an officer reaches into the car, it is completely foreseeable that the driver will attempt to drive away. If the officer reaches deeply into the vehicle, it is likely that he/she will be dragged by the vehicle and therefore be forced to use deadly force. I believe it is time for a change in this training paradigm for the safety of all included.

To be clear, I am not blaming the officer for McKillop's actions of trying to drive away. It is clear McKillop was acting on his own volition in a manner that created an imminent threat of serious bodily injury or death to Mauchin, thereby making the deadly force response appropriate.

— Ed Flosi

Anthony Hill, 27, Black Male

DeKalb County, GA, March 9

DeKalb County received 911 calls reporting that a naked man was banging on doors and crawling on the ground. When Officer Robert Olsen arrived on scene, Hill charged him. Officer Olsen ordered Hill to stop, but Hill continued to charge at Officer Olsen. Officer Olsen fired two shots at Hill. Hill died on scene.[131]

Analysis

The specter of a naked, angry man charging at an officer is alarming, but there are some questions I have about why TASER or other non-deadly force was not attempted. There are just not enough facts here for me to base an opinion.

– Nick Selby

We don't know what the officer was thinking during his encounter with Hill. But what I, as an officer, would have been thinking when I arrived on scene to find Hill completely naked and exhibiting signs of mental instability is "PCP."

People who are under the influence of PCP often shed their clothing and walk the streets exhibiting behavior similar to Hill's. They also tend to exhibit super-human strength and extremely high tolerance for pain. This is a bad scenario for police officers.

Police are taught not to engage in one-on-one confrontations with people exhibiting these characteristic signs. Hill should have picked up on the aforementioned clues and had additional officers respond to this call to assist before engaging with Hill. Hill may have done something to elicit Officer Olsen's immediate intervention. We don't know. But this call could have been handled much differently, absent actions by Hill requiring immediate police intervention.

Having put himself in this position, Officer Olsen was faced with a choice to fight the man charging at him, who appeared to be under the influence of PCP, or shoot. Again, Olsen should have waited for additional officers to arrive before engaging, if at all possible.

– Ben Singleton

Conducting a force analysis without the benefit of critical information is dangerous. There is again, like in so many other cases within this study, not enough information to provide a reasoned opinion. This is not surprising though. It points to the lack of information available to the public and those not actually involved in the investigation. There are valid reasons why some information would not be released but without some basic information, the public and others are forced to draw their own conclusions.

The article reveals a few more details, characterizing Hill as aggressive and saying he lunged at the officer. While this implies that Hill was a threat to some level, this in itself would not necessarily justify the use of deadly force.

While Olsen perceived Hill as a threat, it is interesting to note that some witnesses claimed Hill was no threat as he ran to the police with his hands up. This demonstrates how the same action can be perceived by two people in different ways.

— Ed Flosi

Terrance Moxley, 29, Black Male

Mansfield, OH, March 10

Officers were called to a halfway house in response to a 911 call made by staff members. The staff requested police because Terrance Moxley, a resident of the halfway house, was repeatedly slamming doors, punching walls and attacking staff members. They said: "We need someone as soon as you can get them."[132]

When police and medical personnel arrived, they found Moxley speaking incoherently and saw he had caused damage to the building. Moxley was handcuffed. Firefighters attempted to assess his condition. Moxley attempted to bite firefighters as they performed their assessment.

As officers carried Moxley to the patrol car, Moxley broke out of his handcuffs, and began resisting. Officers deployed the TASER two times, but it had no effect. An officer also received a shock from the TASER during the scuffle.[133]

Toxicology reports indicated the presence of AB-CHMINACA, a synthetic cannabinoid, in Moxley's system. The medical examiner report states that the presence of this substance, "presents a likely explanation for the agitated behaviors observed before and during his interaction with law enforcement" and "also provides a plausible explanation for his sudden cardiac arrest while in the custody of law enforcement."[134]

Analysis

Another case in which the decedent's use of synthetic narcotics caused aggressive behavior and acute intoxication. Breaking out of handcuffs is a very serious level of threat. Officers applied what was intended to be non-deadly force, and Moxley died as a result of cardiac arrest.

– Nick Selby

I think it is important to clarify that when police are called to deal with a man who is actively breaking things and assaulting people, they are expected to remove him. They can't allow him to continue assaulting others and damaging property. The man has to be subdued, handcuffed, placed in a vehicle, and safely transported to the jail or a hospital. In this case, Moxley was obviously intoxicated. He was speaking incoherently, slamming the same door more than 200 times, punching walls, and destroying property.

Moxley broke out of his handcuffs and fought the officers trying to get him to the hospital. TASER, batons, OC spray, and other non-lethal weapons exist to help officers subdue people who cannot be dealt with in other ways. Unfortunately the drugs in Moxley's system, combined with the physical stress resulting from his struggle with the police, killed him.

– Ben Singleton

Halfway house disturbances can create serious threat issues for responding officers. Many halfway houses have trained staff to deal with minor outbursts, but when the problem becomes so severe that these trained professionals cannot handle the patient, the situation is known to be a dangerous one.

It appears that Moxley was initially taken into custody without any significant force. He began to fight the officers and bite at them only after he was handcuffed and was able to break out of them (it would be interesting to know what is meant by he "broke out" of the handcuffs; was there still one cuff attached or did they both come off, or did the chain break). In this, Moxley demonstrated a clear and credible physical threat to the officers. The use of non-deadly force options to take Moxley back into custody would be appropriate and consistent with current law enforcement training and standards.

— Ed Flosi

Antonio Perez, 32, Hispanic Male

Walnut Park, CA, March 12

Perez and a Hispanic female were driving a stolen vehicle when they led police on a car chase. Perez wrecked the stolen vehicle in an alleyway and he and the woman ran from the scene. A police helicopter located the two running through yards in the area. According to a statement released by the department, "When deputies tried to make contact with Perez, he turned on the deputies with his hands in his waistband." Perez was shot by one deputy. He died at the scene[135].

Witnesses to the crash reportedly told deputies that the suspect was armed, but no weapon was found. It was later learned that the suspects broke into two residences and stole property while the police searched for them[136].

Analysis

The facts in this case, the information the police had from witnesses, and the behavior of Perez at the moment of the confrontation with officers lead me to believe that this was a justified use of deadly force.

– Nick Selby

I think it is reasonable to assume that when a person, reportedly armed, who was driving a stolen vehicle and evading police, reaches into his waistband, he intends to remove a weapon and use it against officers.

The deputies were giving orders to Perez: "Stop," "Get on the ground," and "Show your hands." When confronted by the police after such an exhibition of criminal behavior, one must comply with these orders and surrender. Perez did the opposite. He gave the police the universally recognized sign of someone who is "going for a gun" by reaching into his waistband. Anyone who does this, after having engaged in this level of criminal behavior, can't expect the police to give him the benefit of the doubt.

– Ben Singleton

This case illustrates the consideration of the "totality of facts and circumstances" in a very clear sense. The deputies were told by witnesses that Perez was armed. When cornered and given lawful orders to stop and to show his hands, Perez did not comply. One source states that instead, Perez made an overt movement that could lead an officer to believe that he was reaching for a gun. Another source states that the subject turned towards the deputies with his hands still in his waistband. In either case, this action could lead an officer to believe the subject was reaching for a gun, especially considering the fact they had already been advised the subject was armed.

It is important to note that officers need not actually see a gun or have a gun pointed at them in order to reasonably believe the person is armed and presents an imminent deadly threat.

—— Ed Flosi

David Werblow, 41, White Male

Branford, NH, March 15
David Werblow, who had been diagnosed with schizophrenia and had a history of non-compliance with taking his medication, called 911 asking for transport to a hospital by ambulance. He was a resident of a group home for adults with mental health issues.

Werblow, 6'2" and 278 pounds, was delusional when Officer Abley arrived. Officer Abley met with the staff to learn about Werblow and his condition prior to making contact with Werblow. When he did, Werblow walked away from him and toward Abley's police vehicle in the middle of the street. He tried to enter it, but it was locked. Abley called for backup. Werblow walked rapidly down the street, while Abley and a staff member of the facility ordered him to "stop" and "come back."

Werblow continued down the street, attempting to enter numerous other cars along the street. He eventually gained access to a vehicle in a driveway. Despite about 40 requests by Officer Abley to "stop," Werblow entered the vehicle.

Officer Abley deployed his TASER, but it didn't have much of an effect on Werblow. Officer Abley delivered TASER exposures several times while trying to get Werblow out of the vehicle. After several exposures, Werblow began throwing things out of the car at the officers. Abley delivered one more TASER exposure, and with the assistance of another officer, took Werblow into custody.

An ambulance was called to scene per department protocol. Werblow was found to have no pulse. He was transported to the hospital, where he died. Officer Abley was wearing a body camera, which was activated and recording throughout this incident. He was cleared of wrongdoing[137].

Analysis

We mentioned in the introductory chapters the issues that have been raised through a national abdication of responsibility in the treatment of the mentally ill and the huge impact there is when law enforcement officers are called upon to be mental health professionals. While some officers have had the appropriate training, most have not. Whether this is a shortfall in police training is a debate for another forum. In this case, the actions of the decedent posed many challenges to the officer. It's unclear to me why the officer did not have backup, or why he could not have awaited backup. It would seem that if the TASER was not working, repeating what was not working may not have been the best course of action, but I don't think I have enough information to make an informed judgment.

– Nick Selby

Officer Abley was called to a group home that specializes in providing care for people with psychiatric problems, to deal with someone who was having psychiatric problems. Officer Abley is not a doctor.

Werblow was 6'2" and 278 pounds according to a report by the New Haven register. While I don't have any information about Officer Abley's build, Werblow is definitely above average in size, and probably much bigger than Officer Abley. Subduing Werblow by physical force was probably not an option for this officer. At 5'8" 170, I can relate. So, he was forced to use his TASER.

We have learned that the combination of psychosis, often drug-induced, and physical conflict with police can result in death. I believe Werblow's death can be attributed to this phenomenon as well. But I don't believe that Officer Abley used excessive force, or in any way intended to cause Werblow's death.

Based on the information we have, I believe Werblow should have been confined in a secure psychiatric facility where he could have been better cared for and more closely monitored. He needed better treatment.

– Ben Singleton

This case demonstrates the serious mental health problems people have that law enforcement have to deal with on a daily basis. Werblow was a large man who had been acting out. He called 911 to request a transport to the hospital. The officer was dispatched to the location. Werblow did not seem to act violently, nor did he attempt to attack the officer. It appears that Werblow was intent on leaving the location and getting into a car.

It would be important for the officer not to allow Werblow to gain control of a vehicle in his condition, for the danger it created to all those in the area. It is unclear though, what the officer believed Werblow was going to do once in the car and whether the officer believed that Werblow had the ability to start the car, thereby endangering others. Another concern may have been that if Werblow was successful in getting into the car, the struggle it would take to extract such a large man from inside the car would create a greater risk of injury to Werblow and the officers. But once inside the car, this concern is no longer valid.

Due to the known mental illness factor in this case, one must wonder about the exigency to use the TASER "several times" while Werblow was inside the car if there was no indication that Werblow was going to start it. Absent any articulated, credible threat issues, I would have to render the opinion that the use of the TASER device as described would not be appropriate. This is not intended to conclude that the TASER device use had anything to do with Werblow's death. Considering his other medical conditions, it may not be the principal cause.

-– Ed Flosi

173

Sheldon Haleck, 38, Asian/Pacific Islander Male

Honolulu, HI, March 16

Honolulu Police responded to 911 calls about a man running in the middle of the road and acting erratically[138]. Officers arrived and found Haleck, who had a history of mental illness, including anxiety, depression and post-traumatic stress disorder. Haleck was high on methamphetamine at the time officers arrived and was displaying signs of drug-induced delirium. He didn't understand where he was.

Haleck refused orders given by officers. TASER and pepper spray were used, but had no effect on him. Ultimately he tripped and fell, providing officers with the opportunity to subdue him. After being handcuffed Haleck became unresponsive. EMS personnel were called to the scene and he was resuscitated. But he never regained consciousness and was pronounced dead at the hospital. The death was attributed to "multiple metabolic and cardiac complications" stemming from what Honolulu Medical Examiner Christopher Happy described as a "violent physical struggle" with Honolulu police. While the manner of death was listed as "homicide," the autopsy refers to a combination of factors stemming from his altercation with police and his "heightened state of physiological and mental agitation from methamphetamine." The autopsy/toxicology report found methamphetamine in Haleck's system[139].

Analysis

Officers facing a man who is possibly mentally ill or under acute narcotic intoxication or both are faced with a limited range of choices; the TASER application was reasonable, and the officers were not responsible for Haleck's death.

– Nick Selby

This is another death that can be attributed to the combination of methamphetamine intoxication and the physical stress of a fight with the police.

– Ben Singleton

The officer appeared to have a legitimate reason for the contact with Haleck, who was standing dangerously in an active roadway presenting a danger to himself and others. When verbal persuasion failed to get Haleck out of the roadway, the officers used non-deadly force options to try to do it and take him into custody, but they also had no effect. After Haleck fell and was secured, he became unresponsive. The use of the non-deadly force options in this case appears to be appropriate and consistent with current law enforcement training and practices.

– Ed Flosi

Askari Roberts, 38, Black Male

Rome, GA, March 17

Askari Roberts' mother called 911 to report that Askari was being held down by his 64-year-old father, Jackie Roberts, in order to keep him from hurting them. Floyd County officers arrived, and assisted by Jackie, attempted to handcuff Askari. Officers attempted to use a TASER, but Askari grabbed it[140]. Officers were able to deliver several drive-stuns with the TASER, allowing them to handcuff Askari, but he continued to struggle[141].

Shortly after Askari was handcuffed, he became unresponsive. Officers began providing medical care, but Askari died after being transported to a local hospital.

Analysis

We don't have toxicology reports back, but Askari's behavior is consistent with acute narcotic intoxication. I am against drive-stuns in many cases, because it is essentially pain-compliance, which would possibly be accomplished better by going hands-on. I don't have enough to give an opinion.

– Nick Selby

Autopsy and toxicology reports have not yet been released, but there is little doubt in my mind that toxic levels of methamphetamine, PCP, cocaine, or another synthetic drug will be found in Roberts' system. Askari was reportedly claiming that people from Rome were "putting a hit out on him" immediately before this incident took place. This is an example of the kind of paranoia exhibited by people under the influence of mind-altering drugs.

Also, Askari's struggle began before police arrival. We don't know how long Jackie was "holding down" or struggling with Askari before police arrived. I believe this to be another case in which the combination of drugs and physical stress are responsible for the decedent's death.

– Ben Singleton

Roberts was obviously in the throes of a psychotic episode, although it is unknown as to what drove him to this point. There are some missing or vague elements here. The details state the TASER was used "several times" in drive-stun mode. I am unsure what "several times" means, but if Roberts was still actively resisting during the "several times," it could be determined that the use of the TASER was appropriate to use on an "actively resisting" subject.

The TASER in drive-stun mode creates localized pain, only without the benefit of neuro-muscular incapacitation. With that said, there are still some considerations to be made prior to using the TASER in drive-stun mode. If a subject is capable of understanding and complying, a warning should be considered. If feasible, the officer should reassess the need for further cycles after each application.

— Ed Flosi

Brandon Jones, 18, Black Male

Cleveland, OH, March 19

Cleveland Police were called to a convenience store for reports of a break-in. They discovered Brandon Jones walking out of the store carrying a bag of stolen goods[142]. A struggle ensued as officers tried to arrest Jones, and an officer fired his gun once, hitting Jones. He was rushed to the hospital and died the following morning.

One account states that Jones reached for an officer's gun[143]. However, the witness who called 911 stated "The only scuffle is when he first came out the door. They charged him. They got him. They were standing there talking." She said officers were standing with and talking with Jones for four to five minutes before shots were fired[144].

Analysis

This case requires investigation and follow-through by the media and the agency. That this happened more than a year ago and we still have this level of sketchy detail is outrageous.

– Nick Selby

Again, we have too little information. But this is a case that definitely warrants investigation. If Jones merely "reached" for the officer's gun, the use of deadly force would be hard to justify. We just don't have the details necessary to analyze this one.

– Ben Singleton

Given the stark contrast of statements and the lack of details here, it's not possible to render a reasoned opinion on the appropriateness of the deadly force used.

–– Ed Flosi

Jeffrey Jackson, 47, White Male

Williamsburg, KY, March 22

Shortly after arriving at his sister's Kentucky home, Jeffrey Jackson darted out of her house. He stopped a vehicle on a state road and convinced that driver to let him in her car. As they were traveling west, he jumped out of her car, causing road rash injuries to his head and hands. Several more complaints were called in, and troopers were finally able to locate Jackson. Once located, troopers subdued him and handcuffed him, at which time he stopped breathing. He received medical care, but was pronounced dead on scene.

Preliminary autopsy reports showed no signs of trauma[145].

Analysis

This is another case included because officers were attending Jackson and he was technically in their custody at the time of his death. There is no doubt in my mind that his death was caused entirely by his actions prior to officers arriving on scene.

— Nick Selby

Jackson was clearly in an altered mental state, whether drug-induced or otherwise. The physical stress caused by running, jumping out of a fast moving vehicle, and a brief struggle with police, combined with the source of his psychosis (probably drugs) caused his death.

— Ben Singleton

This is another case of a person acting in a bizarre manner for unknown reasons. There are some indications the officers used force to "subdue" Jackson, but it is unknown what type and amount of force was used. We also know that the autopsy revealed no signs of trauma, but this is actually odd since Jackson did jump from a moving vehicle.

While it would certainly be appropriate for officers to use some level of force if Jackson was resistant or assaultive, not knowing what the force response was makes a determination of its appropriateness impossible.

— Ed Flosi

Denzel Brown, 21, Black Male

Bay Shore, NY, March 22

A Suffolk County officer responded to a 911 call about a reported larceny at a Best Buy in Long Island. When the officer arrived, she located Brown hiding outside the store. As the officer approached, Brown took off on foot and began attempting to enter moving and parked vehicles. The officer deployed a TASER, which was ineffective[146].

Brown then attempted to carjack a running car from a couple whose two children, aged four and six, were in the back seat. The officer caught up with Brown as the couple was screaming at him to stop. The officer ordered Brown out of the vehicle, still occupied by two children. Brown began to drive away. The officer fired a shot at Brown, then opened the car door and tried to remove him. The officer unsuccessfully tried her TASER again. The officer fired another round at Brown. Backup officers arrived, and took Brown into custody.

Brown died during surgery at a local hospital[147].

Analysis

Thank God this officer arrived in time to stop this kidnapping. New York law clearly states that it is legal to use deadly force to stop a kidnapping from occurring.

– Nick Selby

In most states, deadly force is authorized to stop a kidnapping in progress, which is what this was. When Brown entered the vehicle with the couple's two children in the back seat and started driving off, the officer heroically shot Brown and rescued the children. This shooting was clearly justified. This officer deserves a medal.

– Ben Singleton

Brown's attempt to escape became an imminent danger when he decided to carjack a vehicle with small children inside. Once the children were outside of the officers' control, the police would no longer have been able to protect them. They were potential hostages, or at the very least now inconvenient witnesses, if Brown was able to escape.

The officer tried to use non-deadly force options, but they proved ineffective. The officers in this case had reason to believe that Brown was an imminent threat of serious bodily injury or death. Based on his actions and behaviors, which demonstrated a complete lack of respect for life, the use of deadly force in this case was appropriate and consistent with current law enforcement training and practices.

–– Ed Flosi

Dominic Wise, 30, Black Male

Fredericksburg, VA, March 30

Wise, believed to be intoxicated, was seen by an officer "walking in circles" in the middle of the street. The officer attempted to get Wise to move out of the street, but Wise took off on foot. Additional officers were called, and Wise was confronted at an apartment complex where officers tried to take him into custody. Wise swung and kicked at officers. A TASER was used with "limited effect." Wise was subsequently subdued with the help of even more officers.

Paramedics were called, and Wise became unresponsive while in their care. One of the officers involved was treated for a broken nose, and bruises[148].

Analysis

One of the things that surprised all of us was the sheer number of these kinds of events, over and over again, throughout the country. Intoxication and possible mental illness, followed by attacks on officers, followed by non-deadly force, followed by some kind of health crisis that ends in death. There is no doubt the officers acted appropriately with non-deadly force given the injuries to one of the officers.

– Nick Selby

A likely intoxicated subject, behaving erratically, fought with the police, and died after a struggle. Again we find the combination of psychotic behavior, likely drug-induced, and the physical stress of fighting with the police immediately before a death. No toxicology report is available at this time. As to the reasonableness of the officers' actions; they were completely reasonable and justified.

– Ben Singleton

Here is another case of a person acting out in a bizarre manner without officers knowing why they do. It is important to note that many of these people are actually in some sort of medical crisis and it would be important to get them medical intervention at the earliest feasible moment.

After the initial contact, Wise ran off. The officers kept a visual surveillance on him as he ran away, eventually catching up him. When Wise fought back, and attempted to strike and kick the officers trying to take him into custody, he became a credible physical threat. The officers used a TASER but it had a "limited effect." Here again it would be interesting to understand why the TASER device had limited effect but it's not necessary to determine the appropriateness of the use. It appears that the use of the TASER in this incident would be appropriate and consistent with current law enforcement standards and training.

— Ed Flosi

Phillip White, 32, Black Male

Vineland, NJ, March 31
Vineland Police responded to a disorderly person call. A violent struggle ensued in the street in which a police K9 was used. White had been taken into custody when he stopped breathing. An ambulance transported him to a hospital where he died[149].

Witness accounts and police reports provide conflicting information. Witnesses claim White was handcuffed, and possibly unconscious, when police struck him and ordered the dog to bite[150]. Autopsy and Toxicology reports have not been released.

Analysis
Once again we see a situation in which the police and the medical examiner's office have failed, after more than a year, to release basic documents and supporting evidence about an officer-involved death. These failures add up, and it is highly frustrating (not to mention almost certainly illegal) for agencies to continue these practices.

— Nick Selby

Few details about this incident have been released. But a thorough investigation is warranted given the witness statements regarding White's condition at the time of the struggle.

– Ben Singleton

Here is another case where limited information and starkly different accounts make it difficult to determine the appropriateness of the use of a Police Service Dog (PSD). Depending on the facts and circumstances revealed by any subsequent investigation, this case could go in any direction.

–– Ed Flosi

APRIL

Donald "Dontay" Ivy, 39, Black Male

Albany, NY, April 2

Donald "Dontay" Ivy was walking home from a convenience store late at night when two Albany police officers made contact with him, citing his unusual gait and that his hands were hidden. Ivy had been diagnosed with schizophrenia as a teenager, and he continued to struggle with the disease. A third officer joined as the officers questioned Ivy. As they patted him down, Ivy became agitated. Officers stated that Ivy, who weighed 274 pounds, "lunged" at them.

Officer Sears fired his Taser at Ivy, but one dart missed and the TASER had no effect. Ivy fled. The officers chased him as he ran toward his residence less than two blocks away. Officers caught up to Ivy, tackled him, and used the TASER to subdue him. The TASER was activated a total of seven times, and may have connected with its target in five of those instances[151].

Ivy was handcuffed. Officers report that Ivy continued to fight and suffered a fatal heart attack while lying on the ground. The autopsy showed Mr. Ivy died of "Cardiac arrhythmia with cardiorespiratory arrest occurring during struggle and altercation," "Significant underlying cardiomegaly [enlarged heart]," and "Atherosclerotic cardiovascular disease." In the words of P. David Soares, the Albany County District Attorney, "Mr. Ivy suffered from an underlying condition that made him particularly susceptible to a heart attack brought on by the stress of the incident with the police." Soares continued that, "in [Forensic Pathologist Doctor Michael] Sikirica's opinion, the TASING of Mr. Ivy by Officer Sears was not the cause of his death, although it was one contributing factor to the overall stress of the event[152]."

In late 2015, the Grand Jury decided to no-bill the officers, and the department cleared all officers involved.

Analysis

In my opinion, officers used the most barely justifiable reasonable suspicion for this stop. Having said that, the neighborhood in which Ivy was stopped is rough, and drugs and criminality are endemic. With 20-20 hindsight, the stop itself probably wasn't justified, but I can see how officers in that agency would believe that Ivy's appearance and demeanor and gait were suspicious, or at least consistent with criminal behavior. I don't like it, and a "suspicious gait" is really thin, but I suppose it is, ultimately, articulable suspicion, at least according to the DA. In my mind it stinks.

After the stop was made, I think the historically strained relationship between Albany Police Department and parts of the community it polices aggravated the reaction of both sides, and both sides read the signals given by the other side through an atmosphere of distrust. Ivy's mental health condition was clearly responsible for his reaction to the officers and their requests (or, rather, their demands). Putting myself in the shoes of these officers, Ivy's reaction to them looked highly suspicious and very much as if Ivy was resisting. This lamentable case must fall under the category of those in which better outreach and training of officers in the fundamentals of neighborhood policing, and especially of more proactive mental health training, might very well save lives.

– Nick Selby

The most troubling part of this case for me is that there is no apparent offense. In order to detain Ivy, the officers involved would have to reasonably suspect that an offense has been, was about to be, or was being committed at the time of the stop. Often, contact is made with subjects in a voluntary context, meaning that the subject of the stop is free to go at any time, but may choose to stay and visit with the officers.

This stop was not voluntary. Ivy was not free to leave. So the question remains: what was the legal justification for detaining Ivy? It may exist. I don't know. But it's the first question that must be addressed.

I am not suggesting that Ivy was selected by these officers for any reason other than their belief that something criminal was occurring. But as police officers who are given incredible power and authority over others, we must make sure that we operate within the confines of what is constitutionally acceptable.

There were three officers present. Why were there seven TASER exposures?

Again, all of this may be articulated in a police report that I haven't seen. But this case is a troubling one for me, based on the available information.

– Ben Singleton

Besides the obvious inquiry into the reason for the stop and whether the officers developed reasonable suspicion to detain Ivy, there are still other questions. If this was a "welfare check," the reason for the stop would have ended as soon as the officers were able to determine that Ivy was okay. It is important to remember that only being mentally ill does not necessarily give an officer a lawful reason to continue a detention. If the detention was to be determined inappropriate at the moment Ivy ran, then that was his choice to leave.

The second question is the legality of the frisk. Absent consent, officers need to articulate a reasonable suspicion that the person may be armed and dangerous with specific and articulable facts, not just a statement like, "For officer safety reasons." Too often I have heard officers state that they will frisk the subject on every stop, regardless if the subject consents or not. They will use the reasoning that by not consenting the subject must be hiding something, and therefore reasonable suspicion exists. This is entirely incorrect. The assertion of one's rights to not be unlawfully searched cannot be used against them.

This also becomes a training issue, as the officer is now searching out of routine, rather than evaluating the subject and then doing a proper search based on real facts and circumstances.

There is not enough information in the material to render a reasoned opinion on the appropriateness of the TASER applications, other than to comment that seven TASER cycles would need to be supported by significant factors.

– Ed Flosi

Eric Harris, 44, Black Male

Tulsa, OK, April 2

During a gun-sales sting, 73-year-old volunteer officer Robert Bates fatally shot Eric Harris, who was running from Tulsa Sheriff's Office deputies. Deputies caught up to Harris and brought him to the ground. Bates shot Harris while he was on the ground and immediately said, "Oh, I shot him! I'm sorry[153]."

Bates said he thought he was grabbing for his TASER when he shot Harris[154]. A controversy regarding Bates' training records raised questions about Bates' status as a volunteer officer[155]. Bates was indicted in the shooting, and charged with second degree manslaughter[156]. Tulsa County Sheriff Stanley Glanz was indicted as well[157], on misdemeanor charges, including one related to falsification of training records of Bates. On April 27, 2016, a Tulsa jury found Bates guilty of second-degree manslaughter. The jury deliberated less than three hours and recommended Bates serve four years in prison, the maximum possible sentence.

Analysis

Bates' accidental shooting of Harris was just that – a tragic accident. That Bates was a reserve officer is a significant issue. There have been many questions about Bates' training and position, which amount to accusations that the sheriff allowed Bates to serve in roles inappropriate for Bates' training and experience. Bates' actions (I have watched the video of the event) and comments he has made since then have convinced me that Bates had absolutely no business on this assignment. He was poorly prepared, not fully trained, and unfamiliar enough with his equipment to the extent that he could confuse a TASER and a pistol – and then defend that action as if it could happen to anyone. The only case I know of that was similar resulted in a conviction of the officer. A retired LAPD captain named Greg Meyer compiled a list of nine similar instances since 2001[158], but Bates was the only officer since 2012 to have made this mistake. To be clear, this is also an agency training issue, but for Bates to imply that this was something that "could happen to anyone" is plain dumb, unsupportable and wrong.

I believe that Bates was appropriately charged with negligent manslaughter, and that the jury was correct in convicting him. Further, having served as a reserve officer alongside officers on a similar task force, it is now my opinion that reserve officers should never be placed in this position.

– Nick Selby

Bates unintentionally shot and killed Eric Harris. He intended to shoot him with a non-deadly TASER, and instead shot him with his revolver. This one is pretty straightforward. The officer screwed up and killed someone. As in any profession, one is expected to be proficient with one's tools. It is clear that Bates was not qualified or prepared for the use of his TASER or firearm.

The questions about Bates' qualifications have to be answered by the head of the department, and the liability for any deficiencies in Bates' qualifications should land on the department head as well.

– Ben Singleton

This is another event where an unarmed man was killed by an officer's unintentional actions. At least one other officer has been convicted in similar cases of involuntary manslaughter, and I was not surprised that the jury convicted in this case.

There have been many documented cases of "TASER confusion" ever since the model M26 was revealed. This is not to imply that the shape of the device is the culprit of the confusion as that is not my belief. Most of the cases I have been made aware of were due to inadequate training or poor deployment policies and strategies by the agency. It is important to note that many officers used to carry their TASER on the same side as their firearm. More progressive agencies have developed training and policies that prohibit this practice, and some have begun to train their officers to use the non-firearm hand to draw to fire the TASER.

– Ed Flosi

David Lynch, 33, White Male

Warner, OK, April 3

A Warner police officer responded to a report of a traffic accident on Highway 64 in Muskogee County, Oklahoma to assist until Oklahoma Highway Patrol officers could get there.

When the Warner officer arrived, Lynch attacked him. He fought the officer, gaining the upper hand and fracturing the officer's eye socket, before the officer used his TASER to regain control of the situation. He handcuffed Lynch, but soon after, he noticed Lynch wasn't breathing and performed CPR[159].

The autopsy revealed toxic levels of methamphetamine in Lynch's system[160].

Analysis

This is yet another methamphetamine-induced psychosis incident in which an officer tried heroically to save someone from himself, only to have the person die because of his drug overdose and exertion.

– Nick Selby

This officer showed a lot of restraint in using non-deadly force after taking on serious facial trauma, and receiving an injury as serious as a fractured eye socket. He likely would have been justified in using deadly force to end this assault, and he chose not to.

It is unfortunate that Lynch died, but in my opinion, his death was a result of the all too familiar combination of methamphetamine use and the physical stress associated with fighting the police.

– Ben Singleton

The officer showed tremendous restraint in his force option choice. It is unlikely that the officer actually understood the nature of his injury, but a fractured eye socket is certainly serious bodily injury and would have justified the use of deadly force if the officer understood the nature of the injury to be that serious. In this case, he used the TASER device and was able to subdue Lynch. The use of the TASER device would be considered appropriate on a person that is an assaultive threat to the officer.

– Ed Flosi

William Dick, 28, Native American Male

Tonasket, WA, April 4

US Forest Service agents responded to a reported robbery of a hitchhiker. Two male subjects and a female reportedly picked up and robbed the hitchhiker at gunpoint before letting him go. The hitchhiker stated that the two males were doing drugs in the van prior to robbing him.

US Forest Service agents located the 3 subjects leaving a campground. A vehicle pursuit, followed by a foot pursuit, led to the confrontation between officers and William Dick[161].

Dick refused orders by officers. A TASER was used to apprehend him. He was placed in handcuffs, and then stopped breathing. Officers administered CPR but were unable to revive Dick[162].

Heroin was found in the vehicle.

Analysis

I believe the use of the TASER was acceptable in this case, given the fact that Dick was the suspect of an armed robbery and was refusing to comply. This is another incident in which the combination of drugs and physical stress caused death.

– Ben Singleton

At face value, the officer's use of the TASER would seem appropriate because, due to the seriousness of the subject's previous violent actions, it could be articulated that Dick was a credible threat. It is not completely clear what Dick was doing at the time of the TASER use. It would be important to know what threat factors were articulated by the officer leading up to and at the moment of the TASER use.

While it is unknown what exactly or how well the officers articulated the threat factors in this case, this serves as yet another good time to remind officers of the importance of good documentation.

– Ed Flosi

Walter Scott, 50, Black Male

North Charleston, SC, April 4

Walter Scott was stopped by Officer Slager of the Charleston police department for a traffic violation. While Officer Slager was running checks of Scott's information, Scott bailed out of his car, and ran off. Officer Slager gave chase, caught up to Scott, and deployed his TASER.

Police alleged that the two men reportedly struggled over the TASER. Scott gained control of the TASER and attempted to use it against the officer. Officer Slager then drew his service weapon and shot Scott.

Scott was pronounced dead on scene. The investigation found that Scott was shot multiple times in the back.

A bystander video was later released in which Officer Slager is seen shooting Scott in the back multiple times as Scott was running away from Slager. Slager can also be seen walking back to pick up what appears to be his TASER, and then dropping it next to Scott's body after the shooting[163].

Dashcam video from Slager's patrol car provides details as to the first half of the encounter. The bystander video starts with Slager drawing and pointing his pistol at Scott who is running away from Slager. Slager fires about eight rounds at Scott, before Scott falls to the ground.

Slager walks over to Scott and puts handcuffs on him. Then he walks back to the position he shot from and picks up an object that is similar in size to a TASER. He walks back over to Scott's body and drops the object next to Scott[164].

The eyewitness who recorded the video said Scott never had the officer's TASER.

A $6.5 million settlement was paid to the family of Scott. Officer Slager was arrested and charged with murder[165].

Analysis

This incident haunts me. Thank God the witness was there to video-record this incident. I know that I have said the media and the public should not jump to conclusions before all the facts are out. I'm about to break my own rule: in my opinion, having watched the video of this incident again and again, I cannot help but reach the conclusion that this officer acted criminally. In this case, my training and experience lead me to seriously doubt that any mitigating circumstances could arise that would possibly justify Officer Slager's actions – especially his cowardly attempt to place his own TASER next to Scott's body. Obviously I will watch the case closely, and if such evidence comes to light, I will seriously consider it.

– Nick Selby

Officer Slager will be tried, and more details will come out. But it appears that Officer Slager unjustifiably shot and killed Walter Scott. A struggle over the TASER may have taken place prior to the shooting. But it doesn't appear that Scott was a threat at the time of the shooting as he was running away empty handed.

The placement of the object, which I believe to be Slager's TASER, is also troubling. I can think of no reason why Slager would move the TASER, or any other object. Officers know that crime scenes are to remain unmolested. Crime scene preservation is common practice. His manipulation of this crime scene appeared to be intentional.

Based on these observations, I believe this shooting was unreasonable and one of the most disturbing acts of a police officer I have ever seen.

– Ben Singleton

This case was very troublesome and appears to be an inappropriate use of deadly force. Certain things are known. The officer chased Scott and eventually caught up to him. There was a TASER probe deployment as one can see the TASER wires clearly in the video. Scott did not possess the TASER as he was running away, although it could be a possibility that Slager believed he did. It is also clear the Slager fired only as Scott ran away, not while they were physically engaged. Slager used the belief that Scott had the TASER device as a premise for his deadly force application.

The TASER was discharged and it appears to me that nobody was affected, and therefore subsequent cycles would likely have the same non-effect. Without the ability to reload the device with a new probe cartridge, the only manner in which the TASER could be used would be drive-stun. In other words, Scott could not have used it against Slager or other officers to achieve neuro-muscular incapacitation, rendering an officer incapable to defend themselves. So, even if Scott was running away with the TASER device, at best he had a stun-gun type weapon, certainly a non-deadly force option. In my considered opinion, even if Scott had the TASER device while running away, it would not justify the use of deadly force.

As pointed out already, the movement of evidence in an officer involved shooting is troubling in of itself, but the manner in which Slager tossed the

TASER device near Scott was reminiscent of seeing a drug user try to pitch his dope without being noticed.

– Ed Flosi

Jared Forsyth, 33, White Male

Ocala, FL, April 6

While at Lowell Correctional Institution participating in firearms training, Officer Forsyth was hit with a round from an accidental discharge. The accident happened in a gun cleaning room. Officer Reghetti's .40-caliber Glock pistol discharged and the bullet hit Officer Forsyth in his chest.

Analysis

This was a horrible accident, and I mourn Officer Forsyth. I feel as terrible as one can for Officer Reghetti and the families of both men.

– Nick Selby

This was a terrible accident. Rest in peace, brother.

– Ben Singleton

There is not intent here, only tragedy for all involved. Even with that said, an investigation will likely reveal some level of negligence on the part of Reghetti, or on the part of his training. It is important that officers follow all safety rules at the range and at the cleaning table to prevent these tragedies.

– Ed Flosi

Michael Lemon, 57, White Male

Lake Isabella, CA, April 8

Kern County deputies were dispatched to a disturbance call. Lemon had reportedly been yelling from his porch all night. Deputies arrived to find Lemon on his porch. Lemon refused to comply with officer orders. The officers tried to use control holds on Lemon, but he punched one in the face. The same officer became covered in feces during the struggle, but how this happened is unknown[166]. The officers subdued Lemon using a TASER, batons, and pepper spray. He was handcuffed and then began complaining of trouble breathing. Lemon was treated by paramedics and transported to the hospital by ambulance, where he died[167].

Analysis

Once again, without critical contextual evidence being released by the department or the ME's office, like the autopsy or toxicology report, we cannot know what happened. If I had to guess, the behavior is consistent with acute methamphetamine intoxication.

– Nick Selby

Autopsy reports have not been released yet, but based on Lemon's behavior, I believe he may have been under the influence of a mind-altering substance, likely methamphetamine. This makes him yet another decedent whose death can be attributed to the combination of a psychotic episode, likely drug-induced, and physical exertion.

– Ben Singleton

The officers attempted to use physical controlling force to take Lemon into custody. Lemon did not comply, but instead punched an officer in the face. This demonstrated a credible physical threat to the officers. The officers used several non-deadly force options that in the 9th Circuit (Kern County is in California and part of the 9th Circuit area) would be considered "non-deadly intermediate" force options. In order to justify the use of these force options, the officers would need to articulate credible threat to the officers or others, which is clearly indicated by at least the first punch. The question is, did the assaultive resistance and threat level remain throughout the use of the force options? If the answer is yes (and if the original "seizure" of Lemon was lawful), then the use of the non-deadly force options would be appropriate.

– Ed Flosi

Freddie Gray, 25, Black Male

Baltimore, MD, April 14

Freddie Gray was arrested by bicycle officers in Baltimore. He was placed in a police transport van in seemingly healthy condition. However, Gray was not belted in, according to department policy.

According to the autopsy report, after the doors were closed, Gray began yelling and banging, "causing the van to rock." The van made several stops. The second stop was made few blocks away, where officers placed an identification band and leg restraints on Gray.

"Reportedly, Mr. Gray was still yelling and shaking the van," the medical examiner wrote. "He was removed from the van and placed on the ground in a kneeling position, facing the van doors, while ankle cuffs were placed, and then slid onto the floor of the van, belly down and head first, reportedly still verbally and physically active."

A third stop was captured on video, which showed the van driver getting out and looking in the back.

During a fourth stop, authorities said the driver called for assistance, at which point Porter got involved.

"The assisting officer opened the doors and observed Mr. Gray lying belly down on the floor with his head facing the cabin compartment, and reportedly he was asking for help, saying he couldn't breathe, couldn't get up, and needed a medic," the autopsy says. "The officer assisted Mr. Gray to the bench and the van continued on its way."

The van made a fifth stop to pick up a second arrestee, when officers checked again on Gray.

"Mr. Gray was found kneeling on the floor, facing the front of the van and slumped over to his right against the bench, and reportedly appeared lethargic with minimal responses to direct questions," the report says.

Gray suffered spinal cord injuries causing his death. The medical examiner concluded that the devastating injuries most likely occurred between the second and fourth stops made by the van driver[168].

Six officers were charged with offenses related to the death of Freddie Gray. The first trial ended in the declaration of a mistrial due to a hung jury. The second trial, after many delays, was set for May 2016 as we went to press[169].

Analysis

This was one of the most controversial cases of 2015, and it is the case that led directly to riots in Baltimore that caused millions of dollars in property damage. Since none of the charged officers has been convicted, it is difficult to answer many questions, because not all the trial evidence has been made public. I know from other large cities that prisoner transport vans operate in similar ways, but deaths have rarely occurred. I don't have enough information to judge whether this was intentional, negligent, or merely common practice of these officers in this case.

– Nick Selby

What this case essentially boils down to is that Grey was not seat-belted in. The medical examiner opined that, "With his hands and ankles restrained, and unable to see out of the van and anticipate turns, he was at a high risk for an unsupported fall."

Whether it was simply an unsupported fall or one caused by rapid deceleration of the van, he died while in police custody because the seat belt policy was not followed, despite repeated memoranda from administrators, training sessions and unannounced audits[170].

– Ben Singleton

Most agencies have a policy that requires officers to seatbelt or secure prisoners in some fashion prior to transport. This can be trickier in a transport van but it's not something that cannot be done. An agency or officer that ignores the reasonable foreseeability of the injuries that could occur open themselves to some serious risk exposure. There are some exclusions to this requirement that are mostly based on the subject's behavior being too dangerous for the officer to do it. The medical examiner's report is fairly compelling in its findings. All that said, I am still uncertain that it should rise to the level of criminal culpability.

– Ed Flosi

Joseph Slater, 28, White Male

Highland, CA, April 15

Highland Officers were called to a Valero gas station in response to a suspicious person reportedly damaging property. A deputy arrived at the store and encountered Joseph Slater. Slater was known to the department, having been previously dealt with for similar offenses. The deputy detained Slater. When he tried to seat him in his police car, Slater resisted. The deputy pepper sprayed Slater, but Slater pushed back. Arriving deputies forced Slater to the ground and gained control of him. Medical aid was summoned to check Slater and decontaminate him.

Slater was eventually placed in the back of the patrol car where he experienced a "significant medical emergency." Fire department personnel provided emergency medical care and he was transported to the hospital where he was pronounced dead[171].

Sources within the Sheriff's Department say officers had repeatedly tried to get help for Slater from Social Services and Mental Health, but he always was released back on the streets[172].

Analysis

It's difficult to see how the pepper spray – which was appropriate based on Slater's resistance to getting into the police car – would have had a toxic effect, but without the toxicology or autopsy, we're flying blind.

– Nick Selby

Toxicology reports have not been released yet. It would make sense if illicit drugs were found in Slater's system, but it is apparent that he had mental health issues as well.

This should be an eye opening case for those unfamiliar with life in law enforcement. Slater is a young man for whom officers "repeatedly" tried to get mental health help. They had probably taken him to several hospitals, referred him to mental health professionals, contacted his family, etc.

Then the same young man died in their custody as a direct result of his mental health struggles. This is an unfair position to put our police officers in.

– Ben Singleton

It appears that the deputies were conducting a lawful detention of Slater for some type of vandalism offense. It is a sad truth that officers are forced to have to continuously deal with the same mentally ill person due to the inadequacy of many mental health organizations and hospitals.

The deputies attempted to place Slater in the rear seat of a patrol car, but Slater resisted their efforts. It unclear if Slater was handcuffed prior to the attempt to place him in the car or if he was unsecured when he was put in. As a reminder, it is not a best practice to place an unsecured subject in the back of a patrol car in most situations. Having information on the status of Slater being handcuffed or not would be important to render an opinion on the appropriateness of the OC Spray use and to help determine the level of threat he posed. Perhaps due to their familiarity with Slater, the officers decided not to cuff him.

If the deputies reasonably believed that Slater was an un-handcuffed physical threat, the use of OC Spray and a takedown technique would be an appropriate force response.

However, if Slater was cuffed and simply refusing the get into the patrol vehicle, the use of the OC Spray would likely be excessive. The takedown would also need further exploration as the takedown of a handcuffed prisoner (i.e., unable to protect the head) can be more injurious than the same takedown of one not cuffed. Again, this is not to imply that the OC Spray or the takedown were necessarily a part of the death, as I believe that is unlikely.

– Ed Flosi

Frank Shephard, 41, Black Male

Houston, TX, April 15

Shephard led Houston Police on a vehicle pursuit after a Houston officer attempted to stop him for a traffic violation. During the pursuit, Shephard called 911 and told dispatchers that he had a child in the car with him. He threatened to harm the child if the police continued to pursue him[173].

Shephard ran through an intersection and slammed into two vehicles, which ended the chase. Shephard got out of the car and began walking toward the officers. Then he turned around and reached inside his vehicle despite officer's commands to show his hands.

Two officers fired a total of 10-12 rounds at Shephard, killing him[174].

Occupants of the two vehicles that were hit by Shephard's vehicle were treated at local hospitals and released. Shephard's claim of having a child passenger in his vehicle was false.

Analysis

I believe that, with the information available to the officers at the time, they made a decision that was fully justified. They had every reason to believe a child was in the vehicle whom Shephard would hurt. As an officer, I would have fully believed that Shephard was making his overtly rapid move to grab a weapon – and especially after he behaved so recklessly, I would have had no doubt that Shephard was murderous.

– Nick Selby

When I read that Shephard dove back into the car after the police ordered him to show his hands, I immediately said in my mind, "the kid is in the car," "the kid he threatened to harm if police chased him."

The officers justifiably stated they feared for their own lives when Shephard dove back into the car. Of course they did. But I think it is fair to add another layer of justification to the incident with the life of the child hostage that police reasonably believed was in the car at the time.

– Ben Singleton

Based on what the officers knew and reasonably believed, Shephard's overt and deliberate movement of going back to and reaching into the vehicle, even after being lawfully ordered to show his hands, would demonstrate an imminent threat of serious bodily injury or death to the officers and to others, especially in light of the child purported to be in the vehicle.

– Ed Flosi

David Kapuscinski, 39, White Male

Rockwood, MO, April 16

Gibraltar police responded to a 911 call reporting an "out of control" subject who was attacking the caller's mother.

The officer arrived on scene and confronted the subject, David Kapuscinski. According to prosecutors, officers heard a noise coming from the bedroom, and then saw Kapuscinski in the nude sexually assaulting the victim in front of a young boy and girl. Kapuscinski yelled that he was going to kill the woman.

Officers ordered Kapuscinski off of her, but he refused to comply. He became combative when officers tried to arrest him. One of the officers used his TASER, successfully separating Kapuscinski from the victim. But he continued to fight, kick, and become increasingly violent with officers. One of the officers used his TASER three times to gain control of him[175].

Kapuscinski began to show signs of medical complication. He was transported to the hospital where he was pronounced dead[176].

His toxicology report revealed that he had 3000 milligrams of amphetamine in his blood system[177].

Analysis

The idea that a person in the process of sexual assault in front of children is not an immediate danger to the safety of others is ludicrous; officers were absolutely, completely justified in their use of the TASER to separate Kapuscinski from his victim. His death is based on his amphetamine use, and is, if anything, distantly related to the TASER – but personally I think it is completely unrelated.

– Nick Selby

These officers did what they had to do to get the sexual assault to stop. When physical force didn't work, they had to use the TASER. Unfortunately we again see that high levels of narcotics in the system of a combative suspect can make for a deadly outcome.

– Ben Singleton

Kapuscinski was in the act of a violent sexual assault, with the additional factor of the children having to witness this horrific event. The officers attempted to use physical force to intervene but were unsuccessful. Kapuscinski was obviously a credible physical threat to the officers and others. The use of a TASER to separate Kapuscinski from his victim appears to be appropriate and consistent with current law enforcement training and standards. It is also appropriate to continue to use the TASER device while Kapuscinski was fighting and assaulting the officers.

– Ed Flosi

Darrell Brown, 31, Black Male

Hagerstown, MD, April 16

Police were called to a residence where Darrell Brown had just kicked in the front door and entered to confront a mother and her four young girls. Witnesses say Brown was "out of control."

When police arrived, they found Brown acting aggressively outside the home. They ordered him to get on the ground and comply, but he refused. Officers used the TASER on Brown and handcuffed him.

He was placed in an ambulance. Officers reported that Brown was still argumentative when being loaded into the ambulance. He was taken away, but later developed a medical emergency and died.

Witnesses supported the officers' decision to use the TASER, citing Brown's aggressive demeanor and his refusal to comply[178].

According to the autopsy report the cause of death was "excited delirium in the setting of police restraint."

The State's Attorney said: "The evidence points to Brown's use of drugs known as "bath salts" as the main factor in his death[179].

Analysis

The officers were clearly justified in their use of the TASER.

— Nick Selby

A toxicology report has not been released yet, but it appears, based on the State Attorney's assessment of the autopsy report, that this may have been a drug overdose, accelerated by a struggle with police.

— Ben Singleton

Brown was obviously a credible physical threat to the officers and others. The use of a TASER in this incident appears to be appropriate and consistent with current law enforcement training and standards.

– Ed Flosi

Norman Cooper, 33, Black Male

San Antonio, TX, April 19

At about 2:00 am, Officers were dispatched to a report of a family disturbance. "As officers arrived, they found an individual that was under the influence of some type of narcotic," San Antonio police Chief Anthony Trevino said. Officers attempted to escort Cooper out of the home, at his family's request, when he became combative.

One of the officers used a TASER on Cooper. Cooper removed the TASER probes, so a second officer deployed his TASER, according to Chief Trevino.

Shortly after the second Taser was deployed, police said Cooper became unresponsive. EMS was called, but Cooper was pronounced dead at the scene[180].

Analysis

This TASER use was justified by the actions of the decedent. When officers are dispatched at the behest of the community and the person is combative and apparently inebriated, officers are within reason to use a TASER to control him.

– Nick Selby

Autopsy and Toxicology reports have not been released. However, the officers believed Cooper was under the influence of some type of narcotic, and this would fit the common and disastrous recipe for an event similar to the others in this book where decedents died as a result of acute drug intoxication combined with physical exertion.

– Ben Singleton

It would be good to know what the officer's intent was in taking Cooper out of the home. If it was for a lawful arrest, then I am fine with their actions. Where it could become tenuous is if Cooper had legal standing in the home and the officers were acting solely on the other resident's request to remove Cooper against his will. Assuming there was a lawful reason articulated by the officers to remove Cooper from the house, when Cooper became assaultive and was a credible threat to the officers, the TASER applications would be appropriate.

– Ed Flosi

Daniel Covarrubias, 37, Hispanic Male

Lakewood, WA, April 21
Police responded to a lumber yard after an employee called 911 to say a man who appeared to be running from police was hiding on top of a pile of wood. The man, Daniel Covarrubias, turned out not to be running from the police, but the employee had made that assumption because she heard sirens in the area. Officers responded to the call and found Covarrubias on a 25-foot stack of lumber. The officers tried to talk with him, but he wouldn't respond.

Covarrubias reached into his pockets, at which point the officers told him to show his hands. Seconds later, according to Chief Zaro, Covarrubias pulled out a dark object in his hand. He pointed it at the officers in a manner consistent with pointing a firearm. Covarrubias then crouched back down, while officers continued telling him to show his hands. He popped up and again pointed the object at the officers, who fired at him.

Covarrubias crouched down, then came up and pointed the object at the officers a third time. The officers fired, and Covarrubias dropped back onto the lumber. Officers climbed a fire ladder to reach him. When they reached the top of the stack, they discovered Covarrubias had been holding a cellphone, not a gun.

Chief Zaro said reports from St. Clare Hospital indicated Covarrubias had methamphetamine in his system the day he was shot, that he had gone possibly three days without eating or sleeping, and that he might have been hallucinating[181].

Further investigation revealed that prior to the shooting incident, Covarrubias had gone to a Lakewood hospital and told staff members he wanted the cameras in his eyes taken out. He told a social worker that he had used meth and had not slept or eaten in three days. Covarrubias left the hospital on foot about an hour before the shooting.

The day before the shooting, Covarrubias called 911 several times to report shots fired, missing family, and then cancelled the report because he said he was "tripping." His father told dispatchers that his son was having delusions. Multiple witnesses said the phone looked like a gun because of the way Covarrubias was holding it and pointing it toward the officers[182].

Analysis

This case was left in our sample because of arguments in which people stated repeatedly that a phone could not be confused with a gun. I professionally disagree, and I'm sure my colleagues here will as well. It is clear that the officers did a great deal to avoid using deadly force, and that the use of force was justifiable. This is another case in which methamphetamine induced psychosis caused a person to behave in a way that turned deadly for him.

– Nick Selby

Covarrubias was clearly in the throes of a drug-induced, psychotic episode. In fact, it's not unlikely he believed that his cell phone was a gun. These officers responded to behavior that was consistent with a legitimate threat to their lives. Their actions were completely reasonable.

– Ben Singleton

This is another tragic example of an officer being forced to believe his life and the life of others were in imminent danger. This case also illustrates the importance of understanding the perception of the officer(s) based on the totality of the circumstances at the time. Although the object turned out to be a cellphone, based on the manner in which it was presented, along with the behavior of Covarrubias, could lead an officer to reasonably believe the object to be a firearm. This falls right in line with those cases where the object was later determined to have been a replica or toy firearm.

There was clearly something amiss with Covarrubias that led him to behave in this matter, but we will never really know. What we do know is what his actions were that led to his own demise.

– Ed Flosi

Steven Davenport, 43, White Male

Meridan, MS, April 21
Deputies received reports of two men fighting at a residence. Upon their arrival at the residence, they tried to deescalate the situation. Davenport became combative, and he and deputies struggled "for some length," according to Sheriff Sollie. One deputy used his TASER during the fight, but it had no impact on Davenport. Two additional deputies arrived and helped to subdue him. After he was restrained, Davenport became unresponsive.

Davenport was taken to a hospital and received treatment, but he ultimately died. Two deputies were transported to the hospital, and received treatment for their injuries as well. All four deputies were wearing body cameras[183].

Lauderdale County Coroner Clayton Cobler said Davenport suffered scratches and bruises but suffered no life-threatening injuries. Cobler said Davenport had heart disease, and that it was possible his heart gave out during the struggle, and that drug use may also have been a contributing factor.

Cobler said the autopsy revealed no indications of Taser use[184]. Toxicology reports have not been publicly released.

Analysis
It astounds me how many people with serious and chronic health conditions get into situations in which they fight or become highly aggressive. This TASER use was reasonable.

– Nick Selby

206

This is likely to be found as another death explained by acute drug toxicity and physical exertion. The officers were completely reasonable in their dealings with this combative subject.

– Ben Singleton

The level of injury reported to the deputies is indicative of the struggle they described once Davenport become combative. The use of the TASER with a subject that is a credible physical threat is appropriate and consistent with current law enforcement training and standards.

– Ed Flosi

William Chapman, 18, Black Male

Portsmouth, VA, April 22
Walmart security called Portsmouth Police regarding an alleged shoplifter leaving the store. The suspect, William Chapman, was approached in the parking lot of the Walmart by Officer Rankin of the Portsmouth Police Department. Witnesses reportedly saw a struggle ensue between the officer and Chapman.

One witness said he saw Chapman "going nuts" and "whaling on the cop." He also said he saw Chapman knock something out of the officer's hand. Then he saw the officer back up about 10 feet. He said, "The guy came at him, and we heard two shots, and the guy went down[185]."

Officer Rankin has been indicted on charges of first-degree murder, and for using a gun in a felony. Officer Rankin shot and killed another unarmed man in 2011. He was cleared by a grand jury of wrongdoing in that case[186].

Analysis
This is troubling, especially because of Officer Rankin's history, which really does affect my judgment of this incident. We don't really have enough information to be certain here. Rankin will be required to articulate, believably, that he reasonably feared for his life when he pulled

the trigger. I don't have enough to state an opinion as to whether he will be successful.

– Nick Selby

There is an ongoing investigation, with a trial pending. Rankin will have to show that he feared for his life and that Chapman posed a significant threat. Based on the evidence we have, I believe that will be hard to do. There are many questions which need to be answered before arriving at any conclusion as to reasonableness. The most important question in my view is; was Rankin injured by Chapman prior to the shooting? If Rankin took several blows to the head and believed he could no longer defend himself, he should be able to articulate a legitimate fear for, and perceived threat to, his life.

But his decision to escalate to deadly force may have been based on an inability to successfully deploy his TASER, and fear alone, when no legitimate threat-to-life existed.

– Ben Singleton

In any deadly force application, there are factors that must be known to render a reasoned opinion as to the appropriateness. In this case, there is simply not enough information in the material to make that determination. The fact that the officer was indicted is compelling, however, because it indicates to me that there is some evidence that the officer not only acted inappropriately, but also inappropriate enough that the actions were seen to be enough to support an indictment.

All we know is that Chapman assaulted the officer. One witness states a TASER was deployed during the struggle. Something was knocked out of the officer's hand that may have been the TASER. If the TASER was used at this presumed close range, it's unlikely there would have been enough spread on the probes to cause anything other than localized pain. Although the TASER use would most likely be deemed as appropriate, the specific facts do not include enough to justify the use of deadly force. The facts may or may not have been present, but at this point it is impossible to tell.

As a training note, there appears to be a pattern emerging with officers using the TASER in probe mode at close range. If the officer is expecting some level of neuro-muscular incapacitation effect, the officer needs to remember that there should be at least four inches of probe spread when the probes are in contact with the subject. That means the subject should be about three or more feet away from the TASER blast doors. A common mistake I have seen is that officers stand about three or slightly more feet away, but then push the TASER forward and towards the subject, thereby reducing the distance. The exception to this would be if the officer attempts to follow-up with a three-point contact application away from the location of the probes.

– Ed Flosi

Hector Morejon, 19, Hispanic Male

Long Beach, CA, April 23
Long Beach officers responded to a trespassing and vandalizing call at a multi-unit residence in the early afternoon. Officers discovered two open windows missing screens. An officer looked through a broken window and saw Morejon standing next to a wall. Police said that Morejon turned toward the officer while bending his knees, and extended his arm out as if he was pointing an object at the officer. The officer believed the object was a gun, and fired at Morejon.

No verbal warning was given to Morejon before the shooting, according to police[187].

Morejon later died at the hospital.

Analysis
This is a really tough case. I can't tell you whether this officer feared for his life, which would be what he would need to have legitimately felt in order for this shooting to be justified.

– Nick Selby

This case is truly tragic. If the officer perceived a genuine threat to his life, this may be a legally justifiable shooting. But it is really unfortunate.

I believe the law enforcement community should be careful about continuing to stretch this idea of the "perceived threat." An officer who cannot deal with fear in a way that allows them to make sound decisions should not be an officer. Most officers will agree that they have experienced many scenarios where they could have legally killed someone, but didn't do so. Deadly force isn't an activity to be engaged in as a matter of following policy or law. It should be used only in the genuine preservation of life.

The officer's justification for this shooting can be summarized with: "he pointed something at me." We need to do better than this.

– Ben Singleton

The law of the land in all use of force cases is Graham v Connor and has been since 1989. The US Supreme Court gave officers guidance on what would be "objectively reasonable" force under the totality of the circumstances. These circumstances include facts known and reasonably perceived by the officer at the time. The known or perceived threat must be supported by objective and articulable facts, and it can't be just a basic blanket statement of, "I was in fear for my life." Another way of looking at "reasonableness" is that the officer does not have to be right; the officer must act in a manner that is the same or similar to another officer with the same/similar training and experience put in a same or similar situation.

If the officer honestly believed, based on all the facts known and perceived, that Morejon was pointing a firearm at the officers, it would be appropriate for the officer to use deadly force to defend against the imminent threat of serious bodily injury or death. Officers are not required to actually see a gun or to be fired upon to reasonably believe a subject is armed. Asking officers to wait to confirm what the object is would create an unreasonable risk to the officer and to others.

Absent that level of threat, the deadly force application would not be reasonable.

– Ed Flosi

David Felix, 24, Black Male

New York, NY, April 25

Two veteran detectives went to a six-story residential building in search of a robbery suspect. They were buzzed inside and told that the building was a half-way house, and that it housed people with mental illness. They were told that the person they were seeking, David Felix, was a paranoid schizophrenic.

When the detectives made contact with Felix, violence erupted. Police officials described a five-minute melee in which Felix ripped a police radio from the belt of one of the detectives, and used it to "bash their heads."

Detective Carter, a 21-year veteran, was bleeding from the head. After five minutes of hand-to-hand combat, he fired a single shot, hitting Felix in the chest. Felix died soon after at a nearby hospital[188].

Both detectives sustained head injuries and were taken to a hospital for treatment. The officer who received the blow from the radio underwent an MRI[189].

Analysis

There are a couple of things to note here, starting with what a dangerous and heavy object a police radio is, and to add that most people would be significantly winded after a fight of two minutes, let alone after five full minutes. These officers seem to have done everything possible to avoid deadly force, and the shooting seems justified.

– Nick Selby

This is another case where the officers appear to have done everything they could have to avoid a deadly conflict. They fought for five minutes with the decedent and sustained serious injuries before resorting to deadly force.

Five minutes is a very long time to be engaged in a fight. The officers were likely winded and continuing to take repeated blows from Felix. Also, detectives don't usually carry the same arsenal of equipment with them as patrol officers do. Detectives often wear plain clothes and carry neither a TASER nor a baton. They probably had limited options in terms of weaponry.

Based on the injuries sustained by the officers in this conflict, and the dire situation that they undoubtedly found themselves in after five minutes of fighting, I believe they were reasonable in their use of deadly force.

– Ben Singleton

Felix engaged the officers in a five-minute struggle. It can be assumed that during this time, based on the intensity described, the officers were likely to be very fatigued and less able to defend against continuing violent attack. Felix removed the police radio from one of the officers and began to beat him about the head with it. This action, in itself, would present an imminent threat of serious bodily injury or death, and it could justify the use of deadly force. While it is unknown at what time the police radio was used as an impact object, what is compelling is the fact that the officers stayed in this fight for five minutes prior to resorting to deadly force.

– Ed Flosi

Billy Patrick, 29, White Male

Bunch, OK, April 26

An Oklahoma state wildlife officer approached three people who were fishing near a pond and asked to see their fishing licenses around 11:10 a.m. One of the men, Billy Patrick, had a warrant from Arkansas for violating the terms of his parole.

Patrick began to fight when the officer tried to arrest him. They fell into a pond, where Patrick attempted to hold the officer's head underwater.

The officer fought his way above the water and shot Patrick. Patrick died on scene.

The officer was treated for minor injuries at a local hospital[190].

Analysis

Outside firing a gun at me, I cannot think of a more obvious deadly threat than someone trying to push my head underwater and hold it there. This shooting is justified.

– Nick Selby

When a combative parole violator holds a police officer's head underwater, one must assume that he is trying to drown and kill the officer. Deadly force is a reasonable response.

– Ben Singleton

This case is a good illustration of the fact that deadly force threats do not always come in the traditional manners one would imagine. An officer in full uniform is at a severe disadvantage in a body of water. The weight of dry equipment can be problematic in some struggles, let alone the weight that being soaked adds. The actions of Patrick demonstrated a clear imminent threat of serious bodily injury or death to the officer, thereby making the deadly force application appropriate and consistent with current law enforcement training and standards.

– Ed Flosi

Dean Genova, 45, White Male

Garden Grove, CA, April 26

Officers responded to a burglary in progress at a pharmacy at about 4:00am. Officers encountered Genova inside the store when they arrived. Genova fought officers when they tried to subdue him. He reportedly bit an officer on the arm before taking another officer's handgun[191].

Genova was told to put down the gun. When he refused, the officer that sustained the bite shot him one time. Genova was taken to a hospital where he was pronounced dead[192].

Analysis

It is unclear to me whether Genova was armed at the moment of his death; this is one of those cases where controversy led to its inclusion.

– Nick Selby

These officers showed great restraint in allowing this incident to escalate as far as it did before using deadly force. Genova was given ample opportunity to surrender. He chose instead to take an officer's gun, and to refuse to drop it and give himself up. He gave them no choice but to kill him.

– Ben Singleton

Genova was caught in progress during a burglary. The officer attempted to lawfully arrest him, but Genova fought back viciously. Genova's actions of biting and disarming an officer are a clear imminent threat of serious body injury or death to the officers. After Genova refused to put the gun down, the officer had little choice, other than to use appropriate deadly force to stop the threat.

– Ed Flosi

Fridoon Rawshannehad, 42, White Male

San Diego, CA, April 30

Police received reports of a man with a knife in an alley behind a theater. Officer Browder arrived minutes later and located Rawshannehad. Browder reportedly gave verbal commands to Rawshannehad but he did not comply. When Rawshannehad advanced, Officer Browder shot him.

Investigators did not find a knife, but did find a "shiny object" in Rawshannehad's hand[193].

Analysis

There is too little information upon which to base any conclusions in this case. But if Officer Browder believed that the shiny object was a knife, and Rawshannehad charged him with it, he could articulate a reasonable fear for, and threat to, his life.

Browder's body camera was not activated, but footage from a private security camera captured the event. It has not yet been released.

– Ben Singleton

The perceptions of an officer can be influenced to prior information received by the officer, especially if the actions of the subject support the previously learned information. The officer was responding to a man with a knife. While it is not known exactly what he saw or did not see in Rawshannehad's hand, it is clear that Rawshannehad was in possession of something that could be reasonably perceived as a knife during the tense and rapidly evolving event. If this was part of the force articulation, it would make the deadly force response more clearly an appropriate one.

– Ed Flosi

MAY

Brendon Glenn, 29, Black Male

Los Angeles, CA, May 6

Officers responded to the Venice Beach boardwalk in response to reports of a "male Black transient" who was harassing customers. When officers confronted Glenn, he walked away toward the boardwalk. The two officers returned to their car, but then noticed Glenn "physically struggle" with someone. According to police, "The officers attempted to detain the suspect, and an altercation occurred between the two officers and the suspect," after which Officer Clifford Proctor, who is black, shot Glenn[194].

Glenn was transported to a nearby hospital where he was pronounced dead. Proctor told investigators that he saw Glenn's hand on his partner's holster. The shooting was captured by a security camera on a nearby building. Chief Charlie Beck said that he was "very concerned" about the incident, after reviewing the recording. Officer Proctor had previously been the subject of an investigation for omitting witness statements in a police report[195]. The Los Angeles Times identified the partner as Jonathan Kawahara, a 10-year department veteran[196].

In a letter dated March 2, 2016, Chief Beck stated that "Video footage from the Townhouse Bar camera captured the struggle between Glenn and the officers and at no time during the struggle can Glenn's hand be observed on or near any portion of Officer [Kawahara's] holster, or capture any actions by Officer [Kawahara] that would suggest [he] was attempting to push Glenn's hand away from [his] holster[197]." Proctor's partner told investigators that he did not feel any "jerking movements", and told investigators he did not know why Proctor shot Glenn[198].

On April 12, 2016, the Police Commission unanimously agreed with Chief Beck, finding that Proctor violated LAPD policies, and declared the shooting unjustified. This is the first time in his tenure that Chief Beck has requested that charges be brought against one of his officers[199].

Analysis

After reading the findings from the Use of Force Review Board, and the Police Commission, this appears to be a case in which the officer made a range of out-of-policy decisions and ultimately was not justified in his use of deadly force. Chief Beck mentioned a range of tactical decisions by the officers, including a failure to coordinate, tactical use of obscenity in an effort by Proctor to gain control that ultimately had an escalating effect, grabbing of Glenn by Glenn's hair, and the firing by Proctor of two rounds while his partner was in the line of fire. My greatest concern in this case is the outright fabrication by Proctor of "justification" for his use of deadly force. The man simply lied. As we mentioned in the About The Data chapter, some cops lie, and the chances of dishonesty being uncovered get higher each year with the increased scrutiny of civil litigation attorneys, investigative reporters, public advocacy groups, and projects including this one. I note that Proctor's partner did not participate in this lie, and told investigators that he did not feel any jerking movements or know why Proctor fired. I consider Proctor's blatant lies in this case to be a total betrayal of the badge, and of the community he swore to protect. In my opinion, Chief Beck is absolutely right to call for Proctor to be criminally charged.

– Nick Selby

Absent an attempt by Glenn to disarm Officer Kawahara, there existed no threat that would justify the shooting of Glenn. Police officers are bestowed with an immense amount of power and authority over others. This power and authority must be handled with exceptional trust and honesty. Proctor killed a man without justification, and then lied in an attempt to justify his actions. This is something we cannot allow to go unchecked. The community needs to know that those in law enforcement will not permit criminal police action by fellow officers, or dishonest attempts to cover up criminal acts. Kawahara had ample opportunity to become complicit in Proctor's false statements in justifying the shooting.

As the great majority of officers would, Kawahara chose to be honest. Proctor should be criminally charged.

– Ben Singleton

There seems to being ample information known to the officers in order to contact and physically intervene in the altercation between Glenn and the bouncer of the establishment. In their efforts to stop the on-view fight from continuing, the officers would have been authorized to use reasonable force options if Glenn had resisted or if Glenn had continued to present a credible physical threat to the bouncer and/or the officers. The decision of the officers to physically engage with Glenn was appropriate.

Once physically engaged, Glenn began to struggle with the officers. Officers are trained that if they can't reasonably control a person in a standing position, they should take the subject to the ground in order to use the ground as a controlling agent. The idea of the takedown was not contested but the methodology seemed to have drawn disapproval. Proctor grabbed Glenn by the hair during the takedown, which in itself is not inappropriate; some schools still teach this as a valid technique. Proctor stated that he didn't recall doing the takedown in that manner and then said it is not the way he would normally do a takedown. I think anybody who has worked the streets understands that the takedowns we learn on the mat do not always translate exactly the same way in a street takedown. That said, the fact that it happened differently than Proctor would normally do it does not create concern for me. Without outright calling Proctor a liar that he didn't recall pulling the hair specifically, it does raise concerns when one takes into consideration the previous investigation of Proctor's alleged misconduct and his first description that he "walked Glenn down to the ground." To put it plainly, the fact that the takedown was performed as seen on video is not the problem, it is the apparent deceitfulness that is.

The video evidence and the statement of the partner is very compelling indeed. These combined with the apparent deceitfulness of Proctor tend to all point towards a conclusion that the use of deadly force was inappropriate based on the preponderance of the evidence.

In order to play "devil's advocate," there are however certain things that strike me as odd in the investigation. To be clear, I do not think these points would exonerate the officer's actions.

There is one point (since the report is heavily redacted, I am assuming this to be the non-shooting officer reporting this) that the officer reports feeling a brief tug on the holster but that the officer didn't see Glenn's hand on the holster. The report is carefully worded to state that at no time did the surveillance video show Glenn's hand on the officer's holster. This may be factually correct but what the statement does not say is whether the officer's holster and Glenn's hands were in full view the entire time. Although very compelling, this statement doesn't dismiss the possibility that the grab happened at a point not visible to the camera and because of a time lag in looking to the holster the non-shooting officer just missed seeing it.

There is also a heavy reliance on the security video. I have not seen the video but if it is standard surveillance video it is most likely shot from a high angle, certainly not from the distance and angle of view experienced from Proctor's position. We understand the importance and value of video evidence. Indeed, all three authors are proponents for body worn cameras. That said, we must also realize the limitations of video evidence. I think many of us have seen the now famous Shreveport, Louisiana officer involved shooting where one in-car camera appears to capture the officers execute a subject whereas the other angle of view clearly supported the officer's actions and perceptions that the subject was armed.

– Ed Flosi

John Kaafi, 33, White Male

Sarasota, FL, May 7

Kaafi was riding in a vehicle with Tim Bess when police stopped the vehicle for a defective tag light. Officers described Kaafi's behavior as erratic. He was reportedly chewing, licking his lips, and acting extremely nervously. Kaafi was found to be in possession of cocaine and spice. He was TASED three times, and struck with a flashlight, during the arrest[200].

After the initial arrest, Kaafi escaped from the police car, and evaded on foot. After officers regained custody of Kaafi, they transported him to the jail, where he told officers that he was having an asthma attack. Officers called medical personnel and said Kaafi was breathing normally and speaking with officers before being transported to the hospital, where he died[201].

Analysis

It would be great to understand what happened between the stop and the use of the TASER.

– Nick Selby

We have no details about what precipitated the use of force by officers on the traffic stop. There are also some concerns about the probable cause cited for the stop, as the tag light appears to be working on the in-car video footage. The officers will ultimately have to justify their actions at every step, beginning with the initial stop. This appears to be another death resulting from the combination of acute drug intoxication and physical stress. An analysis as to reasonableness can't be done until more details are released.

– Ben Singleton

We must have more details to evaluate the appropriateness of the force response in this incident. While it is clear that force options were used, and that Kaafi did die proximate to the arrest process, there is no indication that the force options used were a primary or contributing factor in his death. His objective symptoms displayed and observed by the officer seem to indicate some level of drug intoxication, which combined with other health issues, might have very well played a large role in his demise.

– Ed Flosi

Michael Gallagher, 55, White Male

Enfield, NC, May 10:

Enfield Lieutenant Jerry Powell responded to a reported break-in at a local business. He located Gallagher inside. Lt. Powell and a witness, reportedly a former police officer, got into a physical altercation with Gallagher. Lt. Powell deployed his TASER, and handcuffed Gallagher. Gallagher was later pronounced dead at the hospital.

Gallagher's father has alleged that officers beat Gallagher while he was handcuffed citing reports he received from witnesses[202]. Gallagher was wanted for grand larceny and breaking and entering at the time of this incident.

A preliminary autopsy revealed that Gallagher was in the early stages of liver and heart disease and the presence of cocaine in Gallagher's system. Gallagher also suffered a severe laceration to his ankle and he was bleeding profusely. It is believed that Gallagher suffered this injury while kicking in the door to the business[203].

Analysis

When I compare the likelihood that Gallagher was beaten while handcuffed by a police officer in front of witnesses with the likelihood that someone who had chronic medical conditions and was using cocaine got sick and died after exerting himself, there's just no contest: this is a case in which the suspect died based on his actions prior to custody.

– Nick Selby

I find no corroborating evidence to support claims made by Gallagher's father that officers beat Gallagher after handcuffing him. The evidence does suggest that due to Gallagher's recent ingestion of cocaine and his medical problems, the added physical stress of a fight with police officers prior to his apprehension may have led to his death.

– Ben Singleton

From the material provided, it appears that Powell used the TASER device while in a physical altercation with Gallagher. With the limited details, and if one were to assume that the physical altercation presented a credible threat to Powell, the use of the TASER device would be considered appropriate and consistent with current law enforcement training and standards.

– Ed Flosi

DaJuan Graham, 40, Black Male

Silver Spring, MD, May 12
While conducting a traffic stop, an officer was approached by people who said that a partially clothed man was walking in the street and acting erratically. The officer requested a backup officer, and the two approached the man, DaJuan Graham. A woman, waving her arms, told the officers that Graham had just punched her, cutting her lip. She also told officers that she was under the influence of PCP.

Graham was standing in the street with his hands in his shorts pockets. The officers told Graham to remove his hands from his pockets four times. He refused to comply, and he continued to grunt, raise and lower his shoulders, and assumed a threatening stance. The officers warned him that they would use the TASER if he did not comply. Officers TASED Graham one time, placed him in handcuffs, and rolled him onto his side. An ambulance took Graham to the hospital, where he was conscious and interacting with officers[204]. While at the hospital, Graham assaulted an officer and a member of the hospital security staff. Police left Graham in the care of the hospital staff. The next day, Monday, Graham was transferred to the cardiac care unit due to an elevated heart rate. On Tuesday, he died[205].

Analysis
This is another case where a man with acute narcotic intoxication assaults a civilian and acts in a manner that is threatening and unpredictable to officers. The officer was right and justified in his use of the TASER, and Graham's death was related to his drug use.

– Nick Selby

This is a great example of officers using a tool (TASER) for its intended purpose, and with great care. Graham was most likely under the influence of PCP, based on the description of his behavior and witness statements. This drug is more dangerous to police officers than any other, in my opinion. It turns normal people into fearless, superhuman, seemingly possessed psychopaths. These officers TASERED Graham one time, handcuffed him, rolled him to the recovery position, and called EMS. This was a textbook TASER deployment. They did everything right. Graham died two days later. We don't know why, but symptoms of PCP withdrawal include seizure, coma, central nervous system damage and death[206].

– Ben Singleton

According to the material provided, it appears that Graham had committed a crime of violence and may have been under the influence of PCP. Any working cop that has tried to control a person in the midst of a PCP rage will understand that this is no easy task. Adding to this, Graham was presenting pre-assaultive behaviors demonstrating a clear and credible physical threat to the officers. The use of the TASER device would be considered appropriate and consistent with current law enforcement training and standards.

Beyond that, the officers demonstrated a clear concern for Graham's welfare by moving him to a recovery position as soon as tactically feasible to do so. This is a great training point. Officers should be reminded to move a prone handcuffed subject into a recovery position (side lateral or sitting) as soon as tactically feasible to avoid any allegations of respiratory compromise causing the death.

– Ed Flosi

Lorenzo Hayes, 37, Black Male

Spokane, WA, May 13

Lorenzo Hayes was seen by a witness taking a rifle from his vehicle and hiding it near a home where a woman who had a no-contact order against Hayes lived. After that, he was seen arguing with the woman in front of the home. Officers arrived and said they noticed that Hayes behavior was indicative of narcotics use. Reports said Hayes appeared to be under the influence of narcotics and was sweating profusely.

Officers arrested Hayes for violating the no-contact order and unlawful possession of a firearm, and took him to the County Jail. When they arrived, staff said Hayes was fighting. When the jail staff tried to restrain Hayes, he had a medical emergency. He was taken to the hospital where he died. Police searched his home and found more than a user quantity of methamphetamine inside. Task force officers said Hayes is known to be a mid-level meth and heroin dealer.

Analysis
Other than to point out the drug-related death, my analysis is on the inclusion in this book of this case. While the rifle was involved, Hayes was not armed at the time of his arrest, and the rifle was confiscated. And while Hayes became ill and was transported to the hospital after being transported to the jail, it is my understanding that he had not yet been booked into the jail. To my mind, the illness that ultimately led to Hayes' death began during the period of booking – therefore he was still under police (not jail) custody. There is no doubt in my mind that the methamphetamine and Hayes' health were the cause of his death.

– Nick Selby

This is another death resulting from severe drug intoxication and physical exertion. In this case, TASER was not used. People fear the TASER because they don't fully understand it. But it has no more impact on one's health than pepper spray, or a baton. The common denominator in almost all of these unexplained in-custody deaths is drug use.

Obviously the jail staff did nothing wrong by restraining Hayes, who was fighting staff in the jail. Absent the drug use, Hayes would have lived.

– Ben Singleton

There is no indication of any significant force response by the officers at the arrest scene. There is an indication that Hayes was fighting when he arrived at the hospital, but other than identifying that jail staff was using some type of restraining force, there is no description of what this truly means. If one were to assume it to mean controlling force and body weight, then it would appear to be appropriate for the circumstances. There is more evidence to lead towards a conclusion that the death was more related to acute drug intoxication/overdose.

– Ed Flosi

Denis Reyes, 40, Hispanic Male

New York, NY, May 15

Blanca Sierra, mother of Reyes, called 911 to report that her son was under the influence of alcohol, synthetic marijuana and prescription medication, and that he was acting wildly and being uncooperative[207]. She told reporters that Reyes "lost his mind[208]." Reyes suffered from schizophrenia and bipolar disorder. Wilfred Bracero, Reyes' brother, told police that Reyes was throwing furniture and knocking over lamps.

Police officers and EMS personnel responded. Police arrived first. Police restrained Reyes, who was kicking and fighting. He was handcuffed and his ankles were shackled. When EMS personnel arrived, Reyes was placed in a wheelchair. As paramedics were taking Reyes to the ambulance, he went into cardiac arrest. EMS performed CPR on the way to the hospital, but Reyes later died at the hospital[209].

Analysis

This is another death almost certainly caused by the acute intoxication by a lethal cocktail of alcohol, illegal narcotics and prescription medications of the decedent. The decedent's mental health issues most likely aggravated the agitation caused by this intoxication. All too often, police are called as the last line of defense after multiple societal firewalls (in this case, the mental health system, and family oversight of mental health medication) have failed.

– Nick Selby

It is very unlikely that the police had anything to do with Reyes death. He was clearly in need of medical attention before police arrived. The autopsy report has not been released, but Rayes reportedly took pills, smoked synthetic marijuana, and drank alcohol prior to police arrival. I believe the autopsy will report findings of lethal levels of drugs in Reyes' system.

In 2014, over 47,000 Americans died of drug overdose. Given the illicit nature of drug use and the kind of behavior it tends to promote, police are sometimes present when overdose kills. In fact, police are often present during the treatment of people who have intentionally overdosed, but that doesn't make the police complicit in their deaths.

– Ben Singleton

We don't know if Reyes was experiencing excited delirium, but this incident has all the hallmarks and behavioral cues that would lead a person to believe Reyes was in this state. It is important to note that EMS was initially requested to respond. In cases such as these where an excited delirium scenario may be present, it is important to understand that the person is suffering from a medical emergency and needs immediate medical attention. The officers in this incident did an outstanding job of containing Reyes so that trained medical personnel could treat him as soon as feasible.

It appears that the officers and EMS acted appropriately in their response and actions but unfortunately, Reyes still died. As an instructor of "Excited Delirium Response" at the CIT Academy, I would say that this is exactly what we want our officers and EMS personnel to do.

– Ed Flosi

Marcus Clark, 26, Black Male

Fort Lauderdale, FL, May 20
Deputies were called to a gas station in response to a robbery. The clerk said Clark appeared to be high or drunk. When deputies arrived, they saw Clark

behind the counter and struggling with a clerk. Clark was also blocking the door into the clerk's area, preventing the clerk from escaping and the officers from entering.

A Sergeant climbed over the counter and attempted to subdue Clark. Two other deputies assisted. Clark was holding on to the clerk for the first part of the scuffle. The deputies freed the clerk, and then again began to subdue Clark. Once subdued, the deputies handcuffed him and carried him out of the store.

Clark was taken to a nearby hospital to be evaluated. His temperature was 106.3 degrees Fahrenheit[210]. He died the following morning. Family members acknowledge that Clark had a problem with drugs and was high on "Flakka," but believe that the police killed him.

Analysis

The extremely high temperature and bizarre behavior are now-classic side effects of acute Flakka intoxication, the synthetic drug that has led to hundreds of deaths nationwide. Officers were justified to use the level of force they used to secure Clark from his attack of the clerk, and while the family blame police for Clark's death, the autopsy will likely show acute flakka intoxication and chronic health conditions as the primary cause of death.

– Nick Selby

Autopsy reports have not been released yet. Clark appears to be highly intoxicated in the surveillance footage of the incident. The officers do not appear to strike Clark, or use any unreasonable measures to subdue him. He is extracted from the area behind the clerk's counter and taken to a police car.

Flakka is a new synthetic drug that is wreaking havoc across the country. Small overdoses of flakka can cause violent behavior, spikes in body temperature (105 degrees and higher), and paranoia. Flakka gives users what feels like the strength and fury of the Incredible Hulk[211]. More important, it can cause death. Clark's temperature was 106.3 degrees F according to the hospital. That is a good indication as to Clark's degree of intoxication. I believe Clark died of drug overdose.

– Ben Singleton

Again, little is known about the type and number of force options used in this case so it would be difficult to evaluate the appropriateness, other than to say some level of force would be obviously appropriate to control and arrest Clark. What is compelling to me is the body temperature of Clark. Clark was definitely suffering from hyperthermia at 106.3° F. I have attended many lectures from medical personnel that state unequivocally that hyperthermia is a "harbinger of death." In his condition, it is likely that the force options had little or nothing to do with his demise.

– Ed Flosi

Randall Torrence, 34, White Male

Kansas City, KS, May 27
Police officers were flagged down to investigate calls of a man behaving strangely in the parking lot of a Family Dollar store. The man became combative when EMS personnel tried to treat him[212].

Officers used the TASER on Torrence two times to gain control of him. At some point after the second TASER exposure, Torrence stopped breathing. KCPD Chief Zeigler believes Torrence was high and said Torrence kicked two of his officers during the scuffle.

Torrence's mother said her son lived a troubled life and hung out with the wrong crowd, but was trying to turn his life around[213].

Analysis
We don't know the autopsy results, but based on the information here, this would seem to be violent behavior that was sufficiently threatening to justify use of the TASER.

– Nick Selby

Toxicology reports have not been released. Based on Torrence's violent acts, the fact that his behavior was strange enough to elicit calls from concerned citizens, and his mother's admission that he "lived a troubled life," I believe Torrence was under the influence of one or more mind altering drugs. This combined with the physical stress of a fight with police led to his death.

– Ben Singleton

Based on the description of Torrence's behaviors and actions, it could be reasonably inferred that the officers believed Torrence was a credible physical threat to them at the time of the TASER use. The use of the TASER as described in this incident appears to be appropriate and consistent with current law enforcement training and practices.

– Ed Flosi

Feras Morad, 20, Semitic Male

Long Beach, CA, May 27

Occupants of a Long Beach apartment called 911 to report they had gotten into a fight with a man that lasted about ten minutes, before he jumped through a second story glass window. Long Beach firefighters were called to the scene to respond to a fall from a second floor. Police were dispatched a minute later.

Residents went outside to try to help the man, but he continued to be aggressive. An officer arrived to find three men in an alley. As he exited his patrol car, one of the men, Morad, began to walk quickly toward him. Morad had a large cut across his body and was covered with blood. The officer told him he was there to help him get medical care, and he ordered him to stop. Morad refused to comply with the officer's orders and began to walk more rapidly toward the officer.

The officer used his TASER, his baton, and physical force over a period of several minutes in attempts to get Morad to stop charging. Morad charged again and told the officer he was going to attack him. The officer shot Morad.

He was transported to a local hospital where he died[214].

Morad had taken hallucinogenic mushrooms for the first time, and "freaked out," according to his sister[215]. The family's attorney said Morad "probably had drugs in his system, but said there is no way to say how he ingested it."

Analysis

Two things are surprising here: first, that a Long Beach Officer was left without backup for long enough for this to transpire, and second, that psilocybin (the active ingredient in hallucinogenic mushrooms) would have an effect that rendered Morad so violent. While psilocybin has been known to cause panic attacks and paranoia that can lead to violence, it is relatively rare. The use of force seems to have been absolutely justified, and the officer used restraint in the non-deadly force choices he used until he clearly felt threatened – after even one minute of intense hand-to-hand combat, most people begin to tire.

– Nick Selby

Drugs seem to be the common denominator in a large portion of these cases. But hallucinogenic mushrooms don't typically cause users to exhibit this kind of aggression. The toxicology report, which may provide more answers, hasn't been released yet.

As to the officer's decision to use deadly force, I believe it was reasonable based on the officer's statement of events. The officer used his TASER, his baton, and his body in attempts to get Morad, who was covered in blood, to stop charging him. This took several minutes. After receiving a TASER exposure and strikes from a baton, Morad told the officer that he was going to attack him and charged him again. However, there is no video of the incident. An investigation into the incident, physical evidence, and witness statements should provide a more detailed narrative of events.

– Ben Singleton

Subjects under the influence of mind-altering hallucinogens have been known to behave in very bizarre and unpredictable manners. The officer was by himself with no cover officer to assist. Morad was described to have been "covered in blood" presenting a blood borne pathogen exposure risk, was walking rapidly towards the officer and was ignoring lawful commands to stop. These factors would lead a person to believe that Morad was a credible physical threat to the officer and the use of the TASER device would be appropriate.

The deadly force application is less clear. It is clear that the fight was prolonged and the officer was most likely becoming fatigued. It is clear that the officer attempted non-deadly force options in order to effect the arrest and overcome Morad's resistance. What is not clear are the objective facts that specifically led the officer to believe that deadly force would be justified. It is clear that deadly force cannot be justified simply and only because an officer has attempted to use non-deadly force options.

This is not to say that I believe the officer's use of deadly force was inappropriate or that the details are not articulated in some statement in an investigative file. It does however serve as a chance to remind to officers of the importance of being "detailed and descriptive" in the force response reporting.

– Ed Flosi

Billy Collins, 56, White Male

Louisa, KY, May 29

Billy Collins was arrested by officers near a high school after acting erratically, wrecking his truck into a ditch, and yelling and cursing during the high school graduation. Collins was TASERED twice while at the Louisa Police Department after fighting with officers and barricading himself inside.

Collins reportedly struggled with mental illness for years, and recently had heart surgery[216].

Analysis

We truly don't have enough information here to conclude anything.

– Nick Selby

There is not enough information regarding the incident at the jail to develop an opinion on this case.

– Ben Singleton

In regards to the TASER device use, if Collins was fighting with the officers (i.e., a credible physical threat) then the use of the TASER device would be appropriate, even if used twice as long as the threat continued.

This case though is a good example of how the media tries to "spice it up" a little with death cases proximate to a TASER device use. Reading the headlines it would appear to the layperson that the death was caused by the .TASER device and in the body of the report they write it was used "several times." There is no evidence to lead to the conclusion that the TASER device use was a contributing factor to Collins' death, and the, "several times" is an exaggeration of, "twice."

Looking at his photo, Collins was no small person. In his agitated condition along with his apparent heart condition, a prolonged struggle in itself could expose him to a higher risk of sudden death.

– Ed Flosi

Ebin Proctor, 18, White Male

Cottonwood, AZ, May 30

Ebin Proctor was one of six passengers in a vehicle that police stopped for an equipment violation. During the stop, Proctor fled on foot, leading police on a chase. The deputy pursuing him says they got into a physical fight, and Proctor ended up shot. Proctor died from the gunshot wound. The deputy was treated for non-life-threatening injuries[217].

Analysis

There's not enough information to form an opinion on this case.

– Nick Selby

There is obviously too little information upon which to base any opinions in this case.

– Ben Singleton

There is not enough information in the material to draw any independent, reasoned conclusions as to the appropriateness of the officer's actions. Indeed, it is unknown if the officer fired the shot intentionally or unintentionally during a weapon retention struggle.

– Ed Flosi

Richard Davis, 50, Black Male

Rochester, NY, May 31

Richard Davis, driving a full-sized pickup, struck a parked car and then a church. He exited the truck and fled on foot. Witnesses said he returned to the truck after the fire department and police department arrived. Then, in the presence of the police and fire personnel on scene, Davis ignored commands to stop, got back into his truck, drove backward into a street sign and fence, then forward into a house, destroying the porch and knocking out the gas meter, causing a leak.

When the truck stopped working, Davis refused to get out. After about four or five minutes, Davis aggressively exited the truck and charged at officers with clenched fists. He refused to obey officers' commands. An officer used his TASER to stop Davis.

Davis went down, and officers handcuffed him, but they soon realized that he wasn't breathing and attempted to revive him. Davis died at a local hospital[218].

Analysis

Faced with a 300-lb man in the midst of running amok and destroying property charging at me, it's likely I would have TASERED him as well. The officer's use of force was justified. Davis' death was likely due to chronic health issues or acute drug intoxication, or both.

– Nick Selby

Given the totality of circumstances, I think it is fair to say that Davis was in an altered mental state, whether drug-induced or not. Also, according to family members, Davis weighed almost 300 pounds[219]. An officer who is being charged by an aggressive suspect must take size into consideration. TASER was probably this officer's only reasonable option in combating Davis. Autopsy reports have not been released, but I believe, based on Davis' behavior, the cause of death may be found in the toxicology portion of the autopsy.

– Ben Singleton

This event and the material provided clearly demonstrated that Davis had committed several crimes and was a credible physical threat to the officers. The use of the TASER device in this incident would be appropriate and consistent with current law enforcement training and standards.

– Ed Flosi

JUNE

Ross Anthony, 25, Black Male

Dallas, TX June 8

A number of 911 calls reported Anthony was running into traffic lanes, approaching vehicles and banging on the windows of nearby businesses. Dallas Fire-Rescue paramedics passing by observed this behavior and attempted to assist Anthony. He banged his fists on the hood of the ambulance and entered the vehicle of a passing motorist as officers arrived on scene. Officers tried to talk Anthony out of the car. After a negotiation, Anthony opened the door slightly and officers grabbed him. Anthony resisted as officers removed him from the car, and officer Paul Kessenich used his TASER[220]. Anthony began to show signs of medical distress shortly after he was handcuffed. Paramedics at the scene provided immediate medical attention to Anthony. Dallas Fire-Rescue transported Anthony to Baylor Medical Center at Dallas where he was pronounced dead[221].

Analysis

I suspect mental illness and acute narcotic intoxication, however no releases have been made about the disposition of the four officers involved, nor of the autopsy or toxicology reports of Mr. Anthony. It would appear from the reports and the multiple 911 calls that officers reacted to this behavior, behaved reasonably and attempted to use non-deadly force to end the incident.

– Nick Selby

The officers involved had no choice but to subdue Anthony to prevent him from harming himself or others. The TASER is used to reduce injuries to the officers and the suspect when dealing with a noncompliant suspect. His death was likely a result of excessive drug use, combined with the physical stress of the fight and TASER deployment.

– Ben Singleton

This is another case of a subject acting in a bizarre manner for some unknown reason. When the officers attempted to remove Anthony from the car, a legitimate law enforcement objective, Anthony began to physically resist. Struggling with a subject inside a car can be a dangerous undertaking due to the close quarters and leverage issues. It appears that the officer's use of the TASER device in this incident would be appropriate.

– Ed Flosi

Ryan Bolinger, 28, White Male

Des Moines, IA, June 9

At about 10:17 p.m. Bolinger pulled a 2000 Lincoln Sedan closely alongside a patrol car in a manner that made it so that the officer inside the car couldn't open his door. Bolinger got out and started acting "erratically" in a manner that was described as dancing or making unusual movements in the street, and odd, erratic behavior. Bolinger got back in his car and drove away, with the officer in pursuit at about 35 miles per hour.

About a mile south, Bolinger made a U-turn and stopped abruptly. The officer pulled in front of Bolinger at an angle to stop him from continuing. Officer Vanessa Miller stopped a short distance behind Bolinger's car[222]. Bolinger rapidly got out of his car and charged, or "walked with a purpose," toward Miller's squad car. When he was a short distance from Miller's driver's side window, she fired one round, shattering the rolled-up window and hitting Bolinger in the torso[223].

An internal police investigation cleared Miller, finding that she did not violate any administrative policies in the shooting[224].

Analysis

This shooting may well have violated no policies, but it is shocking to me that Miller would have not been indicted on this shooting. The idea that an officer can open fire at someone for "purposefully walking" towards a police officer stands contrary to everything about this country that protects people.

– Nick Selby

There is a difference between justification and necessity. This shooting was unnecessary. The police response was also tactically unsound.

– Ben Singleton

In order for a deadly force application to be justifiable, the officers must be able to articulate factors that would lead a reasonable officer to believe that the officer (or others) is in imminent danger of serious bodily injury or death. Unless there are some significant facts that we are not aware of, in this case I cannot see how the officer would be able to do that based on the material provided.

– Ed Flosi

Jeremy Linhart, 30, White Male

Findlay, OH, June 9
Linhart was a passenger in a 2003 Ford Focus driven by Ericka Wright when the vehicle was stopped at about 3 a.m. by Officer Andrew Rudnik for a turn-signal violation. Officer Aaron Flechtner assisted. Wright and Linhart were removed from the vehicle so the officers could conduct an inventory of the car's contents[225]. As Flechtner began the inventory, he discovered a Ruger .40-caliber handgun under the front passenger seat. According to the police department's internal investigation, as revealed in the grand jury testimony, Flechtner attempted to put Linhart in handcuffs for the officers' safety. Police said there was a "verbal" exchange between Flechtner and Linhart, and Linhart then resisted.

According to Lt. Robert Ring of the Findlay Police Department, "Flechtner saw the gun when he was conducting the vehicle impound inventory. He looked under the seat to confirm that it was a gun, was able to read Ruger on it, and then he got out of the car. He did not pull the gun out from under the seat, because he felt Linhart was close enough to interfere with Flechtner's clearing the gun. Linhart was standing within 10 feet of him and Flechtner approached Linhart and attempted to secure him in handcuffs. He told Linhart about the gun as he was handcuffing him and Linhart started to resist his handcuffing. Linhart, who had a broken ankle from a drunk driving crash a week earlier, fell as he tried to pull away from Flechtner. When Linhart fell, he was close to the open front passenger door, in the street lawn area. Linhart pulled himself into the front floor board area while Flechtner was on his back trying to pull him out. Flechtner fought with Linhart, striking him multiple times with his fist telling Linhart to submit so he could pull him out. Linhart continued to try and reach under the seat. When Linhart was able to get his right arm and hand under the seat, he was told to stop. Linhart didn't submit so Flechtner disengaged by getting off of Linhart and drawing his duty gun. He told Linhart to drop the gun and show his hands, and Linhart didn't. Flechtner then fired one shot into Linhart's chest. Other officers had arrived by that point (Flechtner called for help on his radio and announced that he had a man with a gun) and pulled Linhart out. The gun was then also pulled out from underneath the seat and secured. Officers rendered aid until EMS arrived[226]."

The gun was later tested at the Ohio Bureau of Investigation crime lab and Linhart's DNA was on the gun[227]. Heroin, cocaine, and methamphetamine were found in the vehicle. The Lucas County Coroner's Office listed the cause of death as a gunshot wound to the chest, with a "significant condition" listed as, "acute combined drug intoxication," and that amphetamine, methamphetamine, cocaine, ephedrine, oxycodone, and phenylpropanolamine were in Linhart's system[228].

Earlier in 2015, Linhart had been arrested on a charge of possession of cocaine. Linhart had been released on bond, but at the time of this incident there was an active warrant for his arrest on charges of violating that bond. No video (dash or body) was used by the Findlay Police Department at the time of the incident. An internal investigation by the Findlay Police Dept. cleared the officers involved of any wrongdoing. The criminal investigation by the Ohio Bureau of Criminal Investigation was forwarded to the Hancock County Prosecutor's Office and ultimately presented to the special Grand Jury, which decided on October 23, 2015 not to indict either officer. Both officers have been returned to active duty.

Analysis

The autopsy tells us that Linhart was on a lethal cocktail of amphetamine, methamphetamine, cocaine, ephedrine, oxycodone, and phenylpropanolamine at the time of his death. This alone would generally lead me to believe entirely the officer's account that Linhart was not behaving rationally and was moving towards where the weapon was. The official department press release[229] on the incident was unclear on certain aspects of the timing, however Lt. Ring clarified the sequence, and I have total confidence that Officer Flechtner was justified in his use of deadly force, and that he attempted everything before using it.

— Nick Selby

I have no problem with Officer Flechtner's use of deadly force in this case. A doped-up drug dealer reached for a gun while fighting the police. Flechtner responded appropriately.

— Ben Singleton

In this incident there were some tactical choices that could be debated. As far as the use of force though, it seems fairly clear. The officer saw a firearm under the front passenger seat where Linhart was seated. When the officers attempted to take Linhart into custody a struggle ensued. Linhart moved back into the passenger side of the vehicle and reached under the seat specifically where the gun was located. Linhart's actions demonstrated a clear intent to recover the firearm, thereby creating an imminent threat of serious bodily injury or death. The use of deadly force in this case would be appropriate.

— Ed Flosi

Kris Jackson, 22, Black Male

South Lake Tahoe, CA, June 15

Jackson was living with his girlfriend at the Tahoe Hacienda Inn. On June 15, 2015, police dispatch received a 911 call reporting a female crying and screaming in the room. Officers were dispatched and arrived on scene at 2:47 am. Two minutes later officers reported someone climbing out the back window of the room. Twenty seconds later, the officer reported shooting. According to media accounts, Jackson had been shot as he attempted to climb out of the hotel room window[230]. An ambulance was requested and arrived on scene six minutes later. Jackson was transported to Barton Memorial Hospital, where he died at approximately 5:00 am. The involved officer, Officer Joshua Klinge, made a verbal statement to supervisors at the time of the shooting that he perceived a deadly threat from Kris Jackson[231]. Klinge is under investigation by the department[232]. After interviews and a search of the crime scene, no firearm or other weapon was located[233]. The police referred several times to prior narcotics arrests of Jackson. Earlier in June, Jackson had been arrested by SLTPD officers for possession of several baggies of cocaine, scales and packaging materials, and on May 21st, 2015, Jackson had been arrested by SLTPD for a Sacramento failure to appear warrant relative to a drug possession charge.

Pursuant to the mutual aid Critical Incident Protocol, the investigation into the incident will be conducted jointly by SLTPD, El Dorado County Sheriff's Office and the El Dorado County District Attorney's Office. The Jackson family filed a wrongful death lawsuit and civil rights lawsuit in February, 2016[234], claiming that the officer never gave a warning, that the cause of death was a gunshot wound as Jackson tried to climb out of the window.

Analysis

That this case looks bad has not been helped by silence from the police department on the case in the months since the case, and refusal to comment publicly by police or district attorney representatives. From the available evidence, which is admittedly scant, this sounds suspicious. An officer waiting on the ground for a person attempting to escape from a window above him is generally not in any mortal danger. The officer has not made any statement about an overt act or movement by Jackson that could have led the officer to feel threatened, and from several media accounts, Jackson was climbing out the window with his legs dangling beneath him when he was shot. This sounds very much like an officer shooting someone for attempting to climb from a window, which would be an unjustified use of deadly force under all but the most specifically articulated of circumstances. We need more information from the police, the toxicology report, an indication of whether video or audio is available, and statements from one of the three separate police agencies that have been investigating this case since June of 2015 to opine further.

– Nick Selby

More information is needed to develop a conclusive opinion on this case. But it is a questionable case, based on the little we know. Unless a clear threat was posed by Jackson as he climbed out of the window, which seems unlikely, this shooting was unjustified.

– Ben Singleton

With the extremely limited information provided in the material, it is difficult to understand why the officer felt Jackson was a deadly threat. Unless some substantial factors are learned later to support the deadly force response, this case appears to have been an inappropriate use of deadly force.

– Ed Flosi

Jermaine Benjamin, 42, Black Male

Vero Beach, FL, June 16

Deputies responded at 3:42 am to multiple 911 calls[235] of a disturbance in the 4300 block of 35th Avenue after a caller said Jermaine Benjamin was "acting crazy" and several people were holding him down[236]. The sheriff's officer reported that calls had been made to this house at least 70 times[237]. Arriving deputies began CPR on Benjamin. Family members claim a deputy who was subduing Benjamin put his knee into the back of Benjamin's neck and kept his face pressed against the ground[238]. Benjamin was transported to the Indian River Medical Center where doctors pronounced him dead. The Medical Examiner ruled that Benjamin died of excited delirium after taking Flakka[239].

Analysis

The idea that this is a police killing is a little insulting. Officers showed up to multiple 911 calls of behavior completely consistent with acute flakka intoxication, to a house that had been the target of 70 prior calls, and according to media and witness accounts officers did what they could to save Benjamin's life. The family's claims of brutality are absurd, and the autopsy results that were released to the media (they have since been removed from the Sheriff's Department Facebook page, and the Sheriff's Office media relations phone went unanswered in March, 2016) stated cause of death was flakka induced excited delirium.

– Nick Selby

The fact that police officers are present when a death occurs doesn't make them complicit in it. Officers were called to the scene of an apparent drug overdose. Benjamin's death is likely a result of the drugs he ingested, combined with the physical stress of his violent episode and the struggle he had with others prior to police arrival.

– Ben Singleton

The officers apparently used some physical controlling force while on the ground to take Benjamin into custody. Officers are trained to take a person into custody in a prone position and to use body weight to help control the subject. Officers are trained to be cautious about placing direct weight onto certain parts of the subject's body including the neck. Even if the officer did do what family members claim there does not appear to be any evidence that those actions had anything to do with Benjamin's demise.

– Ed Flosi

Kevin Bajoie, 32, Black Male

Baton Rouge, LA, June 20

Bajoie was involved in a fight on Avenue C in Scotlandville, where responding officers used TASERs to subdue him. As the first responding officer approached Bajoie, he unexpectedly jumped up and attempted to attack the officer[240]. Observing the incident, two other responding officers, Jace Ducote and Maurice Duke moved in to assist[241]. "After observing the unprovoked, aggressive, erratic behavior displayed by BAJOIE, two different responding officers invoked less than lethal force [sic] by using their TASERs" according to the police press release[242], which refers to non-deadly force. Bajoie died later that day at Lane Regional Medical Center. Dr. William "Beau" Clark ruled that Bajoie's death was an accident due to drug intoxication after he ingested methamphetamine, amphetamine and synthetic marijuana[243].

Analysis

This is a fairly stock-standard account of a death caused by behavior engaged in by someone suffering from acute methamphetamine, amphetamine and synthetic marijuana intoxication. Officers responded with non-deadly force appropriately.

– Nick Selby

This is an absolutely justified use of the TASER. Bajoie died as a result of his drug use.

– Ben Singleton

The officers used appropriate non-deadly force (TASER device) in a situation that Bajoie was a clear and credible physical threat to the officers.

– Ed Flosi

Joshua Dyer, 34, White Male

Indianapolis, IN, June 23

At about 6:30 pm, officers approached an illegally parked vehicle to investigate. The occupants of the vehicle, driver Matthew Cole and passenger Joshua Dyer[244]: "were uncooperative, not providing truthful information, to the officer[245]." Without warning, the vehicle sped off from the officer, who gave pursuit. The vehicle disregarded several stop signs, as it fled officers and drove to North Keystone Avenue, turning east down an alley into the backyard of a residence and crashing into a fence. Officers exited their vehicles and ordered the driver and the passenger out of the vehicle at gunpoint. Cole exited his vehicle, then suddenly returned to the driver's side and put the car in reverse. Officers, fearing for their own safety, fired at the vehicle, hitting Dyer. The vehicle continued in reverse into the side yard of another residence where it became disabled. Cole was taken into custody. Dyer was pronounced dead at the scene.

Cole was initially charged with resisting law enforcement and operating a vehicle without a driver's license. He was later charged with felony charges for possession of an altered gun, and two felony charges for possession of less than 5 grams of methamphetamine, and possession of narcotic drug (less than 5 grams) as an enhancement crime. He was also charged with three misdemeanor charges, including possession of a handgun without a license and an infraction for possession of paraphernalia[246].

Analysis

The officers state that the vehicle was heading towards them and that prompted them to fire, in fear for their lives. The threat was averted when the vehicle changed direction and crashed through another fence. The later arrest of Cole on gun and drug charges might explain the behavior during the stop, but is not relevant to the use of deadly force. The use of force against the driver was justified. It is concerning to me that the passenger was hit. I have reservations about the reasonableness of this case.

– Nick Selby

This case concerns me. The purpose of shooting at the driver is to stop the acceleration of the car, preserving the lives of the officers or others in its direct line of travel. This is the only acceptable use of deadly force that I am aware of for this kind of incident.

To use the fact that the vehicle is being driven in opposition to the police officer's orders, and in the general direction of the officers, as justification to shoot at the car has less to do with the preservation of officer lives and more to do with a preconceived justification to shoot.

What further complicates this case is that the passenger, who did not have control of the vehicle, was shot. Was the passenger targeted, or was his death unintentional? The only acceptable target, if the goal is to stop a vehicular assault, is the driver of the vehicle. Otherwise the officers just recognized that the situation presented the justification needed for sending rounds into the car, regardless of necessity, and did so. Based on my experience, it is likely that the officers were conditioned to respond this way.

– Ben Singleton

This is an unfortunate situation where a subject actually not even causing the threat factors was killed due to the irresponsible and criminal actions of the driver. The officers were attempting to take the occupants into custody with verbal persuasion but Cole chose to change the situation by getting back into the vehicle and reversing it back towards the officers. The officers felt they were in imminent danger of serious bodily injury or death and fired towards the oncoming vehicle, unfortunately striking the passenger.

– Ed Flosi

Spencer McCain, 41, Black Male

Owings Mills, MD, June 25
Police received a 911 call about a possible domestic disturbance at the condominium in the 3000 block of Hunting Ridge Drive in Owings Mills

shortly after 1 a.m.[247]. The caller to 911 stated that her granddaughter resided at the location and had called her because her mother and father were fighting[248]. The caller said that a woman who stated that McCain threatened to beat her, was in the condo with her two young children[249]. Once at the scene, Baltimore County Police Department Officer Wilkes (a six year veteran); Officer Besaw (an eight year veteran); and Officer Stargel (a five year veteran) heard a loud commotion and forced their way into the second-floor condo. After unsuccessfully trying to get someone to answer the door, three officers forced their way inside in fear that someone's life might be in danger[250]. Police say there was a protective order barring McCain from going to the home. Police said the first officer to arrive knew of a history of domestic violence calls at the home[251]. Since 2012, police said, officers responded to 911 calls for the address 17 times, including for several reports of fighting. When police arrived, police say that McCain took a "defensive position," making movements that led officers to believe he had a weapon. Three officers, believing McCain had a weapon, opened fire, but no weapon was found. In an email, the Baltimore County Police Department tells us that the Baltimore County State's Attorney's Office has ruled this shooting justified, and all of the officers involved in this incident are back on full duty status[252].

Analysis

McCain was a known-violent individual threatening serious injury to the people in the home, who had previously demonstrated sufficient fear of McCain that a judge had seen fit to issue an order of protection against him (note that an order of protection is significantly more actionable than a "restraining order," which is a civil, not a criminal, court order). Arriving officers knew McCain – perhaps from the 17 prior calls to the home, that included calls about fighting. So officers were prepared for a violent person. In this context, McCain's actions could easily lead me to believe that officers would believe McCain was acting in a manner that threatened deadly force. It seems from these facts that these officers behaved in a manner that was justified.

– Nick Selby

Domestic violence calls are some of the most dangerous encounters for police officers. The fact that the incidents usually take place in the unfamiliar homes of the involved parties puts police at an immediate disadvantage.

The officers reportedly believed that McCain had a weapon. Unfortunately, McCain was unarmed and the officers were wrong. So the burden is on the officers to adequately articulate the reason that they feared for their lives. While I am sure that the officers' reports of the incident are far more descriptive than reports by the media, they have not been made public. In my view, a "defensive position" does not adequately describe a necessity for the use of deadly force. This is perhaps one of the reasons the public has developed distrust for the police. Although this shooting may have been justified, one can't come to that conclusion based on the description provided by the media.

Officers also need to understand that, when giving a description of events, phrases like "defensive position" are inadequate. If the officer's report stated that "McCain dropped his right foot back, raised his left hand out in front of his body, and reached for the small of his back with his right hand, as if he was preparing to draw and fire a weapon," we would immediately recognize McCain's behavior as life-threatening.

– Ben Singleton

Here is another case where the officer's perceptions may have been influenced by previous information. The officers had several previous contacts with McCain that involved violence. The officers were most likely primed and ready for another violent confrontation with McCain. When the officers went to contact McCain on this incident, McCain took some stance that led all three officers to believe he was armed. It would be good to know more about McCain's body position/movements and whether or not the officers thought they saw an object that in the end was mistaken for a gun. What is compelling is that all three officers fired, thereby indicating a "reasonable officer" standard was in play as to the perceptions.

Based on his actions and behaviors at the time and the prior contacts, it could lead an officer to believe that their life was in imminent danger of serious bodily injury or death, thereby making the use of deadly force appropriate.

– Ed Flosi

JULY

Kevin Judson, 24, Black Male

McMinnville, OR, July 1

Deputy Richard Broyles shot Judson after Judson struggled with him, then jumped into his patrol car and tried to drive away. According to KATU: "As Broyles arrived on the scene, he saw Judson fleeing, pulled his patrol car into a parking lot, parked it and gave chase on foot. During a foot chase the suspect ignored repeated commands to "stop" and "get on the ground[253]." The deputy fired his TASER, but it failed to stop the suspect. The video shows the suspect getting into the deputy's patrol car.

Broyles struggled with Judson for control of the car; the deputy drew his handgun and continued to order the man to give up. At that point Judson gunned the motor, according to witnesses. During the struggle for the car, the suspect's hand was near the deputy's loaded AR-15-style rifle, which was mounted in the car. As Judson began to drive off - with the deputy's hand stuck in the door! - Broyles opened fire. After the first shot hit Judson in the arm, Broyles freed himself as Judson put the car in reverse. Broyles' second shot hit the door jam. The car crashed into an electrical tower. Broyles fired two more times, one bullet hitting the passenger's door, the other striking Judson in the head. Judson died at the scene. According to KATU, "Deputy Broyles at the time he fired his weapon was reasonably in fear for his own life. He too, reasonably believed that to allow Judson to flee in the patrol vehicle, based on all that had transpired, could pose a significant threat to the community…"

Prosecutors released two videos[254] of the altercation and the incident. What can be seen is the deputy in an apparent struggle with someone who steals his car and attempts to drive away.

Analysis

Officers know how many weapons are in police cars, and the idea that a criminal can steal a police car and drive away in it presents multiple dangers. On their own, these might not be sufficient reasons to use deadly force, but Judson went well beyond actions that would be "iffy" – this was an absolutely clear case of the deputy believing that Judson had every intent to continue using deadly force and a justified use of deadly force.

– Nick Selby

This case appears to be a completely reasonable use of deadly force by the officer, and one that is easily justified. The quick release of information and video by the DA is refreshing, and should be emulated by other agencies.

– Ben Singleton

For every rule, there is almost always an exception. As stated before, I'm not an advocate for jumping into a moving (or potentially moving) vehicle unless there are exigent circumstances to do so (February 28, Thomas Allen). This appears to be one of those exceptions to the rule. There have also been previous discussions about the appropriateness of using deadly force against a subject who is simply walking towards (June 9, Ryan Bolinger) or getting into the driver's seat of a police vehicle (January 26, Joshua Garcia). This case differs from the others in critical facts and circumstances.

Judson was not only attempting to control the police vehicle, but the deputy saw the subject placing his hand near the patrol rifle. It would be reasonable to at least physically attempt to prevent the person from taking the police vehicle, since there are many accessible weapons within it. Once his hand was trapped by the closing door and he was physically committed, the situation deteriorated rapidly for the deputy. It would be reasonable for him to believe that he was in imminent danger of serious bodily injury or death as the vehicle moved forward. He fired one shot.

The deputy freed his hand after the first shot, but the threat Judson presented continued with his dangerously reckless and violent behavior. Indeed, the subject had committed a crime involving the threatened infliction of serious bodily injury and would be considered a threat to continue his violence if allowed to escape. It appears that the subsequent shots would be appropriate and consistent with current law enforcement standards and training.

– Ed Flosi

William Jeffries, 57, White Male

Weston, WV, July 1

There's not a lot here: Weston officers were called to a disturbance involving Jeffries, who was believed to be drunk and reportedly urinating in public near a business[255]. Officer Eric Riddle approached Jeffries and asked him to take a breathalyzer; Jeffries refused, and the two scuffled. During the scuffle, as Riddle tried to subdue Jeffries, Jeffries' neck struck the cruiser, breaking it, and Jeffries died. Riddle was suspended pending an investigation, but was cleared by an internal investigation conducted by the Weston Police Department. This was announced in July, 2015, and we cannot find anything further about the incident, nor can we find an autopsy.

Analysis

This was ruled as justified. Sure would be nice to have some facts.

– Nick Selby

This looks like it was an unintended injury sustained during a fight that resulted in Jeffries' death, but we have no details about how it happened.

– Ben Singleton

Although no real information about the "scuffle" was present in the material, this may be a good example of the actual injury not matching the expectations of the officer during the fight. It is important to remember that an officer's force response must be evaluated on the reasonable expectation of injury based on the force option(s) used and the manner in which it was used. That means that in evaluating the force response, we must look at the reasonably expected injury and not necessarily the actual outcome, in this case a broken neck and death. If one uses the actual injury in this case, the officers would have to articulate a deadly force threat in order to balance the force factors with the level of force used. But in this case, it appears that the broken neck and death was not the expected result, and therefore should not be part of the analysis. It appears that the actual injury and the resulting death was not the expected outcome of the struggle or the force used by the officer during the struggle.

– Ed Flosi

Christian Siqueiros, 25, Hispanic Male

Montclair, CA, July 3

NBC Los Angeles reports - in the video, not the written story accompanying the video - that an unnamed witness, "the neighbor who called authorities" who "did not want to go on camera," said that Siqueiros was "acting strangely" and that his eyes were glazed over. Police ordered him to the ground and the man who called in the authorities said that the arrest was orderly and not forceful[256]." NBC continues, "Siqueiros allegedly "became combative" when police arrived, and officers took him into custody, police said. While in custody, Siqueiros went into cardiac arrest and later died at the hospital, police said."

Analysis

This is another case that requires investigation, if only because no autopsy has been released that is publicly available, and no officers have been charged – the case seems to have disappeared. Witnesses claim that Siqueiros was "piled on" by five or six officers and I question whether the healthy 25-year-old could have had a heart attack. I note that the neighbor who called police reported that his eyes were glazed and that he was behaving suspiciously, which is consistent with acute drug intoxication. However the lack of autopsy makes any further analysis impossible.

– Nick Selby

This case may be easily explained, but the lack of available information prevents any substantive analysis.

– Ben Singleton

It appears that the only force options used in this case were controlling force and body weight, which would be appropriate in this situation. It would also be appropriate for several officers to assist in the apprehension process of a person as described in this incident. Any working cop that has tried to control a drug-crazed violently resisting subject will understand the need for more than one or two officers. The witness claim of officers piling on the subject is interesting but not overly compelling. It is highly unlikely that five or six officers would be able to place their entire body weight onto the subject. It would require more investigation to determine if the weight placed onto the subject would clinically impair the respiratory process. It is critical that officers are trained to reasonably modulate and control the amount/type of pressure placed on the subject in order to overcome the subject's resistance and mitigate the possibilities of causing compressional asphyxia.

– Ed Flosi

John Deming, Jr., 19, White Male

Pleasonton, CA, July 5

This is one of two very similar incidents in different parts of the country that ultimately led to the police killing of an unarmed young man with a promising future, but who chose bizarrely to engage in some incredibly uncharacteristic malicious mischief.

John Deming broke into the showroom of Specialty Sales Classics, which sells classic cars, and began to destroy both property and vehicles – kicking, defacing and scratching vehicles, and smashing windows. Specialty Sales Classics salesman Jeremy Bolen says the hood of a 1967 Mustang was scrawled on with a sharpie. The suspect even walked on a Cadillac worth $115,000. "There's a bunch of other damage. Graffiti in the bathroom," he added[257]. NBC Bay Area continues: "Initially police said Deming was found in front of the business, but clarified Tuesday he was still inside but could be seen through the dealership's large front windows. Deming allegedly threw a 50-pound floor jack through the window, which landed on the sidewalk near the officers. Police fired at him with a beanbag round but missed, and Deming refused commands to leave the dealership, police said."

Deming then ran out the back through a broken window[258]. NBC continues, "[Officer Daniel] Kunkel was standing watch in the back of the business and saw Deming jump through the broken window. Kunkel ordered him to stop but Deming kept running, and Kunkel hit him in the back with a Taser, according to police. The Taser didn't stop Deming, and Kunkel started to chase him until Deming turned and charged Kunkel aggressively, police said. Deming allegedly kicked Kunkel in the stomach and punched him in the head, knocking him to the ground. Deming got on top of Kunkel, pummeling his head as he lay on the concrete, police said. Kunkel thought he might lose consciousness and used his Taser again, but again it had no effect, so he drew his pistol and shot Deming once in the torso. However, even that didn't stop Deming and he continued his attack, police said. Kunkel then fired two more rounds, hitting Deming at least once in the face, police said." Later reports stated that the autopsy found Deming free of drugs[259].

Analysis

Like the case of 19-year-old Christian Taylor in Arlington, TX, this is a bizarre situation, but it seems very clear that the officers attempted multiple alternatives to deadly force. It was not until a serious fight with an officer, in which the officer reports being beaten seriously, that the officer used deadly force. This seems very much like justified use of deadly force by the officer in a tragic story.

– Nick Selby

Free of drugs? Deming was a 19-year-old kid who was behaving like a complete lunatic. The likelihood that he was "free of drugs" is extremely minute. There are many synthetic drugs that do not show up in toxicology testing, and many of these synthetic drugs cause users to behave in similarly disturbing ways. Deming appears to have been under the influence of one of these mind-altering synthetic drugs. The officer, taking on serious injury, had no choice but to end the fight. His use of deadly force was reasonable.

– Ben Singleton

We will most likely never truly know what drove Deming to these actions. That being said, his actions and the officers' reactions and force responses are well documented. After several attempts to take Deming into custody with the use of non-deadly force options failed and he was pursued on foot, Deming chose to engage officer Kunkel in a dangerous ground struggle, punching him in the head and kicking him. During the ground struggle, Deming continued his assault on Kunkel up to the point that Kunkel felt he might lose consciousness. Kunkel demonstrated restraint and attempted to stop the assault using the TASER. The two men's close proximity would have lessened the effect of the TASER to cause more than localized pain unlikely to deter a dedicated resister. The use of deadly force in this incident appears to have been appropriate and consistent with current law enforcement standards and training.

– Ed Flosi

Johnny Ray Anderson, 43, Hispanic Male

Hawaiian Gardens, CA, July 5
KTLA reported that, "A 911 caller reported a man was knocking on his or her door and attempting to get inside the house, located in the 12200 block of 216th Street, around 9:40 p.m. Sunday[260]." NBC Los Angeles reported: "The family said Johnny Ray Anderson was knocking on the home's door because he wanted to escape authorities, but authorities said on Sunday that deputies came after the report of a prowler."[261] The Los Angeles Times added: "Johnny Ray Anderson was listed on a gang injunction and didn't want to be arrested, Kathleen Anderson said. At the sight of law enforcement, he climbed over a fence into a neighboring property. About seven hours later, a detective said he was dead."

Analysis

There is so little to go on here that I cannot even hazard a guess. What is more concerning is that as I write this in February, 2016, there is still precious little to be found on this incident. The very paucity of facts this late in the game suggests something's not right. In September, 2015, the Hews Media Group[262] reported that the autopsy in the case contradicted the deputy's account of the incident – the deputy had claimed that Anderson had reached for the Deputy's weapon, but the autopsy is said by Hews to establish that Anderson was six feet from the deputy when the deputy fired. No link was given to the autopsy report.

– Nick Selby

We have got to get better about informing the public. We are losing the public trust because of this secrecy and refusal to release information. No assessment of this incident can be made based on the limited information provided by the agency.

– Ben Singleton

Not enough information is known about this incident to develop a reasoned independent opinion on the force response. All we know is that Anderson was the subject in a prowler incident, who appears to have attempted escape and was shot by the deputy. The autopsy results are not conclusive, as the subject could have attempted to disarm the deputy, but the deputy was able to separate and gain distance. The subject could have then re-advanced at the deputy with the apparent intent to try to gain control of the deputy's weapon.

On the counter-side, if there was a fence between the deputy and the subject after the deputy was able to disengage, it would be considerably more difficult to justify the shooting.

– Ed Flosi

Shane Gormley, 30, White Male

Ogden, UT, July 6

Mr. Gormley was killed by the Utah State patrol when he suffered a heart attack after being TASED four times. Mr. Gormley had been on work-release from jail (where he was serving time on a retail theft conviction) when he escaped. He stole a motorcycle, got stopped by the state police on a traffic charge, and used the motorcycle to escape again. He followed this by stealing a car from Wasatch Front Kia. According to FOX13, police then "went to the apartment where Gormley's girlfriend lives near 24th St. and D Ave. in Ogden. They saw him jump from the apartment window and speed off in her car. Troopers chased Gormley to 21st St., where they boxed him in but he ran from the car and tried to carjack others[263]."

Authorities said he tried to carjack a truck and trailer but didn't get in. After that, according to KSL.com, "Investigators looking for Gormley found him Monday. He attempted to escape by jumping into a car driven by a 53-year-old woman. He punched, scratched and bit the woman in an attempt to get her out of the car, according to the UHP[264]. Troopers used Tasers on Gormley four times before taking him into custody. After he was handcuffed, shackled and taken out of the car, Gormley went into cardiac arrest, according to the UHP. Gormley was taken to McKay-Dee Hospital Center where he was placed in a medically induced coma." He later died. KSL continues, "Tests showed [Gormley] was under the influence of methamphetamine and opiates at the time." FOX13 reports that the medically induced coma was necessary precisely because of the amount of methamphetamine in Gormley's system.

Analysis

An escaped prisoner, motorcycle-and-car-thief, carjacking, female-assaulting, meth-head junkie on a rampage. Thank God the cops were there.

– Nick Selby

"The medically induced coma was necessary precisely because of the amount of methamphetamine in Gormley's system." That pretty much sums it up for me.

– Ben Singleton

In his desperate attempts to escape, and in the course of committing several other different crimes along the way, Gormley demonstrated an intense level of "dedication" to not being recaptured. The violence of carjacking and viciously attacking the person in the car affirms the subject's complete lack of concern for the welfare of anyone else that got in his way, including the public and officers alike.

In this situation, when the subject demonstrated an immediate threat to officers and others, the use of a TASER was completely appropriate and consistent with current law enforcement training and practices. Using the TASER four times might have also been appropriate, as long as the subject remained a threat. While the TASER International guidelines caution against using the TASER device more than three cycles of five-seconds (or 15 seconds total), these are only manufacturer guidelines and are not legal standards.

– Ed Flosi

Jonathan Sanders, 39, Black Male

Stonewall, MS, July 8

Sanders, driving a horse-drawn buggy[265], ran into Officer Kevin Herrington in a subdivision. He pulled into the front yard of a home owned by his cousin, where the two confronted one another. Police Chief Mike Street said in grand jury testimony it was established that Herrington had been monitoring traffic when he saw Sanders' horse-drawn buggy and a vehicle which had pulled alongside it in a suspicious manner that indicated a possible drug transaction. When Sanders saw Herrington, the transaction was moved[266].

Officer Herrington knew the second party and pulled him over because he believed the man had outstanding warrants, but the man produced proof of payment of the warrants. Herrington continued investigating and came to believe that Sanders was in possession of cocaine that he intended to sell. As Herrington patted-down Sanders, Herrington found cocaine in a plastic sandwich-type bag. Herrington placed the bag on the hood of his vehicle and went to continue the pat-down.

Sanders then grabbed the bag of cocaine, stuck it in his mouth, and began to run, Street said. Herrington gave chase, and the two ended up in a physical altercation. Street said Herrington was not able to finish the search on Sanders, so he didn't know if he was armed or not. When Sanders went for Herrington's weapon, the officer put him in a headlock. This ultimately led to the strangulation.

Sanders had a modest arrest record dating to 2001 that included disturbance of the family peace, sale of a counterfeit substance, and domestic violence. The grand jury[267] report said that Sanders' death was a result of "mechanical asphyxia associated with acute cocaine toxicity," and earlier media reports stated that a preliminary autopsy[268] showed "manual asphyxiation," but had been awaiting toxicology results. The grand jury refused to indict Herrington.

Analysis

This case looked far more suspicious than it turned out to be because of the total silence of authorities regarding the reason for the initial stop and the altercation, and the flat-out weirdness of the horse-drawn carriage, and for the leak of information regarding the preliminary autopsy results. Hearing the entire story it seems considerably more plausible and reasonable than prior to learning the details. Still, even after a grand jury no-bill, we still don't have enough details to truly understand the struggle sufficiently to form an opinion. This is preventable, and very frustrating.

– Nick Selby

We would need more details about the struggle to determine whether or not it was reasonable for the officer to strangle Sanders. But if Sanders did attempt to disarm the officer, the use of deadly force would be reasonable.

– Ben Singleton

In this case, as with many others, we begin by looking at the reason for the contact. Was there properly articulated reasonable suspicion during the initial contact to detain Sanders, or probable cause to arrest him. If there is a legal justification for the contact/stop, then we can move on to the analysis of the force response. If not, we have already identified a problem. This is why it is critical for officers to clearly articulate the reason(s) why the contact was made, and articulate the proper standards of a detention or arrest.

The information about what happened during the struggle is varied at best. The information ranges from reports that the subject and officer fighting for control over the officer's weapon to witnesses who state that was no threat present. The autopsy indicates the cause of death to be strangulation. Most experts would agree that strangling a person to the point of causing death is a high level of force response, one that must be justified with a high level of threat and resistance, and not just to keep a person from swallowing drugs (I'm not saying this is what the motive of the officer was, but only using it as an example). With what we know and the lack of any type of reconcilable timeline to evaluate, it would be difficult to make a reasoned opinion on the force response.

– Ed Flosi

Anthony Dewayne Ware, 35, Black Male

Tuscaloosa, AL, July 10

A caller to the East Precinct of the Tuscaloosa Police Department identified Anthony Ware by name and description as standing at a certain place in the city. The caller stated that Ware was wanted on a warrant and for parole violation, and stated that Ware was armed with a "little" .22 caliber weapon[269]. The same caller called back to specify another location where Ware was standing and directed officers to him, and called back a third time to specify Ware's clothing as being a gray shirt, gray black and white camo shorts, and to specify that the .22 was a pistol. The East Precinct officer who had taken the call, Mason, then correctly relayed to 911 the full name and description and location of Ware, on whom Mason had confirmed an active arrest warrant on charges of attempting to elude arrest. The 911 operator sounded familiar with Ware and said she would dispatch several officers, especially due to the pistol[270]. The radio repeated the name and description, and advised officers of the gun. The sheriff's office later stated that there was an open warrant for Ware on charges of domestic violence strangulation, but this information was not passed on to officers. Officers saw Ware, who fled, running into the woods. When he confronted officers, they pepper sprayed Ware and were able to handcuff him and report him in custody at 9:38 pm. Minutes later, it was reported Ware was suffering from shortness of breath. Ware lost consciousness soon after. He was given CPR on the scene by an officer who was cross-certified as a paramedic, and later by medical personnel, and he was pronounced dead at DCH at 10:42 p.m.[271]

The Alabama Department of Forensic Sciences completed its Report of Autopsy. An official police statement read, "The toxicologist indicated that Mr. Ware had recently consumed cocaine, methamphetamine, and alcohol. Based on their examinations and analyses, the medical examiner concluded that Mr. Ware's death was caused by complications of drug toxicity. It was noted that although Mr. Ware had an enlarged heart and thyroid and that these conditions would have caused greater danger to himself by ingesting these types of drugs, there was nothing revealed in the close examination of his lungs to indicate that he had asthma. Finally, the medical examiner also indicated that Mr. Ware had a number of minor and superficial injuries to his upper extremities and a small superficial bruise to his back that likely resulted from his running through rough patches of terrain or bushes and that none of these external injuries were relevant to his death[272]."

Analysis

The Tuscaloosa Police Department exhibited tremendous transparency on this case, releasing all audio and video recordings they had[273]. Listening to these and watching the video one can only conclude that the agency's staff followed procedure, entered a dangerous situation, dealt with a fleeing man as compassionately as possible, handled his medical emergency as professionally as could possibly be expected, without emotion, rancor or anger, and ultimately behaved reasonably in all respects. I strongly urge you to listen to and watch the released documentation. The agency also requested an external investigation by the Department of Justice. At every step of this incident, TPD has been a model to be emulated.

– Nick Selby

As in many other cases, the toxicology report is where we find the cause of death. The officers' response to Ware, reportedly an armed suspect, was appropriate and reasonable. Pepper spray was used to subdue Ware safely and effectively. His death was probably a result of his heavy drug use, combined with the physical exertion associated with a foot chase and physical altercation with police. I second Nick's feelings regarding the handling of this incident by the TPD.

– Ben Singleton

In this event, the responding officers had a lot of intelligence on Ware, including his name, description, location and the fact he was armed. When they attempted to make contact with Ware, he fled into the woods. This is a dangerous situation for the pursuing officers, especially in the hours of darkness during which the subject could easily hide and lay in wait for the officers. When the officers caught up to Ware, they used OC Spray to effect the arrest. Based on the totality of the facts and circumstances known to the officers, it would be reasonable to believe that Ware was a threat and that some force response would be appropriate to effect the arrest. The question lays in the lack of details regarding Ware's actions at the time of the OC Spray application. If Ware was still actively resisting and reasonably perceived as a threat, then OC Spray would be appropriate.

– Ed Flosi

George Mann, 53, Male of Unknown Race

Stone Mountain, GA, July 11
Officers responded around 4:15 a.m. on July 11 to a call reporting an individual acting "crazy" in the caller's garage at 5100 Rock Place Drive in unincorporated Stone Mountain. The caller said "his male neighbor was locked in his garage, was irate and possibly armed."[274] The Atlanta Journal-Constitution reported that, "Officers made contact with the man and "an altercation ensued." "The suspect went unresponsive at the scene and was transported to Eastside Medical Center where he was pronounced dead."[275] The Georgia Bureau of Investigation told the

Gwinnett Daily Post that "Mann was stunned with the TASER when he resisted the officers and went unresponsive at the scene. He was transported to Eastside Medical Center where he was pronounced dead." The GBI also noted that "a gun and suspected methamphetamine were found in the garage where Mann was [arrested]," according to the Daily Post.

Analysis

When an irate man who has methamphetamine and a gun starts fighting with officers and resists a TASER, I suspect methamphetamine-induced psychosis. No autopsy has been publicly released, nor have any officers been charged, however, this looks, sadly, routine in dealing with the national scourge of methamphetamine addiction.

– Nick Selby

I have seen this drug, methamphetamine, turn otherwise good people into the embodiment of all that is evil, dirty, and depraved. Methamphetamine-induced psychosis is known to users as "speed-tripping." It often causes extreme excitability and paranoia. There aren't many details about the altercation, but, given Mann's apparent use of methamphetamines and the state of psychosis the officers found him in, it's likely that his death was a result of the combination of heavy narcotics use, the resulting psychosis, and the physical stress associated with the struggle.

– Ben Singleton

With the limited amount of information available, it appears to have been appropriate to use a TASER. The officers were faced with a subject in the midst of a methamphetamine fueled rage who appears to have struggled with the officers. At some point during the process, the TASER was used. This would be an appropriate force response that is consistent with current law enforcement training and practices.

– Ed Flosi

Salvado Ellswood, 36, Black Male

Plantation, FL, July 12

Officer Erik Carlton was on a foot patrol behind a medical office complex when he encountered Ellswood at about 8:48 p.m.[276] When Carlton ordered Ellswood to leave the property, Ellswood punched him in the face.[277] Carlton fought back and used his TASER to no effect. When Ellswood continued to attack, Carlton fired several shots.

Plantation police Detective Philip Toman told media, including Local10, that Ellswood, who had been released from prison on June 19, "had an extensive arrest record, including acts of violence towards law enforcement officers. He also had an active warrant out for his arrest."[278]

Analysis

On its face, responding with a gun to a punch seems extreme and I would have serious questions about how a punch could be considered deadly force. Other factors, including the physical differences between the men, the layout of the site of the encounter, or several others, are unknown. The officer reportedly attempted to end an assault on his person from a person it would appear the officer knew, with a non-deadly force solution—the TASER—and when that failed and the attack did not stop, the officer fired, killing the man.

– Nick Selby

A punch to the face does not justify the use of deadly force, unless the officer can articulate how the punch caused him to fear for his life. I've done a bit of amateur boxing and can attest to the paralyzing effects of a solid blow to the head. If Officer Carlton experienced disorientation that would severely diminish his ability to defend himself against the attack and cause him to fear for his life, the shooting was reasonable.

– Ben Singleton

While it appears clear that the subject physically attacked the officer and the that officer first attempted to use the TASER to prevent continuing attack, the threat level and resistance of the subject were not fully known. The use of the TASER in this situation would be considered appropriate by most sound-minded evaluators. It is what happens after the TASER being used that isn't as clear.

I am not saying the deadly force application is inappropriate, but I am saying there is not enough information to provide a reasoned opinion. Just because a TASER fails doesn't necessarily make a deadly force application appropriate.

- Ed Flosi

Bruce Stafford, 55, White Male

Hendersonville, NC, July 13
55-year-old Bruce Dean Stafford became combative and fought with officers as he was being booked into jail for stealing puppies[279]. After a brief scuffle Stafford collapsed. Jail staff, as well as Hendersonville firefighters and the county EMS, tried to revive Stafford. He was taken to Pardee Hospital where he was pronounced dead.[280]

In February, 2016, District Attorney Greg Newman announced that no charges would be filed against the officers, stating that the decedent's health was responsible for his death. "I have reviewed the investigative reports provided by the SBI and have concluded that the officers' actions did nothing to cause the death of Mr. Stafford," Newman said in a news release.[281] "Without getting too personal about his medical history, Mr. Stafford's autopsy showed that his heart attack at the jail was caused by the pre-existing conditions of heart disease and from an enlarged heart, among other long standing health issues. No one knows why he was so belligerent with the officers, but clearly he was not a person in good health and the officers gave him every opportunity to handle the situation differently.

Analysis
The incident was video-recorded and investigators found no wrong-doing. That, plus the autopsy finding that the cause of death was health-related, pretty much seals the deal.

Stealing puppies?

– Nick Selby

Fighting with the police is probably not a recommended activity for heart patients.

– Ben Singleton

This is another case where it is impossible to independently opine on the force response, due to the complete lack of information, other than an investigation by the District Attorney's Office concluding no wrongdoing on the part of the officers.

– Ed Flosi

Albert Davis, 23, Male of Unknown Race

Orlando, FL, July 17

Orlando police were called to the pool area of an apartment complex near the intersection of Curry Ford Road and South Conway Road after a fight broke out among five people, including Davis. When Officer Kelvin Vidro confronted Davis, he took off running, but was caught about 100 yards away[282]. Instead of surrendering, "Davis chose to fight with the officer," Chief John Mina said. "Based on the physical evidence at the scene and radio transmissions, it appears there was a very, very violent struggle there," Mina said. "Our officer did use his TASER at some point during the struggle and a lot of his equipment, to include his Taser, baton, gun magazine, wristwatch and ball cap, were strewn about the scene of this violent struggle." Mina said Vidro fired his gun one time, hitting Davis in the chest. Police attempted CPR until paramedics arrived. Davis was taken to a local hospital, where he was first listed in critical condition, then later died."

Analysis

So much of this is consistent with an officer in a fight that got, in the chief's words, "very, very violent." Deploying the TASER before deploying deadly force shows me an officer thinking through his options and escalating his tools as he felt warranted. The length of the struggle and the distance over which the fight took place looks nothing like an officer escalating to use of deadly force without a lot of consideration.

– Nick Selby

Based on the evidence, it appears that Officer Vidro was engaged in a legitimate fight for his life. Police officers do not generally doff equipment while engaging a suspect. The fact that the officer's weaponry and personal items were "strewn about the scene" indicates a very violent struggle.

An officer can also become exhausted very quickly during a 100-yard foot pursuit, while wearing about 30 pounds of equipment and a chest compressing ballistic vest. The fact that the officer fought Davis for as long as he did, and the fact that the officer used his TASER prior to his gun, is a testament to his continued assessment of the situation, and to his ultimate need to use deadly force to end the conflict, which was absolutely reasonable.

– Ben Singleton

The officer chased the subject for approximately 100 yards prior to catching up. Once he caught up, it appears the officer engaged with Davis in a prolonged and violent struggle. The struggle caused the officer to attempt use his TASER, most likely at very close range, which would preclude any neuro-muscular incapacitation effect. In other words, it would have only caused pain. During the continuing struggle, other force options that would have been available were the ones which were "strewn" about. Again, this indicates not only the violence of the struggle, but how the officer lost force options to turn to in his decision-making process. All these factors, combined with how he chased Davis and engaged in the prolonged violent struggle in which Davis refused to yield, could exhaust an officer to a level that would create a risk of his being overpowered, seriously injured or killed. The use of deadly force appears to have been appropriate in this incident and consistent with current law enforcement standards and training.

Darrius Stewart, 19, Black Male

Memphis, TN, July 17

Stewart was pulled over for a broken headlight, and Officer Connor Schilling placed an un-handcuffed and cooperative Stewart in the back of his squad car while Schilling ran Stewart's name. The TBI investigation found two separate warrants for Stewart from two states, including one for sexual assault of a minor, and one for resisting arrest.

The Tennessee Bureau of Investigation says[283] that when Officer Schilling returned to the police car to place Stewart under arrest for the outstanding felony warrants, Stewart resisted and both men ended up fighting. Cellphone video caught part of the fight, and shows both men on the ground fighting.[284] WMC Television reported that, "When the officer opened the back door to handcuff Stewart, he kicked the door and attacked the officer." WMC continued, "During the fight, Stewart grabbed the officer's handcuffs and swung them at him[285]."

In the TBI file, Officer Schilling said it was during the scuffle in the grassy area where he began to fear for his life, as he became winded and exhausted when Stewart grabbed his handcuffs and began swinging them as a weapon. The officer grabbed his gun and shot Schilling, who was transported to a hospital in critical condition where he died. WMC later reported that the Johnson County Iowa Attorney's Office sent reporters court documents showing a 19-year-old Darrius Stewart, who allegedly sexually abused two children under the age of 12 (they were four). According to the petition, both victims (a family member and a family friend) told Child Protective Services that Darrius engaged them in sexual acts on several occasions. Stewart's mother and other family members are denying those claims. Stewart was also charged in Macon County, Illinois, in June 2009 for trespassing and resisting a police officer. A failure to appear warrant was issued on those charges.

Analysis

It sounds as if Stewart's relaxed demeanor left the officer feeling reasonably comfortable that the records check would come back negative, and when it didn't, his task of retrieving the un-handcuffed Stewart from the back of the car became more difficult than he had expected. I mention this because an officer who felt comfortable with someone and then learns that he shouldn't have might be very careful about what he does next, to assure he doesn't get fooled by the suspect a second time. I am, of course, making presumptions here. However, merely knowing the severity of the child sex charges against Stewart, coupled with the charge of resisting arrest, would add to the stress felt by any officer. When Stewart began to fight in earnest, given the totality of these circumstances, it would have been reasonable to believe the officer feared for his life.

– Nick Selby

An officer exhausted to the point of physical and mental weakness can't continue to fight, protect his weapon, or defend his life. The officer must end the conflict at this point or lose the fight. Losing the fight will likely cost the officer his life.

Officer Schilling states that he feared for his life when he became "winded and exhausted." The point at which an officer becomes winded and exhausted is almost entirely dependent on that officer's physical condition. I will not speculate on Officer Schilling's physical condition, nor will I suggest that it has any relevance as to whether or not his use of deadly force was justified. It does not.

But fighting is a very physically demanding activity and, like it or not, it is part of the job. Police officers must be physically fit and proficient in some form of hand-to-hand combat. Officers owe it to themselves, their partners, and the public, to be fit for duty and prepared to fight. They also must be cognizant of their diminishing ability to defend themselves when involved in a prolonged struggle.

Officer Schilling realized he was too exhausted to continue, and ended the conflict to preserve his life. This is a reasonable use of deadly force.

– Ben Singleton

There are a couple training issues here to address. The first would be about placing a subject in the car without handcuffs. Let's be honest, every working cop is likely to have done this at some point, but it is still not a best practice.

The second is to understand the need for training to safely contain and handcuff a person already in the back of a patrol car.

That being said, it doesn't diminish the attack upon the officer, nor does it excuse it. The officer and Stewart ended up on the ground in a prolonged struggle. An officer in a prolonged struggle where injury and/or exhaustion becomes a critical factor is in great danger. Stewart removed the officer's handcuffs and began swinging them as an impact type weapon, with the added threat that the single bar could come loose and create a cutting threat. At close quarters, the handcuffs have a significant risk of causing serious bodily injury or death. Add in the exhaustion factor and the lessened ability to defend against the assault and it makes this an appropriate use of deadly force based on current law enforcement training and standards.

– Ed Flosi

Estevan Gomez, 26, Hispanic Male

Farmersville, CA, July 18

Two officers were booking Gomez into custody on charges of parole violation when he began fighting with police and reached for an officer's weapon. The fight spread into several rooms within the department. A TASER was deployed to no effect. Officers state that Gomez reached for an officer's gun.[286]

Coverage in the Fresno Bee[287] and the Visalia Times Daily[288] state the same basic story: officers were booking Gomez when he attacked them and attempted to take the gun of one of the officers. Officers attempted to TASE, and when this proved ineffective and they were unable to subdue Gomez, they shot him.

Analysis

Fights during booking are rare, but can be very violent. Newspaper accounts state that Gomez was arrested on a parole violation, but leave out the conviction on which Gomez was on parole, which might have added some particular context if Gomez was known to police he was dealing with. There is reason to suspect this is true: later coverage in the Visalia Times linked another man, John Torales[289] (who was also arrested for parole violation and who was in the same car with Gomez when Gomez was arrested) to a string of at least eight armed robberies in Poplar, Kingsburg, Fresno, Earlimart, and at least two in Tipton. The newspapers haven't said whether Gomez was a suspect in those robberies. However, the presence of Torales in the vehicle when Gomez was arrested, and the fact that Gomez was also arrested during the same incident (he had already been locked up when Gomez began fighting officers) leads me to question the relationship between the two, and whether Gomez and the police who were booking him had some kind of prior relationship.

None of the above is, of course, justification for deadly force, but if Gomez attacked as described, resisted the TASER and the fight was as violent as has been reported, the officers' actions would seem to be reasonable under the totality of those circumstances – especially if Gomez actually did reach for an officer's gun. It should be noted that videos of Hispanic prisoners in California jails practicing the defeat of retention holster locks have long been circulated in law enforcement circles, so a Hispanic former California prisoner reaching for an officer's gun might present a more clearly present threat than in some other circumstances.

– Nick Selby

I remain of the opinion that when a suspect attempts to disarm a police officer, that police officer must consider the possibility of that suspect succeeding and the statistical probability of the suspect turning the weapon against the officer if he is successful. The fact that this struggle lasted as long as it did indicates that the officer fought the suspect off for as long as possible, and was probably unable to retain control of the weapon any longer.

– Ben Singleton

We have another incident here in which a subject resisted, officers attempted to use the TASER, the TASER failed, and officers were forced to make a quick decision on how to prevent an officer's firearm from being taken. As stated before, a subject attempting to disarm an officer has only one likely motive, to use it against the officer.

There is no reference as to how the long struggle lasted, but there is evidence of a prolonged struggle, indicated by how the struggle went into several rooms. Gomez was previously incarcerated in a State facility. It is known the prisoners often practice and develop techniques to overcome the safety mechanisms on a holster. This would add to the pace of the event and the need for the officer to make quick decisions.

– Ed Flosi

Troy Goode, 30, White Male

Olive Branch, MS, July 18

Goode was returning from watching a concert, and was reported to have been behaving in a "rowdy" manner when he got out of a vehicle his wife was driving and began wandering down the street, acting erratically, according to media reports.

WHBQ Memphis reports that Goode, "without explanation got out of the car and apparently started acting in an erratic fashion to attract the attention from a bystander, and they called Southaven Police." Southaven Police say they believe Goode was on LSD. Police told FOX13 the 30-year-old was restrained and taken to Baptist DeSoto where he later died. Goode's attorney told FOX13 he had a lot of questions about what happened between the time Goode left the scene and the time Goode's wife got the call two hours later[290].

Goode's attorneys told media that they knew Goode was hogtied and that a witness had stated Goode stated he could not breathe, a charge police deny. WHBQ reported, "We have also learned that the act of "hogtying" someone during arrest is used on a statewide level by law enforcement in Mississippi. It can be used by officers if a suspect could kick or otherwise injure an officer or EMT worker while being taken into custody."

In the days following the incident, the District Attorney made a public statement that Goode had a heart condition, and that all would be made clear when the autopsy was released. On December 2, 2015 PKIC reported on the controversy raised when autopsy and toxicology reports were released[291] in the Goode case, and the assertion in a statement by Erin A Burkhart, the Deputy Chief Medical Examiner, that Goode's death was "Accidental" and blamed it on "acute LSD intoxication" along with other factors. The autopsy report showed 1.0 ng/mL of LSD in Goode's blood, or, about one dose.

This contradicted the earlier statements by the District Attorney and is notable as it is the only death in the database attributed to LSD. LSD deaths are, we are told, highly rare. In January, 2016, the family announced that it had a witness to the police hogtying Goode and would sue. The witness, who is a lawyer, states that he witnessed Goode hogtied, face-down on a stretcher, rearing back in obvious distress[292].

Analysis

This case, frankly, stinks to high heaven. A death from acute LSD toxicity sounds like something out of a 1960s middle school propaganda film – no one I know has ever heard of such a death. And the weirdly contradictory statements about health issues by officials in the case, add a bizarre twist. The lawyer witness is both credible and incredible, because while he admits on camera that he has tried these kinds of cases previously, he also states that he attempted to intervene and was ignored by officials on the scene. But, ultimately, I don't have enough information to form an opinion here.

– Nick Selby

There are no details regarding the escalation of force or the justification for restraining Goode in this way. One dose of LSD is an unlikely cause of death. Although the hogtying of Goode may not be the direct cause of his death, it certainly could have contributed to an excited delirium episode, just as any other form of stress on the body could have.

– Ben Singleton

It's hard for me to opine on the officer's force response without further information. How did the officers get Goode into the "restrained" condition? There is a large degree of confusion in the public mind over "hogtying," which dates to a public debate within law enforcement and medical circles in the late 1980s over something called positional asphyxia that has been widely misunderstood. A widely distributed 1992 paper by Dr. Donald Reay[293] proposed that deaths that had occurred in the rear seat of police cars had resulted from positional asphyxiation.

In fact, current medical and scientific literature on the subject is clear that positional asphyxiation as described in the media in the 1980s and 1990s was a myth - Reay even recanted his own study and findings. A 1998 study concluded[294] and subsequent studies confirmed[295] that, "the hogtie restraint position by itself does not cause respiratory compromise to the point of asphyxiation and that other factors are responsible for the sudden deaths of individuals placed in this position."

Positional Asphyxiation does exist in the medical world, mostly with the infirm and the bed-ridden when they fall off the bed and are trapped in a position that causes asphyxia. In other words, simply placing a person in a prone position that is handcuffed behind their back and has the legs bound and attached back to the cuffs does not clinically affect the respiratory process.

Law enforcement use of tools such as a Total Appendage Restraint Position (TARP) has been shown to have no significant clinical effect on the respiratory process even when 200+ pounds of weight is placed on the person's back. There is a thing called compression asphyxia (sometimes referred to a arrest-related asphyxia). That basically means squishing the person to death, but that's not what happened here. What is clear is that despite the witness accounts, it is unlikely that the officers' use of TARP was the cause of death in this case.

— Ed Flosi

Samuel DuBose, 43, Black Male

Cincinnati, OH, July 19

For more on this case, see the Case Studies chapter at the beginning of the book. An officer pulled DuBose over for lack of a front license plate, and during the stop, the officer and DuBose struggled. Video shows DuBose resisting the officer as he tries to remove him from the vehicle. When the two grappled – DuBose in the driver seat and the officer reaching into the car through the driver-side window, the officer drew his pistol, aimed it at DuBose and fired a single round. DuBose released the officer and accelerated the vehicle away, knocking the officer to the curb. The officer gave foot pursuit, catching up with the vehicle after it wrecked nearby. DuBose was dead at the scene.

The officer claimed DuBose had held onto and dragged him from the moving vehicle. This account was later disproven by body camera footage released by Cincinnati prosecutor Joseph Deters, who announced that murder charges were being filed against University of Cincinnati police officer Ray Tensing.

In an assessment of the officer's conduct, Deters said Tensing had "purposely killed" DuBose and that he "should never have been a police officer[296]"

The Associated Press reported that "Deters says the shooting of motorist Samuel DuBose in a "chicken crap" stop over a missing front license plate was "asinine," and "without question a murder." He also said the university shouldn't be in the policing business at all. The prosecutor said he thinks now-fired Officer Ray Tensing lost his temper because DuBose wouldn't get out of the car."[297]

Analysis

At a minimum, the case is more complex than it has been portrayed in the media. The facts are that Officer Tensing did have intelligence that DuBose's license had been suspended and probable cause to stop the car, and when he gave DuBose a lawful order to get out of the car, DuBose did resist and scuffle with the officer. Tensing's biggest mistake was engaging through the open window, and going hands-on in what was essentially an indefensible position. While deadly force may not have been appropriate it is important to understand that we do not know (even those of us who have watched the video[298] of the incident) exactly what transpired as Tensing reached in through the driver-side window and scuffled with DuBose. It does not appear to me that the scuffle reached the level where I would necessarily fear for my life, but I was not there, and this kind of second-guessing is extremely difficult. I would say that Tensing's much mocked comments, such as, "I just got tangled in the car. I thought I was going to get run over;" and "He just took off on me, man. I thought he was going to run me over," and similar other comments could also be the comments an officer who got in over his head, used his gun to get out of it, and then lied, but, are not in my view necessarily an outright fabrication. They could rather be the result of shock. Ultimately I believe Tensing's actions were not a reasonable use of deadly force. It will be extremely difficult for him to articulate, in a way that will be believed, exactly how he reasonably felt in fear for his life when he fired the fatal shot.

– Nick Selby

There have been past cases in which an officer was dragged by a vehicle and then fired on the driver to prevent further injury or death. In some of these cases, the driver of the vehicle actually pinned the officer's arm inside the vehicle.

In my review of the video in this case, I see Dubose's left hand on the exterior of the driver door and his right hand on the ignition switch, immediately before Officer Tensing fires. It is clear that Dubose intends to flee in his vehicle. Officer Tensing drew his weapon and fired before the vehicle began moving.

Immediately after the incident, Tensing is heard telling fellow officers: "He just took off on me man, I thought I was going to get run over." Whether or not the threat perceived by Tensing was genuine, there did not appear to be an actual threat. That is, I do not believe that Tensing would have sustained injuries had he elected not to shoot Dubose. It is unlikely that Tensing would have been "run over" when the shooting occurred, given his position next to the driver's door.

– Ben Singleton

This case is troublesome from several angles. First, the fact that Deters decided to opine on the stop as "chicken shit" is downright ignorant. The stop was a lawful stop for a verified vehicle code violation. However, saying the stop was valid does not necessarily validate all the subsequent actions of the officer.

In my opinion, the officer was professional and courteous with DuBose throughout the contact, while asking him for standard identification and paperwork. It goes badly when the officer reaches into the car. From here, there's no way to know why the officer said he felt like he would be dragged, but it's not a stretch to believe it may have a little to do with the feeling that DuBose "might" have been able to. Only the officer can reconcile whether this was his true perception or not. All we have is the video, which clearly shows that he wasn't being dragged and that he was (lucky enough to be) able to separate from DuBose prior to being dragged down the road. My personal suggestion is, once again, for officers to stop reaching deeply into cars that are moving (or about to be moving). It's just not worth it in most cases. The fear the officer expressed wouldn't have occurred if he hadn't reached into the car.

– Ed Flosi

Derek Wolfsteller, 31, White Male

Plymouth, MN, July 23
An armed man created a disturbance at a local Arby's restaurant and was detained by employees. Officer Amy Therkelsen was dispatched to a local

Arby's restaurant on a 911 call from an Arby's employee. When she arrived, she saw two employees trying to subdue Wolfsteller, whom she ordered to desist. When the suspect did not submit to Therkelsen's demands, she used her TASER on him, but did not subdue him."[299]

Therkelsen then tried to physically subdue Wolfsteller. A fight ensued and Wolfsteller tried to grab Therkelsen's gun from her holster. Therkelsen drew the weapon, and fatally shot Wolfsteller.

Plymouth Police Chief Michael Goldstein told the Star Tribune[300] that his department had had "previous contact" with Wolfsteller, but he declined to elaborate. Wolfsteller's father said that a day before the Plymouth incident, police were called to Wolfsteller's grandparents' home for a mental health crisis, but Wolfsteller's father said Monday police couldn't take Wolfsteller to the hospital against his will[301].

Analysis

There are several unclear details here around a dynamic and confusing incident, especially around the struggle for Therkelsen's gun. One newspaper implied that Wolfsteller had actually retrieved Therkelsen's gun. If this was the case, this is a clear case of self-defense. If Therkelsen was merely struggling with Wolfsteller and her gun remained secure, things are less clear. What remains clear is that when Therkelsen arrived, she was expecting an armed man. This, in and of itself, changes the dynamics of the incident, and can inform the officer's immediate actions.

It is fairly clear that it would have been objectively reasonable for the officer to feel fear in this situation; her attempt to gain compliance through non-deadly force (the TASER) had failed; the suspect was successfully fighting off the officer and two other people, and then the suspect reached for her gun. There are some other facts missing (such as the nature of previous contacts with the department and the different contextual understanding, if any, Therkelsen may have had as a result of this about Wolfsteller and his capabilities), but on its face, this does not seem an alarming misuse of authority or deadly force.

– Nick Selby

Any attempt to disarm a police officer is a deadly proposition. The officer knows that if an assailant obtains her weapon, the likelihood he will turn it against her is statistically high. This is why gun retention is an area of intense practice and study in police academies throughout the country. This officer recognized the threat posed by that likelihood and responded appropriately.

– Ben Singleton

The original call detailed that the suspect was armed. It is interesting that the officer chose to use the TASER device to take him into custody. We don't know enough to know why she made this decision. Was there an indication that Wolfsteller was not actually armed after the officer arrived? If there was still a belief he was armed, the use of the TASER device might have been an unwise and tactically inappropriate decision.

As for the deadly force application, if a suspect is attempting to disarm an officer, there can be only one logical conclusion as to why. The officer doesn't have to start to lose control of the weapon before making this determination. If Wolfsteller was actively engaged in the act of disarming the officer and she felt her life was in imminent danger, then deadly force was appropriate to stop his attempt.

– Ed Flosi

Zachary Hammond, White Male, 19

July 26

Seneca police were waiting in the parking lot of a Hardee's fast-food restaurant after an undercover officer arranged a drug deal with a female, Tori Morton, who was a passenger in the vehicle being driven by Hammond. Lt Tiller, with his emergency lights flashing, pulled up closely behind Hammond's car[302]. Tiller got out, and saw that Hammond was beginning to reverse as part of an attempt to drive away. Tiller ran toward the vehicle's driver side, just as Hammond put the car into a forward gear and began to drive away. On the dashcam video, we see Tiller, who is in no danger of being hit by Hammond's car, pointing his gun at Hammond, through the driver-side window[303]. As Hammond begins to drive away, Tiller fires at least two shots at the vehicle. After the vehicle drives off camera, we hear Tiller announce that Hammond had tried to run Tiller over. Morton was not injured and later was charged with simple possession of marijuana.

Tiller has said through his lawyer that he thought Hammond was threatening to run him over and fired twice to protect himself. Hammond's family said a private autopsy[304] showed the teen was shot in the side and the back, proving the threat had passed. Tenth District Solicitor Chrissy Adams wrote on October 27, "I have completed my review of the South Carolina Law Enforcement Division's (SLED) investigation into the shooting death of Zachary Hammond on July 26, 2015 in Seneca, South Carolina. After careful consideration of the facts of the case, a thorough review of the State investigation, and an extensive review of all applicable law, I have determined that no criminal charges should be filed against Lt. Mark Tiller at the State level. I met with the Hammond family today and have informed them of this decision.

"A letter issuing my prosecutorial decision and closing the State's investigation has been forwarded to SLED. However, due to a request by United States Attorney Bill Nettles, I will not be releasing any additional information while the federal authorities are making their charging determination[305]."

Analysis

This case shows every possible thing that could go wrong going wrong. In addition to the completely terrible tactics shows by Tiller, and his completely unjustified and unreasonable use of deadly force, we also hear Tiller lying on the dashcam recording, feathering his nest for his ultimate claim of self-defense. Watching this I am totally stunned by the decision of the solicitor, whom I believe was objectively wrong in her failure to prosecute. This means that we can never know what a grand jury or jury would have thought. I know what I think: this killing was unjustified.

– Nick Selby

The in-car video clearly shows Tiller firing as he backed off of Hammond's vehicle, which was not traveling toward him. Immediately after the shooting, Tiller is heard saying, "He tried to hit me", indicating his justification for the shooting was the movement of the vehicle, and not a separate threat from within it. In no way did Hammond pose a threat to Tiller's life. This shooting was completely unreasonable.

– Ben Singleton

Hammond was the driver of a car involved in an undercover dope operation. Tiller pulled in behind the vehicle, likely to block it from escaping. Hammond backed up towards the police vehicle after Tiller had exited and while Tiller was walking towards Hammond's vehicle with his gun drawn. It must be noted that Hammond was reversing and turning the wheel to the right causing the vehicle to reverse towards the front passenger side of the patrol car. This did not seem to cause Tiller to believe he was in imminent danger at this point as he did not fire but instead continued to walk towards Hammond's vehicle while still pointing his pistol at Hammond and telling him to stop. I would agree that the reversing action of Hammond did not pose a threat to Tiller.

Tiller moved forward of the driver's side door and actually touches the area near and below the driver's side mirror as Hammond accelerated forward and to the left. It must also be noted that Hammond did not appear to be attempting to strike Tiller but was trying to escape. Looking at the video, I don't think could Hammond could have struck Tiller had Tiller not put himself into a poor position. We must remember what we had here. Based on the information it was an undercover drug operation that involved the passenger, certainly not a crime involving the infliction or threatened infliction of serious harm. Tiller chose to move into a position that created the danger. There is already case law on point to this issue (Estate of Starks v. Enyart, 5 F.3d 230, (7th Cir.1993)) that warns officers about moving into the path of a moving vehicle and then trying to claim self-defense in crimes that do not involve the infliction or threatened infliction of serious harm.

Indeed, in this case Tiller was not ever truly in danger but for his own actions. Even then, one could debate the seriousness of the danger based on the position of the vehicle and when Tiller chose to fire. This case appears to be an inappropriate deadly force response.

— Ed Flosi

Allan F. White III, 23, White Male

Cleveland, TN, July 28

White was waiting outside the home of a female deputy, allegedly hiding behind a vehicle when she returned to her home in the middle of the night, White "ran out towards her and attacked."

According to WCRB TV, White, "tackled her and they got in a scuffle and he took his hands and put them around her face and tried to kill her[306]," Watson said. The deputy unsuccessfully attempted to TASE White before resorting to deadly force by shooting him. Sheriff Watson added, "He was clearly on her property and close to her front door."[307] Oakley's husband was not at home at the time.

Analysis

This is a textbook example of justified self-defense.

— Nick Selby

Police officers are afforded all of the same basic rights as ordinary citizens, including those of enjoying and defending life and liberty. This officer was clearly defending her life.

— Ben Singleton

This case appears to be an intentional ambush of a law enforcement officer. Whether this incident was driven by a personal vendetta against the deputy or just because she was a cop would be interesting to know, but it also brings new attention to these ambush style attacks. The recent uptick in ambush style attacks on police officers is noticeable and troubling. It increases the awareness officers must have of their surroundings at all times, even when off-duty.

– Ed Flosi

Wilmer Delgado-Soba, 38, Hispanic Male

Worcester, MA, July 29

Delgado-Soba died after he was shocked with a Taser. The Worcester Telegram[308] reported that Delgado-Soba entered a small grocery store and began smashing glass and throwing things. The store's owner, Mike Maranda, said, "police 'tried everything' before using the TASER." The Boston Globe states Delgado-Soba entered the store wearing only shorts, and flew into a rage when he was asked to leave[309]. He smashed a glass and sprinted around the store, clutching the glass and smashing more items. Then he removed his shorts and tried to pour laundry detergent on them, sitting on the floor until police arrived.

Mrs. Maranda said the officers did not strike the man in any way. "They tried very hard to talk to him," she said, noting the man had resisted them by swinging his arms and hands.

The Telegram, which links to the police scanner recording, notes that dispatchers told the responding officers, "He's destroying the store, and he's got a couple bottles in his hands.[310]" Mr. Delgado-Soba had prior convictions for, among other things, assault with a dangerous weapon, breaking and entering in the daytime with intent to commit a felony, assault and battery, and intimidation of a witness. The police chief, Gary J. Gemme, said in a statement, "We are currently awaiting autopsy results for an exact cause and manner of death. However, there is evidence of possible opiate use that may have contributed to his condition. There is also evidence of a possible medical condition that resulted in his irrational and violent behavior. There was no visible evidence or marks of physical trauma[311]." The results of the autopsy were not readily available as of mid-February, 2016.

Analysis

Listening to the dispatch recording and hearing the accounts of the shop owners went a long way to convincing me that the officers recognized Delgado-Soba needed to be controlled, but also that the officers tried very hard to stay within the non-deadly force realm. The reaction described by witnesses and the media of Delgado-Soba to the TASER was a relatively common one with people on drugs; Delgado-Soba's erratic and inexplicable behavior and the chief's statement about "evidence" of opiate use contributes to my opinion that this was a drug-induced rage, and that the drugs were more closely related to Delgado-Soba's death than the TASER.

– Nick Selby

Delgado was apparently in the throes of a psychotic episode, which was likely drug-induced. The officers took Delgado into custody using the TASER, which was the safest method they had available. I believe the outcome would have been no different, with exception to injuries sustained by officers, had the officers engaged in a physical fight with Delgado. This incident was handled appropriately.

– Ben Singleton

This incident clearly demonstrated an appropriate response and use of force options. The subject was apparently in the midst of an emotional episode driven by mental illness, emotional distress, or by drug usage. The environment in which this incident took place and the subject's condition must be taken into consideration. It's a very difficult task to take a naked and agitated person into custody in a close quarter environment with broken glass on the floor. The officers appeared to have attempted verbal persuasion to get the subject to surrender but those attempts failed.

– Ed Flosi

Filimoni Raiyawa, 57, Asian-Pacific Islander Male

San Francisco, CA, July 30

Raiyawa, who was six feet tall and 265 pounds, was the caregiver to 96 year-old Solomon Cohen. Sometime before five a.m. on the day of his death, Raiyawa beat Cohen, who later died from his injuries[312]. Raiyawa died in officer custody in San Francisco after a fight with multiple officers.

According to the San Francisco Chronicle, Raiyawa rear-ended a BMW at 5:30 a.m. on a San Francisco street, pushing the vehicle across the street into a parked car.[313] The victim in the crash got out to talk to Raiyawa, who appeared incoherent and was making disturbing statements about God and "God's will," according to Police Chief Greg Suhr. The victim backed away, police said, and called 911 as Raiyawa got out of his car and approached him in a threatening manner. He chased the victim around the block, but didn't catch him, as the man was able to flee ahead of him. The crash victim jumped into his BMW and escaped, just as police were arriving.

Raiyawa hit a female officer who responded to the call several times about the head and shoulders, beating her nearly unconscious to the ground, and "throwing her partner by the wrist," Suhr said. Willie Gunnari, who lives on Lombard, told the Chronicle that he saw the two female police officers trying to subdue the suspect. Gunnari said the man resisted, flailing his arms as the officers hit him with batons. "Nothing was going to get him to stop moving," Gunnari said.

Prince Tenefrancia witnessed part of the incident from inside a closed IHOP. He heard two police officers yelling, "Get on the ground! Get on the ground!" and then he saw four officers attempting to subdue Raiyawa — one sitting on the man's lower back, two holding his shoulders, and another holding his feet. The officers, according to Tenefrancia, were yelling, "Stop resisting! Stop resisting!" Two injured officers were taken to UCSF Medical Center; the female officer beaten around the head and shoulders was treated for concussion symptoms, while the other officer was put in a soft cast for an injury to the wrist.

Analysis

It's rare to have such a clear case of good officer response and physical control. Two female officers were confronted with an agitated and very large male who had already been violent, and the officers went hands-on without hesitation. When other officers arrived, the escalation came not with deadly force but with non-deadly force, in the form of batons. It would seem to me that the continued attempts to both verbally reason with the suspect as well as apply non-deadly force were in fact continued for longer than some officers would have. Ultimately they were successful in immobilizing and restraining the suspect. We do not – still – have a copy of the coroner's report or toxicology, so any determination of a cause of death is pure speculation. I suspect the cause of death is heart-related, aggravated by an acute mental health condition or acute narcotic toxicity. I have no personal doubt that this was a justified use of force on the part of the officers, and that Raiyawa's death was a medical response to the stimulus he engaged in – namely running around a block, chasing someone and then fighting with officers.

– Nick Selby

These officers showed unbelievable restraint. It is unfortunate that this agency took a useful, and sometimes lifesaving tool from these officers due to public pressure. I believe a properly executed TASER deployment would have ended this incident without unnecessary injury to officers.

The fact that these officers were not equipped with the TASER illustrates the fact that in-custody deaths like these are not necessarily a direct result of TASER use, but are instead a result of physical exertion combined with drug toxicity.

— Ben Singleton

These officers acted quickly in trying to subdue a large, violent subject. They attempted physical control techniques when many officers might have used other more intrusive levels of force. The force options used appear to be objectively reasonable in the eyes of the law, but something still bothers me as a trainer. Was this a case of officers being too leery of using reasonable force options in fear of being overly scrutinized for their choices later?

I can't determine Raiyawa's actions and behavior when the officers went hands-on without further information. The hands-on solution would be tactically appropriate if there was a moment of calm and Raiyawa was not presenting an immediate threat. Based on his size and other factors, it may not have been tactically appropriate to engage physically if Raiyawa was still actively aggressive and threatening. It may have been more appropriate to use non-deadly force options at distance to effect his arrest and overcome his resistance. The rub here is that officers at this particular agency did not carry a TASER due to continuing (and in my opinion unrealistic) public concerns. Officers should be trained on using appropriate force when the situation calls for it rather than trying something lesser to avoid criticism from the Monday-morning quarterbacks sitting in their armchairs.

— Ed Flosi

AUGUST

Joseph Hutcheson, 48, White Male

Dallas, TX, August 1

Hutcheson, a 48-year-old handyman from Arlington, died after he ran into a county office building at around 10:24 a.m. He had been shouting for help[314] and saying that his wife was trying to kill him. He was placed in handcuffs by deputies, lost consciousness, and died. Multiple witnesses said several deputies were on top of Hutcheson; a knee was seen on Hutcheson's neck[315]. According to the medical examiner's office, Hutcheson died from the "combined toxic effects of cocaine and methamphetamine compounded by hypertensive cardiovascular disease [high blood pressure] and physiologic stress associated with struggle and restraint."[316]

Analysis

The deputies' actions require further review to determine whether excessive force was used. The way I have read these articles, the deputies are taking the heat for a series of bad decisions made by a drug addict in poor health who decided to fight deputies rather than surrender. Based on the toxicology and autopsy report, Hutcheson was in the midst of a drug-induced psychotic episode when he ran screaming into the building. The surveillance video recording of the deputies holding him down show me that deputies were attempting to immobilize Hutcheson. Confusion in this case is partly caused by how the word homicide is understood and used by WFAA. The order in which the coroner's report listed the causes of death shows that Hutcheson died first as a result of the cocaine and methamphetamine, second as a result of his chronic condition, and lastly, as a result of the exertion of fighting with deputies. Use of the term "homicide" convinced people to think that the coroner was returning an indictment against deputies, but he was not. WFAA's reporting quotes Jeff Hood, executive director of Hope for Peace and Justice, a social justice ministry as saying: "This was a homicide. The deputies were the precipitating factor in the death of Joseph Hutcheson ... just because someone uses drugs in this country, that it not something we have a death sentence for," near the top of the article. Five paragraphs lower, the article notes, "While Hutcheson's death was ruled a homicide, that does not necessarily mean the death was intentional, or that it was a crime. The distinction — when made by a medical examiner — means another person's actions led to the death of another person."

– Nick Selby

The methods used by the deputies to subdue Hutcheson appear to be appropriate. He posed an obvious threat to himself or others, and he resisted deputies throughout the incident. As in so many other cases, Hutcheson's death can be attributed to the deadly combination of acute drug intoxication and extreme physical stress.

– Ben Singleton

This is another case where it appears the deputies used only controlling force and body weight to subdue a resisting subject. Hutcheson's disturbing behavior troubled others in the lobby, who seemed to scatter from him. As it is, it would be appropriate for the deputies to take him into custody and to control his actions. Watching the video, I don't see anything shocking about the deputies' actions as they struggled to control a good-sized man under the influence of stimulants.

The video does show a deputy with his knee either on the neck or very close to it, as had been claimed. In most cases, this is just not a good practice, as it can lead to a more serious and unintentional injury to the subject. Officers should, as a matter of practice, attempt to stay off the neck of a subject while trying to control him with knee pressure and so avoid claims of excessive force. To be clear, it doesn't appear that the knee pressure had much, if anything, to do with Hutcheson's demise, but it does give rise to questions about the actions of the deputies.

Another claim involves the after-actions of the deputies concerning Hutcheson's medical attention. Although not a part of the use of force evaluation, it's important to remind officers that a subject in their care, custody and control should be given medical attention, if needed, as soon as it is safe and feasible to do so.

— Ed Flosi

Troy Lee Robinson, 33, Black Male

DeKalb, GA, August 6

A police task force working on robbery cases conducted a traffic stop of a vehicle related to a license plate violation.[317] Robinson was riding as a passenger. During the stop, the driver told officers he was armed, and the officers asked the driver to step out of the car. The driver complied and was disarmed by police. As an officer secured that weapon, Robinson fled. There was a short foot chase, after which the Georgia Bureau of Investigation (GBI) recounting of the facts differs from many other media reports: GBI says that, "Robinson climbed a chain link fence and Officer Casey Benton deployed his agency-issued Taser. Robinson attempted to climb over a cement wall and fell to the ground below."[318] Few media reports mention the chain link fence, and it is unclear from the GBI account whether the TASER application occurred when Robinson was on the fence, or while he was on the wall.

In one account, the Atlanta Journal-Constitution reports, "Robinson had an injury in his back which appeared to be from the Taser (sic.). Officer Casey Benton fired the shock weapon after Robinson climbed a chain-link fence, the GBI reported."[319]

Information from the autopsy suggests that Robinson had one injury to his upper back which is apparently where one of the Taser probes penetrated his skin.

It is generally agreed that, in attempting to flee, Robinson is reported to have attempted to scale an 8-foot-high wall (not the chain link fence), and reports agree that Robinson fell from atop the wall.

After Robinson fell from the wall, officers recovered Robinson, who was unconscious, and handcuffed him per police protocol.[320] EMS was called and Robinson was transported to Grady Memorial Hospital, where he died of his injuries. GBI said, "Robinson was unconscious and transported by ambulance to Grady Hospital, where he died."

The GBI is reviewing cellphone video taken by witnesses after Robinson fell off the wall, which documents that Robinson lay on the ground for many minutes before anyone rendered aid, including the many police officers on the scene, who apparently awaited EMS arrival before beginning CPR.[321]

Preliminary findings indicate Robinson died from severe head and neck trauma sustained during the fall.[322] Robinson's father, saying that his son was "not the kind of person to fight with police or shootout with police," added that his son "ran because he had a warrant out on him."[323]

Analysis

I have concerns about the media reporting of this case, and the difference in stated facts between the GBI and media accounts. I am troubled by the allegation that officers did not attempt CPR. We also haven't enough details to understand whether it was reasonable for the officer to deploy the TASER at a man climbing over a fence. There are still open questions about the specifics, and the pacing of this incident. I'm inclined to believe this was unreasonable use of the TASER.

– Nick Selby

A basic level of instruction and training comes with all law enforcement tools. TASER presents a different set of specific uses, risks, and cautions than other tools do. TASER advises on the specific hazards associated with falls, and identifies post-exposure falls as one of the most likely sources of injury.

This risk has to be considered when deploying this weapon. I don't believe it was the officer's intent to cause Robinson to fall from the wall. But I do believe, absent other details regarding the immediate threat posed by

Robinson, negligence and failure to comply with guidelines specific to the use of TASER may have led to Robinson's death.

– Ben Singleton

This case again illustrates the need for post-custody medical assistance. The case law on this is clear and officers can suffer punitive awards against them based on their inactions.

As for the force analysis, this case presents an opportunity to ask, "What was the reasonable expectation of injury based on the type and amount of force used?" The answer must be in reasonable balance to the force factors that drove the officer to respond with force. The use of a TASER in the manner that it is generally used is seen as a non-deadly force option. But just as we take the totality of the circumstances into consideration when we look at the force factors (threat of subject, level of resistance, pace of event, severity of crime, nature of escape), we must also view the totality of the circumstances in this situation to measure the force response.

An officer can reasonably expect a good neuro-muscular incapacitation (NMI) result with a TASER device probe deployment at the distance in this case. A subject in NMI would not be able to brace himself or protect his head from falling from a significant height, as his arms would be locked up. This is the reason that TASER International warns against this practice. The expectation of injury, taking these facts into consideration, is higher than with a standard TASER use. It would require higher factors, specifically related to Robinson, to be deemed justified. If the officer only articulated that Robinson was simply running away from the car stop, it is unlikely the use of the TASER would be deemed appropriate. If there was articulation that Robinson was believed to have been involved with the robberies, and that he was believed to have been armed (based on specific facts), the analysis would be different.

-– Ed Flosi

Matthew Russo, 26, White Male

Hartford, CT, August 7

Police and the Hartford Mobile Crisis Team were called to the home of the parents of Matthew Russo at 8:30 p.m. to deal with a person having a medical and psychological issue, or a "mental health crisis." The police and mental health responders found the 400-lb Russo in the garage,[324] and an argument ensued over whether Russo would go to the hospital[325]. Officers "drive stunned" Russo in an attempt to gain pain compliance and not full neuro-muscular incapacitation[326], after two officers were injured in the scuffle with Russo[327] and the medical team administered "a sedative"[328] to calm Russo down. Russo became unresponsive and was transported to the hospital where he later died. No further accounts or autopsy or toxicology reports have been issued.

Analysis

The presence of the Mobile Crisis Team and the officers, working in tandem to avoid escalation showed a genuine attempt to get Russo to comply without violence. Whether the drive-stun and sedative were necessary or contributed to Russo's death is a question that cannot be answered with the facts at hand.

– Nick Selby

One can only speculate as to what caused Russo's death without an autopsy report. Because a "drive-stun" is a very localized exposure with minimal effects on the body, it is unlikely that it contributed to Russo's death. Sedatives, however, can slow brain function and depress respiration. When combined with other depressants, such as alcohol, these effects can be compounded and even cause death. I suspect the cause of death will be found in the toxicology report.

– Ben Singleton

This case will initially hinge on whether it was lawful and appropriate to seize Russo in the first place. These mental health calls can be tricky for officers having to decide whether they should take the person into custody or not. If they determined Russo was a danger to himself or others, and that he was not able to care for his own well-being due to his condition, then it would have been completely appropriate to take him into custody for a psychological evaluation.

According to the articles, Russo became combative during the process of being taken into custody. Using a TASER device drive-stun in order to overcome the resistance and assist in the seizure of Russo would most likely be deemed reasonable if the officers perceived Russo as a credible threat. Given the prolonged struggle and Russo's condition, it is highly unlikely that the TASER device in drive-stun mode had anything to do with his demise.

This case, however, does bring to our attention the national focus on how officers use force options on mentally ill subjects.

— Ed Flosi

Christian Taylor, 19, Black Male

Arlington, TX, August 7

At about 1 a.m., a security company contracted by the dealership contacted Arlington police on a 911 call to report a possible burglary by a person later identified as Mr. Taylor[329]. The security company reported that its cameras captured Taylor as he drove a sport utility vehicle through the dealership showroom's glass doors.[330] In addition, the now-famous nine minutes of video that were released show Taylor entering the dealership by climbing over a gate, walking down the rows of cars, hitting car windows, jumping on a vehicle's hood, climbing into a vehicle through its sunroof and other vandalism.[331]

There was no video in the building where the confrontation took place between Taylor and Officer Brad Miller, a 49-year-old probationary officer. In a press conference announcing his firing of Miller, Arlington Police Chief Will D. Johnson told reporters that Miller said he confronted Taylor, who had held up a pair of keys and said he was going to steal a car. Taylor then ran towards an exit, and finding it locked, turned back on Miller and walked "aggressively" towards Miller, using profanity.[332] Miller fired four times, striking Taylor at least three times.[333] Chief Johnson stated that officers had seen bulges in Taylor's pockets that turned out to be a cell phone and wallet. "It is clear from the facts obtained that Mr. Taylor was noncompliant with police demands," Johnson said.[334]

Taylor was shot in the abdomen, chest and neck. The Tarrant County medical examiner's office[335] reported Taylor had a synthetic psychedelic drug, 25I-NBOMe, or, "N-Bomb," and marijuana in his system.[336]

According to the National Institute on Drug Abuse, 25I-NBOMe is sold as a legal substitute for LSD or mescaline. These chemicals act on serotonin receptors in the brain, like other hallucinogens, but they are considerably more powerful, even than LSD. Extremely small amounts can cause seizures, heart attack or arrested breathing, and death. A young man in one medical case report published in late 2014 experienced severe hallucinations and panic and attempted suicide after such an ingestion[337].

Analysis

This would seem to be a case of an unjustified use of deadly force by an untrained officer reacting from fear. As we have seen in other cases in this book, people experiencing acute intoxication from these synthetic hallucinogens can act in a highly aggressive, agitated and violent manner. This does not excuse Officer Miller's actions by any means. It does raise the point that, as Chief Johnson fired Officer Miller in the most public of ways, Johnson has inexcusably remained silent on the wider responsibility of his Arlington Police Department in this case. Miller was 49-years-old, but still in the Field Training stage of his career, having only recently graduated from the police academy. His field training officer and his supervisors all bear responsibility for training failures.

Speaking as an Arlington homeowner, in my opinion firing Officer Miller ultimately seems a cowardly thing for the chief to have done. It implies that full responsibility for the tragic series of decisions that were taken rests solely on Miller, not Chief Johnson's department. And it makes it look as if our city does not stand behind its officers until all the facts have been examined. It also sends a terrible message to the grand jurors, that the department has decided the outcome of the investigation – before it had been concluded. Although this is probably a case of the unjustified use of force, it raises further questions about systemic issues in Arlington's training and supervisory processes that may not be publicly answered.

Mr. Taylor, who placed himself, intoxicated, into this situation, did not deserve to die, but neither is he blameless in this incident. Media coverage also exacerbated controversy and scurrilously implied a racial angle that the evidence does not support. Articles written in the days immediately after the incident in the New York Times, Los Angeles Times and Fort Worth Star-Telegram all referred repeatedly to the fact that this incident took place within days of the anniversary of the shooting in Ferguson, MO of Michael Brown by Officer Darrin Wilson. Any connection between these two cases is negligible and there hasn't been a shred of evidence to indicate that officer Miller behaved in a manner indicating racism.

– Nick Selby

Although there were public implications that Officer Miller killed Taylor in an intentional act of predatory racism, it is more likely that he was just scared. Some of the most important skills for police officers to master are the suppression of fear and the control of adrenalin. The facts of this case do not suggest that a legitimate threat to Officer Miller's life was present. Officer Miller may have feared for his life. But fear alone does not make the use of deadly force appropriate.

In my opinion, no training regimen can prepare someone for the fear that comes with the most dangerous aspects of police work. This line of work requires an ability, not found in everyone to face fear with composure and sound judgment.

– Ben Singleton

As stated before, in order to use justifiable deadly force, an officer must believe that he/she is in imminent danger of serious bodily injury or death, based on the totality of facts and circumstances. They would have to be enough to lead another reasonable officer to believe the same. I feel the facts and circumstances in this case would not, therefore the use of deadly force by the officer would not be appropriate.

There are confounding issues at play; first and foremost, we have an officer still in his training program put in this situation basically unsupervised. I am at a loss as to how this officer could be expected to do so without his training officer at least near enough to act as a cover officer if needed. The agency blames Miller for going into the building without his "more experienced" partner which led to "an environment of cascading consequences." I would question why a field training officer would allow his trainee to enter by himself and attempt to apprehend a person acting as Taylor was. It wouldn't be a tactically sound decision to allow the most veteran officers to go in by themselves, let alone a trainee.

— Ed Flosi

Asshams Manley, 30, Black Male

District Heights, MD, August 14

Around 11:30 p.m., Officer Brian Bell heard a car crash. He went to the scene and saw the 6'7" Manley running from the collision. Bell pursued Manley and caught him about a block away, where the two struggled over the Bell's gun, and Bell fired the weapon.[338]

Despite his gunshot wound, Manley continued to fight with Bell. A second officer arrived and used his TASER on Manley multiple times, but it took a third officer before Manley was restrained. No officers were hurt.[339] Manley was taken to a hospital, where he died the next day.

At the hospital, Manley tested positive for opiates and marijuana. Manley suffered from mental health issues. A family member told investigators that he had recently expressed suicidal thoughts[340].

Analysis

This is one of the clearest cases showing how mental health issues and drug use lead to fatal encounters with law enforcement. This use of deadly force seems completely reasonable: when someone is struggling with an officer for his gun, it's really not a question.

– Nick Selby

As I've noted in other analyses, the probability that Officer Bell's weapon would have been turned against him if obtained by Manly is statistically high. I would add to that the probability that Manly would have been able to overpower Bell, given his size. Bell's decision was completely reasonable.

– Ben Singleton

When a person attempts to disarm an officer, they are not truly unarmed anymore. In his attempt to gain control of the officer's weapon, Manley demonstrated a clear and credible imminent threat of serious body injury or death if he were to actually succeed. The use of deadly force to prevent Manley from gaining control would be appropriate and consistent with current law enforcement training and standards.

The use of the other force options listed was clearly appropriate as well, due to the threat and level of resistance presented by Manley.

–– Ed Flosi

John Unsworth, 43, White Male

Hanover, IN, August 15

Deputies responded to multiple 911 calls of a fight in progress at the house in which Unsworth lived. Officers were met in the driveway by occupants of the residence, who said that Unsworth was out of control and had physically assaulted each of them.[341]

Unsworth appeared and charged toward officers in a highly agitated manner. Officers ordered him to stop, but Unsworth continued charging toward deputies. A deputy deployed his Taser and administered multiple cycles, yet Unsworth continued his aggression. Officers say they "utilized a progressive level of force, all of which were ineffective," and after all failed, used deadly force to stop Unsworth. Unsworth was struck at least once and died as a result of the injuries he sustained.[342]

On April 14, 2016, a Jefferson County grand jury issued a no bill as to both deputies involved.[343]

Analysis

The information released by the state police articulates, in almost textbook terms, the escalation of force and fear on the part of the officers leading to use of deadly force. The Indiana State Police investigated and presented to the Jefferson County Grand Jury, whose deliberations are secret. The Prosecuting Attorney, Chad Lewis, stated that the "deputies encountered a horrific set of circumstances leaving them no choice but to use deadly force."

– Nick Selby

The escalation of force is noteworthy in this case. A more detailed articulation of the threat posed by Unsworth, however, would be necessary to conclude that the use of deadly force was reasonable. Unsworth merely charging toward officers does not justify the use of deadly force.

– Ben Singleton

While it does appear that officers in this case unsuccessfully used lesser intrusive methods of force to attempt to gain control of Unsworth, it would not in itself justify the use of deadly force. The force factors must be significant enough to support justifying the deadly force application. What we know is insufficient to render a reasoned opinion as to the appropriateness of the deadly force application.

— Ed Flosi

Oscar Ruiz, 44, Hispanic Male

Baldwin Park, CA, August 15

At about 3:30 p.m., a passerby saw Ruiz lying on a sidewalk next to a Mobil station and called police.[344] Officers didn't find Ruiz on the sidewalk and were told that he stole an 8-foot-tall flagpole[345] with an American flag and swung it at people and cars. Police saw Ruiz, holding the flagpole, in the parking lot of a credit union. Ruiz ran from the officers. During the chase one officer tried to subdue Ruiz with a TASER without effect. Ruiz and the officers struggled, and Ruiz was held down and handcuffed. Ruiz continued to struggle after being handcuffed. Then he became unresponsive. Officers removed the handcuffs and performed CPR; paramedics took Ruiz to the hospital, where he was pronounced dead.[346] Oscar Ruiz Jr., Ruiz' son, said in an email to the San Gabriel Valley Tribune, "My dad was an addict, but he didn't have a violent bone in his body."[347]

Analysis

This is another apparent acute narcotic intoxication/mental illness case. In this case, however, it has been very difficult to find follow up information about Ruiz. In March, 2016, the coroner still listed the cause of death as "deferred pending additional investigation."

– Nick Selby

Ruiz' behavior is indicative of drug intoxication, which is corroborated by his son's statement. Based on this information, this appears to be another example of the deadly effects of the combination of drug intoxication and extreme physical stress.

– Ben Singleton

This may also be a case where the TASER device was discharged, but the subject never received current from the device. Indeed, an officer stated he wasn't sure if the probes actually hit Ruiz.

— Ed Flosi

Richard Jacquez, 40, White Male

San Jose, CA, August 17

San Jose police officers had been tailing suspects, including Jacquez, in the recent murder of 38-year-old Christopher Maxwell Wrenn.[348] Police had obtained a video recording of the Wrenn murder, which showed three men, each armed with a weapon, "terrorizing" Wrenn before he was killed.[349]

The officers had been informed that the suspects planned to kill again the next Monday. Jacquez' intended victim was believed to be a woman who was in the car with Jacquez when officers began tailing him. Officers said that they had "credible information" that Jacquez was going to kill her.[350]

Jacquez, on whom a felony murder warrant had been issued, realized he was being followed by MERGE (SWAT) officers. He led police on a chase that ended when he crashed his car and ran from the vehicle.[351] One officer following Jacquez gave foot pursuit. As Jacquez headed towards a house, the officer shot at him - first when Jacquez' back was turned, and again when Jacquez spun around. In explaining why the officer opened fire, department spokesman Sgt. Enrique Garcia said the officer feared for the safety of those inside the home Jacquez was running toward. Jacquez was declared dead at the scene a short time later.[352]

Analysis

This is one of the best cases in the book to discuss police judgment, dynamics and pacing, and the definitions of terms like "imminent." There were media statements that the officer's initial statement was untruthful. It is my understanding from those with knowledge of the case that the officer did not actually make the first statement that was leaked to the media, and that the officer's original statement was consistent with the facts[353] – that Jacquez had been shot in the back.

To put this into more human terms, cops were following a man they believed to be a heavily armed, sadistic and violent murderer, a man whose next victim they believed was in the car with him right then and there. If you're a cop, you live for this moment!

Further, it appeared that the driver, Jacquez, was conducting (and rather well, actually) counter-surveillance, because he spotted the MERGE team and tried to get away. This very well may have saved the life of the woman in the car with Jacquez. There's nothing provocative that occurs through the pursuit and the foot pursuit. At the moment Jacquez approached the house, things got very important, because the officer believed that at this moment, the lives of the people inside that house were in mortal danger.

First of all this officer was presumably aware of whom he was dealing with and the man's propensity to sudden, very violent action. It is actually quite possible to articulate that this man was fleeing from a crime in progress (kidnapping) which we have good reason to believe may have escalated; that Jacquez had been recently involved in a murder-torture, that this man had just gone to extremes to avoid capture, and that the officer believed that if Jacquez entered the house, there was a high, or even unacceptable, likelihood that Jacquez would endanger the safety of those inside. Those two elements together mean that, if articulated by the officer as his reason, the conditions I just mentioned would be a reasonable and justified use of deadly force under the law.

– Nick Selby

The very foundation of police work is the protection of the innocent. This incident is a profound illustration of this idea.

– Ben Singleton

There are two different types of "scenarios" in which an officer may have to make the decision to use deadly force. The first and most common scenario is a "force-on-force" type. The officer reasonably believes that the subject is about to use, or is actually using, some force on the officer or another person that creates an imminent threat of serious bodily injury or death. The officer using deadly force is doing so to stop the actions, and therefore the threat, of the subject from continuing.

The other scenario, as demonstrated in this case, is of the subject who is trying to escape and the threat of death or serious bodily injury it poses to others if he is allowed to. The officer in this case used deadly force in order to stop the escape and to prevent the threat from becoming a reality. Graham v Connor is still the overriding case law that we look to in these cases, but we can also look to another case that speaks specifically to using deadly force on a fleeing subject, Tennessee v Garner.

In Garner, the SCOTUS set forth guidelines for when officers may use deadly force on a fleeing subject. It is important to point out here that many people, including officers, still mistakenly refer to this standard as the "fleeing felon standard." While it is true that Garner committed a felony in the case (which, of course, the SCOTUS ruled was not sufficient to support the use of deadly force), in the guidelines set forth in the decision, the justices carefully avoided "type-casting" the act of the subject into a classification of crime. Instead, they described the guidelines as follows. An officer may use reasonably necessary deadly force if:

1. The officer has probable cause to believe the subject has committed a crime involving the infliction or threatened infliction of serious physical harm, AND

2. The officer has probable cause to believe the subject poses a threat of death or serious physical harm, either to the officer or others, if allowed to escape (it must be noted that the Court did not put a specific time frame or limit to threat posed here, in other words this differs from the "imminent" standard in significant ways).

As cops we understand what probable cause means. It doesn't mean the officer must be exactly correct in his/her beliefs. It isn't the same standard used to convict a defendant in criminal court; it is necessarily a lesser standard.

Applying the facts known in this case to the Garner guidelines, and based on other significant case law decisions that followed (specifically Forrett v Richardson, 112 F.3d 416, 421 (9th Cir. 1997)) that describe the rationale for the need to prevent the desperate escape of an extremely violent (and murderous subject in this case), it appears to me that the officer's use of deadly force was appropriate and consistent with current law enforcement training and standards.

As to the allegations that the officer changed his statement, this may not be entirely true. There is some information that the "change" was actually created by the "first statement" being given by another person only supposing why the officer may have shot, and the "second statement" is actually the officer's only statement.

— Ed Flosi

Charles Hall, 30, White Male

North East, MD, August 21

Just before 9 p.m., Maryland State Trooper Brackett was heading to a call when he passed a Walmart and recognized Hall, a man he knew was wanted by the Cecil County Sheriff's Office for theft. Brackett stopped his car and attempted to arrest Hall, but Hall resisted arrest and began fighting Brackett. During the scuffle, Hall got into his vehicle and began to accelerate, while Brackett – who was still struggling with Hall – was partially inside Hall's vehicle.[354]

To stop Hall, Brackett drew and fired his pistol, striking Hall twice. Hall died at the scene.[355]

Brackett was cleared of all wrongdoing. Video gleaned from an outside Walmart surveillance camera was studied during the investigation, as well as eyewitness accounts, the autopsy report and physical evidence that had been gathered at the shooting scene. The county's chief prosecutor also reported that Hall's DNA was found on Brackett's agency-issued pistol.[356] This is scientific proof of Hall's sweat, saliva or blood on the gun, and serves to corroborate Brackett's claims of a struggle at close quarters.

Searchers found heroin, cocaine and prescription oxycodone inside Hall's vehicle, packaged in a manner that indicated they had been packaged for street sale.[357]

Analysis

This is a completely credible story, backed up by evidence and surveillance video. The use of deadly force seems clearly justified.

– Nick Selby

While engaged in a fight with Officer Bracket, Hall entered his car and took off, dragging him. It is clear that Officer Bracket used deadly force to end the imminent threat to his life.

– Ben Singleton

As a training issue, it must be noted again that officers should avoid reaching deeply into a moving (or about to be moving) vehicle, absent exigent circumstances. Sometimes the extreme risk to the safety of the officer does not make it worth taking the chance. Hall had a theft warrant, which is hardly worth the extreme risk of being dragged by a vehicle.

– Ed Flosi

Unknown, Unknown age, Male of Unknown Race

Phoenix, AZ, August 21

At about 9:30 p.m., Phoenix police responded to reports of a man making threats to seriously injure the occupants of a home near 68th Way and Bell Road.[358] The residents knew the man, and reported he was on some kind of drugs. As the police responded, the man fled to another residence. He struggled with the officers when they found him. The officers deployed a TASER and the man collapsed. He was transported to a hospital, where he died.[359] A Phoenix police officer was treated for a minor injury sustained during the arrest.[360]

Analysis

We don't have enough information here on which to base any opinion. That is strange – this story has maintained an air of mystery since it occurred. We have checked back multiple times and still cannot find the name of the decedent, or any follow-up on this event.

– Nick Selby

The fact that an officer was injured indicates a struggle. But there isn't enough information to assess the officers' actions or make any conclusions as to their reasonableness.

– Ben Singleton

The use of a non-deadly force option such as the TASER device would be an appropriate force response if the officers articulated that the subject was a credible physical threat. Simply "struggling" with officers or that "an altercation ensued" without further articulation may not be enough to justify the use of the TASER device in this case. We have no compelling evidence in order to answer this question in either way.

–– Ed Flosi

Felix Kumi, 61, Black Male

Mount Vernon, NY, August 28

Kumi was an innocent passerby, unintentionally hit by gunfire from officers who had been robbed during an undercover gun buy. Jeffrey Aristy had contacted an undercover officer with the NYPD and allegedly told them he had weapons for sale. The undercover officer and Aristy met in the Bronx. Aristy got in the car and told the undercover officer to drive to Mount Vernon. When they arrived at the intersection of Beekman and Tecumseh avenues, a second suspect, Alvin Smothers, got into the vehicle. One of the two suspects robbed the officer of $2,200 at gunpoint. The officer signaled his backup team, which opened fire on the suspects. Aristy was uninjured and later captured. Alvin Smothers was hit three times, but two bullets from police guns also struck Kumi, who died from his injuries.[361]

Analysis

This is a tragic accident, and very little about it could have been avoided. Police work, especially undercover police work, is dangerous, and sometimes shots are fired. Officers continue to train in marksmanship, but the fact is, accuracy with a handgun is difficult at the best of times.

Commissioner Bratton expressed his "profound sorrow and sympathy" to the Mount Vernon resident's family. "Mr. Kumi was blameless, and this tragedy has tested and tried his family," Bratton said. "I pray that they may find comfort in their hope of resurrection and awakening, and I tender the Department's support and service in their grief."[362]

The city was forthright about its responsibility and apologized – which really isn't much, and a lawsuit is certainly in the offing, but it *was* one of the city's very rare apologies.[363]

– Nick Selby

Mr. Kumi's death was truly unfortunate. Although cases like Mr. Kumi's are rare, we police officers must respond with compassion and continue to train and improve our ability to mitigate the risks posed to the innocent.

– Ben Singleton

This was a terribly sad incident in a case where officers were using appropriate deadly force, based on the imminent threat of serious bodily injury or death. There was no intent to shoot Kumi and the NYPD did the right thing by accepting responsibility for the death.

–– Ed Flosi

SEPTEMBER

Lucas Markus, 33, White Male

Girardville, PA, September 4

State police responded to numerous complaints at 4:10 a.m., about Markus running up and down in the vicinity of Main Street and Second Street in Girardville. He was yelling and trying to get into passing cars. Police arrived and ordered Markus to stop, but Markus didn't respond to verbal commands from the troopers. Markus was subsequently TASED. As he was being handcuffed, he went into cardiac arrest. Police called for an ambulance and began CPR. Markus was transported by helicopter to St. Joseph Medical Center, where he died at 2:35 p.m. Saturday[364].

Analysis

The autopsy has been completed and the assistant chief deputy coroner in Berks County stated that, aside from cardiac arrest, the autopsy didn't reveal anything conclusive — however, they had not received toxicology results. These still have not been made public. Short of those — which I expect to reveal acute methamphetamine, PCP or synthetic marijuana intoxication — I can only say the troopers clearly intended non-deadly force.

– Nick Selby

This is most likely another death caused by drug-induced psychosis combined with physical stress.

– Ben Singleton

The use of the TASER device would be an appropriate force option if the officer was able to articulate a credible physical threat that Markus presented during the arrest process.

– Ed Flosi

Manuel Ornelas, 47, Hispanic Male

Long Beach, CA, September 5

Around 10:40 a.m., police in Long Beach, California were dispatched to a residence regarding Ornelas,[365] who had been reported by callers to have been acting violently, destroying the residence, and who was possibly under the influence of narcotics. Arriving officers observed Ornelas throwing items from out of a second-story window, including a television. Ornelas also smashed out several windows of the residence. Officers observed that Ornelas was bleeding profusely, possibly from cuts he sustained while breaking out the windows. They requested that the Fire Department respond and stand by, based on Ornelas' bizarre behavior[366].

Officers ordered Ornelas to surrender as he left the house, but instead he fled into the garage. The Officers confronted him and attempted non-lethal means to take him into custody, including continued verbal commands, a TASER, physical force, and a carotid restraint.

Officers were able to take Ornelas into custody after several minutes. While officers were monitoring him, Ornelas went into cardiac arrest. Officers began lifesaving measures, which the Long Beach Fire Department took over upon their arrival. Fire personnel transported Ornelas to a local hospital where he was pronounced deceased a short time later.

Analysis

Despite the reporting of the death of Ornelas as one of "Natural Causes,"[367] we can't find any autopsy[368] or toxicology information to go on. Certainly his behavior was bizarre and his own roommate reported to 911 that Ornelas was under the influence of narcotics. His imperviousness to pain (the broken glass) and TASER is indicative of narcotics. Note that the "carotid restraint" referred to by the Long Beach government is not a choke hold, but rather one designed to limit blood flow to the brain, temporarily, to induce unconsciousness. This is an approved, but highly technical hold, and the user must be trained in its application. Until we have autopsy results we can only say that it appears the officers attempted non-deadly force and control.

– Nick Selby

The officers' handling of this incident could not have been more appropriate and reasonable. Ornelas was destroying property, behaving violently, and bleeding profusely before officers arrived. Many of the decedents in cases like this one die as a result of decisions made prior to police arrival. Police officers are often forced to deal with impossible situations and held responsible for unavoidable outcomes that occur. In this case, their handling of Ornelas was completely reasonable.

– Ben Singleton

The Long Beach Police officers' tactics in this case were very sound. Recognizing that a subject might be in a medical crisis and having medical personnel stand-by is a well thought out plan. The TASER device and carotid restraint options used here are known to be non-deadly force options by most agencies, but they would require that the subject presented a credible threat to the officers to be deemed as appropriate. As this case occurred within the 9th Circuit Appeals Court jurisdiction, this threat articulation is even more important.

It should be noted that many years ago some agencies severely restricted the use of the carotid restraint, or placed it at the level of deadly force, when it was believed that the technique was responsible for many in-custody deaths. Current medical and scientific research has demonstrated that a properly applied carotid restraint has very little likelihood of causing death.

Due to this research, many of those same agencies have repealed those policies that were highly restrictive. The key to maintaining the carotid restraint as a viable force option is quality training in the proper application and post-application care.

– Ed Flosi

India Kager, 28, Black Female

Virginia Beach, VA, September 5

Angelo Delano Perry of Virginia Beach was a person of interest in a homicide. Investigators believed he would commit another act of violence. Perry was inside a car being driven by India Kager when the car was stopped at a 7-Eleven by four uniformed Special Operations officers. Perry was sitting in the front passenger seat of Kager's car, and their four-month-old son was in the back seat. He fired four rounds at officers, hitting one. Police returned fire, killing Perry and Kager.

One of his bullets in Perry's volley passed through the sleeve of the shirt worn by one officer, but no officers were injured by gunfire. Police returned 30 shots into the vehicle, hitting both Perry and Kager.

At the time the police believed that Perry and Kager were the only occupants visible in the vehicle.[369] The child, fortunately, was unharmed.[370]

Police recovered two pistols – the TEC9 and a Kel-Tec – from Perry's vehicle. Ballistics revealed that these guns were used in four violent crimes within several months, including two homicides. Gina Best, Kager's mother, later claimed she was angry at police for shooting her unarmed daughter, and endangering Kager's infant child.

Virginia Beach Police Chief Jim Cervera stated[371] that at the time of the incident Perry was a suspect in two shooting murders, a robbery, an aggravated assault and a home invasion.[372] Cervera stated that over a period of 40 days, six people were shot, two of them killed – and all of the cases can be linked to the guns Angelo Perry used on Sept. 5 to shoot at police. The weapons captured from Perry and Kager's vehicle had been, within a span of 26 days, used to shoot five individuals, killing two of them.

Analysis

This would appear to be one of the most straightforward applications of deadly force – the criminal fired multiple times at police, who returned fire, hitting the criminal and the person who was driving the vehicle in which they were riding.

Ms. Kager shared an infant son and maintained a relationship with Perry, an active murderer and robber in the midst of a violent crime spree. Ms. Kager willingly brought their four-month-old son into a vehicle with an armed Perry – I simply find it impossible to believe she was unaware of his criminal activity, or the fact that he was heavily armed. Had she not been sitting in the front seat next to Perry when he attempted to murder four police officers by firing indiscriminately at them, Ms. Kager would undoubtedly be alive today.

– Nick Selby

Losing a child is extremely tragic and difficult, no matter the circumstances. It is natural for families of loved ones to seek closure, and even retribution. But in extreme cases like this one, their refusal to acknowledge the impact of their family member's poor choices on the outcome is incredibly unfair.

Ms. Kager chose to support criminal activity. In fact, she probably shared in the proceeds. When officers approached her car and Perry reached for his gun, preparing to murder them, Ms. Kager chose to stay by his side. It's unfortunate that Ms. Best lost her daughter. It's even more unfortunate that choices made by her daughter and Perry left a 4-month-old child without a mother or father. The poor judgment and life choices made by loved ones cannot be scapegoated onto the police they put in an impossible situation.

– Ben Singleton

This case presents a few questions. The first question, surrounding the appropriateness of the deadly force application on a subject that is actively firing a gun at officers, is truly a straightforward analysis. Perry presented a clear imminent threat to the officers and therefore deadly force was appropriate at that time to stop his actions.

The second question surrounding the unintentional shooting of Kager is really an unfortunate twist to a clear cut use of force. It is understandable

Kager's family would be upset and asking questions, but they fail to accept certain facts that contributed to the death of Kager.

Perry was a willing passenger in the car. It is difficult for me to believe that Kager was ignorant of Perry's activity, or of the fact there were firearms in the car. If one person is to be held truly responsible for Kager's death, it would most certainly have to be Perry. But for his actions the officers would have not been forced to defend themselves.

Lastly, I am somewhat surprised that there wasn't a controversy about the number of rounds fired. This is a common complaint, people believing officers shouldn't have had to fire as many shots as they did. Although it's not in this study, this type of complaint was recently seen again in the shooting of Mario Woods in San Francisco, CA.

In the Woods case, officers fired about 27 rounds at Woods, striking him 20 times. Some groups charged that it wasn't needed to shoot so many times, although this flies in the face of contemporary law enforcement training and standards.

In a recent SCOTUS decision discussing this question, the opinion summarized that it makes sense that, if officers are justified in firing at a suspect in order to end a severe threat to public safety, they need not stop shooting until the threat has ended (Plumhoff v. Rickard, 2014).

– Ed Flosi

Ben CdeBaca, 45, Male of Unknown Race

Bernalillo, NM, September 6

Police say that the incident began with a "rolling domestic" - a domestic dispute within a motor vehicle; the blue sedan that carried CdeBaca and the female driver was snaking through a McDonald's drive-thru when the fight began. CdeBaca tried to take control of the car from the driver, leading to a crash with another car. Witnesses say CdeBaca then jumped out of the car and made his way into a Walmart across the street. [373] Inside the Walmart, Bernalillo Police say CdeBaca made his way to the electronics section, where he knocked over TVs and electronics, and fought with customers and employees, shouting: "You guys are going to kill me! You guys are going to kill me!"[374]

When police arrived, officers struggled to handcuff CdeBaca. He was restrained, and then police say he suddenly died. Medical crews on scene tried to revive him. [375] The Office of the Medical Investigator conducted an autopsy Monday on CdeBaca, but the police department has not received the results,[376] and as of February, 2016 no autopsy or toxicology were publicly available.

Analysis

If we sense a pattern here, in September, it is because there is one; this is another incident in which a person who appears to be either experiencing an acute mental illness episode or acute narcotics intoxication, or both, engaged in violent and destructive behavior, was confronted by officers who used non-deadly force, and died as a result of his exertion.

– Nick Selby

Unless this is a statistically improbable exception, CdeBaca was in the throes of a psychotic episode, which was probably drug-induced, and exerted himself to death.

– Ben Singleton

This is another case where officers used what appears to have been only controlling force and possibly body weight to subdue a violently resisting subject. Barring other information that might come to light, this would have been an appropriate response.

– Ed Flosi

Richard Cosentino, 63, Male of Unknown Race

Providence, RI, September 6

Police and firefighters were called to the 16-story Carroll Tower apartment building at about 4 a.m., responding to a report of a man stuck in an elevator.[377] On their arrival, firefighters were able to free Cosentino from inside the elevator, but as the doors opened, Cosentino, reported as "highly intoxicated," became combative and agitated,[378] swinging at firefighters, according to both police and firefighters. Police state that Cosentino was handcuffed and placed inside a police car, where he experienced cardiac arrest. He was transported to Rhode Island Hospital, where he was pronounced dead.

Residents described Cosentino as a nice person who would talk to himself.[379] Neighbors described him as suffering from mental illness.[380] It was alleged that Cosentino never actually hit the fire chief he was accused of hitting.

Analysis

What sets this apart from other similar incidents (intoxicated, mentally ill man fighting with police and dying of cardiac arrest) are the allegations that Cosentino never actually struck the fire-chief. From my perspective, attempting to punch someone is as much a cause for physical restraint as actually making contact – this seems to be another case in which the issues surrounding police use of force have been misunderstood by witnesses.

– Nick Selby

Most states have criminal attempt statutes that apply to assaultive offenses. An attempt to assault a public servant is an arrestable offense, so Cosentino's arrest was lawful whether or not the punch landed. It appears that minimal force was used to handcuff Cosentino. I believe his death was the result of factors outside the officers' control.

– Ben Singleton

The force analysis for this case is the same as for the previous one. Using controlling force and possibly body weight to subdue a violently resisting subject would be an appropriate response, again barring other information that might come to light.

Officers are trained, and the law supports the fact, that they need not actually take a punch, hit, or kick to confirm the subject's intent prior to using reasonable force, if the fact and circumstances would lead an officer to believe the person's intent was to attack. This holds true for other threats as well.

– Ed Flosi

Jordn Miller, 24, White Male

Springfield Township, OH, September 8
Officers were dispatched around 3 p.m. to a 911 call about a naked man acting erratically.[381] When officers arrived they encountered Jordn Miller, who had dressed in the intervening time, and was attempting to steal a car. When they tried to remove him from the car, Miller resisted, kicking officers and biting one of the officers on the leg. An officer deployed his TASER, which allowed them to control Miller and handcuff him.[382] After being handcuffed, Miller continued to struggle until EMS arrived, at which point Miller stopped breathing. EMS transported Miller to Akron City Hospital, where he died. The officer wounded by the bite was treated after the incident.

The investigation revealed Miller, whose family states he suffered from mental illness (a bipolar disorder) and battled drug addiction. Miller's fiancé stated that Miller had taken methamphetamine[383] three days before the incident, and that Miller hadn't slept for days, couldn't eat, and was hallucinating and suffering from food poisoning. Summit County Medical Examiner's office notes indicate Miller was prescribed methadone. Miller's mother confirmed that Miller had taken heroin.[384] The Beacon Journal reported that Miller pled guilty in January, 2015 to four counts of felony drug charges in Summit County Common Pleas Court and was sentenced[385] to 24 months of community control, as well as being ordered to refrain from all drug and alcohol use.

Analysis

Like many cases in this month, Miller's actions were precipitated by heavy illegal drug use which likely aggravated a mental illness. Officers used non-deadly force to counteract an attack (bites are extremely dangerous) and Miller's health and drug-addiction conditions caused his death.

– Nick Selby

Although Miller died while in police custody, his death was the result of a chain of events that started days before. Methamphetamine addicts often go days without food or sleep while binging on the drug. This can amplify its hallucinogenic effects, and cause intense paranoia. This combined with the negative health effects of habitual drug use, lack of basic nutrition, and sleep deprivation probably caused Miller's death.

– Ben Singleton

We have some evidence of articulated threat in this case, in the actions of the subject biting and kicking at the officer during the arrest process. The use of a TASER in this incident would be appropriate and consistent with current law enforcement training and practices.

This case provides an opportunity to encourage officers to stay away from catch phrases like "struggling" or "resisting" without providing some context as to what that means. The catch phrases are often overly generic and are subjective in their interpretation. Remember, the force analysis must be based on objective facts and circumstances.

– Ed Flosi

Nicholas Alan Johnson, 32, Male of Unknown Race

Muscoy, CA, September 18

Johnson was wanted by police in connection with a home-invasion and robbery[386] in Devore the day before.[387] When Sheriff's Specialized Enforcement Division deputies recognized and tried to stop Johnson's Chevy Tahoe, Johnson "refused to stop, and a pursuit was initiated at approximately 12:49 p.m. The pursuit continued through Fontana and San Bernardino, reaching speeds in excess of 100 mph with the suspect running several stop signs and red lights, narrowly missing several pedestrians. The suspect then entered the northbound 215 freeway traveling southbound at a high rate of speed into oncoming traffic continuing to jeopardize the safety of the public."[388]

Specially trained sheriff's deputy sharpshooters, in a pursuing helicopter, then fired at the driver compartment of Johnson's Tahoe, striking Johnson with a rifle round. Johnson leapt out of his still-moving vehicle against traffic on the freeway. His car wrecked out in a head-on collision with another vehicle, which contained an adult male, an adult female, and a 13-year-old male juvenile. The male passengers were treated and released. The female was hospitalized with injuries.

Analysis

This incident was controversial because of the shooting from the helicopter at what some have described as an "unarmed" man. Our methodology refers to a person using a vehicle as a weapon as being considered armed, but we have included this here because Johnson did not specifically target people with his vehicle – rather he was using it to escape. Still, Johnson was fleeing a violent crime at 100 mph in a 5,300-lb. vehicle going the wrong way on a crowded freeway. He sent the Tahoe crashing into oncoming traffic. This man, whether he was armed, was by any reasonable conclusion, dangerous and deadly.

Johnson was, in my opinion, engaging in activities that can reasonably be described as those which would clearly lead, without intervention, to deadly results. This justifies the use of deadly force to stop Johnson's actions. The only way deputies could apply this force – they had tried and failed at many maneuvers and other tactics, such as spike-strips — were not practically applicable as Johnson was behaving in such blatant disregard for human life. Shots from the air were, in fact, the only option left to deputies. Deputies who fly for the San Bernardino Sheriff's Department are required to show proficiency at shooting from the sky, a skill they practice every 90 days, minimally, at the academy at Glen Helen Rehabilitation Center in Devore, training for exactly these kinds of scenarios.[389]

The director of the Sheriff's Aviation Unit has said shooting from the air at a vehicle is rare, but it, "is something we've trained for quite a long time. We do qualify on the ground and in the air … We actively train to protect the citizens." Since training for the unit began in 1981, there have been seven deputy-involved shootings from the air, a Sheriff's spokesman said.[390]

This case is fairly easy to evaluate if one keeps in mind the principles of the evaluation factors without getting distracted by the sensational details of this case. We do not see a law enforcement deadly force application from a helicopter upon the driver of a moving vehicle very often. This in itself is so rare of an occurrence that some might incorrectly jump to a conclusion that it is inappropriate. It is here that we must remember that all law enforcement contacts are different and must be looked at within the context of the event.

– Nick Selby

I equate the launching of a vehicle into oncoming traffic to the firing of a weapon into a crowd. One has to weigh the dangers posed to the innocent public when making use of force decisions. The police must, as a condition of their sworn duties, protect the innocent. When Johnson chose to launch his vehicle into oncoming traffic, endangering the lives of the innocent, officers did what they had to do to protect them. The fact that this agency prepared for such an occurrence by training to shoot from the air is a testament to their tactical preparedness and sincere interest in defending their community.

– Ben Singleton

Johnson, in his behavior and actions, was creating a substantial risk of serious bodily injury or deaths to others. While we don't know if this threat was intentionally directed at others, the threat was present and credible. Officers are trained to react to the threat presented.

Given the level of training this deputy successfully completed before taking this very difficult shot, his use of deadly force to stop the threat presented by Johnson would be appropriate and consistent with current law enforcement training and practices.

– Ed Flosi

Cecil Lacy, 50, Male of Unknown Race

Tulalip Indian Reservation, WA, September 18

Two Tulalip Tribal Police Department officers and one Snohomish County Sheriff's Office deputy responded to reports of a man walking in the roadway around 9:45 p.m.[391] When officers arrived they detained Lacy and placed him in protective custody in order to remove him from the road. Lacy began fighting with officers while they tried to place him in the patrol car,[392] and he became unresponsive during the altercation. Officers attempted CPR to revive him until medical aid arrived, but he died at the scene.[393]

In ruling the death accidental, Dr. Daniel Selove said he relied on police and medical investigative reports as well as autopsy and toxicology results.[394] Selove attributed Lacy's death to a heart attack due to methamphetamine in his system and several health-related factors, including an enlarged heart, obesity, hypertension, diagnoses of schizophrenia and bipolar disorder, as well as the struggle with police.

Analysis

This is yet another in a trend of cases in which older, overweight men in poor shape and high on methamphetamine behave in bizarre manners that involve them with law enforcement, and then fight with officers and die as a result of their health condition.

– Nick Selby

If nothing else, I hope these cases will shed some light on the methamphetamine epidemic that started in rural America and has now infiltrated communities across the country, irrespective of affluence or demographics. It has become the most prevalent component of the criminal element. Once created by home cooks, it is now produced in super labs and shipped across the border in tons. As a street cop, and narcotics investigator, I dealt with its wrath on a daily basis. Anyone who claims methamphetamine use is victimless is ignorant of the unspeakable things people are willing to do in pursuit of this drug or while they are under its influence. It absolutely perverts human conscience and morality.

– Ben Singleton

There is no evidence in this case to conclude if Lacy was handcuffed prior to becoming resistive. There is also no mention of what specific force options were used. The case does however bring up some interesting points.

Lacy did not appear to have been arrested for a criminal act, but rather was being taken into protective custody. Officers are trained and understand that they can use reasonable force to effect the seizure of a person being taken for a psychiatric evaluation, but they must also temper that force with the knowledge that the subject's actions involve no criminal activity. The reasonable use of controlling force and body weight would be deemed an appropriate response in most jurisdictions.

There is another training point to illustrate, which working cops will recognize. The moment a person realizes they are going to be put into the back of a police vehicle is one of the more likely times a person will start to resist.

– Ed Flosi

Omar Ali, 27, Semitic Male

Akron, OH, September 21

The 26-year-old mother of Ali's child accused Ali of choking her at the hookah bar Ali owned. The woman told police that at about 4 p.m. Ali became enraged, hit her in the face, choked her and threatened to kill her if she called police. The woman ran down the street and called police. She refused medical attention for the neck injuries the officers observed. The woman signed domestic violence charges against Ali.[395]

Akron drug detectives were already investigating Ali on suspicion of selling drugs at the bar. A SWAT team raided the hookah bar about 8 p.m. and broke down the front door, demanding Ali to surrender. Officers found Ali in the main room of the bar, but he refused to comply with officer's orders. He reached into his back waistband[396] and a SWAT officer fired a single shot, hitting Ali in the torso. After being shot, Ali was treated by SWAT team medics and taken to Akron City Hospital, where he died on October 5.

Officers recovered 2.8 grams of heroin and five unit doses of Suboxone strips hidden in Ali's buttocks.[397] Police suspect Ali was attempting to secrete the drugs in his rectum. Officers also uncovered a gun. Prior to his death, Ali was charged with drug abuse, having a weapon under a disability, domestic violence, domestic violence menacing and assault.[398]

Analysis

This is an example of justified police use of deadly force to combat what appears to be an attempt by the decedent to reach for a weapon, but in which it is later discovered that the person was doing something else. Just because he didn't have a weapon, though, doesn't change the fact that the officer was absolutely justified in his use of deadly force in this case.

There are many cases in which courts have found that officers seeing a person reach in a manner that is consistent with an attempt to grab a weapon are justified in using deadly force to prevent it. It is highly unfortunate for Ali that he chose to secrete drugs in his buttocks and reach for them in a way that would cause any reasonable person to fear Ali was reaching for a hidden weapon. While the fact that Ali had a gun nearby him is not justification for the use of deadly force, it is contextually important to recognize that Ali was known to police as a drug-dealing criminal, was in possession of drugs, and had at least one gun at the time of his death. The police were in fact dealing with a dangerous, weapon-possessing person whom they understood to have just engaged in a violent attack. This may have heightened the officers' sensitivity to the possibility that Ali would introduce a weapon into the situation. Regardless of that context, these officers were well justified in their actions.

— Nick Selby

Police officers are trained to recognize threatening movements and behavior as a matter of survival. By reaching for his waistband near the small of his back, Ali gave the officers the universally recognized sign for "I am drawing my gun." Officers couldn't afford to wait and see what Ali produced from his waistband, as it would then be too late to react if it was a gun.

As a drug-dealing, wife-beating gun owner, Ali cannot be afforded the ability to make these kinds of life threatening movements when confronted by police. Their use of deadly force was absolutely reasonable.

— Ben Singleton

The force analysis must be based on the facts and circumstances known to the officer on scene at the time of the force application. This thought comes directly from the Graham decision and it is followed by yet another very important thought; this is true no matter how compelling that evidence is to be found later. No matter how compelling, revealing, or important is the information found later, after the force application, it can't be part of the evaluation unless the officer knew about it. In this case it may have been determined after the fact that Lacy's reaching actions had nothing to do with drawing a gun - but instead were an effort to hide drugs in his rectum. While compelling in terms of helping us understand Lacy's actions, this was not the stated and reasonable perception of the officers at the moment of their force response.

If the totality of the facts and circumstance known (or perceived) by the shooting officer at the time of the deadly force application led him to believe that Ali was reaching for a gun and therefore presented an imminent threat of serious bodily injury or death to the officers, the use of deadly force would be appropriate and consistent with current law enforcement training and practices, no matter what evidence was discovered later.

– Ed Flosi

William Lemmon, 21, White Male

Akron, OH, September 25

About 1 p.m., Lemmon and another man, who was wearing a mask, entered the Bista Brothers Asian grocery store.[399] The man with the mask could be seen on video holding a gun to a clerk's head while Lemmon kept watch.[400] A clerk threw her purse to the ground, and one of the men grabbed it. The robbers both left, and Lemmon was seen to ride away on a red bicycle.[401]

Officers followed Lemmon to an alley,[402] where he was confronted, and say they warned him several times before shooting him. It is not clear how he allegedly threatened police. No weapon was found.

Analysis

While there is plenty of video of the robbery, we don't have any real sense of what happened during the confrontation in the alley during which Lemmon was shot. It would be impossible to state whether the shooting by the police officers was justified without more information.

– Nick Selby

There is no information regarding the confrontation, and no way to make a determination as to reasonableness.

– Ben Singleton

This case needs more information regarding the actions of the subject at the time of the stop before any reasoned opinion can be rendered. While it is clear that Lemmon was involved in a serious crime, which included a firearm and the threat of serious physical harm, we must know what he was doing at the time of the contact.

– Ed Flosi

Junior Prosper, 31, Black Male

North Miami, FL, September 28

At approximately 5:09 am, Miami Dade dispatched an officer to an accident at an entrance ramp to southbound I-95. The officer made contact with a Road Ranger who advised him that the subject, later identified as Junior Prosper, had been driving a taxi that had crashed, and had run from the scene, south onto I-95. The officer gave chase and attempted to apprehend Prosper. In an ensuing altercation, Prosper bit the officer, almost severing a finger on his left hand.[403] At this point the officer used his TASER, which was ineffective, and finally discharged his service weapon, hitting Prosper. Miami-Dade Fire Rescue pronounced Prosper deceased at the scene.[404] The officer was transported to Ryder Trauma Center where he underwent surgery for his injuries.

Analysis

This is pretty straightforward, with the exception of the response by Prosper's widow, Edeline, who told the local CBS affiliate that her husband was "…a good man. He cared about everybody. He was so nice. The officer shouldn't have killed him."[405] This demonstrates again the failure of police to clearly communicate to the public the circumstances under which officers will apply deadly force. It is also important to note that the officer attempted non-deadly force prior to deadly force.

– Nick Selby

As in some other cases, family members have been unwilling to accept that Prosper's own actions warranted the use of deadly force. Prosper may have been a "good man" who "cared about everyone," as his widow stated, but this doesn't have the slightest bearing on the threat he posed to the officer in this case. The officer killed Prosper because Prosper gave him no other choice when he threatened the officer's life. Anecdotal statements about Prosper's personality are irrelevant in determining whether the officer's response was appropriate. In this case, I believe the officer was reasonable in his use of deadly force.

– Ben Singleton

Prosper had committed a criminal offense and was subject to arrest. When the officers attempted to arrest him, Prosper chose to resist, and then bit an officer so badly he almost lost a finger, demonstrating a clear and credible threat to him. The credible threat makes the use of the TASER in this case appropriate and consistent with current law enforcement training and practices.

– Ed Flosi

Robert Sullivan Christen, 37, White Male

Mora, MN, September 30

Sheriff's deputies received a 911 call from a man stating that he was going to kill someone at a house. Deputy Shanna McIalwain[406] arrived at the house around 9 p.m., and evacuated two children who were in the house. A short time later Christen drove at a high rate of speed and crashed his vehicle into a tree in the front yard of the house. McIalwain came out of the home as Christen was exiting his vehicle. When Christen saw McIalwain,[407] he charged her; the deputy drew her pistol, telling Christen to get on the ground. He continued his charge and attacked McIalwain, repeatedly punching her in the head and face before she fired her gun[408] several times, killing him. McIalwain was treated at the scene for multiple injuries to her forehead and arm. Christen had a history of violence, including at least three Minnesota convictions of assault between 2007 and 2014.[409]

Analysis

A deputy outsized and under attack from a person who has threatened to kill someone, and who then charges without warning, is in a highly dangerous situation. McIalwain repeatedly shouted warnings for Christen to stop and was in danger of being killed herself when she fired.

– Nick Selby

An officer taking repeated blows to the head and face is in a situation that, in and of itself, can warrant his use of deadly force. The fact that Sullivan threatened to murder occupants of the home, crashed his vehicle into a tree at a high rate of speed, and then charged the officer, indicated his intent to make good on his threat. The officer responded appropriately.

– Ben Singleton

The threat presented by Christen was real. He threatened to kill someone; his behavior of crashing his vehicle at a high rate of speed is an indication to his lack of concern for himself or others; and his charging an armed deputy even after she drew a firearm and gave lawful orders to stop; these all contribute to the level of threat posed and resistance Christen was willing to provide in order to complete his threats.

Once the larger and stronger Christen took the deputy to the ground and began striking her in the face, she was faced with making a split-second decision to prevent further attack and serious bodily injury or death, and to save her own life. The use of deadly force in this situation would be appropriate and consistent with current law enforcement training and standards.

– Ed Flosi

OCTOBER

James Joseph Byrd, 45, White Male

Van Nuys, CA, October 3

At 11:36 p.m., Van Nuys patrol officers Zackary Goldstein and Andrew Hacoupian[410] were stopped at a traffic light, when the rear window of their patrol car exploded. Both officers believed that they were being fired upon. They verbalized this to each other and exited their vehicle.[411] They saw Byrd standing on Sepulveda Boulevard right behind it. The officers stated that Byrd was pointing his hand towards them at above waist level, holding an unknown dark object. The officers believed this individual posed an imminent threat to them, and they opened fire.

Paramedics responded and pronounced the suspect dead at scene. No officers were injured during this incident.

A civilian eyewitness provided an account of the suspect's actions that is consistent with him throwing an object from very close range at the rear of the police vehicle. A broken glass bottle was located in the back seat of the black and white police vehicle.[412]

Analysis

Most officers in the position of Goldstein and Hacoupian would have reasonably felt that they were under attack, especially given the circumstances around media coverage of attacks against police officers on duty. And all American law enforcement officers were keenly aware that two NYPD officers, Wenjian Liu and Rafael Ramos, had been assassinated as they sat in their vehicle on a Brooklyn street in late 2014.[413] Additionally, there is a 15-second video that appeared to show a threat to law enforcement officers which had been widely circulated in law enforcement circles, and had even been the subject of briefings by LAPD officials to rank-and-file officers in roll call meetings, which may -have played a part in these officers' situational awareness. The video, taken from a vehicle parked behind a black-and-white police cruiser in downtown L.A., opens with a shot of the patrol car which pans quickly down to show someone holding a revolver. The person shows the gun off for the camera, then the shot cuts back to the patrol car as an officer gets out and walks away.[414] Even had that video not made the rounds (it later proved to be a promotional video for a rap group and not an actual threat against police), the totality of these circumstances would clearly lead a reasonable person to fear for his life.

— Nick Selby

We judge actions by police based on the standard of reasonableness. The risks of assassination, or the baiting of officers into an ambush, are unfortunately real and police officers are cognizant of these threats. When the rear window of a police car explodes, probably making a sound similar to that of a gunshot, officers exit the car to assess the threat and defend their lives. If they see a man pointing an unknown dark object at them, in the way one would point a gun, it is reasonable for these officers to believe that the man is armed, just shot out the back window of their police car, and intends to cause them harm. In that context, their response was completely reasonable.

— Ben Singleton

This is another case that appears to be an appropriate use of deadly force, based on the totality of the facts and circumstances known (and perceived) by the officers at the time of the force application, no matter how compelling any evidence to the contrary is found to be later. Based on the tenor of the situation and how outright threats to the lives of police officers were made by this point, these two officers could have easily perceived themselves as being fired upon. When they exited their vehicle, they reasonably perceived a person pointing an object at them in a manner that a person with a gun would use. While it is a tragedy for all involved that an unarmed man was shot and killed, the actions of the officers would be appear to be reasonable based on their perception of imminent threat of serious bodily injury or death.

It is important to point out that Byrd, although unarmed, is not completely blameless in this incident. His deliberate actions created the situation to which the officers felt compelled to react.

– Ed Flosi

Johnny Rangel, 25, Hispanic Male

Valinda, CA, October 16

Media reports were confusing, initially placing the event in the wrong city and stating that deputies responded to a report that someone had broken into a home shortly after 1:15 am.[415] In fact, the incident had begun earlier, when officers approached a man they believed appeared to be a gang member[416] and he fled. As they followed him, a man and woman came out of a nearby house and told the officers that the man had broken out the sliding glass door leading to their backyard and come inside the house. The male witness was afraid for his elderly parents who were sleeping in one of the bedrooms, and especially for his father, who couldn't walk without assistance. Police said they could hear Rangel moving furniture around and breaking glass. They were under the impression he had taken a hostage, so when the officers entered the house they feared a hostage situation.

Inside, they were met by Rangel. The officers gave him verbal commands, but Rangel refused to cooperate and began to fight with them. According to police, the officers deployed TASERs at least once, to no effect. Police say Rangel charged an officer who had his gun drawn and attempted to take his weapon. During the struggle for the gun, the deputy fired a single shot, which hit Rangel, who died at the scene.

Police say Rangel belonged to a gang in La Puente and had an injunction restraining him from associating with other gang members in the area.

Analysis

Rangel's behavior was consistent with that of someone suffering from acute drug intoxication. A website that tracks the use of methamphetamine has stated that Rangel was high on the drug at the time of the incident,[417] but we couldn't find official reference to this, nor a toxicology report or autopsy. Despite this, Rangel's behavior was erratic and threatening to multiple people, and the grabbing of a deputy's gun is on its face a deadly attack.

– Nick Selby

Although Rangel's alleged use of methamphetamine will probably be confirmed, it's not a necessary component to justify this officer's use of deadly force. As I've previously stated, an attempt to disarm an officer warrants the use of deadly force to prevent the statistical probability that, if obtained by the assailant, the weapon will be turned against the officer. There are not many well-defined examples of justified uses of deadly force against unarmed people. But the attempted disarmament of a police officer is one of them.

– Ben Singleton

In this incident, there were a couple of time frames when different types of force were used. Rangel was a demonstrated threat to others based on his background and his behavior on that day. When he began to fight with the officers, he became a credible physical threat to the officers so the use of the TASER would be appropriate. Once Rangel attempted to take the officer's weapon, he himself changed the nature of the threat with the possibility he might gain control of the officer's weapon, and raised it to an imminent threat of serious bodily injury or death. The use of deadly force in this case would be appropriate.

In this case, as is almost always the case, when a subject attempts to gain control of an officer's weapon, the person demonstrates an inclination toward shooting the officer with his own weapon. Indeed, it is important to point out that the subject need not get full control of the weapon to be a deadly threat.

– Ed Flosi

Paterson Brown, Jr., 18, Black Male

Richmond, VA, October 17

David L. Cobb, an off-duty police officer, drove his car into a car wash to be cleaned. Brown, an employee, got into the officer's car and drove it out of the washing bay. Witnesses told police Cobb ordered Brown out of the car, which belonged to the officer's girlfriend. Cobb apparently pleaded with Brown to get out of the car, and tried several methods to get him out of the car peacefully. A witness told the Richmond Times-Dispatch that "He didn't want to do it…He tried and tried to get him out." The Times-dispatch reports that the officer asked a clerk at the gas station to call police during the incident, but between that call and the arrival of officers, Brown moved suddenly as if reaching for a weapon, and the officer fired a shot.

Surveillance video from the car wash showed Cobb and Brown struggled briefly before a shot was fired. No weapon was recovered from the decedent.[418] Just over year earlier, Brown robbed a James River High School student of some cash and a cellphone at gunpoint in the backseat of a car. He was convicted and his sentence suspended.[419]

In February, 2016, a Chesterfield Grand Jury indicted Cobb on second-degree murder charges in the shooting death of Brown. A prosecutor told Grand Jurors that the fact that Cobb's gun was drawn for over three minutes was evidence that Brown represented no actual threat to Cobb. The prosecutor said that a surveillance showed Brown trying to close the car door and Cobb prevented him from closing it.

Analysis

This case is an example of the difficulty of reaching conclusions based on media accounts and the complexity of judging deadly force cases to those not present during an event, or participating in the investigation. Capt. Brad Badgerow of the Chesterfield County Police Department, having viewed the surveillance video, stated that the account of the officer and witnesses was an accurate account of what had transpired. The witness said the officer was so shaken that he was in tears in the parking lot after the shooting. The bizarre behavior of the young man, the witness and video corroboration of the officer's account, including Brown's inexplicable lunge, combine to create the appearance of a totality of circumstances that would make use of deadly force appear reasonable.

Cobb, who had served as a school resource officer, had no history of violence and since has surrendered his personal firearm and the one issued to him by the RPD. Cobb's trial date has been set for June, 2016.[420]

– Nick Selby

Police officers are never truly off-duty. They aren't privileged with the ability to forget all that they know about the criminal element when conducting their personal lives. When this confrontation started, the officer checked in service, psychologically. He was a cop confronting a criminal.

There isn't enough information regarding the threat posed by Patterson to conclude whether the shooting was reasonable or not, but the officer's decision to intervene was reasonable.

– Ben Singleton

Off-duty officers generally have limited force options available and no immediate access to get assistance from other officers. This places an officer at an extreme disadvantage if he decides to take off-duty action. Indeed, most agencies and trainers discourage taking off-duty actions unless there is a threat to life involved.

The crime initially involved a stolen vehicle. While this crime is a felony by most standards, it is also clearly a property crime. It would be interesting to know why the officer decided to act as he did and if he would have acted the same way if it was someone else's vehicle.

By the officer choosing to act, he should have realized that his only force option available, assuming Brown did not surrender, was his firearm. In choosing to draw his firearm and in choosing to move in at very close quarter, the officer left very little room for error. If this was a life-threatening event, it would be different, but one must remember that at this point the crime was a property crime.

These are all tactical errors on the part of the officer that contributed to the eventual shooting of Brown. As for the actual shooting, it would be hard to ignore Brown's own role in this incident as being at least partially to blame, especially if it is shown that Brown did lunge for the officer's pistol. Without more information, I cannot render a reasoned opinion as to the appropriateness of the officer's use of deadly force.

– Ed Flosi

Ryan [Ruiz|Christopher] Rodriguez, 21, Hispanic Male

Visalia, CA, October 21
At 11:15 am, two officers assigned to the National Family Violence Apprehension detail attempted to serve a domestic violence warrant for arrest on Rodriguez.

Sheriff Mike Boudreaux stated that Rodriguez ran out the back door, and one of the officers told him to stop and tried to stop him. The second officer, a deputy, ran behind the house, and Rodriguez tried to take the deputy's gun. The deputy then struck Rodriguez with the gun, but during the struggle, Boudreaux said, "he's getting the better of the officers,"[421] and both officers opened fire on him. Both officers were injured and were taken to the hospital with bruises and abrasions, the sheriff said. Rodriguez died at the scene.

Rodriguez had six outstanding warrants for domestic violence and one for assault with a deadly weapon.

Analysis
This case is really short on details. It would be nice to know the reaction by Rodriguez of being pistol-whipped by the deputy, the availability to the

officers of non-deadly force options, and perhaps most important, whether the officers were aware of Rodriguez' criminal history (particularly the aggravated assault charge) – which is likely but not certain, and which would absolutely have had a bearing on the officers' demeanor during the encounter. Once again, officer body-worn video could answer many questions that may forever remain unanswered.

– Nick Selby

We aren't privy to the details that are presumably written in police reports, but the officers' injuries indicate they were involved in an intense struggle. The officers would have to articulate how that struggle escalated to the point that they felt their lives were in danger in order to justify their use of deadly force.

– Ben Singleton

This is another case where what we know isn't detailed enough to render a reasoned opinion on the two officer's use of deadly force. There is some information that Rodriguez was attempting to gain control of the initial deputy's gun, which would certainly make him a deadly threat at that moment. Using the pistol as an impact weapon would be an appropriate response.

The question comes in where the information indicates that Rodriguez was "getting the better of the officers," and the officers shot him. This phrase has no substantive value in a force analysis as it is vague and overly subjective as to its meaning. There is some indication of injuries to the officers ("hospital with bruises and abrasions"), but it's not clear how serious, nor what those injuries were.

Although it may be true Rodriguez was getting the better of the officers, and that there may be more details in the investigative files to better amplify what that phrase means, this serves as another good time to remind officers that any articulation to justify the use of force option should be detailed and descriptive, and should include specific and objective facts and circumstances.

– Ed Flosi

Mario Perdigone, 36, White Male

Corpus Christie, TX, October 21

Mario Anthony Perdigone called 911 before 5:30 a.m. asking for help. As officers were headed to the home, another call came in to 911 about a man running in the middle of Leopard Street. The caller said the man was trying to get hit by passing cars. Officers encountered Perdigone, and then struggled with him as they tried to move him out of the roadway. They used a TASER, and then handcuffed him. "The man soon became unresponsive," said KRIS-TV, in the only legitimate media story we can find reporting on the incident."[422] He was rushed to a hospital where doctors pronounced him dead."

Analysis

And that's it. No released autopsy. No police press release. No other media coverage. Hardly any other details, except this: "Mario Anthony Perdigone died Oct. 21, 2015. He was 36. Services will be at 1 p.m. Oct. 29 at Duncan Cemetery." Of 153 killings by police in 2015, this case has by far the least available public information. This is one of the most inexplicably unpublicized cases of 2015.

– Nick Selby

Based on Perdigone's reported behavior, because that is the only available indicator, I believe his death was another one that can be attributed to a combination of physical stress and a psychotic episode, probably drug-induced.

– Ben Singleton

This case is lacking details, but in the force analysis it appears the officers used physical controlling force and a TASER only. The TASER would be an appropriate force response if the officers articulated a credible physical threat created by the Perdigone's struggling. Unfortunately, the only information we know is that a struggle happened. We lack enough details to know the level of the struggle, and don't know what threat the officers perceived at the time of the force application.

– Ed Flosi

Kenneth Schick 48, White Male

Wakarusa, KS, October 23

The county's 911-center received a call from Shawnee County dispatch about a possible domestic disturbance at 1:20 a.m. Tuesday. Deputies arrived at 1:35 a.m. and found a domestic disturbance that included a hostage situation in which Schick was holding his parents hostage. Police used TASERS and pepper spray to gain control of Schick.[423] After some time in handcuffs, officers noticed that Schick was not breathing, and called an ambulance, according to a web-post by Schick's brother, Bob, who notes[424] that Schick "had a chemical imbalance and battled depression, anxiety and paranoia most of his adult life. He responded well to treatment, when he didn't feel 'out of his skin' on the meds." Bob states in his post that after having a pleasant day with his parents, "it was then his chemical imbalance took over, and he began speaking nonsensically about things that didn't make sense to mom and she became scared for him. (This has happened before when he was off his meds and hadn't slept for 3-4 days)."

Bob notes two things of tremendous interest. First, he claims officers TASERED Schick "three to four times," and pepper-sprayed him. He also claims that after police noticed that Schick had stopped breathing, "Removing the handcuffs they then administered CPR for the 30-40 minutes it took for an ambulance to arrive."

Analysis

This is another case involving a mentally ill man with a prior diagnosis of, and medication to treat, serious mental illness. The amount of time involved in this rural call and the presence of Schick's parents might indicate that officers had been made aware of this mental health condition, which might have affected their treatment of Schick. I believe that none of the officers intended to apply deadly force, but I must note that repeated applications of TASER and pepper spray are sub-optimal methods to cope with a person in an acute mental illness episode. Again, our findings of the nationwide need for better training for first responders for the needs of the mentally ill can't be emphasized enough.

– Nick Selby

Irrational, criminal, and deadly behavior sometimes accompanies mental illness. We can only expect police officers to manage the behavior that they were called to deal with in the first place. Sometimes the source of that behavior is impossible to ascertain. In fact, as I read this case, I wonder whether Schick had been self-medicating with illicit drugs, as many people in his condition do. Officers have to make decisions based on the behavior exhibited by the suspect, and by the threats posed by that behavior. We cannot expect police officers to psychoanalyze people engaged in violence to determine the appropriate force response. This is a slippery slope that could lead to unreasonable expectations and unintended consequences.

– Ben Singleton

Deputies arrived to find they were in the midst of an "ongoing" domestic violence event that included a hostage situation, certainly a tense situation that would benefit from a quick resolution. The officers appeared to have used TASER and OC Spray to effect Schick's arrest. It is important to remember that the actions of the subject and the threats created by the subject must be dealt with before any other matter.

If Schick demonstrated a credible threat to the officers while they were involved in trying to defuse the situation, the use of the TASER device and OC Spray would be appropriate.

As for the amount of TASER cycles used, this is something that could be easily reconciled by obtaining the printouts from the device(s). It is important to point out that while some organizations have discussed limiting the number of cycles to a specific amount (absent exigent circumstances), these numbers are still only guidelines, not legal standards.

– Ed Flosi

Anthony Ashford, 29, Black Male

San Diego, CA, October 27

At about 10:45 p.m., nine-year veteran, San Diego Harbor Police Officer Sulimoni Ahfook spotted Ashford looking into vehicles in the parking lot of a local hotel. He approached to Ashford to ask him what he was doing. Police say Ashford "immediately attacked" Ahfook, and both fell to the ground. During the struggle, Ahfook deployed his TASER with the result that both he and Ashford were stunned by the device. Ashford continued to fight and attempted to take Ahfook's handgun from his holster. Ahfook fired a single shot.[425] Ashford died at the scene. Ahfook was briefly hospitalized for "moderate injuries."[426] A homicide investigator said security personnel at the Holiday Inn had ejected Ashford from their lobby for causing a disturbance earlier.[427] Harbor Police are not outfitted with body cameras, so there is no footage of the shooting from the officer's perspective.[428]

Analysis

The sudden attack and the failed attempt to TASER would indicate an officer who felt a genuine fear for his life. It would have been useful if body video had been used, to establish some of the facts of the case and provide a record. There are few facts here to analyze, though the situation of an officer alone, struggling with a suspect who has attacked quickly and without warning, and who has fought for the TASER and the handgun, strikes me as a situation in which an officer would reasonably feel sufficiently afraid to warrant deadly force.

– Nick Selby

This is another case of an officer recognizing the threat of an assailant gaining control of his gun and turning it against him. There is no logical explanation available to someone who attempts to take an officer's gun, except that the person intends to use it against the officer. This is another well-defined and clear example of behavior that will elicit deadly force from police officers. Do not attempt to disarm a police officer!

– Ben Singleton

The subject was seen casing vehicles to possibly commit auto burglaries. When the officer approached, Ashford immediately attacked him. A person who attacks an officer without any warning demonstrates an extreme level of threat behavior. Once on the ground, the officer is at a disadvantage in defending himself, making the situation more dire.

The officer attempted to appropriately use the TASER, but it is unlikely to have had any effect at such close quarter, other than to cause localized pain. It's likely to be ineffective against a person with this level of dedication in his attack.

As Ashford attempted to gain control of the officer's gun, he demonstrated a higher threat level, one that created an imminent threat of serious bodily injury or death if Ashford was to be successful. It would be appropriate and consistent with current law enforcement training and standards to use deadly force to prevent the threat from happening.

– Ed Flosi

Omar Lopez, 24, Hispanic Male

Philadelphia, PA, October 27
Just before 2 a.m., a SEPTA officer escorted Lopez from the Huntingdon Station onto the street. Police noted there was a significant size difference between the two; the cop was 5-6, 155 pounds, while the man was about 5-10 and 185 pounds[429] The officer, armed only with a TASER, was responsible for closing stations along the Market-Frankford Line. Outside, Lopez got into "a heated verbal argument" with another man on the street. The officer observed that the other person was being threatened, so he intervened. At this point, surveillance shows that Lopez suddenly turned on the officer, at one point biting him. The officer called for backup, but there was confusion about his location and it was delayed. The fight went to the ground as the pair struggled. The officer drive-stunned Lopez, and finally gained control over him and handcuffed him.[430]

SEPTA policy is to transport any person who has been TASERED to the hospital for a checkup. During the transport to the hospital, Lopez became unresponsive[431] and later died. In January 2016, the Philadelphia Medical Examiner's Office stated that Lopez died of an overdose of PCP. Court records show Lopez was jailed in 2013 for drug possession and had another drug-dealing conviction that led to probation.[432]

The officer suffered bite marks and bruises during the fight. He was taken to the hospital and treated for non-life-threatening injuries. During his career the officer had never once had an excessive force complaint against him.

Analysis

From the beginning this seemed to be another case sounding very much both like an acute narcotic intoxication incident, and like one in which the officer clearly expressed non-deadly intent, but in which circumstances turned beyond the officer's control and made the encounter deadly. The officer behaved reasonably.

I wish to take this opportunity to point out that the SEPTA Police department sending unarmed law enforcement officers out into their transportation system, unable to defend themselves against attacks greater than this, is a stunning failure of imagination and leadership.

– Nick Selby

It is surprising to me that this officer was able to gain control of Lopez, who had a significant size advantage and was under the influence of PCP. It is also a testament to the value of the TASER. Because Lopez overdosed on PCP, I believe the officer's involvement is coincidental rather than causal.

– Ben Singleton

This case seems like a clearly appropriate use of the TASER device against a person who was a credible threat to the officer.

– Ed Flosi

NOVEMBER

Jeremy David Mardis, 6, White Male

Marksville, LA, November 3

Jeremy David Mardis, an unarmed 6-year-old White male, was killed at around 9:30 p.m. on November 3, 2015, by police who, according to media reports, fired "at least" 18 rounds at the vehicle in which Mardis was traveling. The vehicle was being driven by Mardis' father, Chris Few, and Mardis was buckled in the front passenger seat. Few was also struck by gunfire and seriously injured.

The incident occurred at the intersection of Martin Luther King Drive and Taensas St. in Marksville, LA, and involved four sworn Marshals from the Marksville City Marshals, Ward 2. According to Col. Mike Edmonson, superintendent of the Louisiana State Police,[433] two of these Marshals were arrested, Lt. Derrick Stafford, and Officer Norris Greenhouse Jr., Each was charged with one count of second-degree murder and one count of attempted second-degree murder. Lt. Stafford is an eight-year veteran officer at Marksville Police Department, who worked part-time for the Marshals office. Officer Greenhouse is a reserve (volunteer) officer for the Marksville Police Department. It is unclear whether Greenhouse or Stafford were acting in a paid or reserve capacity for the Marshals office. Louisiana State Police confirm to StreetCred PKIC that the Marksville City Marshals Office (Ward 2) was the agency under whose authority the officers were acting. The two other officers involved, but not yet charged, are Lt. Jason Brouillette, a 13-year veteran with the Marksville Police Department; and Sgt. Kenneth Parnell, who has served 5 years with the Marksville Police Department.

Both officers charged in the incident are Black males.

While early media reports suggested[434] that the car in which the decedent was traveling had struck or attempted to strike a police vehicle or police officers, this has been ruled out by later statements by police officials. No police officer was injured.

At least two of the officers have previously been accused of violence according to court records[435] and media reports. In addition to being named in that July 2015 suit, Lt. Stafford was indicted in 2011 by a Rapides Parish grand jury on charges of aggravated rape.[436]

One of the officers involved in the incident is a reserve police officer.

It is unknown whether the autopsy will show an extant physical illness or condition. No weapon was found in the vehicle in which the decedent traveled. It is unknown whether officers have been fired or resigned. Two officers have been indicted.

Analysis

This case was exactly the sort of case that I hoped to identify and bring understanding to when I established the PKIC database. Because of that, and the tragedy of this case, I chose to dedicate this book to the memory of Jeremy Mardis.

This incident merits more analysis than any other in this book, because, in addition to the apparently wrongful killing by police of a handicapped young boy, the number of problems that existed with this stop, the agency, and other agencies in the city causes this case to rise in my mind to the level of systemic abuse.

The questions raised by this incident – from officer hiring and background checks to suitability of role, policies and procedures, best practices and other fundamental police responsibilities – are the same questions that must be asked nationally. The answers to these questions are indeed predictors of tragedies. Jeremy Mardis was betrayed by a series of incompetent, and perhaps corrupt, decisions and events in and around his hometown that ultimately led to his death.

Initial Questions Raised by These Facts

The most important questions immediately raised are around the engagement itself: it is still unclear why the officers involved chose to contact Mr. Few in the first place. The confusion, along with some issues around the licensing, status and role of the officers and agency(s) involved, should be explored immediately.

Here are issues that need to be answered:

1. Marksville City Marshals Office

A city marshal's duties typically include serving court documents, misdemeanor warrants and papers related to civil lawsuits. Marshals also typically provide court security.

Official statements report the four officers were working "part time" under the authority of the City Marshals office at the time of the engagement leading to Jeremy Mardis' death. Marksville's elected Ward 2 Marshal, Floyd Voinche Sr., could not be reached for comment.[437] It has been reported that Voinche himself is not certified by the Peace Officer Standards and Training Council.[438] While full-time officers are required to undergo basic training and certification, elected leaders of police agencies in Louisiana may be non-certified. The lack of such basic certification is certainly a contextual clue that details relating to law enforcement procedures and policies may be less robust than desirable.

There exists substantial confusion about why exactly the officers were engaging with Few and Mardis, which leads me to believe that the reasons for this confusion may be systemic. Early reports in the media about this incident quoted officials stating that the marshals had sought and approached Few on an arrest warrant.[439]

The service of a misdemeanor arrest warrant with four officers present is unusual, but depends on the context of the relationship between the fugitive and the police department. Typically departments shy away from engaging a misdemeanor fugitive while he is with a minor child. Misdemeanor charges are rarely serious enough to justify such a frightening upheaval in a child's day as seeing his parent handcuffed and brought to jail. It is more disturbing that, later, police and city officials stated that there were no records of warrants issued in Mr. Few's name.

Serious questions about procedures and policies at the agency must be asked when some officials believe a warrant is being served and others don't know of it. Best practices and in many cases state laws dictate that an officer must verify the validity of an arrest warrant with the originating court before attempting to serve the warrant. When a misdemeanor arrest warrant is used to initiate a traffic stop, the officer must be absolutely certain of the warrant's existence and current validity. This is fundamental.

2. Reserve Status of Officer Greenhouse

While three of the four officers involved in the incident were hired officers from Marksville PD, one, Norris Greenhouse, is listed as a reserve officer. A reservist may be able to work for more than one agency. It is not clear, however, in what capacity—paid or volunteer—Greenhouse was working at the time of the shootings. It is crucial to answer this, along with all questions about Greenhouse's qualifications, training currency, licensure, and affiliation, which speak to the Marshals office's policies on hiring, screening, training, and operations.

There are, according to the Bureau of Justice Statistics, more than 29,000 reserve or auxiliary local police officers affiliated with police departments nationwide.[440] The StreetCred PKIC data-set contains two incidents in 2015 in which reserve officers were involved in the killing of an unarmed civilian. Because of these questions about the court and City Marshal agency policies about warrant service, questions about work qualifications and standards at the agency are also important.

3. Reserve Officer Indictments In Killings of Civilians

It is interesting to note that the only other 2015 case involving a reserve officer also resulted in indictments. The first indictment was against reserve Deputy Robert Bates, on a second-degree manslaughter charge involving culpable negligence.[441] The second indictment was filed against Tulsa Sheriff Stanley Glanz, who led the agency that held Bates' commission. Glanz was indicted on two misdemeanor charges, one of which stemmed from the agency's handling of the employment, training, and investigations into behavior of Deputy Bates unrelated to Bates' shooting of Harris. Sheriff Glanz has since resigned[442], and Bates was convicted.

4. Body-Worn Video Is Crucial

Col. Mike Edmonson, superintendent of the Louisiana State Police, said that video exists of the incident[443], and stated in a press conference that the video: "is one of the most disturbing scenes I have seen."[444] The video has not been released publicly however. It is notable that the initial story in several media accounts that Mr. Few had engaged in a vehicular assault on officers was retracted and has now been disavowed. This speaks to the significance of the content of the officer-worn video.

5. Pursuit & Use Of Force Policies

Since national media[445] referred to a brief pursuit between officers and Mr. Few's vehicle prior to stopping and the commencement of gunfire,[446] questions arise about the pursuit policy of the Marshals' office, and even more significantly, its policies about the use of force—especially deadly force. The Advocate has printed a statement that the Marksville Police Department does not have a written use of force policy, which is certainly a departure from best practices, as such policies protect officers, civilians and the city in equal measure.

6. Significant Use Of Force Questions

Coincidentally, the day after the killing of Jeremy Mardis and the shooting of Mr. Few, an entirely unrelated officer-involved shooting took place involving

Marksville PD. In this separate incident, 32-year-old Will Ray Lachney took a shotgun from a hunter in the nearby woods. After being confronted by a passing police officer, he fired it in the air and barricaded himself inside his mother's apartment, about a mile or less from the scene of the Mardis shooting. During the standoff involving Lachney, a Marksville police officer accidentally shot Lachney's mother in the arm after the mother had attempted to convince him to surrender. These two incidents, combined with the filing of a federal lawsuit accusing The City Of Marksville,[447] Chief Elster Smith, Jr., Avoyelles Parish District Attorney Charles A. Riddle, III, Lt. Derrick Stafford; Officer Norris Greenhouse, Officer Joseph Montgomery; Officer Damion Jacobs; Det. Kevin Hill; and Det. Eric Jacobs with excessive force, raise eyebrows about use of force in general in the city and area.

Most disturbing are the accusations against Lt. Derrick Stafford, charged with second-degree murder and attempted murder. Stafford was indicted in 2011 of aggravated rape and held on $300,000 bail.[448]

Investigators must learn about Lt. Stafford's prior and current entanglements with use of force, and pending and past legal issues, and how these may have affected his qualifications to serve as a police officer.

– Nick Selby

A gag order has prevented the public release of important information about this case, limiting any substantive analysis of it. But the limited information that is available is incredibly troubling. Given the swift response by the federal government to the events in Ferguson, Missouri, one would expect some quick action on their part in this case, which reeks of corruption.

– Ben Singleton

We have nothing to indicate this shooting would be appropriate in any way. There are so many red flags associated with this case, as described in Nick's analysis, that even if the marshals were to make a self-defense claim, it would be severely tainted. The fact that the investigation led to the indictment of the marshals makes it seem that a conclusion that the shooting was unjustified has already been reached. This would make any other opinion (with less access to the evidence) unnecessary.

– Ed Flosi

Timothy Gene Smith, 47, White Male

San Diego, CA, November 4

Timothy Smith was a fugitive wanted for felonies in Missouri[449] and he was considered armed and dangerous. He was spotted by an SDPD officer, but the officer lost sight of him after a foot chase. Soon after, another officer saw Smith walking down a street and chased him into an alley. Smith managed to break free from a police dog, and then jumped a fence. When the K9 officer ordered Smith to stop and show his hands, Smith refused to comply and reached into his pocket.[450] The officer states that he believed Smith was reaching for a weapon, and the officer shot Smith.

Analysis

It is unclear whether officers knew that Smith faced a life sentence if re-captured, or, as Smith's companion[451] told CBS8 news, that Smith had said he had no intention of ever going back to jail. It's not clear from the description the manner with which Smith "reached" into his pocket. If it was absent-mindedly, as one would reach for cigarettes, this incident would be less defensible from the officer's standpoint than if Smith did it quickly and with the purpose and manner of someone reaching for a weapon. If the latter was the case, this would seem to me to have been a justified use of deadly force.

– Nick Selby

This is another example of a suspect presenting, to a police officer, a universally recognized sign that is known to elicit a deadly force response. Anyone who confronts an officer, receives orders to surrender, and then reaches for his pockets or waistband should expect the officer to respond with deadly force.

– Ben Singleton

This case demonstrates an escape attempt by a person who stated he wasn't going back to jail. Smith was considered armed and dangerous. He had defeated the attempts of a police service dog and managed to break free and run away. When ordered to stop and show his hands, Smith instead decided to reach for his pocket (i.e., waistband area), an area commonly known to be a place to stow weapons. Based on the totality of the facts and circumstances, if the officers honestly believed Smith was reaching for a weapon, the use of deadly force would be appropriate and consistent with current law enforcement training and standards.

Another possibility is that Smith truly did not want to ever go back to jail. Facing a long sentence with no way to know if his escape would be successful (or for how long it might last), perhaps he might have reached for his pocket to prompt the officers to feel an imminent fear of serious bodily injury or death. It may have been Smith's hasty version of "suicide-by-cop."

– Ed Flosi

John David Livingston, 33, White Male

Spring Lake, NC, November 16

Police arrived at 3:40 a.m. at a house near the intersection of Stage Road and W. Everett Drive to follow up on an assault investigation.[452] Family and friends say that the deputies sought a person who they say no longer lived at the address. When deputies asked Livingston if they could search the trailer, Livingston said "not without a search warrant." Deputies and Livingston fought. Witnesses state that the deputies, "threw him on his stomach ... He was Maced, he was TASERED three to four times. And when he got out on the front porch he was shot four times."[453]

A toxicology report showed "excessive alcohol" and cocaine in Livingston's system, and that the cause of death was three gunshot wounds to the upper chest and limbs.[454]

Analysis

It's difficult to understand the events based on the details, but two elements of the official account are troubling. The first was that officers have said that they followed up on an assault complaint at 3:40 a.m., which strikes me as strange, as the relative exigency of an assault warrant (assault is physical attack, not attack with a weapon – it sounds as if this was a warrant for an earlier fist-fight) doesn't typically warrant a middle-of-the-night investigation or entry.

That Mr. Livingston was inebriated does not seem to be challenged.

There is a key distinction here, between a search warrant and an arrest warrant. Media reports and activist websites have stated that Livingston fought police after he told them that they could not search his house. Police, however, have stated that they were at the house to serve an arrest warrant, and not to serve a search warrant. Mr. Livingston would have been well within his rights to tell the police to come back with a search warrant if they didn't have one in order to search his house for evidence. But that does not seem to have been the case. From media accounts and police statements, police were instead acting on the strength of an arrest warrant. If that is the case, then they would have been well within the scope of a serious misdemeanor or felony arrest warrant to search the house for the presence of a named person they had a reasonable belief was inside the house.

We don't have enough information to conclude anything further.

– Nick Selby

This case concerns me. If the officers possessed the legal authority to enter the residence, why ask for consent? It is akin to an officer asking for consent to search a vehicle, and when denied that consent, searching it anyway, and later stating that he smelled marijuana in the car. One can imagine how that might look. Livingston was asked for consent to search his residence. He refused that consent. The fact that the question was posed to Livingston suggests to him that he had the ability to refuse the search.

How that exchange escalated to deadly force, I don't know. More information is needed to develop an opinion as to the reasonableness of the use of deadly force.

– Ben Singleton

There are several things we know about this incident that create more questions than they answer. Foremost is the question already addressed in Nick's comments about an arrest warrant versus a search warrant. It would need to be determined if the deputies had fresh and reliable information that the person sought on the warrant was currently inside, and if the warrant was valid for service at that time. Absent this, their entry into the house under the authority of the warrant was most likely unauthorized.

Livingston's denial of entry would have been within his rights. An officer cannot use that fact that the person won't consent to the search as part of the reason to go in. In other words, people's assertion of their rights cannot be held against them.

This is where the case goes a little sideways. It seems that after Livingston denied entry, the deputies and Livingston fought. Understanding how the fight was initiated is important. The analysis would be different if Livingston suddenly jumped out and attacked the deputies than if the deputies suddenly decided they were going to push forward through Livingston to search the house. If the first scenario is found to be true, the deputies (although still not on good legal ground to go in to search) would still be appropriate in defending themselves. If the second scenario is found to be true, the deputies would have precipitated the fight through their own unlawful conduct and the force would then be de facto inappropriate.

– Ed Flosi

Jamar Clark, 24, Black Male

Minneapolis, MN, November 16

Police received a 911 call at 12:45 a.m. from party attendees reporting an assault (some accounts state domestic assault).[455] Neighbor Nekelia Sharp, said an ambulance was called after Clark and his girlfriend got into an argument.[456] According to a BCA statement, the responding Minneapolis police officers believed the woman was an assault victim and that Clark was a suspect.[457]

As police were en route, Clark, who had left momentarily, returned to the scene and began to argue and physically confront the paramedics who arrived to aid Clark's girlfriend.[458] When police arrived, they stepped in to protect the paramedics and Clark's girlfriend. Officers tried to calm him, but there was a struggle, during which officers fired a shot at his head. From the official chronology by the Hennepin County Prosecutor on March 30, 2016[459]:

"Officers Ringgenberg and Schwarze approached Clark and noticed his hands were in his jacket pockets. They told him to take his hands out of his pockets. He refused. Ringgenberg then took his gun out and held it down alongside his leg with the barrel pointing to the ground. He did not point it at Clark or anyone else. Clark started yelling, 'What's the pistol for?' The officers again and repeatedly told Clark to take his hands out of his jacket pockets. Clark continued to refuse to do so. Ringgenberg put his gun back in his holster and grabbed Clark's right wrist while Schwarze grabbed Clark's left hand. Schwarze had his handcuffs out but said he was never able to get them on Clark. In the ensuing struggle, Schwarze dropped his handcuffs."

"Ringgenberg had been trained in his prior work as a police officer in San Diego to take a suspect to the ground when he or she resisted being handcuffed because it was believed to be safer. After Clark resisted being handcuffed, Ringgenberg quickly reached his arm around Clark's chest and neck and took him to the ground. This occurred at 12:49:29 a.m. Ringgenberg landed on his side on top of Clark, who was on his back."

"Ringgenberg said he tried to move away from Clark to get in position to handcuff him. Ringgenberg felt his gun go from his right hip to the small of his back and told Schwarze, 'He's got my gun.' Ringgenberg said he reached back to the top of his gun and felt Clark's 'whole' hand on the gun.'"

"Ringgenberg repeatedly told his partner Schwarze, 'He's got my gun, he's got my gun.' Ringgenberg recalled hearing Schwarze tell Clark to let go of the gun or Schwarze would shoot. Ringgenberg heard Clark say, 'I'm ready to die.' Ringgenberg said, 'That was the worst feeling ever because, it just, my heart just sank.'"

"Ringgenberg believed he was going to die at that point because he had no control over his gun. Ringgenberg felt that Clark didn't care what happened to him and remembered thinking that he didn't want his partner to die with his gun. After Ringgenberg heard the round go off he remembered being able to roll away."

An autopsy found the cause of death was a single gunshot wound to the head.[460] In early February, 2016, police investigators sent their findings to prosecutors. Later that month, the Hennepin County Attorney's office returned the file to the investigators, saying it was incomplete.[461] Also in early February, the ACLU of Minnesota and NAACP Minneapolis announced they would file a lawsuit demanding the release of police video footage of the incident under the state's Data Practices Act.[462] Video, photos, chronology, autopsies, DNA, search warrants, narratives and police and ambulance reports were all released on March 30, 2016[463]

Toxicology showed that Clark was legally intoxicated from alcohol (blood alcohol content of 0.093 g/dL; the legal limit is 0.08) and marijuana (his blood cannabinoids panel was positive)[464]. In March, 2016, Hennepin County Prosecutors announced that no charges will be filed against the two officers involved. The DA cited DNA and other evidence showing Clark was not handcuffed during the altercation, and that he refused to let go of an officer's holstered gun during the late-night struggle[465].

A separate federal civil rights investigation into Mr. Clark's death is continuing.

Analysis

The media narrative was highly inflammatory: An unarmed black man was shot by white officers, and reports emerged from the scene, repeated by protesters, that Clark had been handcuffed at the time he was shot. It was made worse by a lack of released video. The result was that this was one of the year's most controversial shootings for its racial overtones, and led to protests and an 18-day encampment outside the police department's Fourth Precinct, near the site of the shooting[466].

After protests intensified, the records of the officers involved were released. The Jamar Clark case is the only case in the StreetCred PKIC data in which an officer involved had a prior complaint of excessive force, and the decedent (Clark) had prior convictions for violent crimes. Yet even before the District Attorney's statements, there was enough in the public domain to raise doubts to the protesters' narrative. The 911 caller described Clark – officers did not profile him or target him because of his race, they responded to a community request for help. There is no question that he was in the process of assaulting his girlfriend when the call was made, nor is there any controversy as to whether he continued to attack paramedics and the officers who responded to assist Clark's girlfriend. That did not by any means justify deadly force in this case, but it did provide context that puts the lie to the protesters' narrative that officers showed up and killed the unarmed Clark for no reason. The full release of the documents in the case, including photographs, video, timelines, narratives, police reports and other documents make clear that this was a justified use of deadly force.

– Nick Selby

Although it became the catalyst for a public uprising and accusations regarding the alleged racially motivated actions of the officers, this case appears to be a reasonable use of deadly force.

The officers repeatedly told Clark to remove his hands from his pockets. This is standard practice in police work for obvious reasons, and it isn't an unreasonable request. Clark refused, which undoubtedly elevated the officers' threat assessment. I believe Officer Ringgenberg removed his gun from his holster for this reason.

Officers had the lawful authority to detain Clark for further investigation, because he was the alleged assailant. Unable to gain compliance from Clark, and recognizing the threat posed by a noncompliant suspect who was now yelling and refusing to take his hands out if his pockets, the officers attempted to grab Clark's hands and detain him. Clark resisted. The officers took Clark to the ground in order to safely handcuff him.

During the scuffle, Officer Ringgenberg felt his gun, which was in his holster, move to the small of his back. This presented Officer Ringgenberg with multiple problems, not the least of which was his inability to see if the weapon was secured in his holster. When he reached back and felt Clark's hand on his gun, he yelled to his partner, "He's got my gun!"

The likelihood that an officer's gun, if obtained by the assailant, will be turned against him is statistically high. Police officers are cognizant of this. Clark's statement, "I'm ready to die," is further evidence of his intent.

Officer Schwarze made a reasonable decision in using deadly force to prevent Clark from obtaining and using Officer Ringgenberg's weapon against them.

– Ben Singleton

The reason for the legitimate law enforcement contact with Clark is described in detail, and it is crystal clear. There was a legitimate reason to ask Clark to take his hands out of his jacket when the officers made their contact with him. When Clark refused, it elevated the concerns to the point that one of the officers removed his pistol from the holster. There is a school of thought that says having the person remove their hands themselves can actually be dangerous, since if the person did have a firearm, it would give them the opportunity to draw it, while appearing to comply with the officers' direction.

The officers eventually did what might be considered safer. They moved in to control Clark's arms and hands instead of having him take his hands out of his jacket. This would have allowed the officers to better control any weapon draw that Clark might have made had he been armed. It also allowed for the officers to move directly into a handcuffing technique.

Once the officers were attached to Clark and attempting to take him into custody, Clark began to physically resist. It does appear that the taking of Clark into custody would be appropriate and justifiable. A person being taken into lawful custody of a police officer has no right to physically resist that effort. Indeed, there are statutory obligations to that effect in some states.

The officers were unable to reasonably control Clark in a standing position. Officers are trained that if they cannot accomplish this that they should take the subject to the ground. The ground acts as a controlling agent to assist in the arrest process. The takedown appears to have been appropriate at the time.

Once on the ground, Clark grabbed Ringgenberg's firearm with such dedication that the holster and gun actually moved from Ringgenberg's hip to his back. Ringgenberg felt to confirm his belief that Clark had grabbed the gun. If the holster and gun were on Ringgenberg's back, it would be more difficult to properly retain the firearm in its holster. Both officers told Clark to let go of the gun, but he did not. Clark made some intense statements that would lead anybody to believe this was going to be a fight for their life.

Ringgenberg had told Schwarze several times that Clark had control of the weapon. Clark himself demonstrated a dedicated threat to disarm the officer. The only reason a subject would want to disarm an officer in a situation like this would be to cause him serious bodily injury or death. Efforts to regain control of the firearm had failed and Clark was still grasping for the weapon. In order to prevent Clark from gaining control of the firearm, deadly force would be appropriate. It is important to point out again that the person need not actually gain full control of the weapon for a deadly force application to be appropriate.

As a training matter, it is also important to point out that if the second officer (in this instance Schwarze) does decide to fire a close-quarter (very near) or contact (in which the muzzle of the pistol is in contact with the skin) shot that would minimize risk to others, it is most likely going to be the best option to ensure that the officer struggling for the weapon is not hit.

– Ed Flosi

Cornelius Brown, 25, Black Male

Opa Locka, FL, November 17

At about 3:30 a.m., a patrol officer near a convenience store spotted Brown, whom he described as behaving erratically. When the officer approached, Brown turned and began to walk away. The officer followed in his patrol car.[467] When Brown reached NW 32nd Avenue, he turned around, jumped on the hood of the officer's patrol car and began punching the windshield. The officer called for backup and a second officer arrived. When they tried to take Brown into custody, he resisted. They tried using the TASER, but it was ineffective. Brown did significant damage to the police car, and was continuing to fight when the officer opened fire.

Brown had a prior diagnosis as a schizophrenic[468]. Some witnesses report that Brown was carrying a broomstick[469] – an item that Brown was known to carry, according to family members.

Analysis

The officers did not mention the broomstick in their main commentary of their articulation of the threat Brown posed, which is why Brown is listed as unarmed. The damage to the patrol car, which may have been accomplished with the aid of the broomstick (I've never heard of a broomstick capable of breaking a vehicle windshield) was clear in photographs, and would have been significant force worthy of defending against by the officers. Most important, this is another case in which a diagnosed mentally-ill person got into a fatal encounter with law enforcement. I have too many questions about this case to opine further.

– Nick Selby

By smashing the windshield, Brown clearly demonstrated his ability to inflict serious injury, and his intent to harm police officers. However, there aren't sufficient details regarding the specific threat posed at the time that officers opened fire. A finding as to reasonableness cannot be made without them.

– Ben Singleton

Brown was acting very odd. When the officer got closer to him, he jumped on the patrol car and began to punch the window. As one can imagine, punching a hard object like a windshield hard enough to break requires a large amount of strength and a high pain tolerance. As the officers attempted to take Brown into custody, Brown continued to physically resist so the officers used a TASER to assist in the arrest. Based on Brown's behavior and threat level to cause serious injury to the officers, a TASER use would be appropriate. Unfortunately it was unsuccessful in stopping Brown.

The details are confusing as to whether or not Brown had a stick at the time and was trying to use it as a weapon against the officers, although witnesses reportedly saw Brown waving something at the officers before he was shot and killed. If Brown did possess a stick and was threatening to use it as a weapon, he was capable of creating a significant risk of serious body injury or death to the officers. Officers do not need to take a hit in order to determine how injurious the stick might be. Using deadly force on a person armed with a long stick and displaying it as a weapon in a threatening manner at close range would be appropriate to stop the threat.

– Ed Flosi

Michael Tindall, 41, White Male

Weatherford, TX, November 17

At 4:16 a.m., an officer observed Tindal driving a tan SUV and running a stop sign, so he tried to pull him over. Tindall did not stop, and a pursuit began, merging onto I-20. At one point during the pursuit, Tindall "slammed on his brakes, put the SUV into reverse and rammed the front of the officer's patrol car."[470] During the chase it became known that Tindall had a felony warrant for aggravated assault with a deadly weapon. The pursuit continued until Tindall wrecked on Bethel Road. Tindall emerged from his vehicle and "walked rapidly toward the driver's side of the lead patrol unit," the department said in a press release.[471]

Tindall was carrying a baby seat in front of him as he approached the police vehicle. Officers were on the passenger side, using the patrol car for cover. When Tindall reached the patrol car, he threw the baby seat into the car and jumped into the driver's seat.[472] In the middle of the front seat was an AR-15 patrol rifle. An officer fired "several times" through the passenger window, hitting and killing Tindall.

After his death, police searched Tindall's home and discovered a natural gas line that had been intentionally destroyed in a fashion consistent with an attempt to create an explosion capable of destroying the house.[473]

Analysis

Tindall was known to the Weatherford PD; he and his wife had, over the years, been in the category of "frequent flyers" with the department, as complainant, suspect, or victim in various low-level criminal, drug and alcohol offenses.[474] The existence of the felony warrant, revealed to the officers during the pursuit, and the vehicular attack on the patrol car by Tindall during the pursuit would tend to make any reasonable officer believe that this person was a clear and present danger to life and limb.

The timing of the death at the patrol car window is, however, something of concern to me, since there is no overt statement that Tindall was actually reaching for the weapon secured within a gun rack between the front seats. Patrol rifles are locked into place by a metal collar, and are typically carried in "Car-ready" condition, which means that there is a loaded magazine but no round chambered, and the safety selector is set to, "Safe." For the officer to blame the reach for the gun as in and of itself a deadly threat would be a stretch; if the weapon was in Tindall's hands and the officer observed Tindall, for example, attempting to chamber a round, this would be a completely different story. But from my understanding, merely reaching towards a secured weapon would not in itself present a deadly threat.

— Nick Selby

The manner in which the rifle was stored in the patrol car is of significant importance. Although many agencies have policies regarding the storage of rifles, many do not. In fact, some agencies allow officers to equip themselves with patrol rifles despite the lack of rifle racks in their police cars. Many officers outfit their patrol rifles with accessories that don't allow the rifles to fit in the storage racks. Whatever the case, if Tindall had access to the rifle and a reasonable person would conclude that Tindall's use of that weapon was imminent, the use of deadly force would be reasonable. If the rifle was locked in the storage rack, the officer would have to articulate how that secured weapon posed a threat.

— Ben Singleton

Tindall's known, prolific criminal history, including an active warrant for aggravated assault with a deadly weapon and his violent actions during his escape attempt, demonstrated he was an extreme danger to others, and to all police officers who might have encountered him in the future. When an officer has an opportunity to arrest this type of person, he/she should not let the opportunity pass lightly.

Tindall deliberately exited his own vehicle with a child seat, presumably to make the officers believe he was holding a child and make them pause in their decisions to use force, and then he walked directly toward their marked police vehicle. Once there, he entered the vehicle, which contained an AR-15 patrol rifle. We don't know the exact manner in which the rifle was stored, but most rifles are locked by a magnetic release button and can be accessed by some sort of mechanical release (some as simple as a handcuff key) in case of electrical failure. In any case, the rifle is not immediately accessible, but is not necessarily inaccessible.

If Tindall was able to leave the scene with the police vehicle and rifle, there's a good likelihood that he would have been able to eventually access the rifle. Indeed, I am aware of a very recent incident where an officer had his patrol unit parked at his home. A thief was able to get into the car and remove the rifle from the car, even though the rifle was properly locked inside. It would have been highly inappropriate for the officers to allow Tindall to leave knowing what they knew, because he could continue his violence with the aid of a high-capacity rifle. Based on the current and potential on-going and significant threat presented by Tindall, it could be deemed appropriate to use deadly force to stop him from his actions.

As a side note, if Tindall had escaped and did gain access to the rifle, using it to kill or injure others in his continued activities, it's not difficult to imagine the fallout against the officer and the agency for allowing Tindall to escape. This demonstrates the "Catch 22" situations that law enforcement in which officers are sometimes forced when making split-second decisions.

– Ed Flosi

Nathaniel Harris Pickett, 29, Male of Unknown Race

Barstow, CA, November 19
At 9:07 p.m. a deputy sheriff, patrolling alongside a citizen volunteer, saw Pickett jump a fence into the parking lot of the El Rancho Motel. The deputy stopped to question Pickett, who gave the deputy a false name and became uncooperative. When the deputy attempted to handcuff Pickett, Pickett tried to run. A fight ensued between the deputy and Pickett that quickly moved to the ground. Pickett struck the deputy in the face numerous times, refusing to comply with repeated verbal commands to stop hitting him and move away. The deputy fired his weapon, striking Pickett, and the assault ceased. The deputy was transported to a local hospital and was treated for multiple injuries, including broken bones.[475] Media outlets reported this account widely[476],[477] but no further updates, including toxicology, were available in February, 2016.

Analysis

Without toxicology or an autopsy, I can't make a stab at motive, but this does sound like a classic situation in which an officer is fighting with a suspect who is overpowering him, which causes the officer to fear for his life and use deadly force. The officer's actions seem reasonable given the facts as we have them.

– Nick Selby

This is another example of why unarmed does not mean non-deadly. This officer not only perceived the threat of, but actually suffered, serious bodily injury before using deadly force. His actions were completely reasonable.

– Ben Singleton

An officer who is taken to the ground and then beaten to the point of having sustained serious bodily injury (and who would most likely be rendered unconscious if the beating were to continue) is in a spot where a mere imminent threat has already passed. The use of deadly force to stop the attack from continuing would be appropriate and consistent with current law enforcement training and standards.

– Ed Flosi

Chase Alan Sherman, 32, White Male

Coweta County, GA, November 20

At approximately 9:09 PM, Coweta County Sheriff's deputies responded to a 911 call made by Sherman's mother from a location off I-85 Southbound in Coweta County. She stated Sherman was suffering from a "psychotic break" as a result of ingesting drugs believed to be spice.[478] Sherman's father and girlfriend attempted to restrain Sherman while deputies were en route to the scene.

During the 11-minute 911 call released by the Georgia Bureau of Investigation, Sherman's mother is heard saying, "He's going to bite us. He's going to bite us!" Mrs. Sherman told dispatchers that they had pulled off the interstate with their flashers on, and the dialogue in the car as the family tries to control Sherman is heard, with quotes like, "Hit him in the head! Hit him in the head! Or in the stomach! Hit him in the stomach!"[479] When a dispatcher inquires whether Sherman is in the vehicle, the mother says, "Listen, he did spice and it messed his brain up."

When the deputies arrived, they attempted to gain control of Sherman. One of the deputies deployed a TASER throughout the struggle in an attempt to control him. Sherman continued resisting the deputies and medical personnel who arrived on the scene. Sherman stopped fighting and went into medical distress, at which point deputies and EMS began performing CPR. Sherman was transported to the hospital where he was pronounced dead.

Analysis

While I haven't been able to read the toxicology report (it was not available in March, 2016), it's pretty clear that this was an acute intoxication of synthetic marijuana, and Sherman's behavior during the incident is a typical reaction to such an event. It is fairly clear that deputies were attempting to control, not kill, Sherman.

– Nick Selby

Sherman was intoxicated, to the extent that he attacked his own family before attacking police officers. The officers used the non-deadly tools and techniques available to them in an attempt to gain control of Sherman safely. I believe he died as a result of his recent drug use and physical exertion.

– Ben Singleton

Although we don't know for certain whether Sherman was under the influence of some illicit drug, his actions were definitely a credible physical threat to the family and to the officers trying to take him into custody. The use of a TASER device on a person who is a credible physical threat is an appropriate force response.

– Ed Flosi

Christopher Lynn Nichols, 24, White Male

Colbert, OK, November 21

Around 7:30 pm, a Colbert officer stopped to speak with Christopher Lynn Nichols, who was walking in town. The officer ran a check on the man and found he had several traffic warrants for his arrest.[480] Nichols ran from the officer when he attempted to arrest him. The two came into physical contact a short distance away, with Nichols on top of the officer, striking the officer in the face.[481] The officer pulled out his gun and fired it several times, hitting Nichols an unknown number of times. Nichols was transported to Texoma Medical Center. He died shortly after surgery.[482]

Analysis

No further details have been released in this incident since the OSBI took over the investigation. OSBI only posts public statements through 2014 on its website.[483] The lack of details, and video make any conclusion too difficult to reach.

– Nick Selby

With the limited information available on this case, it is hard to make any conclusive assessment as to reasonableness. But the fact that the suspect was on top of the officer delivering blows to the face suggests that there may have been a legitimate threat to the officer's life.

– Ben Singleton

This case has similar details to the Pickett case previously, but fewer less specific facts to evaluate. It also appears here that the officer was taken to the ground and the subject was striking the officer in the face. The difference that makes it difficult to render a reasoned opinion is the lack of details as to how many strikes, the intensity of the strikes and the injury level the officer believed he was sustaining. These clarifying facts and circumstances are presently unavailable. An appropriate use of deadly force would require that the officer reasonably believed that actions of the subject created an imminent threat of serious bodily injury or death.

– Ed Flosi

Tuan Hoang, 25, Asian/Pacific Islander Male

Aurora, CO, November 30

An Aurora officer was patrolling when he noticed a vehicle that appeared to be broken down, so he stopped to render aid. The officer made contact with the occupants and began walking back to his patrol car. At that moment, Hoang got out, snuck up behind him, and struck him on the head with an object that left a four-inch gash.

Aurora Police Chief Nicholas Metz told the media: "This was an unprovoked attack, and frankly, I feel very comfortable saying I believe this was an attempted murder."[484]

After the attack, Hoang got into the officer's patrol car and drove away, while the officer was firing shots at him. The injured officer told responding officers Hoang's direction of travel. A patrol car rammed the officer's car Hoang was driving, forcing it to spin out. As officers approached, "[Hoang] got out of the vehicle and he was ordered numerous times to give up, to stop, put his hands up. … He did not comply with those orders and at that time our officer did fire at the suspect," Aurora Police spokesman Lt. Scott Turep said.[485]

Analysis

This is one of the most clearly justified incidents in the database; multiple witnesses corroborated the police account at each stage of the unfolding incident, and Aurora Police took the extra step of proactively releasing audio of the dispatch radio traffic,[486] which allows anyone to follow along. The brutal attack on the first officer would have been clearly cause for deadly force application by the first officer, who fired at and missed Hoang; the ultimate deadly force use was also justified for different reasons – here was a man clearly bent on killing, refusing to show his hands after engaging in deadly behavior. In my opinion, police were absolutely correct and justified in using deadly force.

– Nick Selby

This is a clearly justified and reasonable use of deadly force. I agree with Chief Metz' assessment. This was an attempted murder. Excellent work on the part of his officers in quickly locating, stopping, and confronting Hoang.

– Ben Singleton

Hoang was definitely a dangerous person. He blind-side attacked a police officer with an object that left a severe laceration. This is certainly serious bodily injury and could very well have caused the officer's death. As Hoang fled in the officer's patrol car, it would have been clear that he had committed a crime involving the infliction of serious bodily harm and that he posed a significant risk to others (and especially officers) he might encounter, and be able to cause them serious bodily harm or death. At this point, it would be appropriate for the officer to use deadly force to prevent Hoang's escape.

Hoang then turned around and directed the vehicle in the officer's direction. This action would create an imminent threat of serious bodily injury or death to the officer, especially in consideration of Hoang's previous unprovoked attack.

The appropriateness of the shooting at the end of the pursuit is not as clear. Details are vague as to Hoang's proximity to the officers and as to what Hoang was doing at that moment, other than refusing to comply with commands to stop and put his hands up. Hoang was reported to have had something in his right hand, but what the shooting officer saw or what he may have perceived it is not indicated. Based on the lack of specific details, this shooting is too difficult to call for me. I can think of a few scenarios that would lead to different opinions as to the appropriateness.

– Ed Flosi

DECEMBER

Allen Anthony Pacheco, 32, Male of Unknown Race

Von Ormy, TX, December 2

Pacheco was driving northbound at about 11:17 p.m. when he was stopped by a trooper. Pacheco allegedly told the trooper he was a convicted felon and had a weapon in the vehicle.[487]

"During the contact, the driver stated that he was a convicted felon and had a weapon in the vehicle," said a spokesman for the DPS. "Based on the driver's statement, the trooper attempted to detain the subject."

DPS said that Pacheco resisted, then tried to run back to his car, at which point the trooper deployed his Taser. The Taser was ineffective," the spokesman said. "The trooper was fearing that there's a possibility that the driver might be trying to get back in the vehicle, so the trooper used his weapon."[488]

Pacheco was hit at least once and died at the scene. Investigators found a loaded shotgun on the back seat of Pacheco's car.

Analysis

The trooper understood that he was dealing with an armed felon, and that the felon's gun was in the felon's car. The felon began to fight the officer, resisted the TASER and then he headed back towards the vehicle – where the gun was stored. This trooper's assertion that he was in fear for his life is absolutely reasonable.

– Nick Selby

This account reminds me of Deputy Kyle Dinkheller, who was killed in 1998 in a similar event in which, in spite of Kyle's repeated orders to stop, the suspect reentered his vehicle, removed a rifle, and shot Kyle multiple times, killing him.

The trooper attempted to use his non-deadly TASER to stop the escalation of events. When it was ineffective, and Pacheco continued toward his vehicle, the trooper had no choice but to end the encounter with deadly force.

– Ben Singleton

An officer can only act based on information that is reasonably known, or which he perceives. In this case, the subject told the trooper he was a convicted felon and that he had a weapon in the vehicle. Why Pacheco decided to tell this to the officer and then attempt to move towards the vehicle can only be speculated. It was clearly appropriate for the trooper to use his TASER to stop Pacheco, and it was reasonable for the trooper to believe he was in imminent danger of serious bodily injury or death when Pacheco tried to get back in his vehicle. Therefore deadly force was appropriate.

– Ed Flosi

Miguel Espinal, 36, Male of Unknown Race

Yonkers, NY, December 8

Espinal was driving through the Bronx around noon when two NYPD officers tried to pull him over for speeding and reckless driving. Espinal led them on a wild chase northbound into Westchester County on the Saw Mill River Parkway.[489] Espinal made a U-turn and drove southbound in the northbound lane, causing collisions on the Saw Mill near Cross County Parkway.[490] He then escaped through the car's window and ran into the woods. Officers gave foot pursuit and engaged Espinal in a fight in the woods. During the struggle, one officer's firearm discharged, striking the 36-year-old man in the torso.

Espinal was wanted for felony warrants out of Florida,[491] and had been arrested 14 times in New York; he had served two prison sentences, one for burglary and one for robbery.

Analysis

There's precious little to go on here; the chase and Espinal's aggressive and reckless actions during it demonstrated his danger to human life. It is unclear from the narratives in the media whether the round was fired by accident, though it is telling that the officer had un-holstered and pointed his firearm. This needs investigation.

– Nick Selby

It would be impossible to develop an opinion without more details regarding the fight in the woods. However, a chase lasting this long would have likely exhausted officers and diminished their ability to fight. This could have contributed to the use of deadly force, if it was intentional.

– Ben Singleton

The actions of the officers preceding the shooting are clearly appropriate, and in fact, it is what most would consider good, aggressive police work. However, we don't know enough regarding the intent and perceptions of the shooting officer, or about Espinal's actions at the time, to render a reasoned opinion on the appropriateness of the shooting.

– Ed Flosi

Hector Alvarez, 19, Male of Unknown Race

Gilroy, CA, December 14

Gilroy Police responded to a domestic violence 911 report, in which the caller said a woman was hiding from a man believed to be her boyfriend. The caller said the woman was being pulled by her hair. Officers arrived on scene within four minutes and were listening and observing what they described as a "violent fight"[492] when an officer was confronted by the suspect, who charged at the officer. Based on the suspect's actions and the information the officer was given regarding the domestic violence disturbance and all other circumstances considered, the officer stated he believed he was facing a lethal encounter and fired his weapon.[493] Witnesses reported hearing multiple gunshots.[494]

Analysis

It is not clear whether there was video available; the officer's testimony as to what happened, the totality of the circumstances and the reported sudden attack on the officer would tend to support a justified use of force. The investigation continues.

– Nick Selby

This agency reportedly issues body-worn cameras to its officers. No video has been publicly released, but a review of the video might provide the necessary justification for this officer's use of deadly force. Absent a compelling video, I believe that justification will be difficult to articulate. There have been several cases where an unarmed subject who has not yet attempted or committed an assault on the officer "charges" at him. The burden is on the officer in these cases to describe the specific reasons why the charging of the subject was a legitimate threat to his life.

– Ben Singleton

Based on the very limited information we have, we know that Alvarez was already in the act of committing violent crimes against another person. The officer arrived on scene and took up a surveillance role while waiting for his cover units to arrive. The subject initiated the attack on the officer by charging at him before backup arrived, creating a situation in which the officer was forced to make split-second decisions.

From here, the details provided become vague with respect to the facts and actual circumstances surrounding the officer's perceptions. This is most likely due to the event being fairly recent to this writing and how specific details are not often released to the public prior to legal proceedings. There are some statements that could lead to an evaluation of the deadly force being appropriate ("the information the officer was given regarding the domestic violence disturbance and all other circumstances considered"), but the "other circumstances" might in the end counter this evaluation.

– Ed Flosi

Ruben Jose Herrera, 26, Male of Unknown Race

Torrence, CA, December 19

Herrera had had a run-in with police officers during an encounter at about 8 am, in which he attacked officers and reached for one officer's TASER. Police said they received a 911 call reporting that Herrera was throwing bottles at an apartment building; Herrera then "viciously" attacked the police officers.[495] He was tackled and taken into custody, and both Herrera and the officers involved were taken to hospitals with injuries sustained in the scuffle.[496] In the hospital, during treatment, Herrera was handcuffed to a gurney in the hospital's emergency room, but his cuffs were removed at about 2:30 pm. Herrera jumped up, grabbed a metal chair and began swinging it at staff. When an officer intervened, Herrera grappled with the officer and reached for the officer's gun. The officer fired one shot, killing Herrera.

Analysis

One important fact is that Herrera's mother states that she told officers responding to the initial incident that Herrera was bipolar. The behavior described by the officers and the press are consistent with an acute mental illness episode. An agitated man who had already injured and hospitalized two officers through punching and kicking, who has a steel chair in his hands, and who has reached for their TASER, is by any reasonable measure a deadly threat. The separate question as to whether the hospital should have taken better care to treat Herrera's acute mental illness episode – if one existed – does not change the threat faced by the officer who used deadly force.

– Nick Selby

As previously stated, police officers are cognizant of the statistical probability that their weapon, if obtained by an assailant, will be used against them. Any effort made by Herrera to disarm the officer, should be considered a legitimate threat to life, and warrant the use of deadly force.

– Ben Singleton

It appears that the officers used a good deal of restraint in taking Herrera into custody in the first place, based on the level of resistance and threat that

Herrera presented to them. The shooting at the hospital has to be evaluated based on the immediate situation at hand. An officer actually tried to physically intervene when Herrera grabbed the metal chair and began using it as a weapon and swinging it at staff members, but as he did, Herrera attempted to gain control of his gun. Herrera's actions demonstrated an imminent threat of serious bodily injury or death and therefore, a deadly force response would have been appropriate to stop the threat.

The larger question that looms for me is what reason or need the officers had for removing the handcuffs from a known violent subject. Wasn't it reasonably foreseeable that Herrera might continue his violent actions if released?

– Ed Flosi

Leroy Browning, 30, Black Male

Palmdale, CA, December 20

Just before 3 a.m. deputies responded to a call from Taco Bell employees who said a vehicle had crashed into the restaurant, and that the driver appeared to be unconscious. Deputies made contact with the driver, Leroy Browning, and based on initial observations, they began a DUI investigation. Browning was placed in the rear of a sheriff's vehicle and when deputies decided to arrest him, they opened the car door to handcuff him.[497]

Browning leaped out of the vehicle attacked a deputy, placing him in a bear hug.[498] Other deputies joined the fight, which went to the ground. At some point during the fight, the suspect grabbed the deputy's weapon. The deputy began weapon retention techniques and shouting what was happening, and as deputies fought, Browning did not release the gun; deputies fired, hitting Browning, who died on the scene. A blue-steel pistol and "large" bag of marijuana was later located in the man's vehicle,[499] the Sheriff's Department stated in a news release.

Analysis

Pretty straightforward use of deadly force, with several witnesses; toxicology will likely reveal acute intoxication of alcohol and marijuana. It is not known whether the deputy attempting to arrest Browning knew of the presence of the gun and drugs in Browning's car.

– Nick Selby

As in the previous case, police officers will respond to attempted disarmament with deadly force.

– Ben Singleton

When Browning chose to attack the deputy and attempted to gain control of his weapon, he became an imminent threat of serious bodily injury or death. The use of deadly force would be appropriate to stop the threat.

There is a training concern to be addressed here. As discussed in a previous case, as a profession we need to develop better tactics to handcuff a person placed into the rear of a patrol vehicle who was not previously handcuffed. Remember that this subject is technically contained, so time should be considered an ally in any tactic developed. I have never felt it a good idea to have the subject "step out" in order to be handcuffed. One very effective tactic I have seen is to have the subject remain seated and look away while placing his hands behind his back, effectively presenting his back and hands to the officer for cuffing.

– Ed Flosi

Kevin Matthews, 36, Black Male

Dearborn, MI, December 23

A Dearborn officer was patrolling when he saw Matthews, whom the officer knew was wanted on a larceny warrant, and Matthews ran. A news release said that Matthews had escaped from other Dearborn officers earlier in the day.[500] Police say there was a foot chase through a residential neighborhood on the border of Detroit and Dearborn. The officer and suspect got into a physical encounter, with a struggle taking place over the officer's weapon.[501]

"The officer chased the subject and encountered him several houses away in Detroit, where a struggle ensued," the news release said. "Subsequently, the officer fired his department-issued weapon, striking the subject."[502] Family members said Matthews was on medication for schizophrenia.

Analysis

This is another of the cases in which a mental illness episode may have influenced the behavior of the decedent, however the totality of these circumstances lead me to suspect that this was less a matter of mental illness and more a matter of Matthews attempting to escape custody. I only have media accounts and quotes to go on, but in my experience the family typically uses much stronger language to describe the specifics of mental illness when complaining to the press. Additionally, it's interesting to me that this was the second attempted escape from Dearborn police in a day, with hours between the two attempts. To have an acute mental health incident lasting for hours without any other interaction with civilians does not sound like a plausible scenario.

– Nick Selby

As in the previous two cases, the attempted disarmament of a police officer will elicit their use of deadly force. The fact that Matthews suffered from schizophrenia is irrelevant to the officer who is fighting for his gun, and thus his life.

– Ben Singleton

When a subject chooses to engage an officer in a ground struggle and then attempts to gain control of the officer's weapon, that person is a credible and imminent threat of serious bodily injury or death to the officer. The use of deadly force to stop the threat would be an appropriate response.

– Ed Flosi

Bettie R Jones, 55, Black Female

Chicago, IL, December 26

Bettie Jones was killed accidentally by Chicago police.[503] Police had responded to a domestic violence call regarding Quintonio LeGrier, the 19-year old suspect named in a 911 call for attacking his father with a baseball bat and who had been identified as suffering from a previously diagnosed mental condition.[504] Witnesses state LeGrier had attacked the father with a bat, and when officers arrived they shot at LeGrier, striking and mortally wounding him. Some of the rounds police fired at LeGrier missed and struck Jones, who also died. LeGrier's father states that the officer expressed, immediately after the shooting, "F—, no, no, no. I thought he was lunging at me with the bat."[505]

Quintonio LeGrier was armed at the time of his death with the bat and has not been added to PKIC.

Analysis

It is unclear how Jones became involved in the incident, and whether she was hit by a stray police bullet or otherwise targeted by police. No reports of her involvement in this incident were found. Jones' daughter states that she awoke to the sound of gunshots and found her mother bleeding in the doorway to her apartment. While Chicago Police have faced a number of highly controversial killings of late, in this case they immediately admitted it was an accident, and immediately apologized for killing Jones. They were transparent, proactive, communicative, honest and expressed remorse. It is my belief that this was a terrible accident in which a neighbor was killed by police action targeting another person. What is not clear is whether LeGrier had the baseball bat at the time the police arrived, and the impetus for the officer's use of deadly force against LeGrier. I don't believe that we have enough information to form an opinion as to the reasonableness of the primary use of force against LeGrier.

– Nick Selby

It appears that Jones was hit by gunfire not intended for her. The intended use of deadly force against LeGrier is a separate analysis for which we have too little information. The officer's immediate statement of regret implies a genuine perception of a threat-to-life by the officer, and possibly the absence of an actual threat. We must also know if Jones was hit as a result of poor marksmanship, negligence, or other events outside of the officer's control. We can't leave out the possibility that Ms. Jones was hit as she jumped into the line of fire in defense of LeGrier. This was a heartbreaking event. I commend the Chicago Police Department for their transparency and honesty.

– Ben Singleton

There is no indication that Jones was the intended target for the officer's deadly force response. It appears that the deadly force used on the intended target (LeGrier) would have been appropriate if he was attacking another person with a weapon that would have a significant risk of serious bodily injury or death. Indeed, based on the response of the Chicago PD and the statement of the officer, it appears Jones was not the intended target and that her death was accidental and sad. In these cases, the question of negligence will almost always need to be addressed, but at this time we have no indication either way as to any negligence claim.

– Ed Flosi

AFTERWORD
Clint Bruce

This book needed to be written. The rest of the story needs to be told.

By, "rest of the story" I don't mean a passionate, effective argument purposed to exonerate and justify all deadly encounters involving police officers and unarmed citizens.

No – what I mean is the literal use of the phrase, "the rest of the story." It is impossible to offer right and actionable changes to the way policing is taught and overseen without the whole story. And I think the vast majority of America would agree the media rarely tells the whole story.

Media isn't the bad guy. Media is what it is: an industry influenced and bound by traditional economics. The law of supply and demand influence headlines and content as much (and more at times) than total and complete truth. Reporters are given word limits that restrict their ability to include information they may believe critical to get their "best truth," or most firmly held beliefs published. Editors must make choices based on what readership/viewership wants to consume. Corporations push marketing dollars towards those media efforts that produce the highest volume or readers/viewers.

It is a system: neither good, nor bad. If a bad guy exists in the information ecosystem it is the masses. Us. The casualties of an increasingly fast and entitled American society are critical thinking and the patience to hear not just what we want to hear … but the whole story. Our low intellectual standards and craving for fast and easy-to-swallow morsels of half-cooked facts is compromising our ability to see things clearly.

We increasingly only know how to be fed, and have forgotten how to cook. Absent the completeness of an exhaustive assessment of history, environment, perspectives, and facts ... we limit ourselves to the best of a prepared intellectual buffet without much (or any) insight into what is happening in the kitchen.

Selby, Singleton, and Flosi have invited us into the kitchen. If we are willing and able, we can see (i) how everything gets made, and (ii) how much is left out by current cooks that is truly important.

If this issue is critical (and it should be, and the volume of articles, opinions, and comments say it is) then we ought to be willing to read the rest of the story.

At the Naval Academy we learned that in war, history is neither our friend nor our enemy. It is the great library available to us that can either save us past pain, or doom us to repeated mistakes. The library always tells the truth if we are willing to read everything and consider the whole of things.

Law enforcement differs from the military in that the military has the luxury of post-action review of incidents, which is generally conducted outside the public's view. In the military, we have hyper-intensive periods of action that are followed by seasons of academic review. As we now stand down from our nation's longest period of sustained combat, we are now entering such an academic season.

In contrast, law enforcement agencies must constantly consider the totality of the circumstances, learn the lessons, change the policies, and show results, while they are doing the job. They must build the plane while it is flying, keep the passengers safe and get dinner out, even while other events are continuing. All this is done under the justified scrutiny of the public.

That innocent people die is awful, and we should do everything possible to reduce those numbers of truly innocent casualties. But we must be honest with ourselves and consider the entirety of the story as we assign fault, exonerate actions, and adjust this living and breathing doctrine of keeping the peace, protecting the innocent, punishing the guilty, and respecting the protector.

All lives matter. And this book is the rare but deeply valuable treatise on what actually happens in the microseconds before and after a deadly event.

Does race matter? Yes. Without question. But all races matter and the history of races and race interaction matters - so let's look at all of it.

Does location matter? Yes. Absolutely. But everything that happens on a daily basis in that environment matters - so let's look at all of it.

Does the personal history of all involved matter? Of course. And we need to look at the complete histories of all involved.

Without considering all of these facts - the rest of the story - we are only discussing how what happened makes us feel. But we are not changing the future.

Clint Bruce
Dallas, TX

Clint Bruce is co-Founder of Carry The Load, a non-profit organization dedicated to restoring the true meaning of Memorial Day. Carry The Load provides active ways to honor the military, law enforcement, firefighters and rescue personnel who dedicate their lives to keeping our country safe. Clint was a standout football player at the United States Naval Academy, where he lettered for four years and was named Captain of the '96 Aloha Bowl Champion team. Entering into the elite Navy SEAL Community in 1997, Clint completed BUD/S (Basic Underwater Demolition/SEAL) training with Class 217 and reported to SEAL Team 5. There he had the opportunity to deploy in various positions of command and leadership with three consecutive SEAL Platoons, two of which were post 9-11. Mr. Bruce is also the founder and president of Trident Response Group, a global intelligence and advisory group headquartered in Dallas, Texas.

ABOUT THE AUTHORS

Nick Selby

Nick Selby was sworn as a police officer in 2010, and currently serves as a detective at a police agency in the Dallas-Fort Worth area. His focus is on crimes that leverage the Internet, such as fraud, organized retail crime, identity theft and child exploitation. He is co-author of Blackhatonomics: An Inside Look at the Economics of Cybercrime (Syngress, 2012) and technical editor of Investigating Internet Crimes (Syngress, 2013). Nick has worked in cyber-security and intelligence for nearly 20 years. In 2005 he established the information security practice at industry analyst firm The 451 Group, for whom he consulted more than 1000 information security technology vendors, and a range of Fortune 1000 and government clients. Since 2008 he has focused on law enforcement intelligence and data. In 2012, he co-founded StreetCred Software, Inc. StreetCred provides software for law enforcement agencies, including StreetCred CID, the largest collaboration system currently in use in Texas, which StreetCred makes available at no cost, as a public service to law enforcement. Nick speaks on law enforcement matters regularly on FOX News, FOX Business News, CNN, and other news programs, and is a frequent contributor to newspapers including The Washington Post, USA Today, The Fort Worth Star Telegram, the St. Louis American, and other publications. Follow Nick on Twitter: @nselby

Ben Singleton

Ben Singleton's 10-year law enforcement career included assignments to patrol, traffic enforcement, field training, SWAT, narcotics, and criminal investigations. The latter part of Ben's career has been in criminal investigations, working as a detective. He specialized in narcotics cases, utilizing informants to seize large quantities of illicit substances. Ben designed and implemented a seizure/forfeiture program for his department, which was responsible for the seizure of assets from narcotics traffickers and felons. This program is still in use today, and can be credited for providing necessary funds and equipment to police officers. Ben led his department in felony arrests throughout his tenure, and continues to consult his department in the resolution of major cases. Ben is also a TCOLE-certified law enforcement training instructor, and was responsible for coordinating the training regimen for his department. As a certified TASER instructor, Ben was charged with training the department in the use of TASER, and assisted in developing policies and procedures specific to its use. Ben worked closely with the United States Marshals Service in the Dallas and Fort Worth offices on special assignments which included the Holy Land Foundation trials of 2007 and 2008, and Mexican Syndicate trial in 2009. Ben was also a member of the North Texas Major Case Investigative Team (NTMCIT). Since 2013, Ben has worked as Vice President at StreetCred Software, Inc.

Ed Flosi

Ed Flosi is a retired police sergeant from the San Jose PD (CA). He has been in law enforcement for more than 27 years. Ed has a unique combination of practical real world experience and academic background. He has worked several assignments including: Field Training Program, In-Service Training Unit Instructor, Narcotics Enforcement Team (uniformed), Narcotics Covert Investigations (undercover), Special Operations K9 Handler, Research and Development (Policy and Procedures), Custody Facility Supervisor, and Training Unit Supervisor. Ed was a lead instructor for use-of-force training, as well as defense and arrest tactics for the San Jose Police Department and for the South Bay Regional Public Safety Training Consortium. He has assisted the California Commission on Peace Officer Standards and Training (POST) in providing expertise on several occasions related to use-of-force training. He has been retained in several cases to provide testimony in cases when an officer was alleged to have used excessive force. He has qualified as an expert witness in police practices/use of force in the California Superior

Courts and in the Federal Court. Ed has a Master of Science degree from California State University Long Beach and holds an Adult Learning Teaching Credential from the State of California. He is an adjunct instructor at West Valley College in the Administration of Justice Department. He is currently the President/CEO and Principal Instructor for PROELIA Defense and Arrest Tactics (www.proeliadefense.com or on Facebook). In this capacity he continues to train law enforcement and security personnel as well as to provide consultation and expert witness services in cases that involve an allegation of excessive force.

AUTHOR'S NOTES

Nick Selby

Acknowledgments

Thank you to our editor, Alyssa Harley; to Ben and Ed; Larry Mulvey; Clint Bruce; and of course, Bill Flanagan. I would like to thank Gregg Rowland at StreetCred Software for a range of things including introducing me to Ed, and for holding down the fort while we worked on this intensely absorbing project. Thank you Moeed Siddiqui, for keeping things running, and to Haley Stewart, Jamie Samson, Melissa Westen, and Chris House. Also thanks for early input and critical edits from Eric Olson, D. Brian Burghart, Walter K., Stephen Jones, Ed Hasbrouck, Vishy Venugopalan, John Cannel, Kevin B., Crawford Coates, Jim Glennon and Robert "RoJo" Johnson. At MPD, thank you Tim S., Cody M., Billy S., Mark T., and James D., for your continued support and mentorship. I have endless respect for your experience and talents, and I am honored to serve with you. Thank you also to Stephen C., Cody M., and the ever-patient administrators at my agency. I gratefully thank Amanda Wood and Becker & Poliakoff in Washington DC for sage and wise advice and counsel. And of course, to Corinna and Spijk.

Thank you to the original group that volunteered so many hours in the preparation of the StreetCred PKIC project, especially including D. Brian Burghart of Fatal Encounters & Reno News & Review; Andrew Hay, Eric Olson (again); Roger Lee; James Jelinek; Ed Flosi; Ryan George; Corinna Selby; Wim Remes; boB Rudis; Dean Cornelison; and Elisabeth Nybo.

Ben Singleton

You are an officer assigned to night shift. You're a dedicated officer, interested in making a difference. It is 3:30am and it has been a slow night. You round the same corner for the 8th time tonight as you yawn and think about spending the morning with your kids.

As you round the corner, the dispatcher alerts you to a robbery on that very same corner. You look over and see a man run out of the gas station. He has just committed a robbery, and shot the clerk and 2 customers with a 12-gauge shotgun. He sees you. As you squeal into the store parking lot, he turns and runs into a dark alley. You bail out of your car and see his silhouette disappear into the darkness. He is still armed with the shotgun.

At this point your brain is telling you to get back in your car where it is safe. Your body starts to tremble, as you think about the fact that this guy could kill you as you enter that alley, and there is nothing you could do to stop it. You have a wife and two kids at home. Your heart is racing, and the adrenalin starts to flow as you know you have to make a decision right now.

This moment is what defines a police officer. Any reasonable person would give in to the instinctual urge to seek safety, run away, or call someone else to deal with it.

Fear is something that ordinary citizens think they understand. But to fully understand the fear to which I refer, one must experience it first-hand. There is just no way to explain what it feels like to willfully enter a situation that your brain and body are telling you is unsafe. It is to be truly terrified, but to press on anyway. This is bravery. It is an exercise in psychological and physiological control.

As you read this book, I do not ask that you give the officers the benefit of doubt, or that you approach these cases with anything but objectivity. I only ask that you understand this;

The policing profession exists because there are a precious few who choose not to run away, or seek safety. They choose to protect the innocent. They choose to chase the bad man into the darkness, even though it scares the hell out of them. They need our support, trust, and appreciation to be successful. Please consider giving it to them.

-Ben

Acknowledgments

I would like to thank Nick Selby, for his dedication to the law enforcement profession and his personal sacrifice in building a company that provides life-saving tools to law enforcement agencies and insightful studies like PKIC. I am very proud to be associated with StreetCred, and incredibly privileged to partner with Nick on this project. I would like to thank my mentors, Bill Waybourn and Jerry Vennum, for their guidance and inspiration. And my beautiful wife, Kristen, for her continuous support throughout my law enforcement career and subsequent endeavors. I am so grateful to have all of you in my corner.

-Ben

Ed Flosi

Acknowledgments

I was honored to be asked to participate in this very important project. To be honest, the lion's share of work had been completed and I got to play in the fun part. Use of force training has been my passion for quite some time. It started with taking advanced classes from trainers that I had great respect for and then morphed into a burning ambition to learn everything I could on the topic. I became determined to use my knowledge to help officers better understand: (1) the force decision making process, and (2) the evaluation process. I feel that I have taken another step in the direction of achieving that goal with the opportunity to participate in this critical research and publication. I thank Nick for asking me, and to all the other "StreetCred Software Associates" for allowing me (and sometimes tolerating me) to participate.

There are so many people who have had, and continue to have, a positive influence on my life and that have mentored me that it would take another book to list them and acknowledge all they've done for me. Thank you all, I feel blessed to know you.

ENDNOTES

[1] The utterly excellent Bureau of Justice Statistics (http://www.bjs.gov/), a component of the Office of Justice Programs in the U.S. Department of Justice, has a mission," "to collect, analyze, publish, and disseminate information on crime, criminal offenders, victims of crime, and the operation of justice systems at all levels of government. These data are critical to federal, state, and local policymakers in combating crime and ensuring that justice is both efficient and evenhanded." BJS gathers its primary data from the U.S. Bureau of the Census, the FBI's Uniform Crime Reporting program, and National Incident-Based Reporting System. The BJS Federal Justice Statistics Program collects data from other Federal agencies, including the Executive Office for U.S. Attorneys, the Administrative Office of the U.S. Courts, the U.S. Sentencing Commission, and the Federal Bureau of Prisons.

[2] See, e.g., Radley Balko, Rise of the Warrior Cop: The Militarization of America's Police Forces available on Amazon at http://goo.gl/NgEK1y

[3] http://www.nbcchicago.com/news/local/Officer-Charged-in-Laquan-McDonalds-Death-Due-in-Court-358719021.html

[4] FOX4 Staff. (2016, January 15). Arlington police officer is first transgender officer in department history. Retrieved February 6, 2016, from http://www.fox4news.com/news/75114834-story

[5] See the text in the About The Data chapter on why Hispanic or Latino is particularly problematic as a description – it is no longer considered a race, but rather an ethnicity that is separate from (and combined with) race. Handling this has been rough going. Suffice it to say that in the future, specific government guidance to clarify race from ethnicity in this kind of

reporting will be necessary. According to Dave Hess of Data Bakery, a technology firm that works with StreetCred on software, when discussing the impact of these changes on casual observers, "This may seem like just an interesting definition of little consequence, but the way this was handled has a direct impact on consumers of Census data who are more interested in answering demographic questions where ethnicity and race need to be considered together."

[6] These BJS nationwide police demographic figures do not reference the nation's approximately 29,000 reserve or auxiliary local police officers, of whom two shot to death unarmed civilians in 2015.

[7] http://wreg.com/2016/02/09/craigmont-high-student-tragically-killed-by-12-year-old-brother/

[8] http://kfor.com/2015/12/15/11-year-old-girl-shot-killed-by-12-year-old-classmate/

[9] In fact, this is so common, and has been so common for so long, that it was a significant plot device in the 1988 movie Die Hard. One of the characters laments that his feels so guilty about shooting a child that he has placed himself on desk duty: "I shot a kid. He was 13 years old. Ohhh, it was dark, I couldn't see him. He had a ray gun, looked real enough. You know, when you're a rookie, they can teach you everything about bein' a cop except how to live with a mistake. Anyway, I just couldn't bring myself to draw my gun on anybody again." - http://www.imdb.com/title/tt0095016/quotes

[10] Video of Officer Earomirski confronting McLeod https://www.youtube.com/watch?v=sX371LMLEwY

[11] Leonardatos, Blackman and Kopel (2001) "Smart Guns/Foolish Legislators: Finding the Right Public Safety Laws And Avoiding The Wrong Ones," Connecticut Law Review, 34 Conn. L. Rev. 157

[12] The PKIC project does not draw any conclusions on, or make statements about the "justification" of any incident within the database, except to note, for example whether the killing was "ruled justified" by authorities.

[13]

https://www.gov.uk/government/uploads/system/uploads/attachment_data/file/445667/police-officers-assaulted-mar15.pdf; This includes all physical assaults against officers, including those that led to serious injury. Media reports such as those at http://www.express.co.uk/news/uk/53677/One-police-officer-injured-every-hour indicate rates of some 500 serious physical injuries to officers annually.

[14] One interesting point is how few people in the UK are killed each year in conflicts with police. Having lived and worked in the UK for some years, and speaking anecdotally, I think much of the reason for this is that the UK police are much better, and more frequently, trained in de-escalation and, since they don't for the most part carry guns, accidental killings may be less frequent. But it is also important to understand that UK police don't face the same kinds of threats that American officers face. In an assault against an officer in the UK, it is almost always man-to-man, hand-to-hand combat. While sometimes embarrassing and often stressful, fisticuffs are far more likely to lead to injuries than to death. In America, an officer must understand that the person confronting him (a) understands that the officer is armed and is attacking anyway, and (b) may very well pull a deadly weapon or firearm at any moment, giving the American officer a distinct disincentive to "de-escalate" an attack against him.

[15] WCPO 9. (2015, July 29). WATCH: Police Officer Ray Tensing body cam, Samuel DuBose shooting. Retrieved February 14, 2016, from https://www.youtube.com/watch?v=Z0cdejrSjyc

[16] Ehler, M., Brown, R., Mitchell, D., Nugent, W., & Batty, W. (2015, August 31). Review and Investigation of Officer Raymond M. Tensing's Use of Deadly Force on July 19, 2015: University of Cincinnati Police

Department [PDF]. Report to the Office of General Counsel, University of Cincinnati. New York: Kroll.

[17] Associated Press (2015, August 7) Prosecutor in case of man fatally shot by University of Cincinnati cop criticized for comments | Fox News. (2015). Retrieved February 14, 2016, from http://www.foxnews.com/us/2015/08/07/prosecutor-in-case-man-fatally-shot-by-university-cincinnati-cop-criticized-for.html

[18] eg, http://www.theguardian.com/us-news/2016/jan/18/samuel-dubose-police-settlement-university-of-cincinnati

[19] http://www.kcci.com/news/man-killed-in-officerinvolved-shooting/33497168

[20] http://www.desmoinesregister.com/story/news/crime-and-courts/2015/06/10/fatal-officer-shooting-ryan-bolinger-dancing-man-vanessa-miller/71010592/

[21] http://www.desmoinesregister.com/story/news/crime-and-courts/2015/10/19/dm-officer-cleared-fatal-shooting/74243880/

[22] Ibid.

[23] http://www.kcci.com/news/investigation-officer-cleared-in-shooting-death-of-unarmed-man/35931450

[24] http://www.copblock.org/144423/ryan-bolinger-murder-deemed-justified/

[25] CopBlock maintains a Vanessa Miller collection at http://www.copblock.org/tag/vanessa-miller/

[26] http://www.wpbf.com/news/tripping-man-dies-after-being-subdued-by-deputies/33612230

[27] http://wfla.com/2015/08/13/indian-river-countys-death-linked-to-flakka-deputies-say/

[28] http://www.palmbeachpost.com/news/news/state-regional/police-florida-man-dies-after-tripping-and-acting-/nmdzP/

[29] http://www.wpbf.com/news/tripping-man-dies-after-being-subdued-by-deputies/33612230

[30] http://wfla.com/2015/08/13/indian-river-countys-death-linked-to-flakka-deputies-say/

[31] EMCDDA–Europol Joint Report on a new psychoactive substance: 1-phenyl-2-(1-pyrrolidinyl)- 1-pentanone (α-PVP) European Monitoring Centre For Drugs and Drug Addiction, and Europol Joint Publication; ISSN 1977-7868, 2015

[32] http://cbs12.com/news/local/first-death-attributed-to-flakka-in-indian-river-county

[33] Moskos, P. & Selby, N "Just counting people killed by police won't fix problems. We need better data," The Washington Post, Jan 15, 2016. https://goo.gl/tC2CSs

[34] http://www.washingtonpost.com/sf/investigative/2015/10/24/on-duty-under-fire/

[35] Moskos, P, and Selby, N, "Just counting people killed by police won't fix problems. We need better data." The Washington Post, Jan. 15, 2016. https://goo.gl/tC2CSs

[36] 72.55%

[37] Citizen calls to 911 initiated 69% of non-traffic incidents. Another 21 (19%) involved a citizen flagging down an officer.

[38] 59 of 76, or 77.62%

[39] In the 59 cases in which the incident was initiated by a 911 call to the police, and which included a description of the suspect being reported by the community, 22 (37.28%) of the decedents were black, 18 (30.5%) were white, 10 (16.94%) were Hispanic, six (10.16%) were of unknown race, 2 (3.38%) were Semitic, and one (1.69%) was an Asian or Pacific Islander.

[40] Alpert, Kaminski, Fridell, MacDonald & Kubu (2011) "Police Use of Force, Tasers and Other Less-Lethal Weapons" Research In Brief, Office of Justice Programs, National Institute of Justice (May, 2011) Available: https://www.ncjrs.gov/pdffiles1/nij/232215.pdf

[41] Levinson-Waldman, R and Selby, N (2016) "Body cameras can't solve all our problems," USAToday Opinion, 1 April, 2016; available: http://www.usatoday.com/story/opinion/2016/04/01/police-body-cameras-accountability-exoneration-evidence-column/82484112/

[42] 392 U.S. 1, 30 (1968)

[43] Myers, Richard, Challenges to Terry for the Twenty-First Century (October 24, 2012). Mississippi Law Journal, Vol. 81, No. 5, 2012; UNC Legal Studies Research Paper No. 2166260.

[44] Selby, Nick, "Give Me Your Hunches". Police Led Intelligence. 24 March 2011

[45] Ibid.

[46] We can debate this, but it's generally the case. In the northeast and in agencies with powerful officer unions, this is a different and perhaps more difficult problem, as laws and collective-bargaining agreements have set precedents in the manner in which officers may be identified, and this issue plays directly to this. This can be highly relevant to the conversation about adoption of body-worn video because it in some cases can create a

substantial change in the work environment, which would mean the union would absolutely not be OK with it

[47] https://www.brennancenter.org/analysis/police-body-camera-policies-recording-circumstances

[48] http://www.baltimoresun.com/news/maryland/freddie-gray/bs-md-ci-porter-jury-split-20160115-story.html

[49] http://www.nbcnews.com/id/46082717/ns/us_news-crime_and_courts/t/horrific-murder-no-surprise-us-meth-hub/#.Vw_IDagrKhc

[50] http://www.ncbi.nlm.nih.gov/pmc/articles/PMC2775771/

[51] http://journalistsresource.org/studies/government/criminal-justice/deaths-police-custody-united-states#sthash.BzqcsWAT.dpuf

[52] Glasheen, Hedden, Kroutil, Pemberton & Goldstrom, Past Year Arrest among Adults in the United States: Characteristics of and Association with Mental Illness and Substance Use, Substance Abuse and Mental Health Services Administration, November, 2011

[53] Subramanian, Delaney, Roberts, Fishman, & McGarry, "Incarceration's Front Door: The Misuse of Jails in America" Vera Institute of Justice, 2015.

[54] https://www.youtube.com/watch?v=1E6ywsBBSj0

[55] Parks, Radke, Haupt "The Vital Role of State Psychiatric Hospitals", National Association of State Mental Health Program Directors, Medical Directors Council, 2014, Alexandria, VA

[56] Perry, D and Carter-Long, L, "The Ruderman White Paper On Media Coverage Of Law Enforcement Use Of Force And Disability," The Ruderman Family Foundation, March, 2016, http://www.rudermanfoundation.org/wp-

content/uploads/2016/03/MediaStudy-PoliceDisability_TS-final1.docx

57 Selby, "How tracking police data by race can make unfair laws look like the cops' fault," Washington Post, March 3, 2016

58 https://www.nami.org/

59 National Institute of Mental Health, Any Mental Illness (AMI) Among Adults.

60 Bernstein, R, "Letter to President's Task Force on 21st Century Policing, Office of Community Oriented Policing Services," Judge David L Bazelon Center for Mental Health Law, March, 2015, http://www.bazelon.org/LinkClick.aspx?fileticket=zGdyaep2AjI%3D&tabid=117

61 Sarteschi, "Mentally Ill Offenders Involved with the U.S. Criminal Justice System" Sage Open, July 2013, 1-11. doi: 10.1177/2158244013497029

62 Alpert, Kaminski, Fridell, MacDonald & Kubu (2011) "Police Use of Force, Tasers and Other Less-Lethal Weapons" Research In Brief, Office of Justice Programs, National Institute of Justice (May, 2011) Available: https://www.ncjrs.gov/pdffiles1/nij/232215.pdf

63 Neuromuscular incapacitation (NMI) devices discharge a pulsed dose of electrical energy to cause muscle contraction and pain; for more see McDaniel, Stratbucker and Brewer (2005), Cardiac Safety of Neuromuscular Incapacitating Defensive Devices. Pacing and Clinical Electrophysiology, 28: S284–S287. doi: 10.1111/j.1540-8159.2005.00101.x

64 http://www.miamiherald.com/news/local/community/florida-keys/article5621958.html

65 http://www.miaminewtimes.com/news/key-largo-teenager-dies-after-new-

years-day-tasering-6526364

[66] http://www.keysnet.com/2015/07/17/503669_tased-teen-died-of-drug-overdose.html

[67] http://www.kansas.com/news/local/crime/article22608333.html

[68] http://www.kansas.com/news/local/crime/article5407941.html

[69] http://mynewsla.com/crime/2015/01/07/suspect-dies-tasered-sheriffs-deputy/.

[70] http://www.latimes.com/local/lanow/la-me-ln-taser-death-20150107-story.html

[71] http://www.kcci.com/news/neighbor-blames-dog-for-shooting-that-left-woman-dead/30576424

[72] http://www.desmoinesregister.com/story/news/crime-and-courts/2015/02/27/burlington-police-officer-cleared-fatal-shooting/24161985/

[73] http://norfolkdailynews.com/news/man-who-died-in-police-custody-reported-to-have-been/article_546f0b56-ad47-11e4-bd1c-f729ce80cb9b.html

[74] http://nebraskaradionetwork.com/2015/02/05/mans-death-in-norfolk-police-custody-accidental-officers-in-clear/

[75] http://www.knoe.com/home/headlines/Arkansas-pharmacy-burglary-leaves-one-dead-2-behind-bars-288104941.html

[76] http://www.washingtontimes.com/news/2015/jan/9/arkansas-state-police-investigating-death-of-robbe/

[77] https://www.policeone.com/close-quarters-combat/articles/100228-Cases-

of-Officers-Killed-by-Their-Own-Guns-Likely-Will-Not-Change-R-I-
Policies/

[78] http://www.everythinglubbock.com/news/kamc-news/lynn-co-chase-ends-
in-crash-officer-involved-shooting

[79] http://www.everythinglubbock.com/news/kamc-news/dps-provides-name-
update-after-deadly-officer-involved-shooting-lynn-co

[80] http://www.denverpost.com/news/ci_27394478/denver-police-shoot-2-
suspects-critically-injuring-one

[81]

http://extras.mnginteractive.com/live/media/site36/2015/0605/20150605_
124921_2015letterJordanandGreene.pdf.

[82] http://newsok.com/article/5388814

[83] http://fox2now.com/2015/03/25/female-police-officer-faces-murder-
charges-for-shooting-and-killing-suspect/

[84] http://www.inquisitr.com/2027308/david-kassick-death-video-footage-
allegedly-showing-officer-lisa-mearkle-firing-two-shots-in-unarmed-mans-
back-could-soon-be-released/

[85]

http://www.pennlive.com/midstate/index.ssf/2015/11/mearkle_verdict.html

[86] http://www.texomashomepage.com/news/local-news/update-man-tased-
by-deputies-on-287-has-died

[87] http://www.newschannel6now.com/story/28014585/update-man-tased-
on-highway-287-dies

[88] http://www.abc15.com/news/region-phoenix-metro/south-
phoenix/tempe-police-shoot-2-suspects-near-48th-street-and-baseline-

condition-of-suspects-unknown

[89] http://www.azcentral.com/story/news/local/tempe/2015/02/04/tempe-officer-involved-shooting-abrk/22884251/

[90] http://media.graytvinc.com/documents/Grand+Jury+Case.pdf

[91] http://www.wjhg.com/home/headlines/State-Attorney-FDLE-Finish-Officer-Involved-Shooting—321315491.html

[92]

http://www.newsherald.com/article/20150810/NEWS/150819968/?Start=2

[93] http://www.appeal-democrat.com/da-s-report/pdf_35a8a7a0-46e8-11e5-9385-4fdf8b268cee.html

[94] http://www.appeal-democrat.com/news/man-brain-dead-after-taser-incident/article_0ee17c8c-b804-11e4-83b6-7b653e301058.html

[95] http://www.news-leader.com/story/news/crime/2015/02/18/police-one-dead-in-northwest-springfield-shooting/23604403/

[96] http://www.news-leader.com/story/news/crime/2015/04/22/police-give-evidence-prosecutors-ireland-shooting/26186993/

[97] http://thescoopblog.dallasnews.com/2015/05/tarrant-county-grand-jury-declined-to-indict-in-grapevine-police-involved-shooting-of-mexican-immigrant.html/

[98] http://www.star-telegram.com/news/local/crime/article11225840.html

[99] http://legacy.wfaa.com/story/news/local/tarrant-county/2015/04/21/autopsy-mexican-national-shot-by-police-was-drunk/26131411/

[100] http://www.tulsaworld.com/news/local/autopsy-finds-man-died-of-

cardiac-arrest-after-being-immobilized/article_d7e00dc6-4487-51a7-a0bc-19a6a8d9744a.html

[101] http://osagenews.org/en/article/2015/05/10/no-charges-filed-against-onpd-death-man-osage-casinos/

[102] http://www.miamiherald.com/news/local/community/miami-dade/article21231345.html

[103] http://www.local10.com/news/local/coconut-creek-taser-death-ruled-homicide-by-electrocution-

[104] http://www.ketv.com/news/new-details-released-in-mondays-officerinvolved-shooting/31458074

[105] http://www.wowt.com/home/headlines/293928901.html

[106]

http://media.graytvinc.com/documents/Danny+Elrod+OIS+Press+Release.pdf

[107] http://wthitv.com/2015/03/27/vigo-county-prosecutors-office-ruling-police-action-shooting-justified-veteran-officer-forced-to-respond-out-of-self-defense/

[108] http://www.tristatehomepage.com/news/top-stories/isp-investigating-officer-involved-shooting-in-terre-haute

[109] http://wthitv.com/2015/03/27/vigo-county-prosecutors-office-ruling-police-action-shooting-justified-veteran-officer-forced-to-respond-out-of-self-defense/

[110] http://www.news9.com/story/28195051/okc-police-driver-who-attempted-to-strike-officers-shot-and-killed

[111] http://kfor.com/2015/02/25/police-chase-leads-to-officer-involved-shooting/

[112] http://www.latimes.com/local/lanow/la-me-ln-santa-ana-officer-involved-shooting-20150227-story.html

[113] http://www.latimes.com/la-fg-dead-mexicans-pg-010-photo.html

[114] http://www.stltoday.com/news/local/crime-and-courts/wellston-cop-feared-for-his-life-and-girl-s-when/article_1ab0c618-5eb4-5c33-b604-7fa938713367.html

[115] http://www.stltoday.com/news/local/suspect-in-wellson-police-shooting-dies-of-wounds/article_7572d365-c0d0-515f-a2d5-bc6ab6a2265d.html

[116] http://www.eatoncounty.org/images/Departments/Prosecuting%20Attorney/Press_Releases/Guilford_Press_Release.pdf

[117] http://www.lansingstatejournal.com/story/news/local/2015/06/16/press-conference-eaton-guilford/28801761/

[118] http://www.latimes.com/local/california/la-me-lapd-shooting-20150302-story.html

[119] http://www.latimes.com/local/lanow/la-me-ln-lapd-names-skid-row-shooting-20150319-story.html

[120] https://www.youtube.com/watch?v=T3ejsTMBMKk

[121] http://www.news9.com/story/28233777/man-dies-after-being-tasered-by-okc-police-during-assault-officer-says

[122] http://newsok.com/report-shows-man-who-died-in-police-custody-had-cocaine-in-his-system/article/5419077

[123] https://www.washingtonpost.com/news/the-watch/wp/2015/03/06/another-day-another-drug-raid-fatality/

[124] http://www.wesh.com/news/so-deputy-shoots-suspect-in-face-while-serving-search-warrant-in-deltona/31604946

[125] http://www.news-journalonline.com/article/20150715/NEWS/150719697

[126] http://www.latimes.com/local/lanow/la-me-ln-lapd-pursuit-shooting-burbank-20150306-story.html

[127] Ibid.

[128] http://denver.cbslocal.com/2015/12/30/no-indictment-for-officer-who-killed-unarmed-parole-violator/

[129] https://www.doj.state.wi.us/sites/default/files/MADISON%20-%20TONY%20T.%20ROBINSON%20JR.%20INVESTIGATION,%20MARCH%202015.pdf

[130] http://www.delcotimes.com/general-news/20150309/burglary-suspect-shot-and-killed-by-state-police-in-claymont

[131] http://www.wsbtv.com/news/news/local/dekalb-officer-involved-shooting/nkRY6/

[132] http://www.mansfieldnewsjournal.com/story/news/local/2015/03/11/bci-investigating-voa-death/70172904/

[133] http://www.richlandsource.com/news/no-criminal-charges-in-march-death-of-terrance-moxley/article_4a8029ea-67b9-11e5-a0f0-631f701f77ae.html

[134] http://www.mansfieldnewsjournal.com/story/news/local/2015/10/01/no-criminal-charges-terrence-moxley-death-mansfield-ohio/73097290/

[135] http://homicide.latimes.com/post/antonio-perez-2015-01832/

[136] http://www.presstelegram.com/general-news/20150313/foot-pursuit-in-unincorporated-walnut-park-ends-in-fatal-deputy-involved-shooting

[137] http://www.nhregister.com/general-news/20150821/report-branford-police-officer-exonerated-in-taser-death

[138] http://www.hawaiinewsnow.com/story/28546370/combative-man-dies-following-arrest-near-iolani-palace

[139] http://www.civilbeat.com/2015/07/autopsy-honolulu-man-dies-after-violent-physical-struggle-with-cops/

[140] http://legacy.11alive.com/story/news/local/rome/2015/03/18/floyd-county-police-askari-roberts/24966995/

[141] http://www.northwestgeorgianews.com/rome/gbi-probes-officer-involved-death-of-askari-roberts/article_3574dd54-cd57-11e4-9b46-d3f30165f444.html

[142]
http://www.cleveland.com/metro/index.ssf/2015/03/man_shot_by_cleveland_police_o_3.html

[143] http://www.newsnet5.com/news/local-news/cleveland-metro/brandon-jones-family-of-teen-shot-killed-by-cleveland-police-speak-out

[144] http://www.cleveland19.com/story/28593585/parents-speak-after-son-fatally-shot-by-police-during-robbery

[145] http://www.thetimestribune.com/news/williamsburg-man-dies-in-custody/article_79b2d1d0-d2a5-11e4-ab15-dfce00f6089f.html

[146] https://www.longislandexchange.com/press-releases/suspect-dies-after-officer-involved-shooting-in-bay-shore/

[147] http://blogs.wsj.com/metropolis/2015/03/23/long-island-man-dies-after-

police-involved-shooting/

[148] http://www.fredericksburg.com/news/crime_courts/culpeper-man-dies-after-being-tasered-by-police/article_46debc2a-d727-11e4-a18f-5b06a6f5b1bd.html

[149] http://www.nbcphiladelphia.com/news/local/Officials-Reveal-New-Details-on-Vineland-Man-Who-Died-While-in-Police-Custody—298359361.html

[150] http://www.nbcphiladelphia.com/news/local/Vineland-Man-Dies-After-Being-Taken-Into-Custody-298188581.html

[151] http://www.timesunion.com/local/article/Details-emerge-questions-remain-in-case-of-6473960.php

[152] http://albanycountyda.com/Libraries/Press_Releases/Scanned-image-5_1.sflb.ashx

[153] http://www.tulsaworld.com/newshomepage2/sources-supervisors-told-to-falsify-reserve-deputy-s-training-records/article_a6330f10-a9fb-51e3-ab5e-4d97b03c6c04.html

[154] http://www.nbcnews.com/news/us-news/eric-harris-was-high-meth-when-tulsa-deputy-shot-him-n357926

[155] http://www.tulsaworld.com/news/local/tulsa-sheriff-stanley-glanz-says-two-deputies-reassigned-after-fatal/article_756c7584-c083-5eb2-bec6-9f864cbd7215.html

[156] http://www.cnn.com/2015/04/13/us/tulsa-police-shooting-eric-harris-deputy-charged/

[157] http://www.cnn.com/2015/09/30/us/tulsa-oklahoma-sheriff-indicted/

[158] http://www.aele.org/law/2012all06/2012-06MLJ101.pdf

[159] http://www.newson6.com/story/28721037/sources-suspect-dies-following-scuffle-with-warner-police-officer

[160] http://muskogeenow.com/pdfs/DavidCodyLynchAutopsy.pdf

[161] http://www.seattletimes.com/seattle-news/coulee-dam-man-dies-following-taser-incident/

[162] http://legacy.krem.com/story/news/local/okanogan-county/2015/04/06/hitchhiker-robbed-at-gunpoint-off-hwy-20/25370711/

[163] http://www.huffingtonpost.com/2015/04/07/officer-michael-slager-shoots-man-in-back-video_n_7021134.html

[164] http://www.cnn.com/2015/10/08/us/walter-scott-north-charleston-settlement/

[165] Ibid.

[166] http://www.bakersfield.com/news/2015/05/02/reports-detail-deputies-struggle-with-lake-isabella-man-who-later-died.html

[167] http://www.kerngoldenempire.com/news/top-stories/new-information-on-kcso-in-custody-death

[168] http://www.baltimoresun.com/news/maryland/freddie-gray/bs-md-ci-freddie-gray-autopsy-20150623-story.html#page=1

[169] http://www.sfgate.com/nation/article/2nd-Freddie-Gray-trial-set-fellow-officer-must-6878381.php

[170] http://www.baltimoresun.com/news/maryland/politics/bs-md-police-seatbelt-audits-20151017-story.html

[171] http://nixle.com/alert/5395830/

[172] http://www.highlandnews.net/news/breaking_news/officers-names-released-in-death-investigation/article_712c2f76-e5e6-11e4-9921-777ce68d8709.html

[173] http://www.nydailynews.com/news/national/texas-suspect-shot-dead-live-tv-police-chase-article-1.2186187

[174] http://abc13.com/news/suspect-shot-by-officers-at-end-of-police-chase/661643/

[175] http://thenewsherald.com/articles/2015/08/12/news/doc55ca1fc831698992 120435.txt

[176] http://www.freep.com/story/news/local/michigan/wayne/2015/04/17/gibral tar-stun-gun-death/25925051/

[177] http://thenewsherald.com/articles/2015/08/12/news/doc55ca1fc831698992 120435.txt

[178] http://baltimore.cbslocal.com/2015/04/17/police-man-dies-in-custody-stun-gun-used-during-arrest/

[179] http://legacy.wusa9.com/story/news/local/2015/08/06/autopsy-man-hit-stun-gun-died-drug-delirium/31222289/

[180] http://www.ksat.com/news/man-dies-in-police-custody-following-tasing

[181] http://www.thenewstribune.com/news/local/crime/article26288200.html

[182] http://www.thenewstribune.com/news/local/crime/article28456672.html

[183] http://www.clarionledger.com/story/news/2015/04/21/man-dead-after-altercation-with-deputies/26141147/

[184] http://www.meridianstar.com/news/local_news/coroner-injuries-from-struggle-not-cause-of-death/article_bcd011da-ed4e-11e4-94e8-178137d8683d.html

[185] http://wavy.com/2015/04/22/police-on-scene-of-gunshot-wound-victim-near-walmart/

[186] http://www.foxnews.com/us/2015/09/03/officer-indicted-on-murder-firearms-charges-in-fatal-shooting-in-wal-mart.html

[187] http://www.presstelegram.com/general-news/20150424/police-no-weapon-found-at-scene-of-officer-involved-shooting-in-long-beach-thursday

[188] http://www.nytimes.com/2015/04/27/nyregion/suspect-fatally-shot-by-detective-in-east-village-had-mental-illness-and-a-troubled-past.html?_r=1

[189] http://www.nydailynews.com/new-york/cops-shoot-man-east-village-altercation-police-article-1.2198797

[190] http://www.tulsaworld.com/news/crimewatch/one-dead-after-being-shot-by-wildlife-officer-in-adair/article_f1d11d71-fc0a-5d25-b38c-64356d834739.html

[191] http://www.latimes.com/tn-hbi-me-0430-fv-police-shooting-20150427-story.html

[192] http://www.ocregister.com/articles/fountain-659846-identified-killed.html

[193] http://www.sandiegouniontribune.com/news/2015/may/29/family-files-claim-officer-fatal-shooting-midway/

[194] http://www.troyrecord.com/general-news/20150520/funeral-services-held-for-brendon-glenn

[195] http://www.latimes.com/local/crime/la-me-venice-shooting-20150520-

story.html

[196] http://www.latimes.com/local/lanow/la-me-ln-lapd-venice-shooting-20160412-story.html

[197] http://documents.latimes.com/lapd-chiefs-letter-fatal-venice-shooting/

[198] http://documents.latimes.com/lapd-chiefs-letter-fatal-venice-shooting/

[199] http://www.latimes.com/local/lanow/la-me-ln-venice-wrongful-death-suit-20160209-story.html

[200]

http://www.heraldtribune.com/article/20150513/ARTICLE/150519870/2416

[201] http://www.yourobserver.com/article/investigation-sarasota-arrestees-death-continues

[202] http://www.nbc12.com/story/29032348/midlothian-man-dies-after-police-taser-used

[203] http://wncn.com/2015/05/14/no-answers-from-prelim-autopsy-in-police-custody-death/

[204] https://www.washingtonpost.com/local/crime/man-dies-two-days-after-being-tasered-by-montgomery-county-police-officer/2015/05/15/81106b26-fb55-11e4-9ef4-1bb7ce3b3fb7_story.html

[205] http://wtop.com/montgomery-county/2015/05/death-of-man-after-police-tasing-investigated-in-montgomery-county/

[206] https://www.lakeviewhealth.com/pcp-treatment.php

[207] http://www.nbcnewyork.com/news/local/Man-Dies-Police-Custody-Cardiac-Arrest-NYPD-303850681.html

[208] http://www.theguardian.com/us-news/2015/jun/03/denis-reyes-the-counted-nypd

[209] http://www.nydailynews.com/new-york/bronx-man-died-custody-drinking-sources-article-1.2224115#

[210] http://www.local10.com/news/markus-clark-dies-at-florida-medical-center-after-arrest

[211] http://www.cnn.com/2015/05/26/health/flakka-gravel-illegal-drugs/

[212] http://www.wibw.com/home/headlines/Police-Man-Dies-At-Hospital-After-Shot-By-Police-Stun-Gun-305327711.html

[213] http://www.kshb.com/news/region-kansas/kck/mother-kckpd-chief-speak-about-randall-torrence-man-who-died-after-taser-incident

[214] http://www.presstelegram.com/general-news/20150529/man-killed-by-long-beach-police-was-nationally-ranked-debater-from-woodland-hills

[215] http://www.theguardian.com/us-news/2015/jun/01/student-shot-california-long-beach-police-feras-morad

[216] http://www.wsaz.com/home/headlines/Death-of-Man-in-Police-Custody-Under-Investigation-305777981.html

[217]
http://verdenews.com/main.asp?SectionID=1&SubSectionID=1&ArticleID=65920

[218] http://www.twcnews.com/nys/rochester/top-stories/2015/05/31/police-incident-on-tremont-street.html

[219] http://www.democratandchronicle.com/story/news/2015/05/31/police-holding-press-briefing-tremont-st-incident/28263079/

[220] http://dpdbeat.com/2015/06/09/death-in-custody-5400-north-jim-miller-road/

[221] See http://www.wfaa.com/story/news/local/dallas-county/2015/06/09/man-dies-after-dallas-police-deploy-taser/28726075/; http://dfw.cbslocal.com/2015/06/09/man-dies-in-dallas-police-custody/; and http://crimeblog.dallasnews.com/2015/06/suspect-dies-in-dallas-police-custody.html/

[222] http://www.kcci.com/news/man-killed-in-officerinvolved-shooting/33497168

[223] http://www.desmoinesregister.com/story/news/crime-and-courts/2015/06/10/fatal-officer-shooting-ryan-bolinger-dancing-man-vanessa-miller/71010592/

[224] http://www.kcci.com/news/investigation-officer-cleared-in-shooting-death-of-unarmed-man/35931450

[225] http://www.wtol.com/story/29274441/officer-involved-shooting-kills-findlay-man

[226] Email exchange between Nick Selby and Lt. Ring on 29 March 2016; message from Lt Robert Ring <rring@findlayohio.com> received at 10:46 am ET

[227] https://www.findlayohio.com/fpd-20151023-grand-jury/

[228] Ibid.

[229] https://www.findlayohio.com/fpd-20151023-grand-jury/

[230] http://www.sacbee.com/news/local/crime/article24714634.html

[231] http://www.cityofslt.us/DocumentCenter/View/5539

232 http://mynews4.com/news/local/family-speaks-out-in-deadly-south-lake-tahoe-officer-involved-shooting

233 http://www.cityofslt.us/DocumentCenter/View/5539

234 http://www.laketahoenews.net/2016/02/lawsuit-filed-in-slt-police-officer-shooting/

235 http://www.wpbf.com/news/tripping-man-dies-after-being-subdued-by-deputies/33612230

236 http://wfla.com/2015/08/13/indian-river-countys-death-linked-to-flakka-deputies-say/

237 http://www.palmbeachpost.com/news/news/state-regional/police-florida-man-dies-after-tripping-and-acting-/nmdzP/

238 http://www.wpbf.com/news/tripping-man-dies-after-being-subdued-by-deputies/33612230

239 http://wfla.com/2015/08/13/indian-river-countys-death-linked-to-flakka-deputies-say/

240 http://theadvocate.com/news/12707991-123/zachary-man-32-dies-of

241 http://brgov.com/dept/brpd/news/pdfs/06-22-15_Death_Investigation_Update.pdf

242 http://theadvocate.com/features/13553669-171/death-of-zachary-man-who

243 Ibid.

244 http://www.wowo.com/indianapolis-officer-fatally-shoots-huntington-man-in-chase/

[245] https://nixle.com/alert/5439772/

[246] http://advanceindiana.blogspot.com/2015/06/prosecutor-files-more-charges-against.html

[247] http://www.baltimoresun.com/news/maryland/crime/bs-md-co-police-involved-shooting-20150625-story.html

[248]

http://www.baltimorecountymd.gov/News/PoliceNews/iWatch/DetectivesInvestigatingPoliceInvolvedShootinginOwingsMills

[249] http://legacy.wusa9.com/story/news/local/2015/06/25/owings-mills-police-involved-shooting/29259039/

[250]

http://www.baltimorecountymd.gov/News/PoliceNews/iWatch/DetectivesInvestigatingPoliceInvolvedShootinginOwingsMills

[251] http://www.baltimoresun.com/news/maryland/crime/bs-md-co-police-involved-shooting-20150625-story.html

[252] http://www.usatoday.com/story/news/nation/2015/06/26/police-involved-shooting-unarmed-black-man-baltimore-county/29322373/

[253] http://katu.com/news/local/da-clears-deputy-in-deadly-mcminnville-shooting-after-traffic-stop-releases-video

[254] http://katu.com/news/local/da-clears-deputy-in-deadly-mcminnville-shooting-after-traffic-stop-releases-video#videos

[255] http://wvmetronews.com/2015/07/22/state-police-will-join-investigation-into-death-of-man-who-scuffled-with-weston-officer/

[256] http://www.nbclosangeles.com/news/local/Montclair-Police-In-Custody-Death-311606411.html

[257] http://abc7news.com/news/pleasanton-police-investigate-fatal-officer-involved-shooting/829976/

[258] http://www.nbcbayarea.com/news/local/Man-Shot-Killed-by-Pleasanton-Police-Identified-as-Officers-Son-312270311.html

[259] http://abc7news.com/news/independent-exam-of-man-shot-killed-by-pleasanton-officer-finds-no-drugs/978196/

[260] http://ktla.com/2015/07/06/alleged-prowler-who-was-possibly-unarmed-is-fatally-shot-by-sheriffs-deputies-in-hawaiian-gardens/

[261] http://www.nbclosangeles.com/news/local/Sheriffs-Deputy-Shooting-Hawaiian-Gardens-311707311.html

[262] http://www.loscerritosnews.net/2015/09/15/independent-autopsy-disputes-sheriffs-account-in-johnny-anderson-shooting/

[263] http://fox13now.com/2015/07/07/carjacking-suspect-in-custody-after-assaulting-woman-being-tased-having-heart-attack/

[264] https://www.ksl.com/?nid=148&sid=35397350

[265] http://www.clarionledger.com/story/news/2015/07/10/death-involving-stonewall-miss-officer-investigated/29952949/

[266] http://www.clarionledger.com/story/news/2016/01/11/mississippi-officer-not-indictmented/78627156/

[267]

http://www.al.com/news/index.ssf/2015/08/jonathan_sanders_mississippi_s.html

[268] http://www.clarionledger.com/story/news/2015/07/16/lawyer-autopsy-finds-mississippi-man-strangled-police-encounter/30245669/

269 https://www.youtube.com/watch?v=GIoDDFyhB-8

270 Ibid.

271 Ibid.

272 http://wtug.com/tuscaloosa-police-department-releases-anthony-ware-autopsy-report/

273 See, eg
http://www.al.com/news/tuscaloosa/index.ssf/2015/07/tuscaloosa_police_release_more.html, and
http://www.al.com/news/tuscaloosa/index.ssf/2015/07/tuscaloosa_officers_involved_i.html and
http://www.nola.com/crime/index.ssf/2015/07/alabama_police_probe_use_of_pe.html

274 http://www.gwinnettdailypost.com/archive/gbi-man-acted-crazy-during-deadly-confrontation-with-gwinnett-police/article_fa62ec16-ed24-53f6-810a-c291959611db.html

275 http://www.ajc.com/news/news/crime-law/man-dies-after-altercation-with-gwinnett-cops-gbi-/nmxKw/

276 http://www.sun-sentinel.com/local/broward/fl-plantation-cop-identified-20150713-story.html

277 http://www.sun-sentinel.com/local/broward/fl-plantation-cop-homeless-shooting-id-20150715-story.html

278 http://www.local10.com/news/man-fatally-shot-by-plantation-police-officer-identified

279
http://www.thetimesnews.com/article/20150714/NEWS/150719520/15282/NEWS

[280] http://www.hendersonvillelightning.com/news/4197-arrested-man-dies-after-fight-during-booking.html

[281] http://www.hendersonvillelightning.com/news/4873-d-a-no-charges-in-death-of-man-who-died-after-jail-scuffle.html

[282] http://www.orlandosentinel.com/news/breaking-news/os-orlando-police-suspect-shooting-20150717-story.html

[283] http://www.wmcactionnews5.com/story/30755532/easy-access-tbi-files-in-darrius-stewart-case

[284] http://m.memphisflyer.com/NewsBlog/archives/2015/07/21/memphis-police-officer-involved-in-stewart-shooting-identified

[285] http://www.wmcactionnews5.com/story/29578116/man-dead-after-struggle-with-mpd-officer

[286] http://www.thesungazette.com/article/news/2015/07/22/parolee-is-shot-killed-in-farmersville-police-custody/

[287] http://www.fresnobee.com/news/local/crime/article27864838.html

[288] http://www.visaliatimesdelta.com/story/news/local/2015/07/19/man-custody-killed-farmersville-police-station/30385379/

[289]
http://www.visaliatimesdelta.com/story/news/local/2015/07/24/farmersville-visalia-robberies-police-officer-involved-shooting-fight-john-torales/30626579/

[290] http://www.fox13memphis.com/news/preliminary-autopsy-report-released-in-troy-goode-case/10023624

[291] http://www.fox13memphis.com/news/autopsy-finds-man-died-of-lsd-

toxicity-in-police-custody/10171691

[292] http://www.fox13memphis.com/news/family-of-troy-goode-expected-to-file-lawsuit-this-week/16622227

[293] Reay, Fligner, Stilwell, Arnold. "Positional asphyxia during law enforcement transport." American Journal of Forensic Medicine Pathol. 1992 Jun;13(2):90-7

[294] Chan, Vilke, Neuman. Reexamination of custody restraint position and positional asphyxia." Am J Forensic Med Pathol. 1998 Sep;19(3):201-5

[295] Sudden in-Custody Deaths: Exploring Causality & Prevention Strategies, Flosi, Ed, MS, Forensic Examiner 20.1 (Spring 2011): 31-48.

[296] http://www.foxnews.com/us/2015/08/07/prosecutor-in-case-man-fatally-shot-by-university-cincinnati-cop-criticized-for.html

[297] http://www.wcpo.com//news/local-news/hamilton-county/cincinnati/hamilton-county-prosecutor-to-discuss-samuel-dubose-officer-involved-shooting-death

[298] http://goo.gl/pGjSDY

[299] http://minnesota.cbslocal.com/2015/07/24/police-man-killed-in-plymouth-arbys-officer-involved-shooting/

[300] http://www.startribune.com/father-of-man-killed-in-plymouth-police-shooting-i-just-don-t-understand-it/318734421

[301] Ibid.

[302] http://www.nbcnews.com/news/us-news/no-charges-against-south-carolina-cop-who-fatally-shot-teen-n452301

[303] http://www.liveleak.com/view?i=066_1445960413

[304] https://www.documentcloud.org/documents/2229614-hammond-autopsy.html

[305] http://www.foxcarolina.com/story/30359648/read-full-statement-on-solicitors-decision-not-to-charge-officer-in-hammond-case

[306] http://www.wrcbtv.com/story/29646814/deputy-involved-shooting-in-bradley-county

[307] http://www.timesfreepress.com/news/local/story/2015/jul/28/bradley-county-deputy-shoots-and-kills-man-her-home/316874/

[308] http://www.telegram.com/article/20150730/NEWS/307309660

[309] https://www.bostonglobe.com/metro/2015/07/30/man-critical-condition-after-rampage-worcester-market/JkrgMwQj3EgJeEdSpDuUMJ/story.html

[310] http://www.telegram.com/article/20150730/NEWS/307309660

[311] http://www.worcesterma.gov/wpd-press-releases/update-on-pennywise-market-death-investigation

[312] http://www.sfgate.com/crime/article/Elderly-man-dies-after-being-attacked-by-6417442.php

[313] http://www.sfgate.com/crime/article/Dead-body-probe-on-Lombard-Street-in-S-F-6414831.php

[314] http://www.wfaa.com/story/news/local/2015/08/01/man-unresponsive-after-dallas-jail-scuffle/30986151/

[315] http://www.dallasnews.com/news/metro/20150828-video-shows-arlington-man-struggling-with-deputies-in-jail-lobby-before-his-death.ece

[316] http://thescoopblog.dallasnews.com/2015/08/death-of-man-in-dallas-

county-jail-lobby-ruled-a-homicide-according-to-dallas-county-medical-
examiner.html/

[317] https://gbi.georgia.gov/press-releases/2015-08-10/gbi-investigating-
dekalb-county-police-use-force

[318] Ibid.

[319] http://www.ajc.com/news/news/crime-law/man-who-died-after-dekalb-
officer-shot-him-with-ta/nnFps/

[320] http://www.ajc.com/news/news/crime-law/man-dies-during-police-foot-
chase-in-dekalb/nnFL4/

[321] http://www.11alive.com/story/news/crime/2015/08/08/dekalb-police-
gbi-taser-death-robinson-cell-cellphone-video/31324973/

[322] http://www.cbs46.com/story/29731157/man-falls-off-wall-dies-after-
being-tased-while-running-from-police

[323] http://www.11alive.com/story/news/crime/2015/08/08/dekalb-police-
gbi-taser-death-robinson-cell-cellphone-video/31324973/

[324] http://cnsnews.com/news/article/state-police-probe-death-conn-man-
struck-taser

[325] http://www.nbcconnecticut.com/news/local/Man-Dies-After-Police-
Deploy-Taser-During-Medical-Disturbance-321134371.html

[326] http://www.courant.com/news/connecticut/hc-hartford-matthew-russo-
taser-death-20150808-story.html

[327] http://fox61.com/2015/08/08/combative-man-hit-by-taser-in-hartford-
dies/

[328] http://www.wfsb.com/story/29740899/man-dies-after-being-tased-by-

police-in-hartford

329 http://www.nytimes.com/2015/08/12/us/arlington-tex-officer-is-fired-in-fatal-shooting-of-christian-taylor.html

330 http://crimeblog.dallasnews.com/2015/08/arlington-police-officer-fatally-shot-a-man-early-friday-at-car-dealership.html/

331 http://www.nytimes.com/2015/08/12/us/arlington-tex-officer-is-fired-in-fatal-shooting-of-christian-taylor.html

332 Ibid.

333 Ibid.

334 Ibid.

335 http://www.latimes.com/nation/la-na-texas-officer-fired-20150811-story.html

336 http://crimeblog.dallasnews.com/2015/09/medical-examiner-christian-taylor-had-synthetic-psychedelic-drug-cannibis-in-his-system-when-he-was-killed.html/

337 https://www.drugabuse.gov/emerging-trends/n-bomb

338 https://www.washingtonpost.com/local/crime/pr-georges-police-suspect-shot-after-struggling-with-officer-over-gun/2015/08/15/4d43cfa2-4355-11e5-846d-02792f854297_story.html

339 http://legacy.wusa9.com/story/news/local/maryland/2015/08/15/suspect-shot-police-after-struggle-over-officers-gun/31772861/

340 http://wtop.com/prince-georges-county/2015/08/police-md-man-fatally-shot-during-police-gun-struggle-had-suicidal-thoughts/

[341] http://www.madisoncourier.com/Content/News/News/Article/Hanover-man-dead-in-officer-involved-shooting/178/961/92193

[342] http://www.wlky.com/news/1-dead-after-officer-involved-shooting-in-Hanover-Indiana/34739790

[343] http://wkmnews.com/grand-jury-clears-sheriffs-deputies/

[344] http://www.sgvtribune.com/general-news/20150819/authorities-identify-man-who-died-after-arrest-by-baldwin-park-police

[345] http://www.sgvtribune.com/general-news/20150817/autopsy-pending-for-man-who-died-in-baldwin-park-police-custody

[346] http://www.sgvtribune.com/general-news/20150816/suspect-dies-after-being-shot-with-taser-by-police

[347] http://www.sgvtribune.com/general-news/20150816/suspect-dies-after-being-shot-with-taser-by-police

[348] http://www.nbcbayarea.com/news/local/Suspects-Linked-to-San-Jose-Homicide-Fatally-Shot-By-Police-322238212.html

[349] http://www.mercurynews.com/crime-courts/ci_28656852/san-jose-police-working-officer-involved-shooting

[350] http://www.nbcbayarea.com/news/local/Suspects-Linked-to-San-Jose-Homicide-Fatally-Shot-By-Police-322238212.html

[351] Ibid.

[352] http://www.latimes.com/local/crime/la-me-san-jose-police-20150822-story.html

[353] http://www.mercurynews.com/crime-courts/ci_28668925/san-jose-scrutiny-over-officer-involved-shooting-grows

[354] http://m.cecildaily.com/news/local_news/article_0574528c-b93b-5f10-91f9-79506378a4a1.html?mode=jqm

[355] http://www.baltimoresun.com/news/maryland/bs-md-police-shooting-north-east-20150822-story.html

[356] http://www.stardem.com/news/state_news/article_ea53003f-9dd4-54af-8950-f956a7cf856d.html

[357] Ibid.

[358] http://www.fox10phoenix.com/arizona-news/10925819-story

[359] http://www.trivalleycentral.com/casa_grande_dispatch/arizona_news/man-subdued-by-phoenix-police-with-stun-gun-dies/article_9c39a87c-4a79-11e5-8c8f-bf88cc18df72.html

[360] http://www.azcentral.com/story/news/local/phoenix/breaking/2015/08/22/man-dies-after-altercation—police/32210513/

[361] See, http://newyork.cbslocal.com/2015/08/29/bystander-killed-mount-vernon-police-shooting/ ; https://www.newsday.com/news/new-york/felix-kumi-s-family-won-t-meet-with-mayor-top-brass-after-fatal-shooting-1.10794779 ; and http://www.lohud.com/story/news/local/westchester/mount-vernon/2015/08/28/mount-vernon-shooting-incident-involving-nypd-injures/71333390/

[362] http://www.buzzfeed.com/davidmack/bystander-fatally-shot-by-nypd-officer-during-undercover-op#.kibPonRNy1

[363] http://www.buzzfeed.com/nicolasmedinamora/heres-why-the-nypd-almost-never-apologizes

364 http://republicanherald.com/state-police-probe-death-of-minersville-man-1.1937964

365 http://www.latimes.com/local/lanow/la-me-ln-in-custody-death-long-beach-20150906-story.html

366 http://www.longbeach.gov/Police/Press-Releases/IN-CUSTODY-DEATH-2147470658/

367 http://calwatchdog.com/2016/02/23/deaths-in-police-custody-up-half-attributed-to-natural-causes/

368 http://abc7.com/news/long-beach-man-dies-in-police-custody-sparking-investigation/972064/

369 http://legacy.13newsnow.com/story/news/2015/09/08/va-beach-police—hold-news-conference—people-shot-killed—officers/71883438/

370 http://legacy.13newsnow.com/story/news/2015/09/08/va-beach-police—hold-news-conference—people-shot-killed—officers/71883438/

371 http://www.newsplex.com/home/headlines/Police-Man-Killed-by-Officer-Was-Suspect-in-Two-Slayings-360978851.html

372 http://wtkr.com/2015/12/08/virginia-beach-police-releases-ballistics-results-from-double-fatal-shooting-by-officers/

373 http://krqe.com/2015/09/08/man-who-died-in-bernalillo-police-custody-identified/

374 http://www.koat.com/news/disturbance-at-walmart-ends-with-man-dying-in-police-custody/35138362

375 http://www.kob.com/article/stories/s3899241.shtml

376 http://www.abqjournal.com/641197/news/bernalillo-police-identify-

man-who-died-in-custody.html

377 http://turnto10.com/archive/authorities-identify-man-who-died-in-providence-police-custody

378 http://www.abc6.com/story/29975701/officials-identify-man-who-died-in-providence-police-custody

379 Ibid.

380 http://www.rifuture.org/how-richard-cosentino-died-in-providence-police-custody.html

381 http://www.newsnet5.com/news/local-news/akron-canton-news/springfield-township-police-use-stun-gun-on-man-reported-naked-after-he-bites-officers-leg

382 http://www.newsnet5.com/news/local-news/akron-canton-news/man-struck-with-stun-gun-by-springfield-township-police-dies

383
http://www.cleveland.com/akron/index.ssf/2015/09/man_hospitalized_after_fight_w.html

384 http://www.newsnet5.com/news/local-news/akron-canton-news/man-struck-with-stun-gun-by-springfield-township-police-dies

385 http://dependency5.rssing.com/chan-4043747/all_p582.html

386
http://cms.sbcounty.gov/sheriff/MediaCenter/SheriffPressReleases/PressReleasesfor2015/September/Muscoy-FelonyEvadingOfficerInvolvedShootingTrafficCollision.aspx

387
http://bigstory.ap.org/article/6e9c57eb452240bcbb95e146545dcf7d/author

ities-name-wrong-way-driver-fired-upon-helicopter

388

http://cms.sbcounty.gov/sheriff/MediaCenter/SheriffPressReleases/PressRele
asesfor2015/September/Muscoy-
FelonyEvadingOfficerInvolvedShootingTrafficCollision.aspx

389 http://www.pe.com/articles/pursuit-780943-died-gunfire.html

390 Ibid.

391 http://www.komonews.com/news/local/Officials-Man-dies-during-
altercation-with-police-in-Tulalip-328375921.html

392 http://www.heraldnet.com/article/20150919/NEWS01/150918888

393 http://www.heraldnet.com/article/20150921/NEWS01/150929796

394

http://www.heraldnet.com/article/20151120/NEWS01/151129813/Death-
of-man-in-police-custody-on-Tulalip-reservation-ruled-an-accident-

395

http://www.cleveland.com/akron/index.ssf/2015/10/akron_hookah_bar_ow
ner_shot_du.html

396 http://www.newsnet5.com/news/local-news/akron-canton-news/omar-
ali-man-shot-during-search-of-business-dies-in-hospital

397 http://legacy.wkyc.com/story/news/local/akron/2015/10/06/man-shot-
akron-swat-during-search-dies-two-weeks-later/73455952/

398 http://fox8.com/2015/09/22/detective-finds-heroin-inside-akron-man-
shot-by-swat/

399 http://wksu.org/news/story/44464

[400] http://legacy.wkyc.com/story/news/local/akron/2015/09/25/akron-police-shoot-kill-robbery-suspect/72829710/

[401]

http://www.cleveland.com/akron/index.ssf/2015/09/man_fatally_shot_by_akron_poli_1.html

[402]

http://www.cleveland.com/akron/index.ssf/2015/09/akron_police_fatally_shoot_one.html

[403]

http://www.miamidade.gov/police/releases/PD150928363540_Police_Involved_Shooting.asp

[404] http://www.miaminewtimes.com/news/i-95-snarled-officer-injured-in-deadly-early-morning-shooting-7936729

[405] http://miami.cbslocal.com/2015/09/28/deadly-police-involved-shooting-in-north-miami/

[406] http://www.startribune.com/sheriff-deputy-fatally-shoots-man-attacking-him-in-mora/330238731/

[407] http://www.kare11.com/news/man-fatally-shot-by-deputy-in-mora/13698005

[408] https://dps.mn.gov/divisions/ooc/news-releases/Pages/BCA-INVESTIGATING-OFFICER-INVOLVED-SHOOTING-IN-MORA.aspx

[409] http://www.presspubs.com/kanabec/crime/article_cbf3fca8-6922-11e5-af84-fbe821ca484f.html

[410] http://www.latimes.com/local/lanow/la-me-ln-lapd-beer-bottle-shooting-names-20151105-story.html

[411] http://www.lapdonline.org/newsroom/news_view/59486

[412] http://www.latimes.com/local/lanow/la-me-ln-fatal-lapd-shooting-evidence-20151009-story.html

[413] http://www.usatoday.com/story/news/nation/2014/12/20/new-york-city-police-officers-shot/20698679/

[414] http://www.latimes.com/local/lanow/la-me-ln-lapd-shooting-video-20151006-story.html

[415] http://ktla.com/2015/10/16/homicide-detectives-investigating-deputy-involved-shooting-in-la-puente-lasd/

[416] http://homicide.latimes.com/post/johnny-angel-rangel/

[417] http://fav-meth-head-of-the-day.com/2014/07/01/suspect-johnny-rangel-24-of-baldwin-park-subdued-with-taser-while-fighting-with-west-covina-police-believed-to-be-high-on-methamphetamine/

[418]
http://bigstory.ap.org/article/a32ce97d86864051aec1e16ce09a3119/police-seek-more-witnesses-fatal-shooting-officer

[419] http://www.richmond.com/news/local/central-virginia/article_bfa510bb-f0b3-5319-a774-b6d3b22f5584.html

[420] http://wric.com/2016/02/25/support-rally-planned-at-court-hearing-today-for-richmond-officer-charged-with-murder/

[421] http://www.fresnobee.com/news/local/crime/article40741638.html

[422] http://www.kristv.com/story/30317738/man-dies-in-corpus-christi-pd-custody

[423] http://www.osagecountyonline.com/archives/18642

[424] https://www.facebook.com/BobSchickfan/posts/1071970219481023:0

[425] http://www.latimes.com/local/lanow/la-me-ln-harbor-police-shooting-20151028-story.html

[426] http://www.nbcsandiego.com/news/local/San-Diego-Harbor-Police-Shooting-Fatal-Officer-Involved-337915742.html

[427] http://fox5sandiego.com/2015/10/28/officer-kills-man-during-struggle-outside-point-loma-hotel/

[428] http://www.sandiegouniontribune.com/news/2015/oct/28/fatal-ois-point-loma-harbor-police-struggle/

[429] http://www.nbcphiladelphia.com/news/local/Suspect-Dies-After-Attacking-SEPTA-Officer-in-Kensington-Police-337040801.html

[430] http://articles.philly.com/2015-10-28/news/67793349_1_septa-police-officer-nestel-septa-cops

[431] Ibid.

[432] http://mobile.philly.com/beta?wss=/philly/news&id=366842711

[433] https://www.periscope.tv/w/1ypKdDkZoZVKW

[434] https://www.washingtonpost.com/news/post-nation/wp/2015/11/05/jeremy-was-a-special-gift-from-god-louisiana-6-year-old-is-years-youngest-police-shooting-victim/

[435] http://www.streetcredsoftware.com/wp-content/uploads/2015/11/288815510-Marksville-Police-Lawsuit.pdf

[436] http://archive.thetowntalk.com/article/20111011/NEWS01/110110332/Marksville-police-officer-indicted

437 http://theadvocate.com/news/acadiana/13886147-123/child-shot-multiple-times-in

438 http://theadvocate.com/sports/latestsports/13907799-113/two-of-four-officers-arrested

439 http://goo.gl/Tk7GMO

440 U.S. Department of Justice (May, 2015) "Local Police Departments, 2013: Personnel, Policies, and Practices," U.S. Department of Justice, Office of Justice Programs, Bureau of Justice Statistics, May 2015, NCJ 248677

441 http://www.cnn.com/2015/04/13/us/tulsa-police-shooting-eric-harris-deputy-charged/

442 http://www.nbcnews.com/news/us-news/tulsa-county-sheriff-indicted-resigns-wake-fatal-shooting-deputy-n436481

443 http://www.usatoday.com/story/news/nation-now/2015/11/07/louisiana-officers-shooting-boy/75351174/

444 http://www.periscope.tv https /w/1ypKdDkZoZVKW

445

http://bigstory.ap.org/article/ca2ead6b37fa4ba1ac62435db97147ec/officials-boy-killed-after-city-marshals-shoot-vehicle

446 http://theadvocate.com/news/acadiana/13886147-123/child-shot-multiple-times-in

447 http://www.streetcredsoftware.com/wp-content/uploads/2015/11/288815510-Marksville-Police-Lawsuit.pdf

448

http://archive.thetowntalk.com/article/20111011/NEWS01/110110332/M

arksville-police-officer-indicted

[449] http://www.cbs8.com/story/30483673/pacific-beach-standoff-suspect-to-be-extradited-to-missouri

[450] http://www.nbcsandiego.com/news/local/Pacific-Beach-Reported-Shots-Fired-340456332.html

[451] http://www.cbs8.com/story/30506517/cbs-news-8-interviews-woman-at-center-of-pacific-beach-standoff

[452] http://wncn.com/2015/11/16/deputys-name-released-in-fatal-harnett-co-officer-involved-shooting/

[453] http://wncn.com/2015/11/15/1-killed-in-harnett-co-officer-involved-shooting/

[454] http://www.fayobserver.com/news/crime_courts/autopsy-harnett-county-man-killed-by-deputy-had-gunshot-wounds/article_d189a164-d22b-5e6e-bfe3-b41fa88cc9f1.html

[455] http://www.cbsnews.com/news/protests-erupt-after-black-man-shot-by-police-in-minneapolis/

[456] http://www.startribune.com/what-we-know-about-the-death-of-jamar-clark/353199331/

[457] http://www.mprnews.org/story/2015/11/17/51-arrested-in-shooting-protest-that-blocked-i94

[458] http://www.mprnews.org/story/2015/11/15/minneapolis-police-shoot-suspect

[459] https://www.documentcloud.org/documents/2779903-Speech-Clark-Chronology-3-30-16.html

460 http://www.mprnews.org/story/2015/11/17/51-arrested-in-shooting-protest-that-blocked-i94

461 http://www.fox9.com/news/97456138-story

462 https://www.minnpost.com/politics-policy/2016/02/effort-get-jamar-clark-videos-released-focuses-unique-and-untested-provision

463 http://www.startribune.com/evidence-from-the-jamar-clark-investigation/374007211/

464 https://www.documentcloud.org/documents/2779901-Autopsy-Report-of-Jamar-Clark.html

465 http://www.startribune.com/No-charges-against-police-in-Jamar-Clark-shooting-death/373979481/

466 Ibid.

467 http://miami.cbslocal.com/2015/11/18/deadly-police-involved-shooting-in-opa-locka/

468 http://www.local10.com/news/two-opalocka-officers-involved-in-fatal-shooting/36518156

469 http://www.miamiherald.com/news/local/community/miami-dade/article45318426.html

470 http://www.star-telegram.com/news/state/texas/article45223599.html

471 http://www.mineralwellsindex.com/news/weatherford-police-kill-man-following-pursuit/article_700a26f8-8d60-11e5-91ea-dfd8228fb239.html

472 http://www.mineralwellsindex.com/news/man-killed-by-weatherford-police-identified/article_ca945700-8ebf-11e5-89a4-8b900ad3bea0.html

[473] http://www.star-telegram.com/news/state/texas/article45469116.html

[474]

http://ci.weatherford.tx.us/Search/Results?searchPhrase=tindall&page=1&perPage=10

[475]

http://cms.sbcounty.gov/sheriff/MediaCenter/SheriffPressReleases/PressReleasesfor2015/November/BarstowPoliceDeptinvestigatinganAssaultonDeputyDeputyInvolvedShooting.aspx

[476] http://www.sbsun.com/general-news/20151120/barstow-man-shot-killed-in-fight-with-deputy

[477] http://www.highlandnews.net/news/public_safety/article_aa5569c2-8fa8-11e5-82d7-df412635f2d1.html

[478] https://gbi.georgia.gov/press-releases/2015-11-23/gbi-investigating-use-force-incident-resulting-death-coweta-county-ga

[479] http://bigstory.ap.org/article/c9fbc16c34054e19b1f13a6ffcefb5de/mom-911-son-trying-bite-people-dies-after-struggle

[480] http://www.kxii.com/home/headlines/New-details-released-in-officer-involved-shooting-in-Colbert-352955771.html

[481] http://www.kten.com/story/30590332/family-mourns-loss-of-man-in-officer-involved-shooting

[482] http://durantdemocrat.com/uncategorized/2292/2292

[483] https://www.ok.gov/osbi/Press_Room/index.html

[484] http://www.thedenverchannel.com/news/local-news/officer-involved-shooting-at-i-225-and-kentucky-after-crash-involving-police-at-i-225-and-alameda

[485] http://kdvr.com/2015/11/30/officer-involved-shooting-under-investigation-in-aurora/

[486] https://youtu.be/gmEK3A3Gyfg

[487] http://www.kens5.com/story/news/2015/12/04/investigation-ensues-after-dps-trooper-kills-driver-traffic-stop/76761860/

[488] http://www.kvue.com/story/news/state/2015/12/03/dps-trooper-fatally-shoots-suspect-near-von-ormy/76739410/

[489] http://www.cbsnews.com/news/special-prosecutors-investigate-fatal-nypd-shooting-of-unarmed-man-in-weschester-woods/

[490] http://www.nbcnewyork.com/news/local/Saw-Mill-River-Parkway-Shut-Down-Yonkers-Police-Investigation-360959561.html

[491] http://www.nytimes.com/2015/12/09/nyregion/yonkers-police-chase-off-saw-mill.html

[492] http://www.ksbw.com/news/gilroy-police-kill-man-during-violent-domestic-fight/36980966

[493] https://local.nixle.com/alert/5548309/

[494] http://abc7news.com/news/gilroy-police-fatally-shoot-domestic-violence-suspect/1123132/

[495] http://www.nbclosangeles.com/news/local/shooting-harbor-ucla-medical-center-officer-involved-torrance-363043351.html

[496] http://www.latimes.com/local/lanow/la-me-ln-victim-of-harbor-ucla-emergency-room-shooting-is-identified-20151220-story.html

[497] https://local.nixle.com/alert/5551061/?sub_id=1000000469

[498] http://ktla.com/2015/12/20/sheriffs-deputy-fatally-shoots-person-in-palmdale/

[499] http://www.dailynews.com/general-news/20151220/dui-suspect-fatally-shot-in-palmdale-after-allegedly-grabbing-deputys-gun

[500] http://www.freep.com/story/news/local/2015/12/23/police-dearborn-officer-involved-fatal-shooting/77834122/

[501] http://www.wxyz.com/news/region/wayne-county/dearborn-police-officer-shoots-kills-man-on-whitcomb-street-near-detroitdearborn-border

[502] http://www.fox2detroit.com/news/local-news/61023770-story

[503] http://www.nbcchicago.com/news/local/Police-Involved-Shooting-Leaves-Two-Dead-Family-363547691.html

[504] http://www.chicagotribune.com/news/local/breaking/ct-chicago-police-shooting-20151226-story.html

[505] http://chicago.suntimes.com/news/7/71/1207663/chicago-police-shoot-2-people-austin

This book is distributed by Calibre Press.

Calibre Press began in 1980 with the publication of *Street Survival: Tactics for Armed Encounters*. Today it continues to provide first responders with cutting-edge training that will best serve them, and the communities they serve. Calibre Press offers digital media, live seminar training, and book publishing on a variety of topics, from leadership to cyber crimes to women in law enforcement and more.

For more information, visit

http://www.CalibrePress.com.

DATE DUE

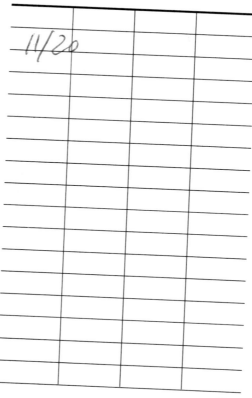

11/20